THE STRUCTURE OF
AMERICAN INDUSTRY

THE STRUCTURE OF AMERICAN INDUSTRY

Eighth Edition

WALTER ADAMS

MICHIGAN STATE UNIVERSITY

editor

Macmillan Publishing Company
New York

Collier Macmillan Publishers
London

Macmillan Publishing Company
866 Third Avenue, New York, New York 10022

Collier Macmillan Canada, Inc.

Library of Congress Cataloging in Publication Data

The Structure of American industry / Walter Adams, editor. —8th ed.
    p.   cm.
    Includes index.
    1. United States—Industries.   I. Adams, Walter (date)
  HC106.8.S78   1990
  338.6'0973—dc20   89-2661
  ISBN 0-02-300771-0   CIP

Printing: 1 2 3 4 5 6 7 8   Year: 0 1 2 3 4 5 6 7 8

To
the small but brave army of young economists
who "prefer to see the truth imperfectly and obscurely
rather than to maintain error, reached indeed
with clearness, consistency and by easy logic but [based]
on hypotheses contrary to the facts."

PREFACE

One of the major transformations in political economy since the first edition of this book appeared in 1950 is a renewed awareness that the power relationships in society — and especially the role of the state — are a matter of profound social concern and require continuing confrontation by public policy makers.

Since then we have lost much of our erstwhile innocence. We have learned some painful lessons about the political economy of power. Over the intervening years, it has become less fashionable to dismiss the Founding Fathers as anachronistic philosophers or to ridicule Lord Acton's warning about the consequences of concentrated power. The excesses of the "imperial" presidency, and the abuse of executive authority to harass and oppress individual citizens, have underscored the importance of a decentralized power structure within a framework of checks and balances. As Madison put it in *The Federalist*, No. 51, "If men were angels, no government would be necessary. If angels were to govern men, neither external nor internal controls on government would be necessary. In framing a government which is to be administered by men over men, the great difficulty lies in this: You must first enable the government to control the governed; and in the next place oblige it to control itself. A dependence on the people is, no doubt, the primary control on the government; but experience has taught mankind the necessity of auxiliary precautions . . ." And these auxiliary precautions, said Madison, require primarily a separation of power between the different branches of government, and secondarily a dispersion of power among the citizenry. The underlying purpose, he wrote, is to prevent the rulers from oppressing the ruled, and to render it improbable, if not impracticable, for one segment of society to oppress another.

This traditional, peculiarly American distrust of concentrated power is, of course, relevant not only to political but also to economic institutions. Despite the recent reemergence of Social Darwinism, there is a persistent recognition that economic power is not merely a decorative status symbol to be passively enjoyed in the counting houses and country clubs. Economic power, we are constantly reminded, may be used with statesmanlike forbearance and diplomatic skill. It may be used only where circumstances absolutely demand it, or when the political climate is particularly propitious. It may be accompanied by sophisticated public relations campaigns to purify its venality or sanitize the corporate image. But the fact remains that, in the long run, the possession of great power and the exercise of such power tend to coalesce. Wherever economic power exists it tends eventually to be used, and for ends chosen by those who control it.

The "Reagan Era" marked a renewed emphasis on the decentralization of economic power. Competition was touted as an instrument for achieving "the best allocation of resources, the lowest prices, the highest quality, and the greatest material progress"; a device to be used by society for social purposes; a blueprint for limited power operating in a comprehensive framework of checks and balances; a network of safeguards against the abuse of power to the detriment of the public; and, perhaps, above all, a regulatory system for the economy which obviates intervention and control by an all-pervasive state.

Unfortunately, the official rhetoric has not always been matched by concrete action. "Deregulation" has often meant the curtailment of government regulations with respect to clean air, pure water, automotive safety, and fuel efficiency rather than the economic deregulation of inherently competitive industries. "Free trade" has meant resistance against the crasser forms of protectionism (e.g., for roses and water beds) but has not been considered inconsistent with "voluntary" import restraints negotiated on a bilateral or multilateral basis (e.g., for steel, textiles, and automobiles). "Antitrust policy" has not been mobilized to stem a rising tide of megamergers and joint ventures which are structurally transforming our industrial landscape. Government still seems content to protect, subsidize, and bail out vested interests which ought to be compelled to live by the Darwinist survival principles they preach to others.

In the context of the current debate over the proper role of government, the virtues of megamergers and corporate giantism, the challenge of international competition, and the need to "reindustrialize" America, the eighth edition of this book seems felicitously timed. It offers a kaleidoscopic view of American industry—a collection of case studies illustrating different types of structural organization, different behavior patterns, and different performance records—with an emphasis on international comparisons, where relevant, with industries in Japan and the European Economic Community. Although each industry is, of course, an "individual," the case studies offer to the student of industrial organization a "live" laboratory for clinical examination, comparative analysis, and the evaluation of public policy alternatives. For that reason the book, I hope, constitutes a useful supplement, if not a necessary antidote, to the economist's penchant for the abstractions of theoretical model building.

Finally, a personal note to acknowledge my indebtedness to President Ronald Calgaard and the faculty, staff, and students of Trinity University, San Antonio, Texas, for providing the stimulating and hospitable environment in which the work on this edition was completed.

East Lansing, Michigan   *Walter Adams*

CONTRIBUTORS

Walter Adams is Distinguished University Professor, Professor of Economics, and Past President of Michigan State University. A member of the Attorney General's National Committee to Study the Antitrust Laws (1953–55), he has been an expert witness before Congressional Committees and the International Trade Commission as well as in antitrust proceedings.

Gerald W. Brock is Chief of the Common Carrier Bureau, Federal Communications Commission. He previously served as a consultant to the Department of Justice and to private firms in matters related to their antitrust suits against IBM.

James W. Brock is Professor of Economics at Miami University (Ohio). He has appeared as an expert witness before Congressional committees and served as a consultant on antitrust matters.

William B. Burnett is Vice President of Charles River Associates, Washington, D.C.

Kenneth G. Elzinga is Professor of Economics at the University of Virginia. He served as Special Economic Assistant to the Chief of Antitrust Division and is co-author (with William Breit) of *Antitrust Penalties, Murder at the Margin*, and *The Fatal Equilibrium*.

Arnold A. Heggestad is William H. Dial Professor of Banking and Finance at the University of Florida. He has previously served as financial economist, Board of Governors of the Federal Reserve System, specializing in public policy issues regarding the banking structure.

Manley R. Irwin is Professor of Economics, Whittemore School of Business and Economics at the University of New Hampshire. He has written and testified on both domestic and international aspects of telecommunications.

Barry R. Litman is Professor of Telecommunications at Michigan State University. He has served as a consultant to various mass media organizations.

Stephen Martin is Professor of Economics at Michigan State University. He has served as an economic expert in antitrust proceedings.

Hans Mueller is Professor of Economics and Finance, Middle Tennessee State University. He has been a consultant on steel industry problems to various government agencies and private organizations. He has also appeared as an expert witness before Congressional committees and the U.S. International Trade Commission.

Willard F. Mueller is William F. Vilas Research Professor (Emeritus) of Agricultural Economics, Professor of Economics, and Professor in the Law School, University of Wisconsin–Madison. He served as Chief Economist and Director of the Bureau of Economics, Federal Trade Commission (1961–68) and Executive Director of the President's Cabinet Committee on Price Stability (1968–69).

Frederic M. Scherer is Professor of Economics at the John F. Kennedy School of Government, Harvard University. From 1974 to 1976 he was director of the Federal Trade Commission's Bureau of Economics. He has also served as a consultant in diverse antitrust, international trade, and defense economics matters.

William G. Shepherd is Professor of Economics at the University of Massachusetts (Amherst). The economic advisor to the Chief of the Antitrust Division (1967–68), he has also been an expert witness in several antitrust proceedings.

Daniel B. Suits is Professor of Economics (Emeritus) at Michigan State University and Fellow of the East-West Population Institute. He has served as consultant to the U.S. Secretary of the Treasury (1961–70) and to a number of other federal and state agencies.

CONTENTS

CHAPTER 1
AGRICULTURE
Daniel B. Suits

I.
INTRODUCTION

As supplier of most of the food we eat and of raw materials for many industrial processes, agriculture is clearly an important sector of the economy. But the importance of the industrial performance of agriculture transcends even this function. In nations where the productivity of farmers is low, most of the working population is needed to raise food, and few people are available for production of investment goods or for other activities required for economic growth. Indeed, one of the factors that correlates most closely with the per capita income of a nation is the decline in the fraction of its population that is engaged in farming. In the poorest nations of the world, more than half of the population lives on farms, as compared to less than 10 percent in Western Europe and less than 4 percent in the United States.

In short, the course of economic development in general depends in a fundamental way on the performance of farmers. This performance, in turn, depends on how agriculture is organized and on the economic context, or market structure, within which agriculture functions. In this chapter, the performance of American agriculture is examined, beginning with a consideration of its market structure.

II.
MARKET STRUCTURE AND COMPETITION
Number and Size of Farms

There are about 2 million farms in the United States today. This is roughly 33 percent of the peak reached sixty years ago, and as the number of farms has declined, the average size has risen. Farms in the United States average about 460 acres, but this average can be misleading. In fact, modern American agriculture is characterized by large-scale operations. Although only 162,000 farms—5.5 percent of the total—are as large as 1,000 acres or more, they include more than 40 percent of total farm acreage. Nearly a quarter of all wheat, for example, is grown on farms of 2,000 acres or more, and the top 2.6 percent of wheat growers raise roughly 50 percent of our wheat.

Sizes of farms vary widely by product, but even where typical acreage is small, production is concentrated. Nearly 65 percent of our tomato crop is grown on farms smaller than 500 acres, but the remaining 35 percent is marketed by the largest 9 percent of tomato growers. Broiler chickens are raised on still smaller farms, with 55 percent coming from farms with fewer than 100 acres. However, more than 70 percent of all broiler chickens are raised by the largest 2 percent of growers.

Size of farm also varies with production technique as this is affected by region, climate, and other factors. In the southern United States, 60 percent of cotton output comes from farms of fewer than 1,000 acres, whereas farms that small produce only a third of cotton grown in the more capital-intensive western states. Over all, however, the largest 3 percent of all cotton growers produced 40 percent of all cotton and cotton seed in the United States.

With the advent of large-scale commercial agriculture, the family farm, long the American ideal, is no longer characteristic. Only about half of all present-day farmers earn their livelihood entirely from farm operations. The others must supplement farm income with industrial jobs or other off-farm employment. Moreover, large-scale agriculture is increasingly characterized by corporate operations. Although only 2 percent of all farms are incorporated, corporations own 12 percent of all land in U.S. farms and market 22 percent of the total value of all farm crops.

Corporate farms are especially important in states like California, where they operate a quarter of all acreage in farms and market 40 percent of the value of all farm crops (including almost 60 percent of all California sweet corn, melons, and vegetables). But even in a state like Kansas, over a third of all farm products are marketed by corporate farms.

Competition in Agriculture

Despite the scale and concentration of production, however, modern agriculture remains an industry whose behavior and performance are best understood in terms of the theory of pure competition. Although agricultural production is concentrated in the hands of a relatively small percentage of growers, total numbers are so large that the largest 2 or 3 percent of the growers of any given product still constitute a substantial number of independent firms. For example, although only 2 percent of grain growers produce about 50 percent of all grain in the United States, this 2 percent consists of 27,000 firms. Numbers like this are a far cry from those for manufacturing. The largest number of firms of all sizes found in any one manufacturing industry are the 10,000 sawmills and planning mills engaged in the production of lumber. However, manufacturing industries typically have many fewer firms — even industries like men's work clothing (277 firms) and cotton-weaving mills (218 firms), which are widely recognized as highly competitive. Thus, even if we ignore the competitive influence exerted by the thousands of smaller farms in each line of production and look only at the very largest, we are still talking about nearly 100 times as many independent firms as are found in the most competitive manufacturing industries.

In any event, the number and size of existing firms are only partial measures of the competitiveness of market structure. An important additional consideration is the extent to which ease of entry generates potential competition beyond the firms engaged in production at any given moment. Not only do the many smaller farms produce and sell in the same market with the larger ones, but there are no special barriers to entry into agriculture. Moreover, many existing farms are adapted to the production of a variety of products and can shift output from crop to crop on the basis of the outlook for prices and costs.

As a result of this structure, even large modern farms are powerless to exert any appreciable individual influence on total output or prices through their own economic behavior. They can only plan production schedules on the basis of their own best expectations, with the knowledge that the ultimate price will be virtually unaltered by anything they might decide. Plans for how much of which crops to grow and by which methods are arrived at on the basis of price and cost expectations. The resulting crop comes on the market and sells at prices that are determined by total volume in conjunction with existing demand.

Demand for Farm Products

Another important element in the structure of agriculture markets is the nature of the demand for farm products. Before exploring farm products in particular, however, it is useful to review some of the properties of demand curves in general. Potatoes are fairly typical farm products and can be used as a convenient illustration.

1. Demand for Potatoes.   In Figure 1-1, the average farm price of potatoes in the United States is plotted vertically against the annual per capita consumption of potatoes, measured horizontally. Each point represents data for a recent year. The downward drift of the scatter of points from upper left to lower right confirms the everyday observation that people tend to buy more at low than at high prices. At the high price of $2.57, for example, average consumption of potatoes in the United States shrank to 133 pounds per person in 1980, whereas at the low price of $1.46, consumption reached 152 pounds per person in 1979. Of course, as a glance at the chart reveals, price is not the sole influence on buying habits. Consumption during 1981 was

Figure 1-1 _____
Demand for potatoes. Prices have been divided by the consumer price index to adjust for inflation.

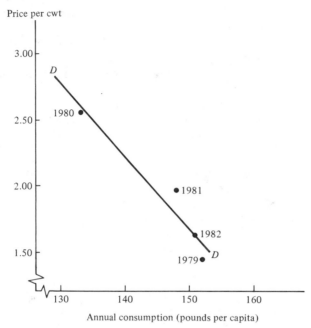

Source: U.S. Department of Agriculture, *Agricultural Statistics,* various issues.

somewhat greater, and during 1979 somewhat less than would have been expected from the price of potatoes alone. Part of this variation can be traced to changes in buyers' incomes and part to changes in the prices of other foods that can substitute for potatoes in the diet. Some of the variation is associated with changes in consumer tastes for potatoes, connected with the shifting popularity of such things as packaged mashed potatoes or "fries" at fast-food outlets.

By the use of appropriate statistical procedures, it is possible to allow for the effects of many of these other influences and to estimate the effect of price alone on potato purchases. The result is shown by the curve *DD,* drawn through the midst of the observations. Such a curve, called a *demand curve,* represents the quantity of potatoes buyers would be expected to purchase at each price, other influences being held constant.

2. *Demand Elasticity.* The responses of buyers to changes in price are measured by the *elasticity of demand,* which expresses the percentage change in quantity purchased to be expected in response to a 1 percent change in price. For example, if a 1 percent price increase induced the buyers of a product to cut their purchases by 2 percent, the elasticity of demand for the product would be expressed as −2 to indicate that percentage changes in quantity purchased tend to be double the percentage change in price. The negative sign reminds us that quantity is altered in the opposite direction to the change in price, a rise in price being accompanied by a reduction in quantity, and vice versa. In a similar fashion, elasticity of −.7 would characterize the demand for a product when a reduction of only .7 percent in purchases would occur in response to a 1 percent price increase. An elasticity of −1 would indicate that percentage changes in quantity and price tend to be equal, and so on.

The elasticity of demand for particular products is readily estimated from fitted demand curves by selecting two prices close together and reading the corresponding quantities shown by the curve. The elasticity is then calculated as the ratio of the percentage difference in the two quantities to the percentage difference in the two prices. For example, careful measurement on the demand curve *DD* indicates that purchasers would be ready to buy about 142 pounds per year at a price of $2.10, but if the price were lowered to $2.00, purchases would expand to about 144 pounds. The price reduction from $2.10 to $2.00 is a change of −5 percent, whereas the increase in purchased quantity from 142 to 144 pounds is a change of about 1.4 percent. This yields an estimated elasticity of demand for potatoes of about 1.4/−5, or about −.3.

We are rarely interested in such exact measurement of elasticity, but we do need a general idea of how elastic the demand for a given product is. For this purpose it is convenient to classify demand curves into broad categories, using elasticity of −1, called *unit* elasticity, as the dividing point. Demand curves with elasticity smaller than 1 (in absolute value) are then referred to as *inelastic* demands. In these terms, the demand for potatoes with an elasticity of −.3 would be classified as *inelastic*.

Demand curves with elasticity greater than 1 in absolute value are termed *relatively elastic*. The demand for lettuce—estimated to have an elasticity of −2.8—is classified as relatively elastic.

3. *Causes of Differences in Elasticity.* Because elasticity measures buyer response to price, it varies widely among products, depending in each case on the characteristics of the product and on buyers' attitudes toward it. Products like potatoes, which many people view as necessities, or food staples, have inelastic demands. Buyers feel that they need a certain amount in their diet and are reluctant to cut back on their use of the commodity as its price rises. By the same token, because buyers are already consuming about as much of it as they feel they need, they have use for only little more when prices fall.

In contrast, products that are viewed as luxuries exhibit relatively elastic demands, for their consumption can be reduced almost painlessly when prices rise, yet buyers are delighted at the chance to enjoy them when lower prices place them within reach of the budget. Among farm products, demands for fruits and fresh vegetables tend to be relatively elastic. The demand for peaches, for example, has been estimated to have an elasticity of −1.49, five times that of potatoes. The high elasticity reflects the ease with which households can do without peaches when the price rises and the welcome accorded the fruit when it becomes cheap.

The elasticity of demand also depends on the relationship the product bears to others. In particular, products that have good substitutes to which buyers can turn as alternatives tend to have relatively elastic demands. Even small percentage changes in price lead large numbers of buyers to choose the cheaper substitute. This is probably one of the reasons that demands for fresh vegetables tend to be relatively elastic. The elasticity of demand for fresh tomatoes, for example, has been estimated at −2.2, and that of fresh peas at −2.8, largely because many other fresh vegetables can be used instead of these if the price is right.

Price elasticities of demand for a number of farm products are given in Table 1-1. Note that demands for basic commodities like potatoes and corn tend to be inelastic, as might be expected from their nature. On the other hand, many individual fresh fruits and vegetables have highly elastic de-

Table 1-1
Elasticity of Demand for Selected Farm Products

Product	Elasticity of Demand	
	Price	Income
Cabbage	−.25	n.a.[a]
Potatoes	−.27	.15
Wool	−.33	.27
Peanuts	−.38	.44
Eggs	−.43	.57
Onions	−.44	.58
Milk	−.49	.50
Butter	−.62	.37
Oranges	−.62	.83
Corn	−.63	n.a.
Cream	−.69	1.72
Fresh cucumbers	−.7	.7
Apples	−1.27	1.32
Peaches	−1.49	1.43
Fresh tomatoes	−2.22	.24
Lettuce	−2.58	.88
Fresh peas	−2.83	1.05

[a]Not available.

Source: Estimated by the U.S. Department of Agriculture.

mands, partly because of their less basic character and partly because of the availability of many close substitutes to which consumers can turn.

4. Elasticity of Derived Demands. A particularly important aspect of demand for farm products is that most are purchased from the farm by canners, millers, and other manufacturers who process the raw product before selling it to final consumers. Wheat is milled into flour and baked into bread before it is purchased for the table; meat is butchered and packaged before consumers buy it; and most fruit and vegetables are canned or frozen before consumers buy them. Even those to be sold fresh require transportation, packaging, and other retailing costs before they can be delivered to the table.

As shown in Table 1-2, only 25 percent of the retail value of food items purchased in the United States consists of their original value on the farm; 75 percent consists of value added by processing and marketing. These percentages vary widely among different farm products. Because of the lengthy production line required for bread and cereal products to reach the final consumer, farm value constitutes only 22 percent of the retail price. The value of the barley, rice, hops, and other farm products in the retail price of a can of beer is even smaller. In contrast, the farm share is 65 percent of the retail price of meat, poultry, and eggs which reach the table more directly.

Because of the value added by processing and marketing, the value of the farm product represents a small percentage of the retail price paid by ultimate buyers, and this tends to make the demand for raw farm products even less elastic. To make clear why this is so, let us consider a processed product with a relatively elastic demand—frozen peas, with a demand elasticity of about -2. This elasticity would mean that a 5 percent reduction in the price of frozen peas would tend to increase consumption by about 10 percent. But if frozen peas are typical of other vegetables, farm value constitutes only

Table 1-2

Shares in Final Retail Value of Food Products

	Billions of Dollars	Percent
Final retail value	$361.1	100
Processing and marketing costs		
Labor	123.7	34
Rail and truck transportation	16.8	5
Power, containers, and other costs	119.8	33
Corporate profit (before taxes)	12.0	3
Farm value of products	89.0	25

Source: U.S. Department of Agriculture. *Agricultural Statistics*, 1987 (Washington, D.C.: U.S. Government Printing Office, 1987).

about 30 percent of the final retail price, so a 5 percent reduction in the farm price of peas would result in no more than 1.5 percent reduction in retail prices for frozen peas. Given the elasticity of -2, this lower price would stimulate only 3 percent greater sales of frozen peas and only a 3 percent increase in the purchase of raw peas to freeze. In consequence, then, a 5 percent price reduction at the farm level stimulates only a 3 percent increase in the quantity of peas bought from farmers, and this gives demand for peas an elasticity of only $-.6$ at the farm level, despite the highly elastic demand for frozen peas by consumers.

The relationship demonstrated for frozen peas holds for all derived demands. In general, the smaller the farm share in retail price, the lower the elasticity of derived demand for the product tends to be at the farm level. Because farm value is only 25 percent of the retail value of foods and other farm products, demand at the farm level would tend to be inelastic even if retail demands for final products were relatively quite elastic. In fact, however, because retail demands for most food products are inelastic even at the consumer level, the small farm share in retail price tends to make demand at the farm level very inelastic indeed.

5. *Commodities with Several Uses.* As we have seen, the elasticity of demand for a product depends on what it is used for, but many commodities are used for more than one purpose. In such cases, demand elasticity varies among the different uses, depending on the degree to which each particular use is viewed as "necessity" or "luxury" and depending on the availability of substitutes to replace the commodity for each purpose. Wheat, for example, has two important uses. It is used not only to make bread and bakery products for the table, but also as a feed grain for poultry and livestock. As a component of bread, wheat is generally viewed as a basic necessity; moreover, because of its gluten content, wheat flour has no good substitutes in baking. Indeed, wheat is so outstanding in this regard that most recipes for "rye" bread, "corn" bread, and other "nonwheat" bakery products call for the addition of wheat flour to the other grain in order to impart cohesiveness to the dough. As a result, the demand for wheat to make into bakery products is quite inelastic. As a feed grain, however, wheat has many fine substitutes in corn, oats, sorghum grains, and other commodities, so that the demand for wheat as feed grain in relatively elastic.

Statistical measurement by the U.S. Department of Agriculture bears out these differences in elasticity. The demand for wheat destined to be made into flour has an elasticity of only $-.2$, whereas the demand for wheat to be used as a feed grain has an elasticity of -3.

Taking all the uses together, the overall elasticity of demand for a product having several uses is the weighted average of elasticities of demand in the different uses, with weights proportional to the quantity consumed in each use. Because wheat is used overwhelmingly for flour, its overall demand is highly inelastic, despite the high elasticity of demand in one of its uses.

6. *Elasticity and Allocation of Available Crop.* Differences in elasticity play an important role in the allocation of farm products among different uses. When supplies are short, the consumption of products must be cut back. Generally, there is some reduction in all uses, but the greatest reduction is in less essential uses, or uses for which the product can readily be replaced by close substitutes. These are, of course, the uses in which demand elasticity is high. Rising prices curtail consumption in these areas, leaving proportionally more for essential uses where replacement is difficult. Response to increased supply is the opposite. As price falls, more of the product is devoted to all uses, but consumption expands proportionally more in the uses that are less essential or where the cheaper product can replace substitutes.

The operation of this principle can be seen in Table 1-3, which shows uses of wheat during a year of high supply and during a year of lower supply. During the year of low supply, wheat consumption for human food was maintained at 96 percent of its higher level, whereas only 67 percent as much wheat was consumed for animal feed. These proportions are about what would be expected from the difference in demand elasticity in the two uses.

Other Factors Affecting Demand

In addition to price, the quantity purchased is affected by income, population, prices of substitute products, consumer tastes, and—for products like soybeans, which have important industrial uses—the state of industrial technology. The influence of change in these factors is generally represented by shifts in position of the demand curve. When, for any reason, consumers begin to buy more of a commodity than formerly at given prices, this fact is represented by a bodily shift of the demand curve to the right. Reduced purchases at given prices are represented by a shift of the demand curve to the left. Curve *DD* in Figure 1-1, for example, shows the location of potato demand when real per capita income stood at the average for the period. The point representing purchases during 1981, however, lies on a curve shifted slightly to the right by the high level of income in that year, whereas the dot corresponding to 1979 lies on a curve shifted to the left.

Table 1-3
Tons of Wheat Consumed in the United States (in millions), 1985 and 1986

Year	Human Food	Animal Feed
1986 (high supply)	700	411
1985 (low supply)	678	274

Source: U.S. Department of Agriculture, *Agricultural Statistics, 1987* (Washington, D.C.: U.S. Government Printing Office, 1987).

1. Income Elasticity. As with prices, the effects of income on buying are expressed in terms of elasticities. The income elasticity of demand is the percentage increase in quantity bought at given prices that occurs in response to a 1 percent increase in income. For example, calculation with potato data indicates that a 1 percent rise in real per capita income increases the volume of potatoes purchased by only .15 percent, and this is expressed as an income elasticity of .15. (Unlike price elasticity, most income elasticities are positive because the consumption of most commodities rises as income increases.)

An income elasticity of 1 characterizes a commodity whose consumption tends to rise in proportion to income. An income elasticity of less than 1 indicates that the quantity purchased grows less than in proportion to income. This is generally characteristic of staples and basic commodities, like potatoes, that even low-income families consume in quantity. An income elasticity greater than 1 characterizes products favored by rich people that poorer buyers cannot afford.

Income elasticity is given for most of the farm products in Table 1-1. As can be seen, basic staples like potatoes and onions have low income-elasticities, whereas cream, fruit, and fresh vegetables are characterized by high income elasticities. The latter represent more expensive, preferred items whose consumption rises more than in proportion to income.

Commodities like cabbage and dried beans are characterized by negative income elasticity. That is, these are *inferior goods* that form an important part of the diet of poor people but are readily abandoned in favor of preferred, but more expensive, substitutes as income rises.

Because of wide differences in the income elasticities of different products, rising income does more to change the composition of demand than it does to increase the total amount of food consumed. That is, rising income increases the demand for more expensive, preferred foods, but it does so largely at the expense of reduced demand for other products. For example, families with incomes exceeding $15,000 (1973 prices) tend to eat, on the average, nearly three times as much sirloin steak as do families with incomes in the $5,000 to $6,000 bracket, but they eat only 20 percent more meat of all kinds, and the difference in total food consumption is even less. Richer families merely eat steak instead of other meat and eat meat instead of other food. In addition, rich families consume a great deal less of such inferior foods as dried beans and cabbage than poor people do.

2. Prices of Other Products and Cross-Elasticity of Demand. The purchase of products that have good substitutes is strongly influenced by the price of the substitute. A rise in the price of beef, for example, stimulates the demand for pork, and vice versa. This influence is measured by what is called the *cross-elasticity* of demand; it is calculated by the percentage change that occurs in the quantity of the item purchased, given its own price, in response to a 1 percent change in the price of its substitute. Research into the demand for meat indicates, for example, that a 1 percent increase in the price of beef tends to increase the purchase of pork by about one quarter of 1 percent. This response is represented by a cross-elasticity of .25 between the demand for pork and the price of beef. Cross-elasticities are a good index of how closely two products substitute for each other in the buyer's consumption pattern. Low cross-elasticity indicates products that are only poor substitutes, for a change in the price of one has little effect on the quantity of the other that is purchased. The more readily products can be interchanged, the higher their cross-elasticities tend to become. In the extreme case of perfect substitutes, any difference in price would lead to consumption of only the cheaper of the two products, a situation that would be represented by an infinitely large cross-elasticity.

In Table 1-4, estimated demand elasticities are given for three kinds of meat. As would be expected, a rise in the price of any one kind of meat reduces its consumption but increases the consumption of its substitutes. Thus, a 10 percent increase in the price of beef tends to reduce beef consumption about 6.5 percent (in keeping with its price elasticity of demand of $-.65$) but increases the purchase of pork by 2.5 percent and the purchase of chicken by 1.2 percent.

3. Individual Commodities Versus Commodity Groups. Demands for individual commodities with close substitutes have high price and high cross-elasticities, so any change in prices causes a substantial change in the proportions in which consumers purchase the several products. When we consider the entire bundle of products as a group, however, we find a much lower response to price changes when the prices of all substitutes change together. For example, the demand for beef has an elasticity of $-.65$ in response to changes in its own price, and cross-elasticities of .01 and .20 in response to changes in prices of pork and chicken, respectively. But when all meat prices change together, the buyer's response is measured not by these individual elasticities but by their algebraic sum. Thus, in response to a 10 percent increase in the prices of all three meats, consumption of beef would show an elasticity of $-.65 + .01 + .20 = -.44$ and would decline only 4.4 percent.

Table 1-4
Elasticities of Demand for Beef, Pork, and Chicken

Product	Elasticity of Demand with Respect to			
	Price of Beef	Price of Pork	Price of Chicken	Income
Beef	−.65	.01	.20	1.05
Pork	.25	−.45	.16	.14
Chicken	.12	.20	−.65	.28

Source: Calculated for the author by students in Economics 835 at Michigan State University.

Similarly, a 10 percent rise in all meat prices would reduce pork consumption by only 4 percent and chicken by only 3.3 percent. In other words, when commodities are considered in groups, the demand elasticity for the group as a whole is substantially lower than the elasticities of demand for individual members of the group. The demand for feed grains as a whole is much less elastic than the demand for corn, oats, or sorghum grains taken individually, and the demand for fresh vegetables is much less elastic than the demands for tomatoes, fresh peas, or green beans taken individually.

Demand Elasticity and Farm Incomes

The general inelasticity of the demand for farm products, especially when major commodity groups are considered as a whole, has important consequences for the behavior of farm incomes. Unlike most manufactured goods, which are priced first with production adjusted to whatever sales materialize, farm crops are grown first and then are placed on the market for whatever price they will bring. Because these prices reflect the size of the crop, normal year-to-year variation in weather, insect pests, and other growing conditions generate year-to-year price fluctuations, the magnitude of which depend on demand elasticity.

The prices of products with inelastic demands fall more than in proportion to increased output, and total dollar value is smaller for a larger crop than it is for a smaller crop. This can be tested in terms of the demand for potatoes illustrated in Figure 1-1. According to the demand curve *DD*, the production of 130 pounds of potatoes per capita leads to a price of about $2.75 per hundred pounds, or a crop worth about $358 per consumer. In a nation of 230 million consumers, the total crop would be worth about $823 million. Increasing production to 140 pounds per person, however, reduces the price to about $2.21 per hundred pounds, making the larger crop worth about $711 million all told. In short, an increase of less than 8 percent in the size of the crop reduces its total value by 14 percent.

Because most farm products — particularly when major commodity groups are considered as a whole — have inelastic demands, it follows that expanded production brings in fewer dollars and reduces farm incomes, whereas contracted production brings in more dollars and raises farm incomes. For this reason, natural year-to-year fluctuations in growing conditions make farming very much a "boom-or-bust" proposition. Poor growing conditions or crop failure in one part of the market mean severe losses to the farms affected but high incomes and prosperity for the other farms. Good growing conditions yield bumper crops but also result in low prices and reduced incomes for everybody.

Beyond the short-run fluctuations, demand exerts important long-run influences on farm incomes. Because demand is inelastic, a rising trend of farm yields means falling dollar receipts and a downward trend of farm income unless demand is expanded by enough to absorb the additional production. Two principal factors operate to expand farm demand. Demand tends to grow in proportion to the number of consumers and also expands as real per capita incomes rise. But growth in population raises demand only in proportion to the number of people (we might say that the "population elasticity" of farm demand is unity), whereas the income elasticity of demand for farm products is considerably less than unity. It thus follows that periods like the last fifty years, in which agricultural productivity grew much more rapidly than population, would also be periods of falling farm prices, diminishing farm incomes, and serious problems for the agricultural community.

The performance of agriculture is not exclusively a matter of demand, however, and before we can explore these problems further, we must turn to an analysis of agricultural supply.

III.
SUPPLY AND THE PERFORMANCE OF AGRICULTURE

Just as demand represents the behavior of buyers in relation to prices, incomes, and other factors, *supply* represents the behavior of producers in response to prices and costs. Like demand, supply can be represented by a curve displaying the relationship between prices and quantities, and the response of quantity to changes in price can be expressed as an elasticity of supply. But there is an important difference between demand and supply, for although buyers tend to adapt promptly to new conditions, producers often require time to revise plans and production schedules or even to acquire new facilities and equipment. For this reason, it is useful to distinguish three different supply situations according to the scope afforded producers to respond to new information about prices and costs.

Harvest Supply—The Very Short Run

Once crops are mature and ready for market, the total quantity available is fixed, and no action on the part of farmers can generate output beyond that total. Nevertheless, the total available is rarely harvested, for it seldom pays to strip fields so carefully that every last particle is collected. Some crops mature over periods of several weeks, and growers must decide when the time is best for harvest and whether it is worthwhile to return to the fields for a second harvest a week or so later. Some crops can be harvested cheaply and quickly but with greater loss of product than would be true of a slower, more expensive harvest. Clearly, high prices at harvest time make it profitable to harvest a larger proportion of the potential crop, whereas low prices make it unprofitable to take great care with picking, and this often results in the outright abandonment of low-yield acreage that would be too expensive to harvest.

Although there is some flexibility in the quantity produced from a given crop, the physical limitation to what can be harvested and the relatively low cost of harvesting (roughly 20 percent of variable cost) severely limit the extent to which output from a mature crop can be varied. Once crops are ready for market, harvest supply is extremely inelastic.

Short-Run Supply and Production Costs

Because the quantity that producers plan to grow depends on expected price in relation to production costs, the properties of short-run supply depend on the structure of costs.

1. Cost Structure. Production costs for farmers—like those of any other business firm—are of two general types. Some costs are fixed regardless of output, whereas others vary with the level of production. *Fixed costs* include taxes, interest on the farm mortgage, depreciation of equipment, and similar expenses that must be incurred whether production is undertaken or not and that do not vary in magnitude as production rises and falls. *Variable costs* are zero as long as nothing is produced, but they rise sharply when production is initiated. The initial increase in variable cost is associated with planning, acquisition of materials, and other general costs that would not be incurred at all if nothing were produced. An important element of this start-up cost consists of the labor of the farm owner and family members, or the salary of managers of corporate farms.

Once start-up costs have been incurred, output can be expanded with relatively small increases in outlays for seed, fertilizer, herbicides, labor, power, and other variable costs; in this range, cost rises slowly as more bushels are produced. There is, however, a limit to the output available from given facilities, and as this capacity limit is approached, variable cost rises more and more sharply. Additional output can be had only by extra care, additional fertilizer, or other inputs to increase yield per acre.

2. Costs of a Corn Grower. Variable costs per acre of corn raised on central Iowa farms are given in Table 1-5. In keeping with modern farming methods, labor cost is low, with chemical herbicides employed in place of labor-intensive cultivation for weed control. Extensive use is made of commercial fertilizer to maintain high yields with little or no crop rotation. All together, variable cost amounted to $41.07 per acre planted. The sources from which the data were taken gave no indication of fixed costs; however, on a national average, fixed costs for farming—largely depreciation of buildings and equipment, interest on farm debt, and taxes—amount to about a third of variable cost. On this basis, we can estimate the total cost of corn grown in central Iowa at about $62.50 per acre.

Table 1-5 _____
Variable Costs per Acre of Corn Production, Central Iowa Farms

Costs	Quantity	Costs per Acre (in 1971 $)
Preharvest costs		
Labor (including owners)	3.78 h	5.82
Seed	.23 bu	3.22
Fertilizer and lime		
Nitrogen	100 lb	5.40
Phosphorus	22 lb	4.58
Potassium	19 lb	.99
Lime	.23 ton	.91
Fuel, lubricants, repairs		3.95
Insecticides		2.18
Herbicides		2.24
Custom work		.85
Hail insurance		.30
Interest on operating expenses		1.01
Total preharvest cost		31.45
Harvest costs		
Labor	2 h	3.08
Fuel, lubricants, repairs		1.81
Custom-hired harvesting and trucking		2.85
Other harvest expenses		1.98
Total harvest cost per harvested acre		9.72
Total harvest cost per planted acre		9.62
Variable cost per planted acre		41.07

Source: U.S. Department of Agriculture, Economic Research Service, *Selected U.S. Crop Budgets, Yields, Outputs, and Variable Costs: North Central Region*, Vol. 2 (Washington, D.C.: U.S. Government Printing Office, 1971).

3. *Average and Marginal Costs.* Total costs are translated into average and marginal costs in Figure 1-2. Marginal cost (MC) is the rate at which total cost rises as production is increased. Once start-up costs have been incurred and production is under way, additional corn can be raised for little more than the cost of the seed and materials needed to cultivate additional acreage. This keeps marginal cost low until production approaches the physical limits of the farm. As this capacity is approached, greater and greater outlays are needed to extract additional output, and marginal cost rises more and more sharply.

Average variable cost (AVC) is high at low levels of production because start-up costs are spread over limited output. As production expands, start-up costs are spread over more and more bushels of corn, pulling down the average variable cost per bushel. As production approaches the capacity of

Figure 1-2
Average and marginal costs of a corn grower (1971 dollars).

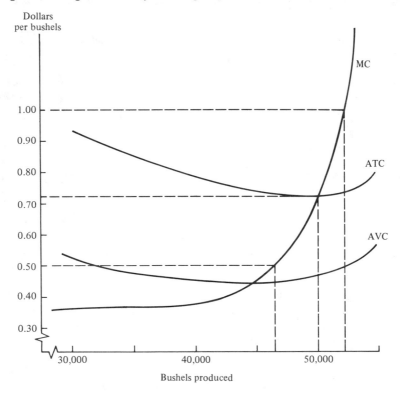

the farm, however, marginal cost begins to rise more than the average start-up cost declines, and at this point average variable cost stops falling and begins to rise.

Because fixed costs are unchanged as output expands, average fixed cost is inversely proportional to output regardless of production. Average total cost is merely the sum of average variable and averaged fixed costs.

4. Profit Maximization and Supply Elasticity. By a familiar proposition in competitive theory, output that brings marginal cost into equality with expected price is the most profitable production plan for a competitive firm—provided only that the expected price is high enough to cover the minimum average variable cost at which the firm can operate. At an expected price of 50 cents per bushel, the farm of Figure 1-2 would plan to raise about 46,500 bushels. If a price of 72 cents per bushel were expected, production would be increased to 50,000 bushels, and a price of $1.00 per bushel would raise the most profitable production to 52,300 bushels.

The cost curves shown are consistent with the cost data of Table 1-5 and are typical of agricultural production. Marginal cost rises so sharply near capacity output that even wide price variations exert little influence on the output of any individual grower, at least as long as he continues in operation. In other words, if a farm operates at all, it functions very nearly at the capacity output afforded by available land and facilities. As Figure 1-2 shows, even a 100 percent price increase—from 50 cents to $1.00—would induce the farmer to add only about 12.5 percent to planned production. This output response corresponds to a supply elasticity of only about .1.

But growers will continue to produce only so long as they expect prices that will cover their average variable costs. Fixed costs are already sunk in the business; they will continue whether anything is planted or not, and the only way to recover them is to operate the farm. Variable costs, on the other hand, are not incurred until the farmer decides to make the outlays; if there is no prospect of recovering variable costs, it is better to keep the money. To operate at all under these circumstances would result in losing not only fixed costs, but also some part of the variable cost in addition.

This proposition can be tested in terms of Figure 1-2. The 52,300 bushels produced at a price of $1.00 would entail an average total cost of about 74 cents per bushel and would leave nearly $13,600 as profit above cost. But production of 46,500 bushels at a price of 50 cents would involve an average total cost of about 73 cents per bushel, so the farm would sustain a loss of about $10,700 for the year. Even so, this would be better than shutting down the farm, for with no production at all, the farm would lose its entire $13,500 fixed cost. Because the 50-cent price is above the minimum average variable cost at which the farm can operate (about 44 cents per bushel), the farm is $2,800 better off when it produces at a loss than when it shuts down.

If, however, the price of corn should fall below the 44-cent minimum average variable cost to, say, 40 cents per bushel, marginal cost would be equated to price at an output of about 43,000 bushels. At this level of production, average total cost would be about 76 cents per bushel, and the operation would generate a loss of nearly $15,500. This would be about $2,000 more than the farm would lose if it simply stopped production and settled for the loss of all fixed costs.

Because farms in operation tend to operate very close to capacity regardless of price, the principal supply response to falling price occurs when farmers find it no longer profitable to produce the crop. Similarly, the principal supply response to rising prices comes when farmers find prices moving back into the profitable range and again take up production of the crop.

Variable costs differ widely among growers, depending on soil type, climate, length of growing season, and skill of the producer. During the same year that growers in central Iowa incurred an average variable cost of 47

The Structure of American Industry

cents per bushel of corn, Nebraska farmers produced corn at an average variable cost ranging from 49 cents per bushel in the lowest-cost district to 71 cents in the highest-cost area, and similar cost differences are characteristic of all other crops.

Figure 1-3 shows the striking variation in average costs among cotton growers in the United States. The curve shows the percentage of cotton production that was produced by cotton growers whose average costs were lower than those indicated on the vertical axis. For example, the average variable cost line indicates that whereas practically all cotton growers had an average variable cost below 39 cents per pound, only about 75 percent of

Figure 1-3 ———————————————————————

Percentage of total U.S. upland cotton crop raised by growers with average costs below those specified. Each point on the curve represents the percentage of U.S. cotton production (on the horizontal axis) raised by growers whose average costs were below the figure given on the vertical axis.

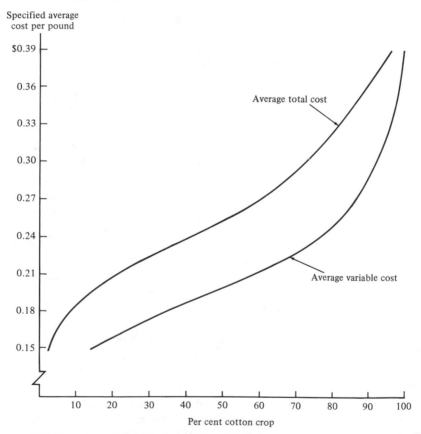

Source: U.S. Department of Agriculture, *Costs of Producing Upland Cotton in the United States,* Economic Research Service, 1967.

cotton was grown by farmers with an average variable cost below 24 cents, and barely more than a third of all cotton was produced at an average variable cost below 18 cents.

Because no grower will plant cotton unless he expects price to cover at least his average variable cost, the distribution of average variable costs among growers gives a good indication of the elasticity of the short-run supply of cotton. For example, because practically all cotton grown in the United States was produced by growers with an average variable cost below 40 cents, but only about 92 percent by growers with an average variable cost below 30 cents, a 25 percent reduction of price from 40 cents to 30 cents would cause about an 8 percent reduction in cotton output, corresponding to a supply elasticity of about .3 for the short term.

Still another source contributing to the elasticity of short-run supply is the shifting composition of the output of multiple-product farms. For several reasons, many farms produce several different crops. Hog farmers, cattle feeders, and poultry growers need grain for feed, and it is natural for them to raise some of their own feed requirements. Other farmers raise crops that ripen at different times in order to spread harvesting over a longer period. This avoids the high harvesting costs that would be incurred if the entire crop had to be brought in within a few days and reduces fixed cost by employing a smaller investment in harvesting equipment operated over a longer period, rather than a large investment that is used only briefly each year. Although it is less significant in these days of commercial fertilizer than it once was, crop rotation is another reason for multiple-product farms. Finally, producing several crops provides some degree of insurance against such natural calamities as blight, which can ruin yields for any one crop, and against the economic calamities that can result from unfavorable marketing conditions for any one particular commodity.

Regardless of the reason, however, the proportions in which different crops are grown are not fixed, but vary in response to expected prices. The expectation of cheap corn and high-priced hogs, for example, leads hog raisers to increase the number of hogs, while planning to buy, rather than raise, extra feed requirements. Expectation of high prices for corn and low-priced hogs, on the other hand, induces growers to reduce hog production, while planning to sell, rather than feed, some of the high-priced corn. In a similar fashion, a division of acreage between corn and soybeans, the choice between planting more tomatoes or more sweet corn, and other planting decisions depend on expectations about the relative prices of alternative crops and therefore contribute to their supply elasticities.

Market Equilibrium and Adjustment Cycles

The interaction of short-run supply with demand for farm products governs the year-to-year behavior of production and prices. This interaction is depicted in Figure 1-4, where supply, *SS,* and demand, *DD,* determine a

Figure 1-4

Short-run market equilibrium.

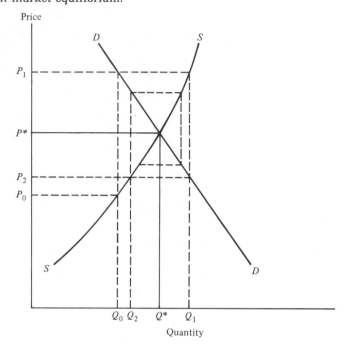

market equilibrium represented by price P^* and quantity Q^*. The P^* and Q^* values are equilibrium values in the familiar sense that no other combination of price and output could simultaneously satisfy the desire of consumers to buy—as indicated by the demand curve—and conform to the production plans of growers—as shown by the supply curve. At any price higher than P^*—at P_1, for example—farms would expand planting in keeping with the supply curve and would bring to market a total output equal to Q_1, greater than Q^*. Yet, consumers, faced by a high price like P_1, would purchase only Q_0, an amount smaller than the equilibrium quantity and considerably less than the amount farmers would be bringing to market. Resulting unsold surpluses would make it impossible to maintain the higher price, and the market would be forced back toward equilibrium. By the same token, any price below P^*—say, P_2—would lead farmers to cut production back to Q_2, whereas the lower price would induce consumers to try to purchase a larger quantity, Q_1. The resulting inability of the market of satisfy demand would drive price and production upward toward the equilibrium values.

Equilibrium price and quantity comprise a kind of "target" for the market, marking values toward which actual price and output are continually being pushed, but it should be understood that day-to-day price and quantity are rarely observed at their equilibrium values. For one thing, supply deals with production *plans* rather than actual outcome. The most a farmer can do is to plant and tend his crop in a manner calculated to yield the most profit under normally expected conditions. Actual output invariably depends on vagaries of weather, insect damage, blight, and other factors that affect yields.

In addition, supply relates production plans to *expected* prices, and growers' expectations are not always exact. Indeed, the fact that they must plant for next season on the basis of price expectations derived from last season's experience sometimes leads to a systematic cycling of prices and output around equilibrium. For example, suppose farmers initially expect the low price P_0 and, consequently, plant the restricted output Q_0, in keeping with short-run supply. When this limited quantity reaches market, however, price would be driven up to P_1, in keeping with demand. But on the basis of the high price P_1, growers would be induced to plant Q_1 for the next season, and price subsequently would fall to P_2. The producer response to this would be an output of Q_2, which would again force price up. Under these circumstances, as can be seen in Figure 1-4, price and output would be observed to perform a series of diminishing cycles as they approached equilibrium. The spiral adjustment path marked out by the dotted lines in Figure 1-4 reminds some people of a cobweb, and for this reason the cycles of price and output observed in such markets are called *cobweb cycles*. Figure 1-4 is a highly simplified version of what actually happens. In the first place, production is not neatly divided into discrete stages but is subject to more or less continuous adjustment. Crops, once planted, can be cultivated or sprayed more intensively when prices are observed to be rising, improving yields beyond what had initially been planned; or acreage can be abandoned before maturity if it appears that low prices will make it impossible to recover the additional costs that otherwise would be invested in it over the remainder of the growing season.

The length of time between high and low prices or between low and high prices in the cobweb cycle depends on the length of time between the initial planning and the marketing of the finished product. Crops such as onions and potatoes that have annual growing seasons also tend to have prices that oscillate annually, whereas products such as hogs that take longer to raise have prices that oscillate more slowly.

The history of hog prices in the United States exhibits cycles that are readily apparent in Figure 1-5. Because corn is the principal variable cost of hog production, the price of hogs is shown divided by the price of corn. The figure shows four complete price cycles in the 17-year period, beginning with the peak in 1969. This works out to an average of roughly four years for the price of hogs to complete a cycle from high to low and back again. The relatively long period of this cobweb cycle reflects the time required for hog raisers to respond to high prices by building up their herds of broodsows and the additional time that must elapse after the sows are bred before mature hogs are available for market.

Figure 1-5
U.S. hog prices, 1968–1986.

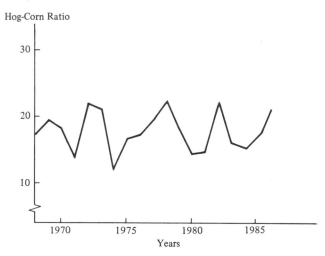

Source: U.S. Department of Agriculture, *Agricultural Statistics*, selected issues.

1. Ironing Out Price Fluctuations. The basic cause of systematic cycles in price and production is that farmers are forced to formulate production plans on the basis of past conditions, rather than on the basis of conditions at the time the crop will be ready for harvest. When farmers have advance information about market conditions, cycles are much less severe or are eliminated entirely. One way growers can obtain such information is by contracting with buyers in advance about prices and quantities, and this is common in many lines of agriculture. For example, 98 percent of all sugar beets, 85 percent of vegetables grown for processing, and 95 percent of all fluid-grade milk are sold to processors under contract. Contract marketing also covers 90 percent of all broiler chickens, 55 percent of citrus fruit, 45 percent of potatoes, and 42 percent of turkeys. This contrasts with barely 1 percent of hog production sold in advance.

A second way to iron out price fluctuations is by vertically integrating farming into the food-processing industry. Integrated farms are not independent producers at all, but operate as subsidiaries of food-processing firms. Vertical integration is especially common in cane sugar, where 60 percent of all cane grown comes from acreage owned by sugar-manufacturing firms. (The other 40 percent is grown under contract.) Similarly, 30 percent of citrus is grown in groves operated by processors, 35 percent of potatoes are grown on processor-owned farms, and 30 percent of vegetables commercially grown for fresh market are grown by subsidiaries of supermarket chains.

A third way to eliminate cycles in price and production is government action to stabilize prices by means of price-support programs. Essentially, these programs provide an advance guarantee to farmers that prices will not fall below a specified minimum, regardless of market conditions at time of harvest. The most important purpose of government agricultural price supports, however, is not to smooth out fluctuations, but, rather, as the term suggests, to maintain a level of farm prices higher than market equilibrium. We explore the operation of these programs at a later point.

Long-Run Supply

1. The Role of Average Total Cost.   Farms that cover variable costs but fail to recover all their fixed costs can remain in business for short periods by allowing buildings and equipment to go unrepaired and by digging into savings to meet family living costs. Sooner or later, however, a time arrives when buildings become unusable or equipment must be replaced. At this point, farmers must decide whether to continue in operation. Unless prospects are so strong that additional investment will not only be recovered but will yield a profit, it is obviously better to shut down rather than invest more money in what is already a losing proposition. In the long run, in other words, supply depends on the ability of farmers to cover not just variable costs but total cost of production. The long-run elasticity of supply, then, depends on the distribution of average total costs among growers. For cotton production, this distribution is shown by the average total cost curve in Figure 1-3, each point on which indicates the percentage of total cotton production (on the horizontal axis) grown in the United States by producers whose average total costs are less than the figure indicated on the vertical axis. For example, 92 percent of all cotton was grown by farms with an average total cost below 39 cents, 88.2 percent was grown by those with an average total cost below 36 cents, and so on.

Naturally, the quantity of cotton that could be grown by farms that can cover average total cost at any given price is considerably smaller than what can be grown by those farms that could temporarily stay in production by covering average variable costs. The chart shows, for example, that whereas growers of 95 percent of the cotton in the United States could cover average variable cost at a price of 33 cents, growers of only 81 percent of the cotton could cover average total cost at that price. If price persisted at 33 cents, output would immediately fall to 95 percent; however, in the long run, producers of only 81 percent could afford to stay in operation. This greater long-run responsiveness of production is reflected in supply elasticity. Whereas practically all growers had an average total cost below 40 cents per pound, growers of only 73 percent of the cotton had an average total cost below 30 cents. Thus, the long-run effect of a 25 percent decline in price from 40 cents to 30 cents would be accompanied by a 27 percent decline in output, corresponding to a long-run supply elasticity of about 1.

Although supply in Figure 1-3 is treated only at prices below 39 cents per pound, similar relationships hold for supply at higher prices. Prices above 39 cents attract higher-cost growers to production, resulting in a larger long-run response to price than that obtained in the short run.

2. Long-Run Adjustments to Shifts in Demand. An important aspect of the performance of any industry is how effectively output is adjusted to shifts in demand. But because of the three different supply situations, adjustment of price and output is not a once-and-for-all process; it is a sequence of events that may require many years for completion. Buyers whose demand has risen, for example, find themselves initially confronted by a very inelastic harvest supply. Although rising prices signal a greater demand for the product, growers have little power to satisfy it, for they are locked into the results of production plans laid many months previously and can harvest no more than has been grown. The most they can do to satisfy increased demand is to strip fields with greater care than would have been profitable at lower prices and to harvest low-yield acreage that would otherwise have been abandoned.

Although rising prices do little to elicit additional output, they nevertheless perform two important functions. In the first place, rising prices reallocate available supplies among alternative demands. Buyers who are in a position to do so are forced to resort to (now) cheaper substitutes or to go without the product entirely. The reduction of purchases by these buyers, in keeping with their highly elastic demand for the crop, leaves a larger quantity available for uses in which it is essential or for which satisfactory substitutes are unavailable.

Second, higher prices for the harvest encourage growers to plan a greater output in planting for the next season and to shift some of their fields from other crops to the more profitable use. By the time of the next harvest, these efforts will have expanded output, and prices will decline somewhat from the initial peak reached just after the upsurge in demand.

In the still longer run, as higher prices persist over the next several years, production is expanded further as farmers invest in additional equipment and as new farms are attracted to the profitable crop. This long-run expansion of output is accompanied by a gradual decline in price, but so long as the price remains high enough to attract new capacity, expansion continues. Expansion slows, however, and approaches a halt as prices approach levels that just cover average total costs of the least efficient, highest-cost farms engaged in production.

This adjustment mechanism has profound economic significance. The production of crops requires that resources be diverted from other uses and devoted to the purpose. Consumers who want the crop signal their willingness to provide the required resources by their willingness to pay prices. But time is required to transfer resources from one employment to another. At harvest time, the most producers can do is to apply a few extra labor- and machine-hours and a little extra gasoline and other costs to increase recovery of the crops already in the fields and thus squeeze out as much as possible for the consumer. Even so, the resources needed to do this raise harvest costs sharply.

Given more time, growers can plan expanded production and bring prices down from the peak reached at harvest. In the longer run, resources can be shifted in a more efficient way, and equilibrium price will settle to the lowest level that will permit all growers of the new equilibrium quantity to cover the average total costs of operation.

The response to a reduction in demand would be the reverse. Reduced consumer desire for the crop would be signaled by sharply falling prices, indicating that consumers would prefer fewer resources devoted to production of this crop. But because most resources have already been irretrievably sunk in production, the most growers can do at harvest time is to divert some small amount of resources away from the harvest by the abandonment of low-yield acreage and by a less intensive harvest of the remainder. Output declines but little, and few resources are saved. In planning for the next season, growers who find they can no longer expect to cover average variable costs shift labor, fuel, and materials to other crops or release them for employment elsewhere in the economy. At this point, nothing can be done about the resources already sunk in farm equipment and buildings. In the long run, however, as capital equipment wears out, it is not replaced, and labor and other resources that would otherwise be devoted to the production of farm machinery and buildings are freed for employment elsewhere.

IV.
IMPROVEMENT IN TECHNOLOGY

It is not enough for an industry merely to move resources around in response to consumer demand. It also must see that the productivity of those resources is kept as high as possible. One way to raise the productivity of resources in use is by the introduction of new, more efficient methods of production, and an important criterion of the performance of any industry is the rapidity with which it improves its technology.

In analyzing the behavior of agriculture in this regard, however, we must remember that there are two distinct aspects to the problem. One question is how fast the industry itself originates and develops new methods of operation. The other question is how rapidly the industry adopts and puts into use new methods as they become available, regardless of where the ideas originated.

On the first count, the record of agriculture has been rather poor. The intensively competitive structure and the relatively small scale of operation characteristic of farming simply do not lend themselves to the research and development of new ideas. The expensive laboratories and large research budgets that are commonplace in many large industrial firms could not be supported by even the largest wheat or cotton farm, hog grower, or cattle raiser. If improvements in agricultural technology had to wait until they could be developed on the farm, agricultural productivity today would be little ahead of what it was a century ago.

Fortunately, however, we have not had to depend on the farm to develop its own technical improvements, for the job has been undertaken by others. One major source of new technology has been the government-subsidized laboratories of state universities and agricultural experiment stations. To a far greater extent, however, improvements have originated in agricultural equipment firms, chemical firms, and in other industries that supply input to modern agriculture. For, if farmers have done little themselves to raise their own productivity, they have provided a ready market for any improvement in method, once it has been developed and demonstrated. The result has been a rate of growth in productivity that has outstripped the rest of industry.

The Profit Incentive

The strong incentive to adopt better methods derives from the profits that are available to the first growers to implement them. A grower who can reduce the cost of his 30,000 bushels of corn from $28,000 to $23,000 immediately adds $5,000 to his annual income. His individual behavior cannot affect the price of corn, for his individual contribution to total supply is insignificant. Until others take up the new method, the entire $5,000 is pure profit.

Innovation and Prices

Unfortunately for the grower, however, the new profitable situation carries within it the germ of its own destruction. For, when other growers see this demonstration of the cheaper method, their own eagerness for greater profit leads them to imitate it. The spread of the new method produces a general increase in supply with a consequent fall in price to a new equilibrium level commensurate with the new lower cost of production.

This fall in price, which is the long-run consequence of technical innovation, has a number of important effects. In the first place, it means that exceptional profits are received only temporarily by the first growers to put the new methods into practice. As other farmers follow suit, extra gains from the lower-cost methods are wiped out as price is reduced by the rising supply of the product.

Falling prices also mean that in the long run growers have no effective choice about whether or not to adopt the new methods. As prices approach the new lower-cost levels, farmers still using the old, higher-cost methods are no longer able to cover the average total costs of production and are compelled to adopt the new methods if they are to survive. Those farmers who hold back too long are simply driven out of business.

Above all, as prices fall to the lower-cost levels, the entire gain from the new method is passed on to consumers. Growers who first adopted the method for the sake of extra profits, and those who followed along later in self-defense, have combined in an action that has not only increased the productivity of resources but also has passed the cost saving onto society at large in the form of lower prices.

Broiler Chickens—An Example of Innovation

The continual improvement of production methods is one of the most striking features of American agriculture. A good example is the revolution in the production of broiler chickens, shown in Table 1-6. Forty years ago, broiler chickens were raised commercially on farms where they ran at large in yards, competing with one another for food, with heavy losses from accident and disease and heavy labor costs for care. In those days, it took 16 weeks and 12 pounds of feed to raise one 3½-pound chicken, and labor cost ran as high as 8.5 hours per 100 pounds of chicken raised. It is probably difficult for modern readers to realize that in those days chicken was too expensive for everyday use and generally was served only on holidays and other special occasions.

In about 1950, a revolution began in commercial broiler production: The chickens were raised indoors in individual cages. This eliminated wasteful

Table 1-6
Production Cost, Output, and Price of U.S. Broiler Chicken, 1934–1980

Year	Production Cost per 100 lb. of Chicken		Production (Lb. per Capita)	Relative Price per Pound ($)[a]
	Feed (Lb.)	Worker-Hours		
1934	n.a.[b]	n.a.	.76	.457
1940	420	8.5	3.13	.394
1950	330	5.1	12.82	.342
1960	250	1.3	32.76	.164
1970	219	.5	52.27	.135
1980	192	.1	68.48	.109

[a]Price of chicken divided by Consumer Price Index to adjust for inflation.
[b]Not available.

Source: U.S. Department of Agriculture, Economics Research Services, and *Agricultural Statistics, 1983* (Washington, D.C.: U.S. Government Printing Office).

competition among birds for feed, greatly reduced losses, permitted auto-
mated delivery of feed, and lowered labor costs. By 1960, a 3½-pound
chicken could be raised in only 8 weeks on 7.5 pounds of feed and at labor
cost of only 1.3 worker-hours for 100 pounds. By 1980, labor costs had been
cut to barely 1 percent of their level of 40 years earlier, and birds were ready
to market in 47 days.

As a result of this great increase in supply, prices of broilers, adjusted for
changes in the Consumer Price Index, declined from 46 cents per pound in
1934 to 10 cents per pound by 1980. The fall in price, partly assisted by the
increased demand arising out of growing population and income, resulted in
a one hundred-fold increase in consumption of commercial broilers. Chicken
is no longer a special holiday dish, but has become the cheapest meat in the
store; outside the home, chicken sold in franchise outlets has become a rival
of the hamburger.

Table 1-7 emphasizes that the story of commercial broiler chicken is by
no means unusual. The continual search for a more profitable operation has
sharply reduced production costs in virtually every line of agriculture. It takes
only 10 percent as much labor per acre of corn today as it did 75 years ago,
yet output per acre has quadrupled. Three times as much wheat can be raised
per acre with one-sixth the labor, and a worker-hour of effort produces nine
times as many pounds of hogs, thirteen times as much milk, and one hundred
times as many pounds of turkeys as could be produced 75 years ago.

Technology and Scale of Operation

Most modern technical innovations have reduced farming costs by replacing labor with mechanization or other capital-intensive methods. Innovations of this kind reduce variable costs of operation at the expense of higher
interest, depreciation, taxes, and other fixed costs. As a result, they generally
require greater output than less capital-intensive methods if they are to
realize their potential for lower average total cost.

Techniques of broiler production in general use in 1960 reached a
minimum average total cost of 16.4 cents a pound at an annual output of
20,000 birds per farm. Subsequent technical improvements permitted cost to
fall to 10.9 cents, but only if growers could produce and market an annual
output of 116,000 birds each. If the improved methods were used to grow
the same number of broilers per farm as in 1960, the average total cost would
be considerably higher than even the 1960 level. Thus, the same forces that
press for innovation and lower cost also bring irresistible pressure for larger-
scale output.

When farms get larger, what happens to the total number in operation
depends on demand. Falling prices expand total consumption in keeping with
demand elasticity, and demand itself rises with population and income. When
demand is sufficiently elastic, or rises sufficiently rapidly, markets for output

Table 1-7
Productivity of Labor and Land in U.S. Agriculture: Selected Crops and Livestock, 1910–1986

Crop	1910– 1914	1935– 1939	1945– 1949	1955– 1959	1965– 1969	1982– 1986
Corn						
worker-hr per acre	35.2	28.1	19.2	9.9	6.1	3.1
bu per acre	26.0	26.1	36.1	48.7	71.1	109.3
Wheat						
worker-hr per acre	15.2	8.8	5.7	3.8	2.9	2.5
bu per acre	14.4	13.2	16.9	22.3	25.9	37.1
Potatoes						
worker-hr per acre	76.0	69.7	68.5	53.1	45.9	32.6
cwt per acre	59.8	70.3	117.8	178.1	205.2	283.9
Sugar beets						
worker-hr per acre	128.0	98.0	85.0	51.0	35.0	20.0
tons per acre	10.6	11.6	13.6	17.4	17.4	20.4
Cotton						
worker-hr per acre	116.0	99.0	83.0	66.0	38.0	5.0
lb per acre	201.0	226.0	273.0	428.0	505.0	581.0
Soybeans						
worker-hr per acre	n.a.[a]	11.8	8.0	5.2	4.8	3.2
bu per acre	n.a.	18.5	19.6	22.7	24.2	30.7
Milk						
worker-hr per cow	146.0	148.0	129.0	109.0	84.0	24.0
cwt per cow	38.4	44.0	49.9	63.1	82.6	127.3
Hogs						
worker-hr per cwt	3.6	3.2	3.0	2.4	1.6	0.3
Turkeys						
worker-hr per cwt	31.4	23.7	13.1	4.4	1.6	0.2

[a]Not available.

Source: U.S. Department of Agriculture, *Agricultural Statistics* (Washington, D.C.: U.S. Government Printing Office, appropriate issues).

may expand enough to maintain or even to increase the number of farms in operation, despite larger scale. But inelastic demand that rises only slowly results in a smaller number of farms as size increases. The trend toward a smaller number of larger-scale producers in the broiler industry is evident in Table 1-8. During the period 1959–1982, the average output per farm rose nearly tenfold, but total sales only tripled, reducing the number of farms by half. Even this remarkable performance understates the effect of technology on farm numbers and size, for it is estimated that the largest five producers ship 40 percent of all birds marketed.

Growth in the average size of farms has been continuous throughout the history of the United States. Some idea of the development can be had from the trend in number and average acreage of farms shown in Table 1-9.

Table 1-8

Number, Size, and Output of U.S. Broiler Producers

Year	Number of Farms	Average Output per Farm (Number of Chickens)	Total Production (Millions)
1959	65,314	18,985	1,240
1964	41,778	45,193	1,888
1978	31,743	96,462	3,062
1982	30,104	116,596	3,510

Source: U.S. Department of Commerce, *Census of Agriculture* (Washington, D.C.: U.S. Government Printing Office, appropriate issues).

Improvements in agriculture came slowly during the first 40 years of the period shown, and average farms were only 11 percent larger in 1920 than they had been in 1880. Moreover, growth in demand had greatly exceeded the rate of growth in farm productivity, and there were more farms in 1920 than there had been 40 years earlier. The high point in number of farms occurred in 1920. In more recent decades, the tempo of technical improvement has greatly accelerated, but the rate of population growth has slowed, leading to a rapid rise in average farm size accompanied by rapidly falling numbers. In the period 1960–1982, the average size of farms, in the United States doubled, but the total number was reduced 60 percent.

Technology and the Displacement of Farm Labor

The same forces that affect the size and number of farms also affect labor cost and the number of people engaged in agriculture. When new technology raises the productivity of farm labor, any given quantity of farm

Table 1-9

Number and Size of Farms, and U.S. Farm Employment, 1880–1986

Year	Number of Farms	Average Acreage per Farm	Farm Employment (Thousands)
1880	4,008,000	133.7	10,100
1900	5,740,000	146.6	12,800
1920	6,453,000	148.5	13,400
1940	6,104,000	174.5	11,000
1960	5,388,000	215.5	7,100
1970	2,730,000	389.5	4,200
1986	2,173,410	461.0	3,204

Sources: U.S. Department of Commerce, *Census of Agriculture* (Washington, D.C.: U.S. Government Printing Office, appropriate issues). 1986 data from U.S. Department of Agriculture, *Agricultural Statistics, 1987* (Washington, D.C.: U.S. Government Printing Office, 1988).

product can be produced with fewer people than before. As a result, unless consumption expands in proportion, rising productivity reduces the number of people needed. Higher productivity increases the supply of farm products, and the resulting decline in prices automatically expands consumption, but because of the very low demand elasticity for farm products, consumption will increase much less than in proportion to the productivity increase. The net result of the increase in productivity, therefore, is a reduction in the demand for farm labor.

It is the market that keeps the number of people engaged in agriculture in balance with demand. Reduction of demand cuts earnings of farm labor below what could be earned in other industries, and farm people with the necessary skills leave for more promising jobs in other industries. Those farm laborers without alternative employment for their skills find themselves trapped in low-paying farm occupations or are forced off the farm into the city where, without marketable skills, they are added to the welfare rolls.

The fate of farm labor is an excellent illustration of two important aspects of the operation of competitive markets. Competition generates inexorable pressure to extract greater output from available resources and passes the gains of this greater productivity on to the consumer in the form of lower prices and higher standards of living. But, in so doing, the market operates without regard to the fate or feelings of the people involved. The supply and demand for farm labor are rigorously balanced by the competitive market, regardless of what happens to farm families who are caught in the adjustment.

Other Social Costs of Modern Agriculture

The increasing scale of operations needed to apply modern farming methods has brought other profound changes to agriculture. Considerably more farming is being undertaken by large corporations, and commercial farming of specialized crops is replacing the more diversified agriculture of the family farm.

Moreover, modern agricultural methods are seen by some people as leading to an overspecialization in production, which increases the danger of soil exhaustion as single-crop agriculture replaces crop rotation. In addition, heavy reliance on chemical fertilizers puts water tables in danger of contamination, and the intensive use of sprays increases risks to consumers. Crop varieties are also being adapted to the requirements of mechanical harvest, storage, and shipping rather than to improved flavor and nutritional value.

Some of these objections reflect more on the tastes and preferences of American consumers than they do on farm technology. If people are willing to buy cheap tomatoes with the flavor and consistency of red baseballs rather than pay more for flavorful tomatoes that are too delicate for anything but hand harvest, competitive agriculture will provide for their preferences.

Others of these concerns, however, derive from problems that are fundamental to competition. The most important deficiency of competitive industry is that no account is taken of social costs that are external to the accounts of the individual firm. In the struggle to cut cost, the individual firm evaluates only its own costs. If reduction of costs of the firm also results in the imposition of higher costs on society as a whole, the competitive market provides no mechanism to balance one against the other.

The adoption of circular irrigation systems provides, in some areas at least, an example of this kind of problem. These irrigation systems enhance crop yields by doing for the fields what a lawn sprinkler does for a home garden. Hence, the adoption of the system is highly profitable to the individual farm. Yet widespread adoption of the technique has serious detrimental effects on the water table, which may even raise the long-run cost of agriculture in the area. None of the unfavorable wider consequences is directly presented to individual firms as part of the cost of irrigation, with the result that the individual farmer sees only the short-run profit potential of circular irrigation. The result is that pursuit of profit by individual farms can yield severe environmental impacts as well as cheaper food.

Similar external costs arise when insecticides and chemical fertilizer run off the fields to pollute streams and endanger water tables, or when antibiotics used in animal feeds create serious health problems for meat consumers. If the farm industry is to be properly regulated by the forces of competition, these costs must be somehow taken into account. Some part of the answer lies in action by government to limit the type and amount of spray that can be applied, and to monitor the use of the common water table. Thus, the environmental impact of DDT has resulted in laws forbidding its use for most agricultural purposes.

A thorough assessment of the problem of environmental pollution goes far beyond the scope of this chapter, but it is important to recognize that one important aspect of the behavior of any industry is its impact on the environment. In this respect, unmodified competition as exemplified by agriculture has a poor record.

V.

EVALUATION OF AGRICULTURAL PERFORMANCE

Left to itself, agriculture is a highly competitive industry. As such, its performance is, in many respects, almost ideal. Indeed, it is difficult to imagine a system better adapted to carry out the purely technical functions of production and allocation of products:

1. Although harvest is subject to the vagaries of random events, available supplies are rationed among competing uses in accordance with consumer priorities as expressed by demand elasticities.

2. At each stage of production, the most is extracted from available resources. In the very short run, when most costs have been already sunk into crops, relatively little can be done to adapt to consumer desires; however, given time, the investment in production closely follows up demand, with matching shifts in output.
3. In addition, the industry has demonstrated a remarkable history of rapidly increasing the productivity of the resources it employs and of passing this increase on to consumers in terms of lower relative prices and increased standards of living; at the same time land, labor, and other resources have been released for the production of other products.
4. All of this has been accomplished with virtually no conscious collective planning, administrative direction, or political processes. Competitive pressure toward improvement is inexorable. It is unnecessary to debate new methods; they simply impose themselves.
5. The same competitive process, however, appears inexorably to move along its own way regardless of the fates of the people involved. When productivity grows more rapidly than the demand for farm products, people who have devoted their lives to agriculture are driven off the farm to fend for themselves, as best they can, in urban areas.
6. By the same token, the absence of social costs from the accounts of the individual farm means the search for cheaper farming methods can result in the destruction of the environment.

VI.
GOVERNMENT POLICY TOWARD AGRICULTURE

Price Supports

The severe dislocation wrought in agriculture by untrammeled technical innovation proceeding in the face of slowly increasing demand has generated overwhelming pressure for governmental intervention. This intervention has largely been directed toward efforts to hold up farm prices. Price-support programs were initiated during the New Deal of the early 1930s and, although repeatedly modified as to detail, they have maintained much the same general character.

Any program to support prices must somehow define a target level at which to support them and then devise methods for enforcing the supports. Support levels for farm prices are usually defined in terms of "parity" prices. These are prices that are calculated for each commodity; they bear the same relationship to the average price of things that farmers buy (the "prices-paid" index) that the price of that same commodity did during some base period.

As originally defined, parity prices were to bear the same ratio to the average prices-paid index that they had during the base period 1910–1914. For example, if the price of cabbage had been $1.10 per hundredweight as an average during 1910–1914, when the index of prices paid by farmers averaged 100, then the parity price of cabbage would be defined for any later year by multiplying the prices-paid index during that year by .011. Many years later, when the prices-paid index reached 350, this calculation would yield a parity price for cabbage of $3.85 per hundredweight. In subsequent legislation, definitions of parity have been altered to refer to more recent base periods, and more complicated formulas are applied in the calculation of parity prices for individual commodities.

Once parity prices are defined, government policy then undertakes to support the prices of a number of key commodities at a specified fraction of their parity price. The fraction at which prices are supported varies from commodity to commodity and from time to time. Regardless of the level of support, however, one difficulty is encountered, for when prices are supported at levels higher than market equilibrium, government must somehow contend with the resulting gap between supply and demand. The problem is illustrated in Figure 1-6. Because the support price P exceeds the equilibrium price P^*, farmers tend to produce and bring to market a total quantity Q_s that exceeds the amount Q_d that consumers are willing to buy at that price. If market price is to be maintained at P, something must be done about this gap.

Figure 1-6

Problems of price supports.

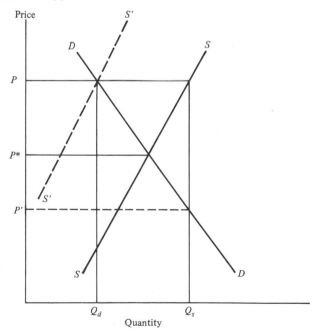

Restriction of Supply

There are three alternatives: (1) government might induce farmers to restrict supply to $S'S'$ so that the desired support price becomes the new market equilibrium; (2) government might purchase the output (Q_s-Q_d) that farmers cannot sell at the support price; or (3) the entire output might be sold on the market at whatever price it would bring (P'), and government would make up the difference between P' and P by a subsidy paid directly to growers.

Historically, government price-support programs have involved a mixture of the three techniques. Supply has been restricted, usually by paying farmers to "set aside" part of their acreage, or to divert part of their acreage into "soil-conserving" crops, or to place acreage in a "soil bank." In the early years of price supports, acreage diversion was the most important weapon of government policy. At its peak in 1966, a total of 63.3 million acres was diverted from cultivation. This amounted to nearly 6 percent of all farm land in the United States and entitled farmers to more than $1 billion in government payments. More recently, however, outright payments to farmers for acreage diverted have been replaced increasingly by the use of acreage limitation as a criterion for receipt of other price-support payments.

The Commodity Credit Corporation

Any surpluses that remain after supply has been reduced have generally been dealt with by crop loans issued to farmers by the Commodity Credit Corporation (CCC). The CCC is a government agency that, under the direction of the Secretary of Agriculture, each year designates a loan rate on each commodity to be supported. The loan rate is the amount per unit that the CCC stands ready to lend to farmers in good standing with the price-control program who want to borrow on their crops. For example, when the loan rate for corn is $2.65, farmers are entitled to borrow $2.65 for each bushel of corn they grow, regardless of its actual market value. Now, if too much corn is grown and the market price begins to sink below the $2.65 loan rate, the farmers are privileged to default on their loans, letting the CCC take the corn. On the other hand, if the market price should rise above the loan rate, the farmer can reclaim the crop, repay the loan, and sell the corn at the higher market price. Although the CCC is set up as a lending organization, its principal function is to provide a roundabout way for farmers to sell to the government any output that cannot be sold on the market at the price defined by the loan rate.

The Commodity Credit Corporation must, by law, extend loans on six "basic" commodities: corn, cotton, peanuts, rice, tobacco, and wheat, and on a group of designated "nonbasic" commodities that includes, among other things, butter, honey, tung oil, rye, and wool. In addition, from time to time, as directed by the Secretary of Agriculture, the CCC extends price-support loans on an extensive and diverse list of crops ranging from staples such as dry peas, soybeans, and potatoes to such things as almonds, cotton seed, and olive oil.

The volume of crops acquired depends on loan rates in relation to production and demand levels. At the end of 1986, the CCC owned a total of $13.8 billion of farm commodities, including 1,265 million bushels of corn, 987 million bushels of wheat, and 2,140 million pounds of butter, cheese, and dried milk.

Huge bumper crops harvested in the face of recession-level demand can leave large, unsold surpluses in government hands. During the recession of 1958–1959, the CCC spent nearly $2 billion to acquire unsold commodities, including more than 25 percent of the wheat crop for that year. From 1959 to 1963, the CCC owned an entire year's production of wheat.

Agricultural Subsidies

The third method of price support involves direct subsidy payments to growers of corn, wheat, cotton, sugar, wool, and a number of other commodities to make up the difference between market price and support level. In terms of Figure 1-6, for example, support of the price at P would induce farmers to grow Q_s bushels. When this output arrived on the market, the market price would be driven down to P', but the price difference would be made up by payment to growers of a subsidy equal to $(P-P')$ dollars per bushel.

In their current versions, most price-support programs integrate direct subsidies with acreage limitation and CCC loans in a rather complicated package. In general, farmers who agree to limit their acreage are offered price-support subsidies designed to bring the prices they will receive for only a designated portion of their output up to the full support level. Beyond this specified portion, production is subject to support at CCC loan rates set below the full support level. For example, in recent years, the support price of corn has been $2.86 per bushel, and the CCC loan rate has been $2.65. This has meant that farmers participating in the corn-production program were guaranteed a price of $2.86 on a specified number of bushels, whereas the remainder of their crop was supported by the CCC loan rate, at a minimum price of $2.65. Similar programs have been in force for wheat, cotton, barley, and grain sorghum.

Because price supports of any kind make it difficult for farm products in the United States to compete in foreign markets, the government sometimes pays special export subsidies on commodities shipped abroad. The Export Enhancement Program (EEP) provides certain foreign buyers of U.S. farm products with free bonuses of CCC-owned commodities to reduce the price they pay for U.S. exports. In 1986 the value of these bonuses reduced the price of wheat an average of $25 a ton and of wheat flour, $80 per ton. During the period from May 1986 to March 1987, the EEP contributed to sales of 11 million tons of wheat and flour; 2.8 million tons of barley and barley malt; as well as quantities of dairy cattle, frozen poultry, rice, eggs, and other commodities.

All told, the several price-support programs have absorbed huge government outlays. The cost of price support to the American taxpayer rose to almost $26 billion during 1986.

Other Price-Support Measures

Not all prices are supported by direct governmental action. Prices of a broad array of commodities, ranging from citrus fruit to nuts, are set by *marketing orders* issued by the Secretary of Agriculture. These orders enable producers to organize *marketing boards,* which are given wide powers to control the production and marketing of designated commodities. Aside from certain professional sports, marketing boards are the only unregulated legal monopolies permitted in the U.S. The boards limit production, sometimes by restricting the quality or sizes of product that can be shipped. Some boards prop up prices by assigning quotas to individual producers and by requiring that any additional output be placed "in reserve," usually to be disposed of by exporting at low prices.

The price of milk is supported by a combination of marketing order and CCC intervention. A marketing order by the Secretary of Agriculture sets the prices that dairies must pay farmers for fluid milk destined for human consumption. Because demand is elastic, the higher this price is raised, the less milk the dairies will buy, but the marketing order cannot control production. To deal with this problem, all milk that farmers cannot sell at the price established by the order is marketed as "manufacturing-grade" milk and is sold at whatever price the market will bring. The demand for manufacturing-grade milk is supported, however, by means of CCC loans extended on such manufactured dairy products as dry milk, butter, and cheese.

The government accumulated so much cheese, butter, and dried milk that in 1982, 1983, and 1984 it became necessary to pass it out to poor recipients to forestall extensive spoilage. The milk program has recently been modified to compensate dairy farmers who agree to reduce production below their normal rate of output.

Who Benefits from Price Supports?

Because the clear result of agricultural price-support programs has been higher prices to consumers and higher taxes for taxpayers, one might well ask who benefits from these programs. Presumably, the rationale for farm policy has been to relieve some of the suffering that resulted from rapidly rising agricultural productivity. Yet, oddly enough, practically nothing about government farm policy has benefited the people who need it the most.

The history of agriculture has been a continuous story of small farmers driven out and people pushed off the farm. But even most farmers who remain on the farm get few benefits from farm programs. In fact, the very nature of price supports concentrates the benefits among the largest, most powerful growers, rather than among the poor and weak who really need help.

In 1982, the smallest 50 percent of farms received less than 8 percent of total government price-support payments. This amounted to an average of only $250 per farm. In contrast, the largest 12 percent of all farms received 48 percent of all government payments. The largest 5 percent of all farms received 24 percent of all payments, with an average receipt of almost $7,000 per farm. Payments to the few very largest farms ran to millions of dollars each!

This highly unequal distribution of benefits is a direct consequence of programs that pay for acreage diverted, buy up surpluses, and subsidize production. When farmers are paid to divert acreage, the farms with the largest acreage receive the largest payments. When price-support subsidies are paid, those with the largest output receive the most support. In short, all price-support benefits are inevitably distributed in direct proportion to the size of the operation, which, in the very nature of things, is inversely in proportion to human need. Moreover, this is only part of the picture, for gains to farmers extend beyond what they receive directly from the government. When acreage is restricted, farmers not only receive payments for that reason but the products that they grow on their remaining acreage sell at higher prices, providing a second benefit; but nobody knows how large this part of the benefit from the government program is. It has been estimated at many times the value of the direct payments, but—whatever it is—it is distributed in proportion to the size of the operation and is concentrated in the hands of the largest producers.

Farm Policy in the European Economic Community

The U.S. is by no means alone in its program to support prices. The problems encountered by farmers are common to all developing economies, and many provide aid along similar lines. The European Economic Community (EEC or "Common Market") was established shortly after World War II to bring to the people of Europe the same economic advantages that the U.S. has always enjoyed with our continent-wide market. Formation of the EEC, however, was accompanied by a Common Agricultural Policy (CAP), to assure high farm prices. The CAP established the European Agricultural Guidance and Guarantee Fund, to provide common financing of price supports.

The Fund supports a wider variety of products than does the U.S. program, including grains, dairy products, beef, sugar, oil seeds, olive oil, wine, fruits, vegetables, protein crops, and some fibers. The Fund provides price support by entering the market and purchasing whenever the market price of a farm commodity falls below its specified intervention price. Support is combined with a system of flexible tariffs on imported farm commodities, which are varied, sometimes daily, to maintain the resulting price of imports to European buyers higher than the intervention price.

Since production controls are generally absent, farmers produce much more than European consumers will buy at the high target prices. As much as possible of the resulting surplus is disposed of by exports, which are made possible by flexible export subsidies, set to make up the difference between the intervention price and the much lower prices exporters receive on the world market. With the continual increase in farm productivity, however, the expansion of output has outstripped the capacity of the export market to absorb surpluses, and the burden on the Fund has reached staggering proportions.

Regulations establish a production "threshold" which, if exceeded by a three-year average of actual production, is supposed to trigger downward adjustment of price-support levels to discourage output. In fact, however, annual setting of support prices remains in the hands of the EEC Council of Ministers of Agriculture. The result has made price reduction politically almost impossible, and the problem of supporting European farm prices is becoming a severe burden on EEC finances.

It is ironic that this heavy cost buys little for consumers but, on the contrary, effectively deprives them of the full benefit of the specialization that such a wide European market would permit. High, artificially supported farm prices encourage the employment in agriculture of workers and capital equipment that would be much more productively employed in other occupations. The result is substantial gain for large farmers, but at the expense of lower living standards for taxpayers and consumers.

Rapidly rising agricultural productivity has generated a serious problem of human displacement and has been associated with serious human suffering. Public policy toward agriculture, however, has done practically nothing about this problem. It has, instead, subsidized the largest farms. It is the ultimate irony that agriculture, the industry whose operation is best understood in terms of purely competitive behavior, is subject to expensive governmental intervention to forestall the benefits of that very competition and to protect the revenues of large corporate growers.

SUGGESTED READINGS

Harris, Simon, Alan Swinbank, and Guy Wilkinson. *The Food and Farm Policies of the European Community.* New York: John Wiley and Sons, 1983.

Heady, Earl O. *A Primer on Food, Agriculture, and Public Policy.* New York: Random House, Inc., 1967.

Lin, William, James Johnson, and Linda Calvin. *Farm Commodity Programs: Who Participates and Who Benefits?* U.S. Department of Agriculture, Agricultural Economic Report No. 474, Washington, D.C., 1981.

Newman, Mark, Tom Fulton, and Lawrence Glaser. *A Comparison of Agriculture in the United States and the European Community.* U.S. Department of Agriculture, Economic Research Service, Foreign Agricultural Economic Report No. 233, 1987.

Roy, Ewell P., Floyd L. Cortz, and Gene D. Sullivan. *Economics: Applications to Agriculture and Agribusiness* Danville, Ill.: The Interstate Publishers, 1971.

Ruttan, Vernon W., Arley D. Waldo, and James P. Houck, eds. *Agricultural Policy in an Affluent Society.* New York: W. W. Norton & Co., Inc., 1969.

Schultz, Theodore W. *Transforming Traditional Agriculture.* New Haven, Conn.: Yale University Press, 1964.

CHAPTER 2

THE PETROLEUM INDUSTRY

Stephen Martin

After the days of luxury, we have become
A lamb in the midst of the jungle.
Like a gang, the wolves of the market
Swirl around us.

—Sheik Mani Said al-Otaiba
Oil Minister, United Arab Emirates[1]

I.

INTRODUCTION

Just as fossilized footprints mark the passage of a great dinosaur long after the dinosaur itself is gone, so the record of fluctuations in the price of crude oil marks passages in the world petroleum market. The traces of major political events can be seen in Figure 2-1: the Arab–Israeli War of October 1973, the fall of the Shah of Iran in January 1979. Changes in market structure, which occur less abruptly, also underlie the movements depicted in Figure 2-1: the shift in ownership and control over Mideast crude-oil reserves from vertically integrated, Western-based international oil companies to local governments; the subsequent reduction in the growth of energy demand; and the development of new oil supplies, outside OPEC control.

We will examine the economic and political forces that have determined the performance of the world oil market and the U.S. submarket. Some of the questions we shall address are: What industry characteristics have allowed the exercise of market power, and by whom? What structural characteristics limit the exercise of market power? What has been the role of the major oil companies in the market and that of smaller, independent companies? How have government policies in the consuming nations affected the market? What does industrial economics suggest concerning likely future market performance?

41

Figure 2-1 _____

Official price of Saudi Arabian light (34°) crude oil.

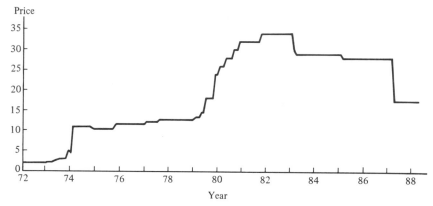

Source: *Basic Petroleum Data Book*, Volume VIII, No. 1 (January 1988), Section VI, Table 11; *Petroleum Economist*, various issues.

II. _____
STRUCTURE

The petroleum industry includes four distinct vertical levels: production, refining, marketing, and transportation. Production involves the location and extraction of oil and natural gas from underground reservoirs; these may be so close to the surface that their oil seeps up through the ground, or they may require extensive drilling from platforms located miles offshore. The refinery segment manufactures finished products ranging from petroleum coke to motor gasoline and jet fuel. Wholesale and retail marketers distribute these products to consumers. Connecting these three vertical levels is a specialized transportation industry, including pipelines, tankers, barges, and trucks, which moves crude oil from fields to refineries and finished product from refineries to marketers. Vertical links connecting the different stages of production have been and promise to be critical in determining overall market performance.

Crude Oil

1. Domination by the International Majors. During the decade or so following World War II, the world oil market was dominated by the seven vertically integrated major oil companies. Five of these "Seven Sisters" were based in the United States;[2] the other two were British Petroleum and Royal Dutch/Shell. An eighth firm, Compagnie Française des Pétroles, was an additional player on the market.

Together, these eight firms controlled 100 percent of 1950 world crude-oil production outside North America and the Communist bloc. Twenty years later, their combined share remained slightly above 80 percent.

The basis for this control was the system of joint ventures—partial horizontal integration—under which the vertically integrated majors divided ownership of the operating companies that exploited Middle East oilfields, the richest in the world.

This interconnecting network of joint ventures developed with the support of the home governments of the international majors, each concerned —for reasons of national security—to ensure the access of domestically based firms to crude petroleum reserves. Thus, the U.S. Department of State induced American firms to take part in the 1928 "Red Line Agreement," which formalized control of the Iraq Petroleum Company. The French government set up Compagnie Francaise des Petroles to exploit its share of the Iraq concession.

The British government was similarly involved in the 1934 agreement that divided the Kuwait operating company between Gulf and British Petroleum. The U.S. government was instrumental in the 1948 reorganization of the Arabian–American Oil Company (Aramco) as a joint venture of Exxon, Texaco, Chevron, and Mobil to produce Saudi Arabian crude. The Iranian consortium—which delivered Persian oilfields into the hands of the seven majors, CFP, and a handful of American independents—was established after a CIA-backed coup returned the Shah of Iran to power in August 1953 (reversing the nationalization of Iranian oil by the Mossadegh government). The fact that such a joint venture involving five American firms was contrary to U.S. antitrust law was put aside, on the urging of the Department of State, for reasons of national security.

Table 2-1

Ownership Shares in Middle East Joint Ventures (Percent)

	Aramco	Kuwait Oil Company	Iranian Consortium	Iraq Petroleum Company
Exxon	30		7	11.875
Texaco	30		7	
Gulf		50	7	
Chevron	30		7	
Mobil	10		7	11.875
Royal Dutch/Shell			14	23.75
British Petroleum		50	40	23.75
CFP			6	23.75
Others			5	5

Note: CFP = Compagnie Française des Pétroles

Source: S. A. Schneider, *The Oil Price Revolution.* Baltimore: Johns Hopkins, 1983, p.40.

The continual contacts required for the management of these joint ventures resulted in a sharing of information and a communality of interest that is not characteristic of "arm's-length" competition:[3]

> Every major company was linked to practically every other one through a series of joint producing and refining ventures, long-term bulk purchasing agreements, and long-term reciprocal supply arrangements. Where joint facilities existed, they normally required joint operating decisions; the output of Aramco in Saudi Arabia, for instance, as well as that of the Iraq Petroleum Company, was partly determined by an intricate bargaining process among the major companies.

The Mideast joint ventures were operated under restrictions that had the effect of ensuring output limitations. For example, partners in the Iraq Petroleum Company were obliged to file their requirements for crude oil five years in advance. Each partner thus gained definite information about the plans of every other partner. A firm that filed requirements for expanded output would telegraph its plans to rivals, exposing itself to immediate retaliation.[4]

With its restrictive network of horizontal and vertical linkages, the world oil market for roughly the first decade after World War II was one in which[5]

> . . . the seven companies controlled all the principal oil-producing areas outside the United States, all foreign refineries, patents and refinery technology: that they divided the world markets between them, and shared pipelines and tankers throughout the world; and that they maintained artificially high prices for oil.

During this same postwar period, U.S. government regulations insulated the United States from the world market. Of course, the same suppliers dominated the world market and the U.S. submarket.

From the 1930s until the 1950s, controls on oil production by state governments (importantly, the Texas Railroad Commission) held crude-oil prices in the United States at artificially high levels. These prices proved attractive to foreign suppliers, and by 1948 the United States became a net importer of refined oil products. Three congressional investigations of the matter in 1950 conveyed to the oil companies a congressional preference for low imports. When domestic oil producers raised the price of U.S. crude oil in June 1950, the U.S. coal industry, with the support of the petroleum industry, sponsored a bill to place import quotas on petroleum. The Eisenhower Administration set up "voluntary" import-restraint programs in 1954 and 1958, and when these proved ineffective, imposed mandatory quotas in 1959.

These formal and informal restrictions on the flow of oil into the United States meant higher prices for U.S. consumers, perhaps by as much as $3 to $4 billion a year.[6] At a time when the price of crude oil on the Eastern seaboard was about $3.75 a barrel, a Cabinet task force estimated that the elimination of oil-import quotas would reduce the price of crude oil by $1.30 a barrel.[7]

Although the quotas had been justified on national security grounds, the effect of high U.S. prices in a shielded market was to encourage the extraction of relatively high-cost U.S. crude oil, accelerating the depletion of U.S. reserves and conserving lower-cost reserves elsewhere in the world. It became clear, in 1973, that U.S. national security would have been better served if the pattern of extraction had been reversed.

2. Rise of Independent Companies. The domination of the world oil market by the international majors set in motion a process of entry by new firms in search of profit. This process occupied the period from the mid-1950s through 1973, which marked a transition from a market dominated by the international majors to a market dominated by the governments of producing countries.

The first step was the 1954 Iranian consortium, when the United States government insisted that the majors make room for nine independents. Having gained a toehold in the Middle East, the independents sought to expand their access. Just as the majors had once been able to play host nation against host nation by shifting production from country to country to resist pressure to expand output, so host nations gradually gained the option of playing independent companies against major companies.

In 1956, Libya granted concessions to 17 firms. Independents subsequently accounted for half of Libyan output, and in due course products refined from this oil found their way to European markets.[8]

The activities of Enrico Mattei, head of the Italian national firm Ente Nazionale Idrocarburi (ENI), had far-reaching consequences. He sought access to oil supplies in Iran and elsewhere and ultimately found it in the Soviet Union. After 1959, products refined from Russian oil joined the flow of independent oil onto world markets.

The increased flow of oil from these various independent sources created an excess supply at prevailing prices, despite rapidly expanding demand. The result was downward pressure on prices, which the international majors could not resist. But the governments of the oil-producing nations collected taxes based on a "posted price" for oil, a price largely divorced from the reality of transactions in the marketplace. This presented no problem for the majors, as long as the market price of oil was rising. A falling market price combined with unchanging posted prices meant that an increasing share of profit went to host countries in the form of taxes.

In August 1960, Exxon reduced its posted prices for oil. In due course, the remaining major firms followed suit. This reduction in the posted prices for oil was no more than a reflection of reductions in transaction prices. The reduction in transaction prices was the consequence of a more rapid expansion in supply than in demand. The more rapid expansion in supply than in demand was, in turn, a direct result of the actions of the host countries, which had granted independents access to crude supplies as a way of breaking the grip of the Seven Sisters on the world oil market.

The reduction in posted prices was, therefore, an inevitable consequence of the actions of host countries. But it appeared to them as a unilateral reduction in their own tax revenues, imposed on sovereign nations by international corporations. The reaction came at a September 1960 meeting of Saudi Arabia, Iran, Iraq, Kuwait, and Venezuela, when it was agreed to establish the Organization of Petroleum Exporting Countries — OPEC.

The thirteen years that followed the formation of OPEC saw a long dance between the two loosely coordinated oligopolies, one of the international majors and one of producing countries. At the start of this period, the balance of power lay with the companies; by the end, it lay with the countries.

Although OPEC member nations were beneficiaries of this shift in power, OPEC did not actively initiate it. The international companies had a long history of effective cooperation, and they were better at it than the producing countries. By negotiating on a country-by-country basis, the major companies were able to prevent the countries from combining their bargaining power. OPEC was able to prevent further declines in the posted price but was not able to reverse the reductions that had induced OPEC's formation.

The catalyst for change was the interaction of independent companies and the revolutionary government of a relatively new oil province — Libya. Colonel Qaddafi's government took power in September 1969 and soon set about renegotiating the terms of Libyan oil concessions. As we have already remarked, these concessions involved independent firms in an important way, and independents were in a much weaker bargaining position, vis-a-vis the host countries, than the majors. Any one of the integrated majors, faced with an unattractive proposal from a producing country, could credibly threaten to reduce output in that country and turn to supplies elsewhere around the world. Independent companies often had no such alternative.

In August 1970, Occidental Petroleum Company acceded to Libyan demands for higher prices and higher taxes. This example inspired other oil-producing nations. In February 1971, oil companies agreed in Teheran to the higher price demanded by the Shah of Iran. The major oil companies revised the terms of their arrangement with Libya in April 1971.[9]

The oil-producing countries had demonstrated their ability to control the terms upon which oil was lifted from their territories. But it was the major companies that, through their joint ventures, owned the operating companies (see Table 2-1). This too was to change.

Again it was the radical states, rather than OPEC, that led the way. Algeria nationalized 51 percent of French ownership in Algerian reserves in February 1971; Libya nationalized British Petroleum's interests in November 1971; the Iraqi Petroleum Company was nationalized in June 1972. Long negotiations between Saudi Arabia, represented by Sheik Zaki Yamani, and Aramco followed. Aramco agreed to yield an initial 25 percent of its Saudi Arabian concession to Saudi Arabia.[10]

In the absence of intervening political developments, the transfer of world market control from the international majors to the producing countries would likely have continued at a gradual pace. The producing countries would have slowly replaced the international majors, with little change in market performance. In such a world, the Western "man in the street" might have remained blissfully unaware of the nature of the world oil market. Events unfolded rather differently.

3. Domination by OPEC. The 1970s opened with the demand for oil increasing throughout the industrial world. The first column in Table 2-2 shows the growth of the U.S. market for crude oil in the 1960s and early 1970s. Similar growth took place in Europe and Japan. In 1973, with simultaneous booms in North America, Europe, and Japan, world demand for energy—and oil—was at an all-time high.

At the same time, supply and the control of supply were increasingly concentrated in the low-cost Middle East. In 1970, proved reserves of crude oil in the Middle East were 333,506 million barrels—in contrast to 64,431 million barrels of proved reserves in the Western Hemisphere and 19,396 million barrels in Africa.

Location and development of crude reserves is a time-consuming process, particularly when oil fields are located offshore or in other hostile climates. Thus, the 1970s opened with a relatively small short-run supply of crude oil available from fringe, non-OPEC suppliers. These fringe suppliers operated at substantially higher cost than Middle East producers.[11] This situation is illustrated in Figure 2-2(a).

In such circumstances, a dominant firm or perfectly colluding oligopoly would maximize profit by selecting an output that equates marginal revenue along the residual demand curve—the market demand curve after subtracting fringe output—to marginal cost. In Figure 2-2(a), the corresponding cartel output is q_1, which would sell at price p_1.

Since the economic interests of the OPEC member nations diverge in fundamental ways, it was difficult for OPEC to cooperate as an effective cartel. It was a political rather than an economic event that triggered coordinated OPEC action and allowed OPEC to take advantage of the demand–supply relationship depicted in Figure 2-2(a). In reaction to Western support for Israel during the Egypt–Israeli War of October 1973, Arab nations imposed production cutbacks and an embargo of crude oil supplies to the West.

The international oil companies were based in the West, and they had long benefited from the political support of their home governments, governments that sought to protect their perceived national security interest in a

Table 2-2
Import and OPEC Shares of U.S. Market

	U.S. Market (Thousand Barrels/Day)	Import Share of U.S. Market (Percent)	OPEC Share of U.S. Market (Percent)
1960	9,807	18.5	11.8
1961	9,985	19.2	11.7
1962	10,409	20.0	12.6
1963	10,753	19.7	11.9
1964	11,033	20.4	12.2
1965	11,523	21.4	12.5
1966	12,096	21.3	11.9
1967	12,569	20.2	9.9
1968	13,404	21.2	9.6
1969	14,149	22.4	9.1
1970	14,709	23.2	8.8
1971	15,225	25.8	11.0
1972	16,379	28.9	12.5
1973	17,321	36.1	17.3
1974	16,665	36.7	19.7
1975	16,336	37.1	22.0
1976	17,475	41.8	29.0
1977	18,446	47.6	33.6
1978	18,864	43.5	30.5
1979	18,530	45.3	30.4
1980	17,071	40.2	25.2
1981	16,121	35.6	20.6
1982	15,358	32.2	14.0
1983	15,233	31.6	12.2
1984	15,728	33.3	13.0
1985	15,726	32.2	11.6
1986	16,281	37.9	17.4
1987	16,556	39.1	18.0

Source: *Basic Petroleum Data Book*, Volume VIII, Number 2, May 1988.

safe supply of oil. But the international majors administered the embargo of Western nations in accordance with OPEC directives, going so far as to provide Saudi Arabia with information on the shipment of refined oil products to U.S. military bases around the world.[12]

As the producing countries cut back the international majors' supplies of crude oil, the majors cut back supplies to independent companies. With their survival threatened, the independents turned to the market for oil not tied up by long-term contracts—the relatively narrow spot market. Independents bid up the spot-market price of oil, and official OPEC prices soon followed. The immediate result was the 1973 rise in official prices shown in Figure 2-1.

Figure 2-2 _____

Demand and supply in the world oil market.

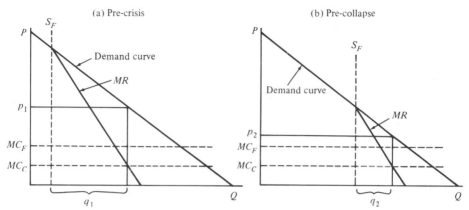

Notes: q_1 = profit-maximizing cartel output in pre-crisis market

q_2 = profit-maximizing cartel output in pre-collapse market

P = price Q = quantity S_F = fringe supply

MR = marginal revenue facing cartel

MC_F = fringe marginal cost MC_C = cartel marginal cost

From this price increase flowed longer-run changes. OPEC revenue from the sale of oil rose from \$13.7 billion in 1972 to \$87.2 billion in 1974. Real U.S. gross national product, which grew 5.2 percent in 1973, fell 0.5 percent in 1973 and 1.3 percent in 1974.

Aside from the accelerated shift in control of production to the producing nations, there were remarkably few structural changes during the period following the first price increase. As shown in Table 2-2, the size of the U.S. market fell slightly in 1974 and 1975 but then rose to new heights by 1978. The share of imports in the U.S. market, and specifically imports from OPEC, peaked in 1977 but remained higher than in 1973. The pattern of consumption and supply was much the same in other industrialized countries. As shown in Figure 2-3, OPEC's share of world crude-oil production fell only about 5 percent over the period 1973 to 1979. World production of crude oil grew throughout this period, but OPEC's production was essentially level: 30,989 thousand barrels per day in 1973, and 30,911 thousand barrels per day in 1979.

Because of the length of time needed to develop new petroleum reserves and to install energy-saving residential and industrial equipment, the underlying market conditions that greeted the fall of the Shah of Iran in January 1979 were essentially the same as those that had greeted the Arab–Israeli War of 1973: peak demand, concentration of supply in the Middle East, and absence of spare capacity in the West.

The impact of the course of events on the market was similar. Supply was

The Structure of American Industry

Figure 2-3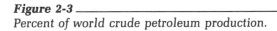

Percent of world crude petroleum production.

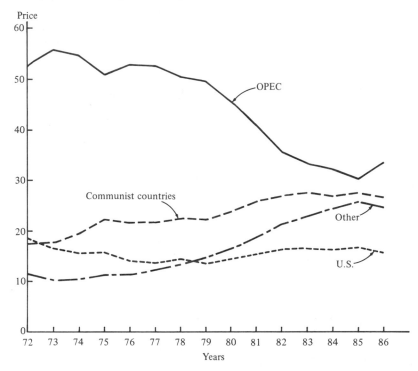

disrupted. Independent refiners had their crude supplies cut off. Desperate for crude oil, they turned to the spot market. The spot-market price shot up and the official price, as shown in Figure 2-1, followed.

4. Rise of Independent Oil-Producing Countries. The response to the second oil-price shock, however, was substantially different from the response to the first oil-price shock. Differences occurred on both the demand side and the supply side of the market.

As shown in Table 2-2, the size of the U.S. market fell over the period 1979 to 1983 and remained smaller in 1987 than in 1973. Part of the reason for this decline was a decrease in the "energy intensity" of the U.S. economy. U.S. energy use (measured in British Thermal Units consumed per dollar of gross national product), which fell from 23 in 1973 to 21 in 1979, sank to 17 by 1987. This illustrates the long response time required to realize changes in the demand for energy resources.

For example, at the time of the first oil-price shock, the electric power-generation industry was a major U.S. purchaser of petroleum. In the production of electricity, it is of course possible to substitute other fuels for petroleum (such as coal). But the lead time for construction of a fossil-fuel electric plant can be five years. Many petroleum-fired power plants came on line in the period following the first oil price shock simply because they had been planned during the period of cheap oil. Substantial reductions in petroleum consumption by the U.S. electric-power-generation sector did not begin until 1980—after the second oil-price shock. There is every reason to believe that the decline in the demand for energy is a permanent change. The full effect of the installation of energy-saving equipment (and insulation in homes) has yet to be felt.

There is a matching effect on the supply side of the market, described in Table 2-3. Crude oil production in the United States and Canada declined slightly from 1973 to 1986. For the United States in particular, this trend is likely to continue. Long isolated from the world market by quotas, the United States has been thoroughly explored. Large future discoveries of low-cost reserves are unlikely, although additional offshore and Alaskan developments are possible. For example, in April 1988 Amoco and Exxon announced a major Gulf of Mexico oil and gas find, in water three times as deep as any currently exploited. This oil field will not be developed as long as the price of oil remains relatively low. But it will be waiting, in the event that the price of oil rises.

Output from Western Europe increased sharply over this period, as the North Sea oilfields of Britain and Norway came into production. North Sea oil output will have peaked by the early 1990s and will decline thereafter.

Output in Latin America rose over this period, and this trend is likely to continue. Venezuela, although a charter member of OPEC, continues to expand its oil reserves. In addition, Venezuela has aggressively acquired a network of refineries, to ensure outlets for its oil. In June 1988, Brazil

Table 2-3 _____
World Crude Production by Area, 1973 and 1986 (Millions of Barrels)

	1973	1986	Change
United States	3,360	3,168	− 192
Canada	648	537	− 111
Western Europe	139	1,395	+1,256
Latin America	1,895	2,190	+ 295
Asia	816	1,176	+ 360
Communist nations	3,603	5,403	+1,800
Africa	2,161	1,820	− 341
Middle East	7,745	4,639	−3,106
Total	20,368	20,329	− 39

Source: American Petroleum Institute, *Basic Petroleum Data Book*, Volume VIII, Number 2, May 1988.

announced a major oil discovery. Because it is Brazil's best hope of repaying its international debt and financing future development efforts, this oil will find its way to market.

Crude oil output from the Third World, including China and various less developed countries in Africa, can be expected to increase. This reflects a convergence of interest between LDCs and the international majors. The international majors have been cut off from the Mideast oilfields, which were for generations the foundation of their dominant market position. They will explore anywhere outside OPEC's sphere of influence for new reserves, which they can feed into their existing refining and marketing networks. They will do so as long as the new reserves can be developed at or below the spot market price for oil.

At the same time, LDCs know from bitter experience that it is their development efforts that are torpedoed by dependency on foreign sources of oil. For political reasons, LDCs will encourage the development of local oil supplies even if the cost seems likely to exceed the spot market price of oil. Their national security, and often the lives of their leaders, depend on it.

The international majors will, therefore, be welcome in the new oil provinces around the world. The supply of oil from less developed countries will increase, and to some extent this increase will result from political rather than economic considerations.

A consequence of the OPEC-induced oil price shocks of the 1970s and early 1980s is that OPEC now operates in a market with substantial fringe reserves. Table 2-4 reports estimates of the quantity of reserves available, at various prices, outside OPEC and Communist countries. Because these reserves are costlier to produce than OPEC reserves, potential fringe supply rises sharply as price rises. OPEC will be able to keep these reserves in the ground by holding the price of oil below $20 a barrel. At higher prices, OPEC will lose sales to higher-cost suppliers. The presence of higher-cost fringe suppliers limits the ability of OPEC to raise the price of oil.[13]

The Soviet Union, long the world's single largest supplier of crude oil, will sell oil to the West as long as it has a need for hard currency, which is to say for the foreseeable future. Supplies of crude oil from the Soviet Union

Table 2-4

Non-Communist, Non-OPEC Crude Oil Reserves

1986 Dollars/Barrel	Billion Barrels
10	340
20	560
30	720
40	860
50	1,000

Source: Theodore R. Breton and John C. Blaney, "Outlook for OPEC's Competitors," *Petroleum Economist*, October 1987, p.361.

are not likely to increase substantially (Siberia is no more hospitable to industrial activity than the North Slope of Alaska), but neither are substantial decreases to be expected.

Corresponding to the substantial increases in crude oil production outside OPEC are the reductions in African and Middle East output indicated in Table 2-3. The decline in African output is marginal and reflects a combination of output restrictions by OPEC members and new supplies from Syria, Egypt, South Yemen, and elsewhere. The real restriction in output has come from the Middle East, which is home to the largest and least expensive oil deposits in the world.

By mid-1985, OPEC found itself in the kind of market illustrated in Figure 2-2(b). Fringe supply, after a decade of development efforts, was relatively large. Demand, after a decade of conservation efforts, had grown much less rapidly than expected. The residual part of the market left for OPEC was substantially reduced, compared with the situation of Figure 2-2(a). In such circumstances, the best OPEC could do would be to set a price p_2, much lower than p_1, and market a substantially smaller quantity q_2.

Just as the international majors' long domination of the world oil market created an incentive for the entry and expansion of independent oil firms, so OPEC's somewhat briefer period of control created an incentive for the entry of new oil-supplying countries. The entry of independent firms undercut the power base of the international majors, which reacted by seeking new supplies of oil. The entry of new oil-producing countries has undercut the power base of OPEC member nations, and they have reacted by seeking secure outlets for their oil.

5. The U.S. Submarket. The U.S. crude market is relatively unconcentrated, by conventional measures. In 1985, the largest four U.S. crude producers had a combined share of 26.1 percent of U.S. crude production. The 1985 Herfindahl index for the U.S. crude industry was 0.02766, suggesting a level of concentration equivalent to an industry with 36 equally sized firms.[14]

Students of industrial organization justify their interest in market concentration figures on the ground that such figures provide information on the likelihood that leading firms will come to recognize their mutual interdependence and act in a way that is likely to maximize joint profit. Two factors suggest that domestic concentration figures for the U.S. market understate the likelihood of recognition of interdependence.

The first is the common use of joint ventures among U.S. firms, which in a local sense replicates the use of joint ventures by international majors in the Mideast. From 1970 to 1972, 4 of 16 major U.S. oil companies made no independent bids for offshore oil leases but submitted a total of 863 joint bids with 14 alternative partners. Chevron submitted 79 individual bids and 108 joint bids with 9 alternative partners; Cities Service made 7 independent bids and 372 joint bids with 4 alternative partners. Among the 16 majors, only Exxon made no joint bids during this period, although it made 80 independent bids.[15] A similar pattern of joint ventures occurs in the management of pipelines.

The partners in this overlapping network of joint ventures, to the extent that they profit from the same enterprises, have an incentive to avoid competition. The operation of the network of joint ventures provides each company with myriad bits and pieces of information about the market strategies of its fellows. No single firm could contemplate noncooperative behavior without expecting that this behavior would be promptly detected by other firms.

The second factor that suggests that U.S. domestic concentration figures understate the likelihood of noncompetitive behavior is the current wave of mergers among major U.S. firms and between U.S. firms and international majors. Table 2-5 outlines the recent merger activity of the (1986) eight largest U.S. oil companies. Four of the eight majors took over other major firms during this period, and two were themselves taken over by foreign firms. A similar consolidation is taking place among smaller U.S. oil companies. The U.S. market, long protected by formal and informal trade barriers, is today part of the world market. The long history of joint ventures, cooperation, and collusion on the world stage suggests the likelihood of similar conduct in the United States.

6. Refining. The refining segment of the petroleum industry transforms crude oil into a variety of final products, ranging from gasoline and liquefied petroleum gases to residual fuel oil and petroleum coke. Refining involves not only the distillation of crude petroleum into refined products, but a number of upgrading processes by which lower-value refined products can be transformed into higher-value products (lead-free gasoline, for example).

Table 2-5

Consolidation Among U.S. Oil Companies

Company	1986 Revenue (Billions)	
Exxon	$76.6	
Mobil	49.9	Acquired Superior Oil Co., 1984
Texaco	32.6	Acquired Getty Oil Corp., 1984[a]
Chevron	24.4	Acquired Gulf, 1984
Amoco	18.3	Acquired Dome Petroleum Ltd., 1987
Shell Oil Corp.	17.4	Acquired by Royal Dutch/Shell, 1985
Atlantic Richfield	14.5	
Standard Oil Co.	10.0	Acquired by British Petroleum, 1987

[a]A consequence of this acquisition was the 1985 breach-of-contract suit by Pennzoil against Texaco, Texaco's 1987 passage through bankruptcy proceedings, Texaco's $3 billion settlement with Pennzoil, and Carl Icahn's unsuccessful 1988 takeover attempt against Texaco. So it goes.

The most striking recent development on the world refining market has been the forward vertical integration of OPEC member nations into refining, and indeed forward still further into marketing.

Through a subsidiary of the Kuwait Petroleum Corporation, Kuwait owns two European refineries with a capacity of 135,000 barrels per day, together with 4,800 retail gasoline stations in seven different European countries. Kuwait has acquired a 22 percent ownership of British Petroleum, much to British government concern, and has sought refining assets in Japan.

Venezuela has employed joint ventures to acquire partial interest in refineries in West Germany, Sweden, Belgium, and the United States. The latter interests include retail outlets that can handle the equivalent of 200,000 barrels per day in gasoline.

In June 1988, in the midst of an unsuccessful takeover attempt by Carl Icahn, Texaco Inc. announced its intention to sell a half-interest in its refining and distribution network in the East and Gulf Coast areas to Saudi Arabia for $1.28 billion. The three refineries involved have a capacity of 615,000 barrels per day; the distribution network includes 11,450 retail gasoline stations. With this investment, the largest source of crude oil in the world moves to secure a market for its product. It also acquires an interest in maintaining profitability at the refining and distribution levels of the market, as well as the crude level.

The motives for this forward integration are partly political and partly economic. A move forward into refining is a way of broadening the local industrial base while taking advantage of existing assets and skills. At the same time, a refinery associated with a national oil company of an oil-producing state has an almost insuperable advantage when compared with an independent refiner. The real cost of crude oil to the integrated refiner is the cost of crude production (regardless of the transfer price from the crude division to the refinery division). But the cost of crude oil to an independent, nonintegrated refiner is the much higher market price for crude oil. Refining and distribution networks associated with producing nations will always be able to undersell independents. When there is a surplus of crude oil, it will be tempting—and profitable—to do so.

A consequence of this forward integration by oil-producing nations is a persistent excess capacity at the refining level, as illustrated in Table 2-6. Oil-producing nations integrate forward for economic and political reasons, while (in some cases at least) restraining crude output. International majors retain the bulk of their refining operations, which are the heart of their distribution network, while seeking to develop access to crude oil outside OPEC control. Refining capacity expands and crude reserves expand rapidly, while crude production grows slowly if at all. (World production of crude oil was essentially the same in 1973 and 1986). The result is excess refining capacity.

Table 2-6
Worldwide Refining Capacity (Thousand Barrels Per Day)

	1973	1987	Demand (1986)
United States	13,671	15,288	12,716
Other Western Hemisphere	8,176	8,857	6,740
Europe	16,827	14,127	10,095
Middle East	2,757	4,146	2,950
Africa	825	2,630	2,095
Asia–Pacific	7,916	10,274	7,400
Sino–Soviet Bloc	9,110	17,610	14,280
World	59,282	72,933	56,276

Source: American Petroleum Institute, *Basic Petroleum Data Book*, Volume VIII, Number 2, May 1988.

7. Marketing. Marketing channels differ, depending on the class of final consumer served. Nearly all jet fuel is sold by refining companies to their customers, who are principally the Department of Defense and commercial airlines. Most refiner sales of residual fuel are made directly to large utility and industrial customers, with the remainder going to large terminal operators and dealers.

In contrast, no more than one-third of distillate fuel-oil sales is made directly to customers from refiner-owned facilities, whereas two-thirds goes through independent marketers.

The retail market for gasoline, like all levels of the petroleum industry, has been severely affected by the structural changes that have occurred since 1973. Table 2-7 indicates the substantial decline in service stations since that time. In part, this reflects the shift from full-service to convenience store distribution (with an estimated 37,500 convenience stores retailing gasoline in the U.S. in 1988). In part, the decline in the number of outlets signals an increase in the scale of operation:[16]

> The stations that are disappearing are generally on the smaller side — 30,000 to 40,000 gal./month. In their places are being built the big superstations — the 100,000- to 200,000-gal./month-plus pumpers that are more economical to operate and frequently are on a seven-day, 24-hour basis.

Table 2-7
U.S. Service Station Population

	Number	Company-Owned	Franchisee-Owned
1973	215,880	47,176	172,704
1988	112,000	21,160	91,840

Source: *1987 National Petroleum News* Factbook Issue and *National Petroleum News*, February 1988.

In part, the decline in outlets reflects a high level of concentration of retail gasoline sales in local markets (where the combined share of the largest four firms typically ranges from 40 to 60 percent). This concentration can be expected to increase, as vertical integration from crude production through distribution (by OPEC members and major companies) clones the obligopolistic structure of the crude segment of the industry at levels closer to the final consumer.

These changes bode ill for the independent retail outlet. As competition from independent retail outlets has always been an important factor in forcing competitive pressure vertically backward from the retail level, they bode ill for the consumer as well.

8. Transportation. Pipelines are the most important mode of transportation in the United States, where large volumes of oil must be moved overland.[17] In any oil field, a network of small-diameter "gathering lines" collects crude oil from individual wells in an oil field and transmits the field's output to a larger-diameter "trunk line" for shipment to a refinery. Pipelines later move refined products to marketing centers.

Bulk shipment of oil in trunk lines is a classic example of a technology that exhibits decreasing cost per unit of output. Pipeline construction cost is roughly proportional to pipeline radius, while pipeline capacity is proportional to the square of the radius. If pipeline radius is doubled, pipeline capacity increases by a factor of four. Construction and operating costs per unit of capacity decline, therefore, over the entire range of technically feasible pipelines. Petroleum shipment over pipelines is for this reason a natural monopoly.

It is not surprising, therefore, that major oil companies dominate pipeline transportation. Nearly 90 percent of crude-oil pipeline shipments reported to the Interstate Commerce Commission in 1976 originated in lines that were owned or controlled by the 16 major U.S. oil companies. At the same time, nearly 75 percent of refined-product shipments that originated in refineries (in contrast to those received from connecting carriers) went into pipelines owned by the major companies.

Pipeline transportation is inherently a local activity, moving from one point to another:[18]

> Concentration in major crude oil transport corridors (i.e., specific pipeline markets) is extremely high. In the Texas–Cushing, Oklahoma corridor, for example, the four largest pipeline companies together account for 76% of total crude carried. Three pipeline companies control all crude oil shipments in the Gulf Coast–Upper Mid-Continent corridor . . . in 1979, the four-firm concentration ratio for pipeline shipments in the nation's major crude carriers averaged 91%.

This high degree of concentration is intensified by the use of joint ventures in pipeline management. As with joint ventures in offshore oil and Mideast exploration, such joint ventures are not conducive to "arm's length" competition.

The implications of this concentration of pipeline ownership and control are clear:[19]

> A pipeline rate set well above the competitive cost of transporting crude oil . . . imposes no burden on the majors who own the pipeline. For them, the high price is simply a transfer of funds from the refinery operation to the pipeline operation. To the nonintegrated refiner, however, an excessive pipeline charge is a real cost increase that he cannot recoup elsewhere and that places him at a competitive disadvantage vis-a-vis his integrated competitors.

Vertical integration from refining into pipeline transportation allows U.S. majors to apply a vertical price squeeze to refiners who are not integrated forward, much as vertical integration forward into refining allows crude-oil-producing countries to apply a price squeeze to refiners who are not integrated backward into production.

III.
CONDUCT AND PERFORMANCE

It is sometimes asserted that the price increases of 1973 and 1979–82 reflect no more than the working of competitive forces. In this view— favored in particular by oil-producing nations—a price of oil at or near extraction cost fails to reflect the scarcity that current consumption imposes on future generations. A price substantially above marginal extraction cost, in this view, is to be desired, because it encourages conservation and spreads consumption of a finite resource over a long time period.

This argument might explain the price increases observed in 1973 and 1979–82. It cannot explain the price declines since then. Oil is, after all, as much a finite resource as it ever was, and if future scarcity would produce a high price in 1982, it would, seemingly, produce a still higher price in 1988. Statistical tests do not support the argument that OPEC pricing is competitive.[20]

Some analysts have suggested that the world oil industry is driven by a single dominant firm—Saudi Arabia. According to the figures in Table 2-8, Saudi Arabia holds nearly 19 percent of world proven reserves, which can be extracted with current technology at current prices. It is widely believed that Saudi Arabia substantially understates its reserve holdings. Saudi Arabia's proven reserves may actually be twice as great as indicated in Table 2-8. This quantitative description does not capture the fact that Saudi crude is by far the least expensive in the world, with an estimated cost of 30 to 60 cents a barrel.

These reserve holdings establish that Saudi Arabia will be a factor on the

Table 2-8
Estimated Proven Reserves of World Oil, 1988 (Billion Barrels)

Saudi Arabia	167
Iraq	100
Iran	93
Abu Dhabi	92
Kuwait	92
U.S.S.R.	59
Venezuela	56
Mexico	49
United States	25
Libya	20
World	887

Source: American Petroleum Institute, Basic Petroleum Data Book, Volume VIII, Number 1, January 1988.

world oil market as long as there is a world market for oil. If Saudi Arabia were to act as a wealth-maximizing dominant firm, it would in principle restrict output and raise price above the cost of production. It would then gradually give up market share, as other producers expand output to take advantage of the opportunity for profit created by the price increase.[21]

A variation on this theme suggests that although no single OPEC member has sufficient control of reserves to exercise control over price, OPEC, as a group, is able to act as a collusive price leader. The predicted market performance is much the same as under the dominant-firm model. OPEC's share of the market should decline over time as independent producers respond to the incentive created by a price above the cost of production.

Figures 2-1 and 2-3 suggest that the dominant-firm and dominant-group models have a certain degree of explanatory power vis-a-vis the world oil market. OPEC's share of world crude-oil production fell very slowly from 1973 to 1979. As already noted, this is a reflection of the long lead times in discovery and development of oil reserves. OPEC's market share has fallen precipitously since 1979, bottoming out at 30 percent of the world market in 1985. Price has fallen as OPEC's market share has fallen and the share of other producers has increased.

What the dominant-firm and dominant-group analyses fail to capture is the oligopolistic interactions that have flavored OPEC behavior. When price is raised above the cost of production, individual OPEC member nations (not just independent producers) have an incentive to increase their own output.[22] The problem of OPEC, like any cartel, is to achieve agreement on a course of action (raising price to some level) and then securing adherence to the agreement. As is the case with any group, differences make for disagreements. The two principal differences that have plagued OPEC have involved product differentiation and the rate of time preference for income.

In an industry that produces a differentiated product, a successful cartel must confront the problem of controlling differentials between the prices of alternative varieties, as well as the general price level. Before OPEC domination of the world crude market, low-density, low-sulfur crude oil sold at a premium compared with heavier, high-sulfur oil. Light, low-sulfur oil yields a more valuable mix of refined products, at lower cost and with less corrosion to refineries. The initial OPEC price scheme built the traditional price differential—higher prices for light, low-sulfur oil—into the official price schedule.

Before the 1973 oil price increase, refineries were designed to process relatively specific types of crude oil. U.S. refineries, for example, were largely designed to handle low-sulfur, "sweet" African crudes, which could be refined into motor gasoline at a relatively low cost. When the supply of oil tightened, such refineries had few alternative sources of supply. Since that time, Western refineries in general, and especially those in the United States, have installed expensive upgrading equipment, which allows them to process heavier, high-sulfur ("sour") crudes in a cost-effective way. The effect of the investment at the refining level is to increase the demand for heavy, high-sulfur oil relative to the demand for light, low-sulfur oil.

Negotiations within OPEC to reduce the price differential between sweet and sour crude had been a persistent source of difficulty. Thus (in January 1985):[23]

> OPEC oil ministers, gathering here for an emergency meeting that begins Monday, seemed today to be heading for a collision over how to cope with a glut of oil that has been eroding prices.
>
> At the heart of the dispute are differences over how to change OPEC's official price structure to enable members to sell all of their allotments. . . .
>
> The so-called price differential is a premium OPEC adds to the price of its more valuable light crude oils, with their high yields of valuable derivatives such as gasoline, to increase the competitiveness of heavy crudes. . . .
>
> But the lower price of heavy crudes, their easy accessibility in near-surface locations and new refining technology . . . have increased demand for these oils at the expense of the lights.
>
> Complicating matters, much of the new oil that has poured onto the world market for producers such as Britain and Norway is light crude.
>
> As the price of light has gradually eroded, OPEC has tried to halt the slide by narrowing the gap between its light and heavy crudes. . . .
>
> African countries that produce mainly light crude oils have called for more increases in heavy crude prices. . . .
>
> Strong resistance to an increase in the heavy crude price, which is no longer competitive, is expected from Saudi Arabia, OPEC's largest heavy-crude producer.

Another persistent source of disagreement among OPEC members involves the substantial differences in the urgency with which OPEC members desire revenue from oil sales. Countries such as Saudi Arabia, Kuwait, and the United Arab Emirates have small populations, high GNPs per capita, and political circumstances that are well served by modernization at a slow pace.

Their massive oil reserves ensure that they will earn oil revenue for the foreseeable future. Other OPEC members, such as Indonesia, Nigeria, and Algeria, have larger populations, smaller GNPs per capita, and substantially smaller oil reserves. Their best hope for economic development is through the maximization of short-run oil revenues. Political pressures reinforce this economic incentive. More than once, governments of OPEC nations have been overturned because of mismanagement of the oil sector, and the ousted leaders often do not survive to collect retirement benefits. Arguments between OPEC members who place great weight on short-run revenue and OPEC members who place great weight on the long run have persistently complicated OPEC negotiations:[24]

> . . . For more than four years, the search for a solution to the problems of declining prices and plummeting sales amid a world-wide oil glut has been thwarted by infighting between the cartel's "rich" and "poor" factions. . . . Within OPEC, the Saudis increasingly are viewed as the rich landlord in a slum. Resented for their wealth, the Saudis are seen as preying on poor members who can't afford to sacrifice much more of their revenue by cutting prices or trimming production. The Saudis, for their part, feel they have sacrificed enough to prop up sagging oil prices, allowing their production to fall to two million barrels a day—from 10 million barrels a day a few years ago—while other members cheat on prices and production quotas.

Differences like these, reinforced by the Iran–Iraq war, have made the OPEC of the mid-1980s a textbook example of cartel collapse:[25]

> The classic breakdown sequence is (1) incremental sales at less than the collusive price, with incremental revenues for the cheaters; (2) matching of price cuts, with the bigger cartelists, reluctant to cut, losing market shares to the smaller; (3) accusations, confrontations; and then (4) renewed agreements among the cartelists, but with mutual suspicion and readiness to retaliate.

By 1985, OPEC's market share had fallen to 30 percent, mostly on the strength of output cutbacks by Saudi Arabia, which enjoyed an OPEC quota of 4.353 million barrels per day but was estimated to be producing only 2.5 million barrels a day in September 1985. OPEC's official price remained at $28 a barrel, but the spot-market price for oil was no more than half the official price.

At this point, Saudi Arabia introduced a system of "netback pricing," under which the price paid for Saudi crude oil was determined by the market prices of the products refined from the crude. The immediate effect of the netback pricing system was to eliminate risk for the purchaser of Saudi crude: If the price of refined products should fall, the price of crude would fall proportionately. The consequence was a sharp increase in the demand for Saudi oil, output of which reached six million barrels a day by July 1986.

Two explanations have been put forward for the Saudi expansion of output in late 1985. The first explanation viewed Saudi behavior as directed toward its fellow OPEC members. By expanding output and compelling a lower price, in this view, Saudi Arabia hoped to persuade other OPEC members to adhere to their output quotas.

The second explanation viewed Saudi behavior as directed toward non-OPEC producers, with their generally higher costs, and oil customers. By lowering the price of oil, Saudi Arabia would make oil more attractive relative to other energy sources (such as coal and nuclear energy). This would increase the size of the market to be divided by oil producers.

Further, a lower oil price would, eventually, affect the supply side of the market. North Slope and North Sea oil, profitable at $28 a barrel, is unprofitable at $14 a barrel. Much of the capacity installed when prices were at $28 a barrel would continue to produce at the lower price. But lower prices would cause companies to cut back on exploration and development activity. Five to seven years after a price decline, fringe supply will be reduced. In this view, Saudi Arabia in late 1985 hoped to move the world oil market from a situation like Figure 2-2(b) back to Figure 2-2(a).

Other OPEC members soon adopted their own netback pricing schemes, and oil prices fell as low as $6 a barrel. By August 1986, OPEC members, with the exception of Iraq, which held out for a quota equal to Iran's, reaffirmed their support for the quota schedule that they were all violating.

It was clear by this time, however, that OPEC was reduced from being able to direct the market to trying to react to the market.[26] Disputes between rich and poor OPEC member nations continued, and the war between Iran and Iraq continued to spill over into cartel activities. Effective January 1987, OPEC quota output was reduced from 16.639 to 15.8 million barrels per day, with a reduction in official price to an average of $18 a barrel.

For one brief shining moment, the new agreement seemed to hold. But by the end of February 1987, with reports of overproducing by OPEC members, spot market oil prices were $2–$3 below OPEC's official price. Saudi Arabia resumed its role as the "swing" OPEC producer, cutting output to 2.5 million barrels a day, far below its quota output of 4.133 million barrels a day, but this was not enough to hold total output down. OPEC quota output for the last half of 1987 was 16.6 million barrels a day, but actual output reached 19 million barrels a day. At the end of 1987, OPEC oil continued to sell $1–$3 below the $18 official price.

The Iran–Iraq war also interfered with cartel agreement. Iraq refused any agreement that gave it a smaller quota than Iran. Non-Arab OPEC members refused to reward Iraq, a consistent overproducer, with a higher quota.

1988 saw OPEC, by its actions, admit that it could no longer control the market. A projected 5 percent cut in OPEC output was abandoned, in view of expected increases in output from non-OPEC producers. Some non-OPEC producers also reached the conclusion that OPEC could not control the market. In April 1988, representatives of Saudi Arabia, Venezuela, Nigeria, Algeria, Kuwait, and Iran met with representatives of non-OPEC countries China, Egypt, Mexico, Malaysia, Columbia, Oman, and Angola. Also on hand to observe discussions on joint action to raise oil prices were observers from Norway and Brunei, as well as Texas Railroad Commissioner Kent Hance.

In due course, the non-OPEC countries put forward an offer to reduce their exports of oil 5 percent, or 200,000 barrels a day, in return for a 700,000-barrel-a-day cut by OPEC. Railroad Commissioner Hance, taking it upon himself to speak for the Texas oil industry, allowed that " 'under the right conditions, 5% could look attractive' to some U.S. producers."[27] There is little doubt that Commissioner Hance was correct in this view, but no agreement between OPEC and non-OPEC countries was realized:[28]

> The Saudis, along with Kuwait and Nigeria, think that OPEC has already sacrificed a substantial part of its oil output in recent years in order to prop up prices. And they complain that other oil-producing nations responded to the OPEC cuts by increasing production and stealing market share from OPEC.

Saudi Arabia managed to block an accord between OPEC and non-OPEC producers. The lure of profitable collusion being what it is, there is little doubt that contact between OPEC and non-OPEC oil-producing nations will continue. The lure of profitable cheating on collusion being what it is, there is little reason to think that a world cartel of 20 or more oil-producing members would be any more successful than the 13-member OPEC cartel.

The most recent OPEC dialogues have focused on the sort of minutia that would be easily passed over if OPEC were able to determine the course of events on world oil markets. Iraq will not adhere to a quota scheme that grants it a smaller production level than its battlefield rival, Iran. Thus the OPEC agreement excludes Iraq. Saudi Arabia and Kuwait deliver the proceeds from the sale of 300,000 barrels a day in the Neutral Zone to Iraq; this output escapes the quota system. The United Arab Emirates, a perennial overproducer, declines to adhere to its quota on the ground that the quota system is unfair. Kuwait and others press for a more precise definition of oil: Venezuela produces the equivalent of 180,000 barrels a day of crude oil in oil condensates, which are excluded from the quotas because they are not "oil." By mid-1988, OPEC can secure the agreement of 11 out of 13 members to maintain official quotas, which most ignore, and official prices, which all undercut.

IV.

GOVERNMENT POLICY

U.S. Antitrust Activity

Antitrust policy has been the traditional approach to the preservation of competition in the United States. In 1911, the Supreme Court upheld a finding that the Standard Oil Company had violated the Sherman Antitrust

Act while acquiring a dominant position in the refining, marketing, and transportation of petroleum. The Court imposed a structural remedy, ordering the parent holding company to divest itself of controlling stock interests in 33 subsidiaries.[29] This first case was also the last successful major case involving the U.S. oil industry.

To be sure, the oil giants have from time to time attracted the attention of antitrust enforcers. In 1940, a case so broad that it became known as the "Mother Hubbard" case was filed.[30] Twenty-two major oil companies, 344 subsidiary and secondary companies, and the American Petroleum Institute were charged, in a Justice Department civil suit, with violating both the Sherman and Clayton Acts. The case was postponed because of the onset of World War II and thereafter languished until it was dismissed in 1951 at the request of the Justice Department.

Throughout the postwar period, in fact, antitrust action against U.S. oil firms was suspended on grounds of national security. In the closing days of the Truman Administration, the government accused the five U.S.-based international majors (along with British Petroleum and Royal Dutch Shell, which were beyond the jurisdiction of U.S. authorities) of seeking to restrain and monopolize crude oil and refined petroleum products, in violation of the Sherman Antitrust Act. But the State Department urged that the oil companies receive antitrust immunity for their cooperation in setting up the 1954 Iranian consortium, and this immunity weakened the cartel case, which dragged on for years. Exxon, Texaco, and Gulf eventually settled for consent decrees, and charges against Mobil and Socal were dismissed. The last parts of the case were dropped by the Justice Department in 1968.[31]

By 1985, OPEC's market share had fallen to 30 percent, mostly on the strength of output cutbacks by Saudi Arabia, which enjoyed an OPEC quota of 4.353 million barrels per day but was estimated to be producing only 2.5 million barrels a day in violation of the Sherman Antitrust Act. But the State Department urged that the oil companies receive antitrust immunity for their cooperation in setting up the 1954 Iranian consortium, and this immunity weakened the cartel case, which dragged on for years. Exxon, Texaco, and Gulf eventually settled for consent decrees, and charges against Mobil and Socal were dismissed. The last parts of the case were dropped by the Justice Department in 1968.[31]

Much of the vitality of American antitrust law derives from the possibility of private enforcement. A private antitrust suit filed in 1978 by the International Association of Machinists and Aerospace Workers (IAM) sought to apply U.S. antitrust law to OPEC. OPEC declined to appear when the case was heard, and the Department of Justice declined to submit the *amicus curiae* brief requested by the District Court. The District Court declined to hear the case on technical grounds, among others that the IAM did not have "standing" to sue OPEC since IAM was not a direct purchaser from OPEC.

IAM appealed this dismissal to the Circuit Court of Appeals, which upheld the lower court's refusal to hear the case on the ground that the case would interfere with U.S. foreign relations. Once again, conditions of national security short-circuited the application of the antitrust laws.[32]

Government Policy Responses to OPEC

The fact that the oil crisis of 1973 was repeated just six years later is testimony that Western governments generally were unable to develop adequate energy policies. The founding of the International Energy Agency (IEA) in November 1974 suggests government recognition of the importance of cooperation among consuming countries. However, France refused to join the IEA, apparently preferring bilateral government-to-government negotiations with oil-producing nations. Such government-to-government negotiations became common during the tight crude markets of 1978–1980, when security of supply was a matter of concern. Since that time, with crude oil in excess supply at official OPEC prices, sales with government involvement have declined. Supplies can be acquired on the spot market, and generally at prices below the official OPEC levels.

Three interrelated aspects of the continuing debate over proper government policy toward the petroleum industry merit discussion. All reflect a failure to understand the way markets work.

1. The International Energy Agency.[33]   Twenty-one Western nations are members of the International Energy Agency. They are pledged to share oil supply if it is determined that a shortage of oil has occurred or is likely to occur. "Shortage" is defined in terms of a physical interruption in supply, and it seems clear that the focus of the IEA is embargoes imposed for political reasons. Price increases, however, have been an important aspect of past oil shocks. It would be desirable to alter IEA procedures so as to facilitate a response to a sharp price increase as well as to a sharp supply decrease.

2. The Strategic Petroleum Reserve.   In 1975, Congress established a Strategic Petroleum Reserve (SPR) as insurance against future interruptions in foreign supplies. Targets, set in later detailed plans, were for 500 million barrels in storage by 1980 and a billion barrels by 1985. The current target, set in 1986, is 750 million barrels. The March 1988 total, stored in salt caverns around the Gulf of Mexico, was 545 million barrels. U.S. imports of oil from all countries were something under 6 million barrels per day during 1987. Hence the SPR is large enough to replace all U.S. imports for about 90 days.

Increasing the SPR to a billion barrels, at current prices, would cost roughly $6.5 billion. A $10 per barrel increase in the price of oil would cost $58.4 billion.[34] The added insurance seems worth the price, but the old story about repairing a hole in the roof when it isn't raining makes it seem doubtful that the insurance policy will be taken out in a timely manner.[35]

Policy for the use of the SPR focuses on interruptions in supply. Before the SPR can be used, the President must declare an oil supply emergency. An alternative procedure, which would allow the market to signal the need for additional supplies, would be to sell oil from the SPR at any time, at a modest premium above the current spot market price for oil. Under such a regime, SPR oil would reach the market before supply shortages triggered severe price increases, and there would be no need for an explicit Presidential finding of emergency.[36]

3. Low Price or Energy Independence?

The U.S. government has been unable to come to grips with the constraints imposed by the market on its policy options. What is striking is that OPEC member nations suffer from a symmetric analytical failure.

Figure 2-4 shows a stylized demand curve for the world oil market. In the long run, a monopolist or complete cartel can be anywhere on the demand curve. The constraint imposed by the market is that price and quantity are inversely related: high price—low quantity demanded; low price—high quantity demanded.[37] It is clear from endless public statements that OPEC oil ministers want desperately to be at a place like X in Figure 2-4. They want to charge a high price for oil and sell a great deal of oil, and over the long haul the market will not let them.

But it is not proximity to rich oil reserves that brings about fuzzy thinking. The debate on U.S. policy toward the petroleum industry has long been bedeviled by a similar failure to come to grips with the limitations imposed by the market.

U.S. policymakers have long recognized the ills associated with a high oil price. Supply shocks mean short-run bursts of inflation, which eventually raise interest rates. A high oil price raises the cost of all energy-intensive activity, by consumers and by industry. Economic growth is slowed, and the U.S. trade balance—because the high price applies to a good for which the U.S. is a net importer—is made worse.

Figure 2-4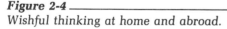
Wishful thinking at home and abroad.

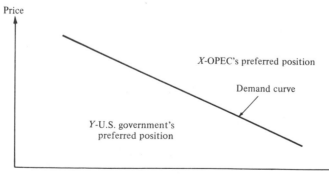

One might think, therefore, that an oil price collapse, like that of 1986, would be welcomed by U.S. policymakers. But no! A low price for oil encourages U.S. dependence on foreign suppliers and increases the likelihood of future oil crises. No less a figure than the Vice-President of the United States travels to Saudi Arabia to make a[38] "plea for stability of the marketplace," and states:[39]

> . . . the interest in the United States is bound to be cheap energy if we possibly can. But from our interest, there is some point where the national security interests of the United States say, "Hey, we must have a strong, viable domestic industry."

In short, a recurring theme in the U.S. policy debate would very much like to have the U.S. at a point like *Y* in Figure 2-4: a low price for oil, but we don't buy much of it.

Some of this is simply the putting of parochial interests ahead of national interests, as when the governor of Texas sits on the lap of Santa Claus and asks for "$25-a-barrel oil."[40] More important, however, is the failure to think through the implications of dependence on domestic supplies for long-run national security.

National Security: The Short Run

Current consumption of U.S. oil always makes future dependence on foreign oil worse — barrel for barrel. The only way to avoid this is permanent tariffs or quotas that artificially raise the price of oil in the United States and distort input/consumption choices in less efficient and productive ways. It is not in the national security interest of the United States to be protected from foreign oil that is cheaper than domestic oil.

The specter is raised of unending Middle East reserves (Table 2-9) and vulnerability of a cutoff of oil supplies from a politically unstable region of the world. The response to this contingency points to the increase in supplies elsewhere (Table 2-3), an increase that will intensify as the price of oil rises (Table 2-4).

There is no long-run U.S. security interest in avoiding the current consumption of cheap foreign oil. There is a short-run U.S. security interest in neutralizing runups of oil price due to sporadic supply interruptions, and that is a problem that can be addressed, in the event, through proper use of the Strategic Petroleum Reserve.

National Security: The Long Run

Secure energy supplies need not lie in oil reserves around the world. They may also lie in alternatives to conventional oil and natural gas — shale oil, coal gasification, solar power, nuclear fusion, and others. Experience shows that this sort of research cannot be left entirely to market forces. The costs of commercial-scale plants are far higher, and the development times far longer, than commercial enterprises can support. If government investment in a Strategic Petroleum Reserve to maintain short-run energy security is appropriate, then government support for the long-term—twenty- or fifty-year—research needed to ensure long-run energy security is also appropriate.

V.
PUBLIC POLICY CHALLENGES

The oil price increases of 1973, 1979, and 1981 induced a permanent change in world demand for energy. The demand for energy will grow as the world economy grows, but much less rapidly than would have been the case if the OPEC-administered price increases had never taken place. As the price of oil falls, the use of oil relative to other energy sources will increase, but industry will maintain the flexibility to reduce the use of oil in the event of oil-price increases. The demand side of the world oil market, therefore, is permanently changed in a way unfavorable to any would-be cartel.

There is a corresponding change on the supply side of the market—the expansion of fringe or non-OPEC supply as oil companies and less developed countries seek secure oil supplies. It will take a prolonged period of low oil prices—five or six years, not the few months enforced by Saudi Arabia in 1985–86—to shrink non-OPEC supply and move the market toward, but not to, the precrisis situation of Figure 2-2(a). Some of the increased fringe supply is politically rather than economically motivated and will not leave the market even in the face of extended low prices.

A critical change in structure is the expanded number of players. For generations, the world oil market was dominated by the Seven Sisters—the vertically integrated majors. For something more than a decade, the world oil market was dominated by the 13 OPEC member nations. For the foreseeable future, events on the world oil market will reflect the actions of the OPEC member nations (integrating forward toward the final consumer), the international majors (integrating backward through the development of non-OPEC reserves), new supplying nations, and independent oil companies. These various firms and nation-firms will collude when they can and compete when they must. The expanded number of suppliers reduces the likelihood of successful long-run collusion.

Nonetheless, when the growth of demand and the reduction in fringe supply present an opportunity to OPEC or an expanded "World OPEC," it will be taken. Periodically, supply will be cut back and oil prices will rise. There will be future oil price shocks.

Governments can—if they will—mitigate the effects of these shocks.

The policy to do so will use the market as a trigger to release reserves over the short run and to share reserves among industrialized countries, and supplement the market to develop long-run alternative sources of supply. Policies that fail to use the information provided by the market in the short run, and that rely on the market to develop new technology over the long run, will exacerbate future oil shocks.

NOTES

1. Youssef M. Ibrahim, "Crumbling Cartel," *The Wall Street Journal*, January 11, 1985, p. 1.

2. Among which survivors of the 1911 breakup of the Standard Oil Trust: Standard Oil of New Jersey, now Exxon; Standard Oil of New York, now Mobil; and Standard Oil of California, now Chevron.

3. R. Vernon, "An Interpretation," *Daedalus*, Volume 104, Number 7 (Fall 1975).

4. M. A. Adelman, *The World Petroleum Market* (Baltimore: Johns Hopkins, 1972), pp. 84–87. Relevant here is Stigler's theory of oligopoly: The more rapidly cheating is likely to be detected, and therefore subject to retaliation, the less likely cheating is to occur. See George J. Stigler, "A Theory of Oligopoly," *Journal of Political Economy*, Volume 72, Number 1 (February 1964), pp. 44–61, reprinted in George J. Stigler, *The Organization of Industry* (Homewood, Illinois: Richard D. Irwin, Inc., 1968), pp. 39–63.

5. Anthony Sampson, *The Seven Sisters* (New York: Bantam Books, 1975), p. 147, describing the findings of the Federal Trade Commission report "The International Petroleum Cartel."

6. S. A. Schneider, *The Oil Price Revolution* (Baltimore: Johns Hopkins, 1983), p. 46.

7. Subcommittee on Antitrust and Monopoly, Cabinet on the Judiciary, United States Senate, *The Petroleum Industry: Part 4, The Cabinet Task Force on Oil Import Control* (Washington, D.C.: U.S. Government Printing Office, March 1970).

8. Sampson, pp. 174–175.

9. Sampson, pp. 253–272.

10. Sampson, pp. 278–282.

11. The average cost of Persian Gulf oil is about 60 cents a barrel. Average cost of U.S. oil ranges from $4 to $12 a barrel, and the cost of offshore oil can reach $24 a barrel.

12. Louis Turner, *Oil Companies in the International System* (London: Allen & Unwin, 1983), p. 136.

13. The limit price model is due to Joe S. Bain, *Barriers to New Competition* (Cambridge, Mass.: Harvard University Press, 1956). For discussion, see Stephen Martin, *Industrial Economics* (New York: Macmillan Publishing Company, 1988), Chapter 4, pp. 61–96.

14. The inverse of the Herfindahl index gives the number of equally sized firms that would produce the level of concentration measured by the Herfindahl index. See M. A. Adelman, "Comment on the 'H' Concentration Measure as a Numbers Equivalent," *Review of Economics and Statistics*, Volume 51 (February 1969), pp. 99–101. The concentration and Herfindahl figures are computed from output data reported in the *National Petroleum News* 1987 factbook issue.

15. Walter Adams, "Vertical Divestiture of the Petroleum Majors: An Affirmative Case," *Vanderbilt Law Review,* Volume 30 (November 1977), pp. 122–123.

16. *1984 National Petroleum News* factbook issue, p. 103.

17. Pipelines assume an increasingly important role in the Middle East, where they provide a way of moving oil that avoids the Persian Gulf and (some) of the hazards of war.

18. Walter Adams and James W. Brock, "Deregulation or Divestiture: The Case of Petroleum Refineries," *Wake Forest Law Review,* Volume 19 (October 1983), pp. 711–712.

19. Adams and Brock, pp. 1134–1135.

20. James M. Griffen, "OPEC Behavior: A Test of Alternative Hypotheses," *American Economic Review,* Volume 75, Number 5 (December 1985), pp. 954–963.

21. Darius Gaskins, "Dynamic Limit Pricing: Optimal Limit Pricing Under Threat of Entry," *Journal of Economic Theory,* Volume 3 (September 1971), pp. 306–322; Norman J. Ireland, "Concentration and the Growth of Market Demand," *Journal of Economic Theory,* Volume 5 (October 1972), pp. 303–305.

22. For general discussion, see Martin, Chapter 6.

23. John Tagliabue, "OPEC Facing a Dispute on Policy for Glut of Oil," *The New York Times,* January 27, 1985, Section 1, p. 4.

24. Youssef M. Ibrahim, "OPEC Makes Small Cuts in Crude Prices, but Move Seen Unlikely to Steady Market," *The Wall Street Journal,* July 26, 1985, p. 3.

25. M. A. Adelman, "Oil Import Quota Auctions," *Challenge* (January–February 1976), pp. 17–22.

26. Ironically, a factor holding up prices during the 1985–86 price war was a strike by the caterers' union serving Norwegian offsea oil platforms. The strike eventually cut off output of 900,000 barrels a day, which slowed the decline in oil prices as Saudi output tripled.

27. "Likelihood Dims for World Oil Cartel, but Limited Output Accord Is Possible," *The Wall Street Journal,* April 26, 1988, p. 4.

28. Youssef M. Ibrahim, "Saudis Resist Cuts in Output," *The New York Times,* April 28, 1988, p. 25.

29. Martin, Chapters 4 and 16; John S. McGee, "Predatory Pricing: The Standard Oil (N.J.) Case," *Journal of Law and Economics,* Volume 1 (October 1958), p. 138.

30. *U.S.* v. *American Petroleum Institute et al.,* Civil No. 8524 (D.D.C., October 1940).

31. B. I. Kaufman, "Oil and Antitrust: The Oil Cartel Case and the Cold War," *Business History Review,* Volume 51, Number 37 (Spring 1977); Sampson, pp. 150–159.

32. Irvin M. Grossack, "OPEC and the Antitrust Laws," *Journal of Economic Issues,* Volume 20, Number 3 (September 1986), pp. 725–741.

33. See Douglas R. Bohi and Michael A. Toman, "Oil Supply Disruptions and the Role of the International Energy Agency," *The Energy Journal,* Volume 7, Number 2 (April 1986), pp. 37–50; David R. Henderson, "The IEA Oil-Sharing Plan: Who Shares with Whom?" *The Energy Journal,* Volume 8, Number 4 (October 1987), pp. 23–31; and George Horwich and David Leo Weimer, eds., *Responding to International Oil Crises* (Washington, D.C.: American Enterprise Institute for Public Policy Research, 1988).

34. Taking 1987 U.S. petroleum use as 16 million barrels per day, annual use is 5.84

billion barrels. A $10/barrel increase in the cost of oil would mean an increased cost of $58.4 billion. The actual increase would be less, as the increased price induced a cutback in the use of petroleum products.

35. A $2/barrel import fee dedicated toward financing the SPR would pay for raising the SPR to a billion barrels in under two years.

36. M. A. Adelman, "Coping with Supply Insecurity," *The Energy Journal,* Volume 3, Number 2 (April 1982), pp. 1–17; and "Keeping OPEC Off Balance," *The New York Times,* May 16, 1988, p. 19.

37. By discussing a complete cartel, we abstract from the difficult—for OPEC—problem of fringe supply. See Figure 2-2 and the accompanying text.

38. Robert D. Hershey, Jr., "U.S., in Shift, Seems to View Fall in Oil Prices as a Risk, Not a Boon," *The New York Times,* April 3, 1986, p. 1.

39. UPI, reported in *The New York Times,* April 7, 1986, p. 1.

40. John Badan, "A Welfare Plan for U.S. Oil," *The Wall Street Journal,* December 18, 1987, p. 22.

SUGGESTED READINGS

Adams, Walter. "Vertical Divestiture of the Petroleum Majors: An Affirmative Case." *Vanderbilt Law Review,* Volume 30, Number 6 (November 1977).

Adelman, M. A. *The World Petroleum Market.* Baltimore: The Johns Hopkins University Press, 1972.

Horwich, George, and David Leo Weimer, eds. *Responding to International Oil Crises.* Washington, D.C.: American Enterprise Institute for Public Policy Research, 1988.

Sampson, Anthony. *The Seven Sisters.* New York: Bantam Books, 1976.

Schneider, Steven A. *The Oil Price Revolution.* Baltimore: The Johns Hopkins University Press, 1983.

Turner, Louis. *Oil Companies in the International System,* 3rd ed. London: George Allen & Unwin, Ltd., 1983.

CHAPTER 3

THE STEEL INDUSTRY

Walter Adams and Hans Mueller

I.

INTRODUCTION

For almost three-quarters of a century, the steel industry was a quintessential prototype of a tight oligopoly whose concentrated structure militated toward oligopolistic behavior and resulted in lackluster economic performance.

Until the 1960s, a handful of vertically integrated giants dominated the industry. Their well-honed system of price leadership and followership was marked by a consummate insensitivity to changing market conditions. Their virtually unchallenged control over a continent-sized market made them lethargic bureaucracies oblivious to technological change and innovation. Their insulation from competition induced the development of a cost-plus mentality, which tolerated a constant escalation of prices and wages and a neglect of production efficiency. Eventually all this made their markets vulnerable to invasion by newcomers—both domestic and foreign. In the 1960s, when these newcomers finally appeared, the industry found itself in disarray and desuetude. It was saddled with a jumble of largely obsolete and poorly located plants; high production costs; and, worst of all, it was without the expertise to deal with competitive challenges. The only solution for this malaise, the industry thought, was to demand government protection from foreign competition. It is a strategy that the industry has pursued for the last 20 years and that is still the central issue in the public policy debate concerning the steel industry.

A brief look at the industry's history throws some light on these dramatic changes.

History

Prior to the formation of the U.S. Steel Corporation in 1901, the industry was the scene of active and, at times, destructive competition. Competition for market shares was vigorous, often taking the form of aggressive price cutting. Companies that failed to adopt the best technology or anticipate market shifts fell by the wayside. Unlike the British steel industry, which was becoming conservative and defensive, innovative American managers and an industrious work force were creating a dynamic industry that was highly cost-competitive in international markets.

In this early period, various gentlemen's agreements and pools were organized in an effort to control the production of steel rails, billets, wire, nails, and other products, but the outstanding characteristic of these agreements was the "frequency with which they collapsed." Their weakness was that, inherent in any pool or gentlemen's agreement: "60 per cent of the agreers are gentlemen, 30 per cent just act like gentlemen, and 10 per cent neither are nor act like gentlemen."[1]

With the birth of U.S. Steel, these loosely knit agreements were superseded by a more stable form of organization. In the "combination of combinations," U.S. Steel merged more than 65 percent of the nation's steel-producing capacity into a single entity. Under the leadership of Judge Gary, its first president, it inaugurated the famous "Gary Dinners," which were a transparent form of collusion among competitors. Cooperation replaced competition, and U.S. Steel held a price umbrella over the industry, which was high enough to accommodate its much smaller, even marginal rivals.

This policy of "friendly competition," of course, was not without cost. It permitted the Corporation's rivals to expand and to gain an increasing share of the market. But the Corporation seemed content with this tradeoff between high and stable prices in exchange for loss of market share. Over time, this policy led to the transformation of an asymmetrical oligopoly, dominated by a giant firm, into an industry with a more balanced oligopolistic structure. Friendly competition had one other fundamental consequence. Eventually, when the oligopoly felt entrenched enough to pursue a policy of constant price escalation—in good times and bad—in periods of declining as well as rising costs—it attracted newcomers.

The challenge to the steel oligopoly, starting in the 1960s, came from two principal sources: foreign competition and the appearance of the minimills. Against the former, the industry's primary defense was to plead for government protection in the form of a variety of trade restraints. Against the latter, the primary response was the gradual abandonment of industry segments in which the minimills had established themselves as the low-cost producers.

By the 1980s, the steel oligopoly seemed moribund—a collection of helpless giants begging for government relief from self-inflicted injury.

II.

MARKET STRUCTURE

Before analyzing the structure of the American steel market, it is important to note some of the characteristics of that market. First, there are about 10,000 distinct iron and steel products, including pig iron; semifinished steel (billets, blooms, and slabs); rolled products (bars, rods, structurals, hot- and cold-rolled sheets, coated sheets, and plates); and steel products with a very high unit value—forgings and castings.

Second, even very narrowly defined products are often further differentiated according to metallurgy, physical properties, and surface conditions. In addition, differences in quality of the more sophisticated products (such as cold-rolled and coated sheets) have become important enough to make steel buyers quite selective concerning the reputation of their suppliers, both domestic and foreign.

Third, the term *market* connotes the interaction of buyers and sellers in a geographical trading area. In a pure oligopoly, theory tells us, a slight difference in price can cause a sale to be switched from one producer to another. But in the vast expanse of the North American continent, steel—a relatively heavy good—is also differentiated by the location where it is offered for sale. A steel user in San Francisco is economically (that is, in terms of freight costs) closer to Japan than to Pittsburgh. No matter how identical in other respects, tonnages of steel in those two cities are not homogeneous. The geographical area of the United States is, therefore, not necessarily synonymous with the "home market" of the American steel industry.

Mindful of these caveats, the structure of the steel market in the United States can be described as an oligopoly that is dominated by large integrated companies but that also includes minimills, imports, and a specialty steel segment (producing primarily alloy, stainless, and tool steels). The growing relative importance of minimills and imports over the last three decades is portrayed in Table 3-1.

The Integrated Sector

The integrated companies produce most of their steel from iron ore smelted in blast furnaces. For technological reasons, most integrated plants have a capacity in excess of three million tons of raw steel a year. The staple products of these mills are plates, hot- and cold-rolled sheets, coated (for example, galvanized) sheets, and heavy structurals (such as large I-beams). Some also produce pipes and tubes, rails, pilings, and a variety of other products.

Historically, this segment of the industry has been shaped by mergers and consolidations; it has also undergone a structural transformation from an asymmetrical to a symmetrical oligopoly. When U.S. Steel—the "combination of combinations"—was organized in 1901, it accounted for 65 percent of all the steel produced in this country. By 1938, its share had dropped to approximately one half of that and, by 1988, its share of raw steel output had dwindled to 15.6 percent (12.7 percent of total steel consumption in this country—see Table 3-2).

The relative ascendancy of U.S. Steel's fellow oligopolists was largely

Table 3-1

Market Shares, Share of Domestic Shipment and Tonnage Shipped of Various Suppliers of the U.S. Steel Market, 1956, 1979, and 1988 (in Percent and Millions of Tons of Steel Products)

	1956			1979			1988		
	Market Share (%)	Share of Domestic Shipments (%)	Tons[a] (mill)	Market Share (%)	Share of Domestic Shipments (%)	Tons[a] (mill)	Market Share (%)	Share of Domestic Shipments (%)	Tons[a] (mill)
Imports	1.7	—	1.3	15.2	—	17.5	20.3	—	20.9
Specialty Mills	4.5	4.5	3.6	4.8	5.6	5.5	4.9	6.1	5.0
Minimills	1.1	1.1	0.9	11.5	13.5	13.2	17.0	21.4	17.5
Integrated Mills	92.7	94.3	74.9	68.5	80.8	78.9	57.8	72.4	59.4
Apparent Consumption			80.8			115.0			103.6

[a]Data for domestic producers do not include export shipments.

Source: Donald F. Barnett and Robert W. Crandall, *Up From The Ashes* (Washington, D.C.: Brookings, 1986), pp. 12, 98, and 102; also our own estimates.

Table 3-2

Concentration of Raw Steel Production Shares

Year	U.S. Steel	Four Largest Firms	Eight Largest Firms
1904	60.8	74.2	83.5
1920	45.8	58.5[a]	65.7[a]
1938	33.1	62.0	79.0
1947	33.7	63.5	79.9[b]
1961	25.7	54.6	75.5[b]
1976	22.1	52.8	73.4
1984	16.6	46.6	65.0
1988	15.6	45.3	63.1

[a]Shares of firms 2 to 8 computed from capacity data.
[b]National's share was estimated.

Sources: Federal Trade Commission, *The United States Steel Industry and Its International Rivals* (Washington, D.C.: 1977), p. 157; Charles Bradford, *Steel Industry* (Merrill Lynch, Jan. 1989), Table 73; and International Iron and Steel Institute, *World Steel in Figures* (1988), p. 2.

attributable to mergers. In the 1920s, these "independents" took part in an aggressive consolidation movement. Bethlehem, Republic, and National consummated a series of major mergers which enabled them to grow rapidly— not only in terms of absolute company size, but also in terms of market share. The gains in market share were made largely at the expense of U.S. Steel.[2]

In the period after World War II, the merger trend was temporarily stalled by government antitrust objections to Bethlehem's acquisition of Youngstown, a merger that would have combined the second and sixth largest steel producers. In the late 1960s, however, when the merger movement resumed momentum, several integrated firms began to buttress their positions through horizontal consolidations. The following combinations took place:

1. 1968—Wheeling Steel (10th largest) and Pittsburgh Steel (16th largest).
2. 1971—National Steel (4th largest) and Granite City Steel (13th largest).
3. 1978—Jones & Laughlin (7th largest) and Youngstown (8th largest).
4. 1983—Jones & Laughlin (3rd largest) and Republic (4th largest).

The two mergers involving Jones & Laughlin (J&L) also had conglomerate aspects. In 1968, both J&L and Youngstown were taken over by conglomerates, the former by Ling-Temco-Vaught (LTV), which had aerospace, meatpacking, and sporting-goods operations, and the latter by Lykes, which was primarily active in ocean shipping. Neither LTV nor Lykes infused badly needed capital into their steel properties. Ten years later, both companies were in a precarious financial condition, and the Attorney General felt compelled to approve the merger of the two conglomerates and their sizable steel subsidiaries by relying on the "failing company" exception under the antimerger law.

The 1983 merger of the enlarged LTV company with Republic Steel was at first rejected because, in the view of the Justice Department, the new company would obtain unacceptably high market shares in two important product lines, sheet-steel products and specialty steel. Two former Republic plants—at Massillon, Ohio and Birmingham, Alabama—therefore had to be sold. This was the first major case in which international competition was an important consideration in the government's enforcement of the antimerger law.

LTV is now the third largest steel producer in the United States. With a capacity of about 13 million tons, it follows U.S. Steel (19 million tons), and Bethlehem (15 million tons). Other integrated majors in order of their relative importance in 1988 are: Inland (7 million tons), Armco (6 million tons), and National (6 million tons).

Aside from the creation of a symmetrical oligopoly, other structural changes in the integrated steel sector are noteworthy. First, the diversification movement that began in the 1960s led to a number of acquisitions outside the steel industry: a chemical firm (by U.S. Steel); a large nonmetallic composite firm (by Armco); a builder of prefabricated homes (by Inland); an aluminum firm (by National); and a producer of plastic products (by Bethlehem). More recent acquisitions included a California savings and loan association (by National); an insurance holding company (by Armco); and—the largest of all—Marathon Oil Company (by U.S. Steel). Its ownership of Marathon Oil means that U.S. Steel now derives more revenues from petroleum than from steel. (The company's name change to USX reflects this new reality.) Several of these acquisitions have been unprofitable, if not disastrous (such as Armco's venture into the reinsurance business) and a few have subsequently been spun off.

Second, increasingly intensive competition from minimills and foreign producers has generated a "restructuring" of several integrated companies. This restructuring, which began in 1977, involved the closure of facilities that should have been shut down during the 1950s, or, at the latest, in the 1960s. Some of the plants that were partially or completely closed were originally built in the last century. Although their technology and scale had been updated to some extent, their structural features—such as location and the flow of materials—reflected the best-practice standards of a bygone era.

Many of these closures occurred in the eastern Ohio—western Pennsylvania area, between Youngstown, Pittsburgh, and Johnstown. Others affected primarily northern New York (Buffalo and Lackawanna) and South Chicago. The suddenness of these closures wrought a great deal of hardship on communities and workers in these regions. Much of this harm could have been avoided had these plants been phased out during the growth stage of the industry, when workers would have had little difficulty finding employment in an expanding steel industry or in other manufacturing industries. One company, National Steel, attempted to shed all of its steel operations. It managed to sell its largest steelworks at Weirton, West Virginia, to the employees of that plant. The company decided that the future earnings potential did not justify large investments to replace worn equipment.

Finally, there are two recent developments that will have a substantial, but as yet unpredictable, impact on the integrated steel sector. One is the acquisition by major Japanese steel producers of equity shares in several integrated firms. Nisshin, Japan's sixth largest steel producer, bought a 10 percent interest in Wheeling-Pittsburgh, one of the smaller integrated firms; Nippon Kokan (NKK), the second largest Japanese steel company, bought a 50 percent share in National Steel; Kawasaki, the fourth largest Japanese producer, acquired a 25 percent share of a new company, California Steel Industries, which was formed to reactivate the rolling facilities of the former Kaiser integrated steelworks near Los Angeles; Kawasaki acquired a 40 percent share in Armco; and Kobe, the fifth largest Japanese producer, acquired a 50% stake in the USX Lorain works in Ohio.

In addition, joint ventures have been organized to build and operate new steel installations. These took the form of partnerships between Bethlehem and Inland, U.S. Steel and Rouge (the Ford Motor Company steel plant), Inland and Nippon Steel (Japan's leading producer), and LTV and Sumitomo (the third largest Japanese steel producer).

Both of these developments—financial and managerial participation by Japanese firms, as well as joint ventures—can be expected to lead to new alliances. However, it remains to be seen whether they will add to or detract from the monolithic structure of the integrated segment and what their lasting effect will be on the industry's competitive behavior.

The Minimill Sector

Since the early 1960s, minimills have made dramatic inroads into the market position of the integrated steel giants; at the same time, they have captured a share of the market once held by imports. There are now 32 such companies operating 51 mills (of which 11 were built or acquired by foreign firms) and they account for 21.4 percent of domestic steel shipments.

Minimills are relatively small, nonintegrated companies that convert scrap into finished steel products.[3] They typically operate modern electric furnaces, continuous casters, and rolling mills to achieve maximum efficiency. Specializing in narrow product lines, they have sprouted up across the country in the past two decades. They are controlled by genuine entrepreneurs, whose fiery independence has kept many of them from joining the American Iron and Steel Institute or any other trade association.

These entrepreneurs show disdain for fleets of company jets and limousines and chic executive dining facilities. Occupying Spartan headquarters, they share the rigors and rewards of the marketplace with their employees by means of productivity incentives and profit-sharing programs. In minimills, says a trade magazine, "personalities and personal management styles dominate and stand in sharp contrast to the bureaucracies that long throttled competition, decision-making, and accountability in the integrated sector. And labor is regarded as a resource, not merely a cost."[4]

Low labor and capital costs have enabled minimills to wrest market shares from their competitors in those product lines — bars, small shapes, and wire rods — where they were not handicapped by their small-scale operations or the limitations of their scrap-based technology. Their expansion during the 1960s and 1970s was all the more remarkable because it took place despite a shrinkage in total steel industry capacity.

By the mid-1980s, however, minimills found that there was little market share left for them to conquer, except from each other. Several among them, notably North Star and Birmingham Steel, continued to grow by acquiring financially weak or bankrupt rivals. Nucor, the most enterprising of the group, decided to break out of its traditional niche by way of technological innovation. With a Japanese partner, it built a new plant to compete head-on with Bethlehem, USX, and Inland by producing large I-beams. Drawing on the innovative skills of a German equipment supplier, Nucor also built a plant to produce hot- and cold-rolled sheets — products that had been the traditional preserve of the steel majors.

Because of persistent problems with metallurgical impurities, Nucor's products cannot yet be used in such applications as outer panels of automobiles and appliances. But ongoing developments in the area of small-scale smelting of iron ore may well overcome this handicap. Before long, perhaps by the mid-1990s, the integrated steel producers are likely to find themselves again embroiled in a tenacious struggle for market share, if not for survival. A massive entry of minimills into the market for flatrolled products would no doubt also affect trade flows in the world steel market.

Imports

Steel imports increased from a trickle of mostly low-quality products in the 1950s to a flood of high-grade steel in the mid-1960s. From 1968 to 1980 imports fluctuated widely around a long-term average of roughly 16.5 percent of the U.S. market. Currently, imports enjoy a market share of roughly twenty-one percent.

Several developments contributed to the growing market share of imports during the early 1980s. One was the rising international value of the dollar, which widened the cost and price gap between domestic and foreign steel. Another was the "oil shock" of 1979 which led to a deep recession in major Latin American industrializing nations, forcing them to increase their exports in order to earn the necessary foreign currency for servicing their enormous foreign debts. Brazil and Argentina managed to turn abruptly from being net steel importers to becoming major steel exporters. A third development was a tenfold increase in the purchase of imported semifinished steel (slabs) by American steel producers and a lack of domestic capacity to produce oil pipe, galvanized sheet, and continuous-cast steel products.[5]

The function of imports in the American steel market is well described in a study by the Department of Commerce: "Imports serve to meet shortfalls in the U.S. capacity for particular regions, products, and time periods. They are largest relative to demand in regions where the are capacity shortfalls. For those regions with capacity overhangs, import penetration is typically well below national averages."[6] A comparison of import statistics by destination bears out those conclusions. In 1968, two-thirds of all imported steel came into ports on the East Coast and the Great Lakes and only one-third into Gulf and Pacific ports. By 1982, shipments of imported steel to Gulf and Pacific ports had increased to 60 percent of total imports, while shipments to other ports had declined correspondingly. With respect to products sold primarily by integrated mills (sheet, plate, heavy structurals, and pipes), the import dependence of Western and Southwestern regions has grown even more, largely because the integrated domestic producers do not have much (efficient) capacity in those regions.

Imports also meet shortfalls in particular products. A 1980 survey by the International Trade Commission showed that customers had switched from domestic to foreign suppliers in nearly half of all the instances because domestic supply was not available.[7] More than 13 percent did so because they could not find domestic products of the required quality, and 7 percent preferred multiple sourcing. Only 28 percent switched to imports because of price considerations. In the same year, a General Accounting Office survey of domestic-steel users found that, for products other than those supplied by minimills, salient motives for buying imported steel were better quality, assured availability, and marketing help.[8] Although the big steel producers claim to have caught up with their foreign rivals (or even surpassed them) on this score, a 1988 investigation by the International Trade Commission reveals that many deficiencies in product quality and customer service still persist.[9]

Table 3-3 shows the changing structure of imports. As a result of trade litigation and pressure by the U.S. government, the share of steel imports from the European Community and Japan declined between 1964 and 1984, but Canada, Spain, Turkey, a multitude of nations from the Third World, and even Eastern Europe began to ship significant amounts of steel into the U.S. market. In addition, the product mix of imports has changed over the long run, in the direction of higher-value products (such as cold-rolled and coated sheets, as well as tubular products), because foreign mills have an incentive to increase the value-added content of their exports.

Table 3-3
United States Steel Consumption and Imports, 1960–1988

Year	Consumption (Million Net Product Tons)	Domestic Shipments	Imports (Million Net Product Tons)	Share of Total U.S. Imports (Percent)				Import Share of U.S. Market (Percent)
				Japan	EC	Canada	Rest	
1960	71.5	71.1	3.4	17.9	62.4	6.3	7.4	4.7
1965	100.6	92.7	10.3	42.5	47.3	6.2	4.0	10.3
1968	107.6	91.9	18.0	40.6	46.8	6.9	5.7	16.7
1971	102.5	87.0	18.3	37.7	46.5	7.0	8.8	17.9
1975	89.0	80.0	34.3	12.0	48.6	8.4	8.7	13.5
1978	116.6	97.9	21.1	30.7	35.3	11.2	22.8	18.1
1981	105.4	88.5	19.9	31.3	32.6	14.6	21.6	18.9
1983	83.5	67.6	17.1	24.8	24.1	13.9	37.1	20.5
1984	98.2	73.7	26.2	25.3	24.2	12.1	38.4	26.6
1988	102.8	84.0	20.9	20.5	29.8[a]	15.2	34.5[b]	20.3

[a]These figures reflect the entrance of Spain and Portugal into the European Community in 1986.
[b]Preliminary.

Source: AISI Annual Statistical Report, various years.

Some International Comparisons

1. Firm Size and Concentration. An international comparison of firm size and concentration lends some perspective to our discussion of market structure. In 1988, the four largest steel firms in Japan turned out 62 million tons of steel products, compared to 38 million tons by the four largest producers in the United States and 53 million tons by the four largest producers in the European Community. The eight largest firms produced 78 million tons in Japan, 55 million tons in the United States, and 77 million tons in the European Community.

There is also a marked contrast in the concentration ratios of the three steel-producing industries. Thus, the four-firm concentration ratio in Japan (58.4 percent) is larger than that in the United States (42.8 percent) and the European Community (42.2 percent). Indeed, the four-firm ratio in Japan exceeds the eight-firm ratio in the European Community. The eight-firm ratios for Japan and the United States are much closer.

2. Plant Size and Economies of Scale. Taken by itself, an international comparison of firm size and concentration yields little information about industrial efficiency, because in an industry like steel the primary unit of efficiency is the individual plant rather than the firm, and the largest firms do not necessarily operate the largest plants.

Of the 24 integrated plants operating in this country in 1988, 14 (or 58 percent) had an annual raw-steel capacity of less than 3 million tons — the capacity generally considered to be the minimum efficient scale for a plant with a narrow product range. The comparison with Japan and the European Community, portrayed in Table 3-4, is not flattering to the United States.

Large plants do not necessarily make good use of best-practice economies of scale. The efficiency of a steel-making operation is also influenced by the location of the plant; the size, layout, and flexibility of the various interrelated processes; and the degree of product specialization. In these respects, however, the efficient new plants built in Japan, the EEC, and the newly industrializing countries enjoy a distinct advantage over many integrated steel plants operated in the United States.

Summary

Since World War II, the U.S. steel industry has experienced a profound structural transformation. The power of U.S. steel, which once dominated the industry, has greatly diminished, and the market share of the large integrated producers has been significantly eroded by the entry of minimills and the dramatic increase in steel imports.

Table 3-4
Changes in the Plant Size of Integrated Steel Producers

Plant Size	1952 U.S.	1952 E.C.	1952 Japan	1960 U.S.	1960 E.C.	1960 Japan	1988 U.S.	1988 E.C.	1988 Japan
above 6 mNT	—	—	—	3	—	—	2	4	10
4 to 6 mNT	4	—	—	6	—	—	3	7	2
2 to 4 mNT	7	—	—	18	4	3	15	15	6
1 to 2 mNT	20	7	2	23	16	6	4	8	1

Source: William Haller, "Technological Change in Primary Steelmaking in the United States, 1947–64," Hearings, Subcommittee on Antitrust and Monopoly, Committee on the Judiciary, September–October 1967, pp. 3186–3197; Louis Lister, Europe's Coal and Steel Community (Twentieth Century Fund, 1960). Appendix E; Eurostat, Iron and Steel, 1970 Yearbook Table 11-8; Institute for Iron and Steel Studies, Commentary (Jan. 1983); Metal Bulletin, Iron and Steel Works of the World, 9th ed. (1988), and company annual reports.

III.

MARKET CONDUCT

Business conduct or behavior is closely related to industry structure. A tight, oligopolistic structure is generally expected to lead to nonaggressive pricing behavior. An absence of competitive pressures may also lead to a lack of progressiveness which, over the longer term, will cause severe inefficiencies in the industry's structure and performance.

The "Administered Price" Era

From the turn of the century until the early 1960s, the U.S. Steel Corporation was the acknowledged price leader of the steel industry and, for the most part, the other oligopolists followed in lockstep. Prices were generally uniform; rigid; and, over the years, steadily escalating.[10] The pricing discipline observed by the large American steel producers, even during severe recessions, became the envy of foreign steel producers, who often experienced great price instability during periods of weak demand. Although this "administered pricing" helped to create an environment of stability and predictability, it had harmful effects over the longer term. It exposed the industry to external challenges that eventually resulted in a significant erosion of its oligopoly power.

During the administered price era, steel prices were characterized by remarkable rigidity and uniformity.[11] Price stability was obtained at the expense of instability in output and employment. Unless impelled by sharp increases in direct costs or dangerous sniping by rivals, U.S. Steel generally preferred to resist both price increases and decreases and to sacrifice stability "only when the decision [was] unavoidable."

After World War II, this price policy was transformed into one of "upward rigidity," that is, a pattern of stairstep price increases at regular intervals. At times this upward flexibility was achieved in the face of declining demand. This rigidity in steel prices was reinforced by price uniformity. With or without resort to the conspiratorial basing point system, the integrated giants matched each other's prices with monotonous consistency. They maintained a lockstep price uniformity by punishing any major mill that showed deviationist tendencies.[12]

The "Competitive" Era

Beginning in the mid-1960s, this policy of price uniformity and upward rigidity came under pressure, primarily due to competition from minimills and imports. In wire rods, for example, Paula Stern (then a member of the International Trade Commission) found it "obvious why the integrated producers lost so much of the market to the minimills. . . . The efficiency of their technology, management, and cost control techniques enable minimills to keep their prices low." According to Stern, price data showed "that the average delivered price paid for rod from nonintegrated firms was well below that price paid for rod from integrated firms in most regions and in most of the period of investigation. But even more significant is the fact that these efficient U.S. mills were able to sell wire rod at a price that, on average, was below the average price of imported wire rod."[13]

Like the minimills, imports have had a moderating influence on the administered pricing policy of the domestic oligopoly. Between 1959 and 1969, the Council on Wage and Price Stability found that "there were limiting forces which operated to prevent U.S. steel companies from increasing prices and maintaining the previous higher profit levels. *Chief* among these was import competition."[14] The Federal Trade Commission came to the same conclusion.[15]

The "Protectionist" Era

Predictably, the domestic oligopoly did not view these competitive challenges with complacency. While it could do little to curb the competition of minimills, it launched an orchestrated political campaign to neutralize the threat of foreign competition. The result was a succession of "voluntary" import quotas imposed on foreign producers.

1. The Voluntary Restraint Agreement (VRA), 1969–1974. Under this agreement, steel imports from Japan and from the European community were each limited to 5.8 million tons annually, compared with their then current levels of 7.5 million and 7.3 million tons, respectively. The agreement also provided for an annual growth factor of 5 percent in the allowable quotas.

The price effects of the VRA were dramatic. According to one study, between January 1960 and December 1968, a period of nine years, the composite steel price index rose 4.1 points—or 0.45 points per year—indicating the moderating effects that surging imports had on domestic prices. In the four years between January 1969 and December 1972, while the VRA was in effect, the steel price index rose 26.7 points—or 6.67 points per year—which was twice as much as the index for all industrial products (including steel). Put differently, since the import quotas went into effect, steel prices increased at an annual rate 14 times greater than in the preceding nine years.[16]

Another study showed that the products that had been subjected to particularly hard import pressure prior to the VRA evidenced greater price increases than other steel products after the VRA became effective, again highlighting the anticompetitive effects of the quotas.[17]

Yet another study estimated that the VRA caused steel prices to increase by $26 to $39 per ton, meaning that the price of steel would have been 13 to 15 percent lower in the absence of the VRA.[18]

2. The Trigger Price System, 1978–1982. The lapse of the VRA in 1974, plus falling demand, caused prices to be very competitive again for a few years. But after a plethora of complaints by the domestic oligopoly before the International Trade Commission, the Carter Administration granted the industry a novel form of protection in the form of the Trigger Price Mechanism (TPM). For all practical purposes, the TPM set minimum prices for all carbon steel products imported into the United States. The "trigger prices" (so called because undercutting by foreign suppliers was to trigger antidumping proceedings by U.S. authorities) were based on estimated Japanese production costs plus freight costs from Japan. In exchange for administrative protection, the steel industry agreed to refrain from filing antidumping, subsidy, or import-injury complaints before the International Trade Commission.

By forcing up import prices, the TPM gave domestic producers an opportunity to raise their prices as well. A sizeable gap developed between U.S. and world market steel prices, and by 1981 American manufacturers were paying $100 to $150 more per ton of steel than their foreign competitors.[19] Especially hard-hit were firms producing items for which the cost of steel amounted to a significant portion of total production costs, such as wire rope, fasteners, transmission towers, bridge components, oil rigs, and automotive parts. Many of them responded by purchasing these items abroad or by switching production to foreign subsidiaries. American "indirect" steel trade, that is, trade in steel-containing goods, turned sharply negative during the TPM period.[20]

The TPM not only maintained American steel prices significantly above world market levels. It also distorted patterns of steel pricing and consumption in the United States. Traditionally, domestic steel prices had been low in the Great Lakes region, where the most efficient American integrated plants are located, and high on the West Coast, which lacks adequate domestic capacity. Trigger prices, however, because they were calculated on the basis of Japanese production and freight costs, were lowest in the Western states and highest in the Great Lakes region. The distribution pattern of steel imports changed accordingly, as foreign producers—even remote British, German, and Brazilian suppliers—shipped more to the West Coast and less to the northeastern states.

It is noteworthy that the impact of the TPM system was intimately linked to exchange-rate fluctuations and that this eventually caused the system's demise when the value of the dollar reached inordinately high levels. In fact, the entire episode serves as an excellent illustration of the effect that currency relations have on the international competitiveness of national industries.

3. The "Reagan" Quotas, 1984–1989. The lapse of TPM came at the worst possible time for the domestic industry. Demand for steel was falling precipitously, while several newly industrializing countries, attracted by a strong dollar, were sending record volumes of low-priced steel into the U.S. market.

To remedy this situation, the Reagan Administration, in September 1984, began to negotiate a set of voluntary restraint agreements. By March 1985, American negotiators had concluded quota agreements with nearly every major steel-exporting nation in the world, including Brazil, Mexico, Yugoslavia, Poland, and Rumania. As a result of these agreements, the total market share of imports declined from 26.6 percent in 1984 to about 21 percent in 1988 (see Table 3-3).

However, unlike the experience during previous periods of import controls, steel prices continued to weaken. The main reason was a widening rift among the large integrated producers—due in part to the turmoil that accompanied restructuring, in part to the favorable labor contracts negotiated by some of the companies, in part to divergent positions on trade policy and in part to a plan (later aborted) by U.S. Steel to import semi-finished steel from the British Steel Corporation. Whatever the cause, open dissent repeatedly erupted between the large producers and pricing discipline seemed to collapse completely.[21] The increasingly large discounts from list prices posted by the big companies well into 1986 resulted in huge financial losses. Only the shutdown of U.S. Steel by a labor dispute from August 1986 to January 1987 put an end to this infighting.

Since then, the steel market has recovered, so much so that supply shortages developed in the fall of 1987 and persisted throughout most of 1988. Domestic producers, taking advantage of the tight market, raised prices by 5 percent in 1987 and by a further 8 percent in 1988. The Reagan quotas caused particularly severe distortions in the market for semi-finished steel, comprising mainly slabs and billets. Restructuring had raised the demand for these products by rerollers and small steel producers while, simultaneously, it had led to a significant reduction in the number of domestic suppliers.

Ironically, U.S. Steel, whose earlier plan to import semis from Great Britain was the principal reason for including slabs and billets in the VRA, now emerged as a dominant force in this market. Its quota-given market power enabled the company to charge exorbitant prices for these products.[22] While this behavior may be shrugged off as nothing more than an effort to maximize profits during the "breathing space" provided by the quotas, there may have been a more sinister motive. The company may have deliberately attempted to put its slab customers, who are also its competitors in the sheet, plate, and pipe markets, at an economic disadvantage.

Summary

Assigning quantitative limits to troublesome foreign competitors facilitates pricing coordination among the domestic suppliers, if only by making it easier for them to read each other's signals. Except in those product markets where they compete against efficient American minimills, the integrated producers are likely to achieve the main objective of their intensive trade litigation and political lobbying: to stabilize and, ultimately, raise steel prices. This explains why, in spite of the generally propitious conditions of the domestic steel market, the major producers insisted that import quotas be renewed for another five years upon their expiration in the fall of 1989. An extension of the Reagan quotas was vigorously opposed by a group of steel users, led by Caterpillar, who had been severely injured by the import restraints and the distortions they caused. Nevertheless, on November 4, 1988, just four days before the Presidential election, then candidate Bush announced his intention to have the quotas renewed.

IV.
MARKET PERFORMANCE

An industry's performance is nothing more than the product of its structure and conduct. It is a measure of how well—how efficiently—it functions to serve consumer needs and contributes to the welfare of the national economy. Obviously, a precise quantitative assessment of performance is difficult, but international comparisons can yield valuable insights and guidelines for public policy.

A principal index of performance is technological progressiveness. This index measures an industry's ability to keep up with the latest advances in "best-practice" operations or to be in the forefront of such advances. Judged by this criterion, the U.S. steel industry, except for its minimill and specialty-steel segments, has lagged rather than led in the post-World War II period. Consequently, it has suffered serious erosion of its cost competitiveness, not only in world markets but even in its domestic market.

Historically, according to the American Iron and Steel Institute, "The steel industry in this country has adopted most new technologies, wherever they were developed, at least as rapidly and probably more rapidly than steel industries in other parts of the world." The industry's spokesmen were quick to label anyone who dissented from this view as "simply misinformed."

That the large steel companies have been slow to adopt state-of-the-art technology is no longer a matter of dispute. It is recognized not only by the industry's academic critics but also by financial analysts and even by some steel company executives.

R&D Expenditures

In a study released in 1980, the Congressional Office for Technology Assessment (OTA) reported that "The number of R&D scientists and engineers per 1,000 employees is smaller for steel than for any other industry except for textiles and apparel, about 15 percent of the average for all reported industries." The OTA also noted that "foreign steel producers spend more on R&D than those in the United States."[23] The U.S. steel industry's steel-related R&D expenditures have been about 0.4 percent of sales in recent years, compared to over 2.0 percent in Japan. Furthermore, the ratio of research personnel to total steel industry employment is less than 1.0 percent in the United States and nearly 4.0 percent in Japan.[24]

Process Innovation

Among the large number of process improvements that have been made in basic steelmaking during the last 30 years, two undoubtedly deserve to be characterized as technological breakthroughs: the *basic oxygen furnace* (BOF), a fast technique for converting iron to steel, and the *continuous caster,* a process that bypasses both the laborious ingot-pouring process and the energy-intensive reheating of ingots and primary rolling. Other major developments during this period were methods to produce steel products of higher quality by removing impurities from liquid steel and by improving the dimensional accuracy, flatness, and surface quality at the rolling end of the steelmaking process.

1. The Basic Oxygen Furnace (BOF). The oxygen furnace was first put into commercial use in a small Austrian steel plant in 1950. It was first installed in the United States in 1954 by a small company (McLouth) but was not adopted by the steel giants until more than a decade later: U.S. Steel in December 1963; Bethlehem in 1964; and Republic in 1965. As of September 1963, several of the largest steel companies, together operating more than 50 percent of basic steel capacity, had not installed a single BOF furnace, whereas smaller companies, operating only 7 percent of the nation's steel capacity, accounted for almost half of the BOF installations in the United States.

By the late 1980s, the industry had replaced all but 5 million tons of its open hearth furnaces with BOFs. However, many of these meltshops still lag behind those of major foreign competitors with respect to such modern features as combined blowing and full process control. Steel producers in Japan, the EC, and Canada are also ahead in the installation of ancillary equipment (e.g., vacuum degassing and other "ladle metallurgy" practices) that further help remove impurities and thus improve the quality of steel products.

The most likely explanation of the hesitant adoption of the Austrian converter by the large American firms is that their managements were still imbued with Andrew Carnegie's motto: "Invention don't pay." Let others first assume the cost and risk of research and development and of breaking in a new process; then we'll decide. The result was that during the 1950s, the American steel industry installed 40 million tons of melting capacity which, as *Fortune* observed, "was obsolete when it was built."[25]

2. Continuous Casting. The belated adoption of continuous casting by the American steel giants is a further illustration of their technological lethargy. Again, it was a small company (Roanoke Electric), with an annual capacity of 100,000 tons, that pioneered in introducing this European invention in the United States in 1962. Other small steel companies followed, so that by 1968, firms with roughly 3 percent of the nation's steel capacity accounted for 90 percent of continuous-casting production in the United States.

By 1978, the U.S. steel industry (taken as a whole) was continuously casting 15.2 percent of its steel, less than one-third the 46.2 percent achieved in Japan. But these totals conceal a curious fact: American minimills, with a rate of 51.2 percent, were already ahead of the Japanese average, whereas the integrated U.S. mills were producing only 11 percent of their output by the continuous-casting method.[26] The latter managed to boost their average to 46 percent by the end of 1988, but by that time Japanese producers and U.S. minimills were achieving rates of over 90 percent.

Over the years, continuous casting technology has been steadily im-

Table 3-6

Continuous-Casting Adoption Rates, 1969–1988 (in Percent of Steel Production)

Year	U.S.	E.C.	Japan	Brazil	South Korea
1969	2.9	3.3	4.0	0.1	na
1971	4.8	4.8	11.2	0.8	na
1973	6.8	9.4	20.7	3.2	na
1975	9.1	16.5	31.1	5.7	19.7
1977	11.8	25.4	40.8	17.4	32.0
1979	16.9	30.9	52.0	27.6	30.4
1981	20.3	45.1	70.7	36.6	44.3
1983	31.2	60.4	86.3	44.4	56.6
1984	39.6	65.4	89.1	41.3	60.6
1988	59.9	83.0	93.2	46.1(e)	88.5(e)

Sources: International Iron and Steel Institute, *Steel, Statistical Yearbook*, 1978 and 1982; IISI, *World Steel in Figures*, 1988; and Charles Bradford, *Steel Industry* (Merrill Lynch, January 1989), Tables 1, 36, and 49.

proved with respect to casting speed and product quality. Indeed, the majority of steel users now specify steel made by this process. Most notable, perhaps, is the breakthrough by Nucor (an American minimill) which enables it to produce much thinner slabs (under 2 inches) than was previously possible (the minimum had been over 8 inches). This innovation greatly reduces the barriers that so far have blocked minimill entry into the enormous market for hot and cold rolled sheets. If it succeeds, it will present a formidable challenge both to the integrated mills and to foreign competitors.

3. Other Processes. On other aspects of steel technology and innovation the integrated segment of the U.S. steel industry has likewise fallen behind the standards achieved elsewhere in the world, especially in Japan. In 1988, the International Trade Commission released a detailed comparative analysis of steel industry performance in several countries. The report confirms that "[t]echnological leadership in the integrated sheet and strip industry, in terms of both development and application, has passed to offshore competitors. . . . Major new developments in ore reduction, steel making, and casting have come from Europe (especially West Germany) and Japan, and most rolling technology originates in Japan. . . . The greatest challenge facing U.S. modernization efforts in this regard is that foreign competitors have comparatively more modern equipment than the U.S. industry. . . . Japan sets the world standards on installed technology, although West Germany, France, Korea, and Canada do have certain facilities or operating units that utilize the most advanced equipment."[27]

The Problem of Organic Technological Progress

Technological progressiveness is an organic rather than a piecemeal process. It is not enough simply to add a modern continuous caster to an antiquated open-hearth furnace or to install a new BOF in a plant that is poorly located with respect to raw material sources or markets. Efficiency, in the best-practice sense, requires a coordinated approach to modernization.

Some of the defects afflicting many of the integrated American steel companies can be traced to the manner in which they were created: independent firms were combined into a few large empires by multiple, often helter-skelter mergers. Eventually, when they embarked upon a major expansion program, enormous amounts were spent by U.S. firms on the piecemeal expansion of many poorly located and poorly laid out plants. Because of differences in efficient size, work speed, and quality standards, the grafting of new equipment onto an old process rarely made for a good fit.

In 1983, a steel consultant at Arthur D. Little commented: "you've got a mishmash — 100-year-old stuff fitted into two-year-old stuff," and a company executive told *Iron Age:* "All the multi-plant mills have scattered good facilities in with bad. We've screwed things up so they'll never get untangled."[28]

Additional restructuring since then has resulted in the closure of several of the worst-integrated facilities and the streamlining of others. But technologically unbalanced plants remain a problem. As the International Trade Commission points out: "Some excellent hot-end facilities are teamed with mediocre or poor rolling and finishing facilities. However, in other cases, the situation is reversed. To some extent, this has been caused by the need to retrofit existing facilities, as opposed to building complete new plants. . . . As new foreign mills are built, they incorporate state-of-the-art technologies that give those mills great advantages in terms of cost and productivity. New process technologies generally have different requirements in terms of space, flow lines, and organization than those of older technologies. Placing newer technology in an existing plant can result in non-optimal performance."[29]

The industry's lagging performance in the area of efficient plant structure and technology cannot be attributed to insufficient spending on plants and equipment. In the 1960s and 1970s, the industry had invested more than $40 billion (measured in 1978 dollars) on steel-related operations. What is remarkable about this effort is that, per ton of steel capacity installed or replaced, the industry had outspent its European and Japanese rivals.[30] Moreover, in view of the fact that during the same period about 15 percent of total investment expenditures were channeled into non-steel operations, the lag can be blamed with even less justification on inadequate financial resources.

A more plausible explanation is that the costly investment effort made by the U.S. steel industry foundered on the lack of comprehensive organic company planning with respect to plant structure and organization. Rather than concentrating its funds on plants that held promise of being transformed into world-class operations, the industry had spread available funds over too many plants, many of them of marginal efficiency.

Other Factors Affecting International Competition

Spokesmen for the domestic steel industry are wont to blame plant closures and the layoff of employees on unfair competition by foreign suppliers. They maintain that, in their home markets at least, the integrated steel companies could compete successfully "on a level playing field," i.e., if all market participants observed the rules of "fair" competition.

Such complaints fail to take note of the following facts. First, since the early 1970s, the integrated mills lost more market share to aggressive domestic minimills (about 15 percent) than to imports (8 percent until 1984). Second, more than 90 percent of the drastic workforce reduction occurring during the 1980s can be attributed to restructuring, modernization, and the elimination of many outdated work rules. These changes enabled the integrated producers to turn out more finished steel in 1988 than in 1980 with less than half the number of employees.[31]

There has been no significant finding of unfair competition regarding the largest steel exporters to the United States—Japan, Canada, West Germany, and South Korea—which traditionally accounted for nearly 60 percent of all imports. These exporters used to possess sufficient steel-making capacity to make up for any reduction in shipments by foreign suppliers who might have been forced to withdraw from the U.S. market following the imposition of stiff antidumping and antisubsidity penalties.

With respect to subsidization, it is indisputable that all national steel industries are subject to a variety of government policies that affect their ability to compete in international markets. On one hand, some have benefited from direct government contributions to operating funds, loans at reduced interest rates, loan guarantees, area-redevelopment programs, manpower training programs, investment tax incentives, buy-domestic rules, and import quotas. On the other, they have been injured by price controls, the overvaluation of their country's currency, interference with decisions on investments and on plant location, denials of permission to close obsolete plants or to lay off redundant employees, as well as by the uncertain enforcement of environmental regulations. Economic theory suggests that it is only the *net* effect of both the favorable and the burdensome interventions that can modify an industry's comparative advantage and hence distort its competitive position vis-à-vis other national steel industries.[32] Yet, under U.S. trade law, the definition of subsidies is confined to the *benefits* and excludes the injuries resulting from government interventions. Furthermore, the International Trade Commission has found subsidization to violate American law even where the subsidy margin was clearly negligible and where it clearly did not distort the competitive advantage of foreign over domestic producers. Such decisions go far beyond protection of domestic producers against trade-distorting policies by foreign governments. They constitute protection of domestic producers from foreign competition.

Summary

In spite of its sizeable investments since World War II, the integrated U.S. steel industry never achieved a degree of modernization comparable to its foreign rivals. Most of the investment effort consisted of an endless "rounding out" of existing plants. Moreover, the legacy of a concentrated market structure, nonaggressive inter-firm rivalry, and technological lethargy continued to be an impediment to modernization and international competitiveness.

In the 1980s, however, the industry has started on the road to at least a partial comeback. The large producers have embraced a strategy of rationalization. They have shut down anachronistic facilities and, in cooperation with the United Steel Workers, they have brought labor costs under control and modified unrealistic, cost-inflating work rules. At the same time, the precipi-

Table 3-7

Cost to Produce Class 1 Cold-Rolled Sheet in U.S. and Abroad as of November 1988 (dollars per metric ton shipped)

	Typical U.S. Major Mill	West German Mill @ 1.75DM/$	Japanese Mill @ 125Y/$	Canadian Mill @ 1.23C/$	S. Korean Mill @ 694Won/$	Brazilian Mill @ 517Cru/$
Iron Ore	42	32	29	39	29	18
Met Coal	56	66	63	59	63	75
Hot Metal	134	143	135	142	126	97
Liquid Steel	192	190	195	190	177	138
Slab	240	230	230	230	202	161
H.R. Coil	320	300	305	310	250	210
C.R. Coil	405	375	397	388	293	256
S.G.&A.[a]	46	40	50	42	30	36
Financial	33	58	105	40	95	130
Total Pretax	$484	$473	$552[b]	$470	$418	$422

[a]Sales & General Expenses and Administrative Costs.
[b]The Japanese mills are planning major reductions in debt and in the number of workers.

Source: Peter Marcus of Paine Webber. Prepared in conjunction with Donald F. Barnett.

tous decline in the value of the dollar—from 239 yen in 1985 to 125 yen in 1988—has given the industry a welcome respite from the intensity of foreign competition. The combined impact of these developments, according to some observers, has been to make the industry cost-competitive vis-à-vis its major international competitors (See Table 3-7).

V.
PUBLIC POLICY

Given the lackluster performance of the integrated steel producers, what direction should public policy take? Specifically, should antitrust enforcement be relaxed in order to facilitate mergers and encourage a "rationalization" movement among the integrated giants? Should the government—in the national interest—maintain its import-restraint policy in order to assure the survival of an integrated steel sector in the American economy? We now turn to a brief examination of these issues.

Antitrust Policy

In examining the application of the antitrust laws to the steel industry from 1890 to the present, it is fair to say that the law has had a minor impact on the structure and the conduct of the industry. The Sherman Act did not block the formation of U.S. Steel and its achievement of market dominance in 1901; it did not result in the dissolution of U.S. Steel in 1920; it did not block the emergence of a tight oligopoly through a series of mergers among the erstwhile "independents"; it did not interdict the recent mega-mergers between LTV and Youngstown or LTV/Youngstown and Republic; and it did not prevent oligopolistic coordination among the leading firms of the industry, either under the conspiratorial basing-point system or other mechanisms designed to ensure collective action among ostensible competitors.

The outstanding antitrust success in the steel industry was prevention of the proposed merger between Bethlehem (then the industry's second largest firm) with Youngstown Sheet and Tube (then the industry's sixth largest firm) in the mid-1950s. The net result of this action was that Bethlehem decided to build a modern greenfield plant at Burns Harbor, Indiana, in order to compete more effectively in the Chicago market. In other words, the law forced Bethlehem to expand by "building" rather than by "buying"; to expand without substantially lessening competition in an already overly concentrated industry. Incidentally, the law "forced" the corporation to build a plant that even today still ranks as the most modern and efficient steel-producing unit in the Bethlehem empire. One can only speculate whether a tougher antitrust stance, especially toward acquisitions and mergers, would not have helped the industry avoid some of its current difficulties in trying to remain internationally competitive, and thus obviated its dependence on government protection.

Import Policy

The major stimulus to competition in steel has come not from antitrust but from import competition and, to some extent, from the appearance of the minimills. As Douglas Yadon, publisher of the *Preston Pipe Report* put it: "If we don't have imports, we have given the domestic mills a license to steal and to return to poor quality. There must be competition."[33] Not surprisingly, the major public policy battles, at least since 1960, have revolved around the industry's efforts to obtain protection from import competition. These efforts consisted of political lobbying and intensive trade litigation. As a rule, the industry argued that it needed import restraints because unfairly traded (dumped and subsidized) imports had deprived it of an opportunity to modernize as rapidly as its foreign rivals. Such restraints were to provide the breathing space for the industry to raise its efficiency and regain its former cost competitiveness. The idea was simple: limit imports in order to permit the industry to raise prices, so that it can earn higher profits, and so that it has more investment funds to put into new, modern facilities, which will enable it to stand on its own feet and compete effectively with best-practice firms around the world.

Critics of the industry argued that the high costs and technological backwardness of the large domestic steel firms were not attributable to a lack of funds, but to poor investment decisions and the diversion of funds into non-steel activities; that much of the imported steel was neither dumped nor subsidized; that the steel companies actually reduced investment during periods of import protection; and that protection of steel would place a heavy burden on American steel-using industries.

The basic policy dilemma is that import restraints, which are essentially a price-support program for the domestic industry, seldom achieve the objectives that were originally proclaimed to justify them. As J. Paul McGrath, the Chief of the Antitrust Division in 1984, told a Congressional Committee:

> Despite the existence of import restraints during most of the 1970s, integrated steel producers did very little to reduce their costs, to improve their product mix and to modernize and consolidate their facilities. It has only been with the competitive pressures of the marketplace during the last two or three years that integrated steel producers began to consider truly significant changes in their operations.[34]

He advised Congress that to "remove those pressures now would be to ensure a return of the policies of the past that are largely responsible for many of the problems that currently face the industry."

Steel trade restrictions have been particularly harmful to "downstream" manufacturing, i.e., industries for which steel is a major input. (For the wire-drawing industry, the cost of steel amounts to 60 to 70 percent of total production costs; for heavy-equipment makers, it is about 25 percent.) As mentioned earlier, higher steel prices and other market distortions caused by protectionist interventions have forced some of these firms to abandon product lines to foreign suppliers, or to relocate their businesses to countries where steel is available at lower cost. Indeed, the decline in steel imports resulting from trade restrictions has been more than offset by rising imports of steel-containing goods.[35] Somewhat paradoxically, protection of the steel market has boomeranged against its intended beneficiaries—the steel industry and its workers. At the same time, however, it has exacted a staggering cost (estimated at between $1 billion and $7 billion annually) from American steel-using industries and ordinary consumers.[36]

Conclusion

Our analysis of the U.S. steel industry has, we believe, illustrated the beneficial effects of competition on industrial performance. It has also documented the high cost of the erstwhile oligopoly structure and of oligopolistic behavior, not only to the national economy but to the industry itself. It would be prudent, therefore, to make competition the lodestar of public policy regrading the steel industry. Once competition is abandoned or seriously crippled—and this is the necessary consequence of import restrictions and large-scale mergers within the industry—a surrogate for the competitive process will have to be devised. Some new regulatory device will have to be invented to assure efficient performance and to induce technological progressiveness. Such a *deus ex machina* is not yet on the drawing boards.

NOTES

1. H. R. Seager and C. A. Gulick, *Trusts and Corporation Problems* (New York: Harper, 1929), p. 216. This book is an excellent source on the early history of U.S. Steel. See also Ida M. Tarbell, *The Life of Elbert H. Gary* (New York: Appleton, 1930), p. 205.

2. For a history of the early merger movement in the steel industry, see U.S. Congress, House, *Hearings Before the Committee on Small Business, Steel Acquisitions, Mergers, and Expansion of 12 Major Companies, 1900–1950*, 81st Cong., 2d sess., 1950.

3. Donald F. Barnett and Louis Schorsch, *Steel—Upheaval in a Basic Industry* (Cambridge, Mass.: Ballinger, 1983), and Donald F. Barnett and Robert W. Crandall, *Up From the Ashes: The Rise of the Steel Minimill in the United States* (Washington, D.C.: Brookings, 1986).

4. *33 Metal Producing*, February 1987, p. 27.

5. *The New York Times*, June 30, 1986, p. D1; *Iron Age*, October 1988, pp. 17–24.

6. U.S. Department of Commerce, *The Structure of Steel Markets in the United States* (unpublished study, 1979), p. 2.

7. ITC, *Certain Carbon Steel Products from Belgium, the Federal Republic of Germany,*

France, Italy, Luxembourg, the Netherlands, and the United Kingdom, Publication 1064 (May 1980), pp. A-81, A-96, A-111, A-124, and A-138.

8.   General Accounting Office, *Report by the Comptroller General, New Strategy Required for Aiding Distressed Steel Industry* (January 8, 1981), Chap. 3, pp. 4–11 (hereunder, GAO Steel Report).

9.   ITC, *U.S. Global Competitiveness: Steel Sheet and Strip Industry,* Report to the Committee on Finance, U.S. Senate, January 1988, Table 12-15, p. 12–29.

10.   U.S. Congress, Senate, Subcommittee on Antitrust and Monopoly, *Administered Prices in Steel,* S. Rept. No. 1387, 85th Cong., 2d sess., 1958, pp. 17–26 (Kefauver Committee Report).

11.   A. D. H. Kaplan, J. B. Dirlam, and R. F. Lanzilloti, *Pricing in Big Business* (Washington, D.C.: Brookings, 1958), p. 175.

12.   Council on Wage and Price Stability, Staff Report, *A Study of Steel Prices* (Washington, D.C.: U.S. Government Printing Office, July 1975) p. 1.

13.   ITC, *Carbon and Certain Steel Products,* Publication 1553 (July 1984), vol. 1, p. 110.

14.   Council on Wage and Price Stability, op. cit., pp. 9–10 (emphasis supplied).

15.   Federal Trade Commission, *The United States Steel Industry and Its International Rivals* (Washington, D.C., 1977), pp. 168, 240, 524 (hereunder, FTC Steel Study).

16.   Cited in Comptroller General of the United States, *Economic and Foreign Policy Effects of Voluntary Restraint Agreements on Textiles and Steel,* Report B-179342 (Washington, D.C., 1974), p. 23.

17.   See testimony by Walter Adams in ITC, Stainless Steel and Alloy Tool Steel, Investigation No. TA-203-3 (Washington, D.C., September 1977), p. 11 (mimeo).

18.   Ibid., pp. 11–12.

19.   Peter Marcus and Karlis Kirsis, *Steel Strategist #13,* Paine Webber, March 30, 1987, Table 3.

20.   International Iron and Steel Institute, *Indirect Trade in Steel, 1962–1979,* (Brussels, 1982), pp. 17, 128–129.

21.   *American Metal Market,* October 24 and November 3, 1983; *Business Week,* "Steel Giants Split over Import Protection," November 28, 1983, p. 40.

22.   *The Wall Street Journal,* December 30, 1987, and February 23, 1988; Hans Mueller, "Protection and Market Power in the Steel Industry," *Challenge* (September–October 1988), pp. 52–55.

23.   Office of Technology Assessment (OTA), *Technology and Steel Industry Competitiveness* (June 1980), pp. 275, 277–78 (hereunder, OTA Steel Report).

24.   International Iron and Steel Institute, Committee on Technology, summarized in "Worldwide Steel Industry Research," *Advanced Materials and Processes;* also ITC, 1988, op. cit. pp. 9–15, 11–90.

25.   *Fortune,* 74 (October 1966) p. 135; for an analysis of the BOF innovation episode, see Sharon Oster, "The Diffusion of Innovation Among Steel Firms," *The Bell Journal of Economics* (Spring 1982), pp. 45–56; and Leonard Lynn, "New Data on the Diffusion of the Basic Oxygen Furnace in the U.S. and Japan," *Journal of Industrial Economics* (December 1981), pp. 123–135.

26.   OTA Steel Report, p. 290.

27.   ITC, 1988, op. cit., pp. 12-12, 12-13.

28.   *The Wall Street Journal,* April 4, 1983, p. 11; *Iron Age,* October 21, 1983, p. 58.

In 1979 Norman Robins, research manager of Inland Steel, gave the following report after a visit to Japan ["Steel Industry Research and Technology," *American Steel Industry Economics Journal* (AISI) (April 1979), pp. 49–58]:

> I was in the Fukuyama plant last year, and one of the most impressive things about it was the lack of truck and train traffic. Inland's plant, on the other hand, was begun in 1902 and undoubtedly was not conceived at that point in time to grow to the size that it has since become. Presently, there are blast furnaces in two locations and a new one being built in a third location, steelmaking at four different locations and a great deal of material handling and transportation required to move steel through the finishing facilities.

29. ITC, 1988, op. cit., p. 12–13.

30. Calculated from data compiled in the following sources: OTA Steel Report, p. 123, and various issues of *Tekko Tokei Yoran,* Japan Iron and Steel Federation, *Iron and Steel Yearbook,* Eurostat, and *Investment in the Community Coalmining and Steel Industries,* European Coal and Steel Community.

31. Calculated from *Annual Statistical Report,* American Iron and Steel Institute, various years.

32. Federal Trade Commission, "Comment in the Matter of Certain Steel Products from Belgium, Brazil, the Federal Republic of Germany, France, Italy, Luxembourg, the Netherlands, Romania, South Africa, Spain, and the United Kingdom," (mimeograph, 1982), p. 8; Hans Mueller and Hans van der Ven, "Perils in the Brussels-Washington Steel Pact of 1982," *The World Economy* (November 1982), p. 265. For an economic analysis concerning the effects of subsidies on prices, see John Mutti, "Subsidized Production, World Steel Trade, and Countervailing Duties," *Southern Economic Journal* (January 1984), pp. 871–880.

33. *Pipeline,* March 1988, p. 12.

34. Total U.S. trade in steel-containing goods (indirect steel trade) changed from a slightly positive balance of 84 thousand tons (steel-weight equivalent) in 1979 to a negative imbalance of 9.3 million tons in 1986. See International Iron and Steel Institute, note 20 supra, and *Iron Age,* January 1988, p. 28.

35. Total U.S. trade in steel-containing goods (indirect steel trade) changed from a slightly positive balance of 84 thousand tons (steel-weight equivalent) in 1979 to a negative imbalance of 9.3 million tons in 1986. See International Iron and Steel Institute, note 20 supra, and *Iron Age,* January 1988, p. 28.

36. Robert W. Crandall, *Steel in Recurrent Crisis* (Washington, D.C.: Brookings, 1981), pp. 134–139; Gary Hufbauer, "Wean the Steel Barons from Protection," *The Wall Street Journal,* December 27, 1988, p. A10.

SUGGESTED READINGS

Books and Pamphlets

Acs, Z. J., *The Changing Structure of the U.S. Economy: Lessons from the Steel Industry.* New York: Praeger, 1984.

Adams, W., and J. W. Brock, *The Bigness Complex.* New York: Pantheon, 1986.

Barnett, D. F., and R. W. Crandall, *Up From the Ashes.* Wash., D.C.: Brookings, 1986.

Barnett, D. F., and L. Schorsch, *Steel—Upheaval in a Basic Industry.* Cambridge, Mass.: Ballinger Publishing Co., 1983.

Crandall, R. A., *The United States Steel Industry in Recurrent Crisis: Policy Options in a Competitive World.* Washington, D.C.: Brookings Institution, 1981.

Hogan, W. T., *World Steel in the 1980s — A Case of Survival.* Lexington, Mass: D.C. Heath Co., 1983.

———, *Steel in the United States: Restructuring to Compete.* Lexington, Mass.: D.C. Heath Co., 1984.

———, *Minimills and Integrated Mills.* Lexington, Mass.: D.C. Heath Co., 1987.

Jones, K., *Politics vs. Economics in World Steel Trade.* Lundon: Allen & Unwin, 1986.

Tiffany, P. A., *The Decline of American Steel — How Management, Labor, and Government Went Wrong.* New York, Oxford University Press, 1988.

Government Publications

Congressional Budget Office. *The Effects of Import Quotas on the Steel Industry.* Washington, D.C., July 1984.

General Accounting Office. *Report to the Congress of the United States by the Comptroller General: New Strategy Required for Aiding Distressed U.S. Steel Industry.* Washington, D.C.: U.S. Government Printing Office, January 1981.

International Trade Commission, *U.S. Global Competitiveness: Steel Sheet and Strip Industry.* Report to the Committee on Finance, U.S. Senate, USITC Publication 2050, January 1988.

National Academy of Engineering, Committee on Technology and International Economic and Trade Issues, *The Competitive Status of the U.S. Steel Industry.* Washington, D.C., National Academy Press, 1985.

United Nations, Economic Commission for Europe, *Structural Changes in International Steel Trade.* New York, United Nations, 1987.

Journal and Magazine Articles

Aylen, T., "Privatization of the British Steel Corporation," *Fiscal Studies,* August 1988.

Adams, W., and J. B. Dirlam, "Steel Imports and Vertical Oligopoly Power." *American Economic Review,* 54, September 1964.

———, and J. B. Dirlam, "Big Steel, Invention, and Innovation." *Quarterly Journal of Economics,* 80, May 1966.

———, and J. B. Dirlam, "The Trade Laws and Their Enforcement by the International Trade Commission," in *Recent Issues and Initiatives in U.S. Trade Policy,* R. E. Baldwin (ed.). National Bureau of Economic Research, 1984.

Dirlam, J. B., and H. Mueller, "Protectionism and Steel: The Case of the U.S. Steel Industry." *Journal of International Law,* 14, Summer 1982.

Kawahito, K., "Relative Profitability of the U.S. and Japanese Steel Industries." *The Columbia Journal of World Business,* 19, Fall 1984.

Lynn, L., "New Data on the Diffusion of the Basic Oxygen Furnace in the U.S. and Japan." *Journal of Industrial Economics,* 30, December 1981.

Mueller, H., "Protection and Market Power." *Challenge,* 31, September–October 1988.

———, and H. van der Ven, "Perils in the Brussels-Washington Steel Pact of 1982." *The World Economy,* 5 (November 1982).

Mutti, J., "Subsidized Production, World Steel Trade and Countervailing Duties." *Southern Economic Journal,* 51, Jan. 1984.

Schorsch, L. L., "Can Big Steel Change Bad Habits?" *Challenge,* 30, July-August 1987.

CHAPTER 4

THE AUTOMOBILE INDUSTRY

Walter Adams and James W. Brock

I.

INTRODUCTION

The automobile industry is one of the most concentrated oligopolies in the American economy. As such, it affords an excellent opportunity to examine how industrial concentration shapes corporate behavior and, ultimately, results in suboptimal performance. How to remedy such deficient performance confronts the nation with a host of vexing public policy dilemmas.

The history of the industry can be divided into distinct periods: the era of the independents; the emergence of the Ford Motor Company as the dominant producer; the shift of dominance to General Motors and progressive industry concentration; and, finally, the era of foreign competition.

The automobile, as we know it today, first took shape in the 1890s. Gasoline engines, steam engines, and electric motors were all tried as sources of propulsion. By 1900, more than 4,000 cars had been sold.

Production expanded rapidly thereafter and, by 1910, 187,000 automobiles were sold annually. Entry into the industry was comparatively easy. The manufacturer of automobiles was largely an assembler of parts. The new entrepreneur needed only to design a vehicle; announce to the public its imminent appearance; and contract with machine shops and carriage makers for the engines, wheels, bodies, and other components. The assembled autos could be sold for cash to dealers or directly to customers. The capital requirements for a new company were not steep. Prices varied widely (from $650 up), and both entry and exit rates were high.

The next decade marked the emergence of the Ford Motor Company as the dominant producer. Henry Ford's goal was to provide an inexpensive car that would reach a large market. Standardization, specialization, and mass production, he felt, were the keys to lowering manufacturing costs, and constant price reduction the key to tapping additional layers of demand. "Every time I reduce the charge for our car by one dollar, I get a thousand new buyers," Ford said. His strategy seemed simple enough: to take lower profits on each vehicle and thereby achieve larger volume. As Ford saw it,

101

Figure 4-1

Historical evolution of auto industry structure.

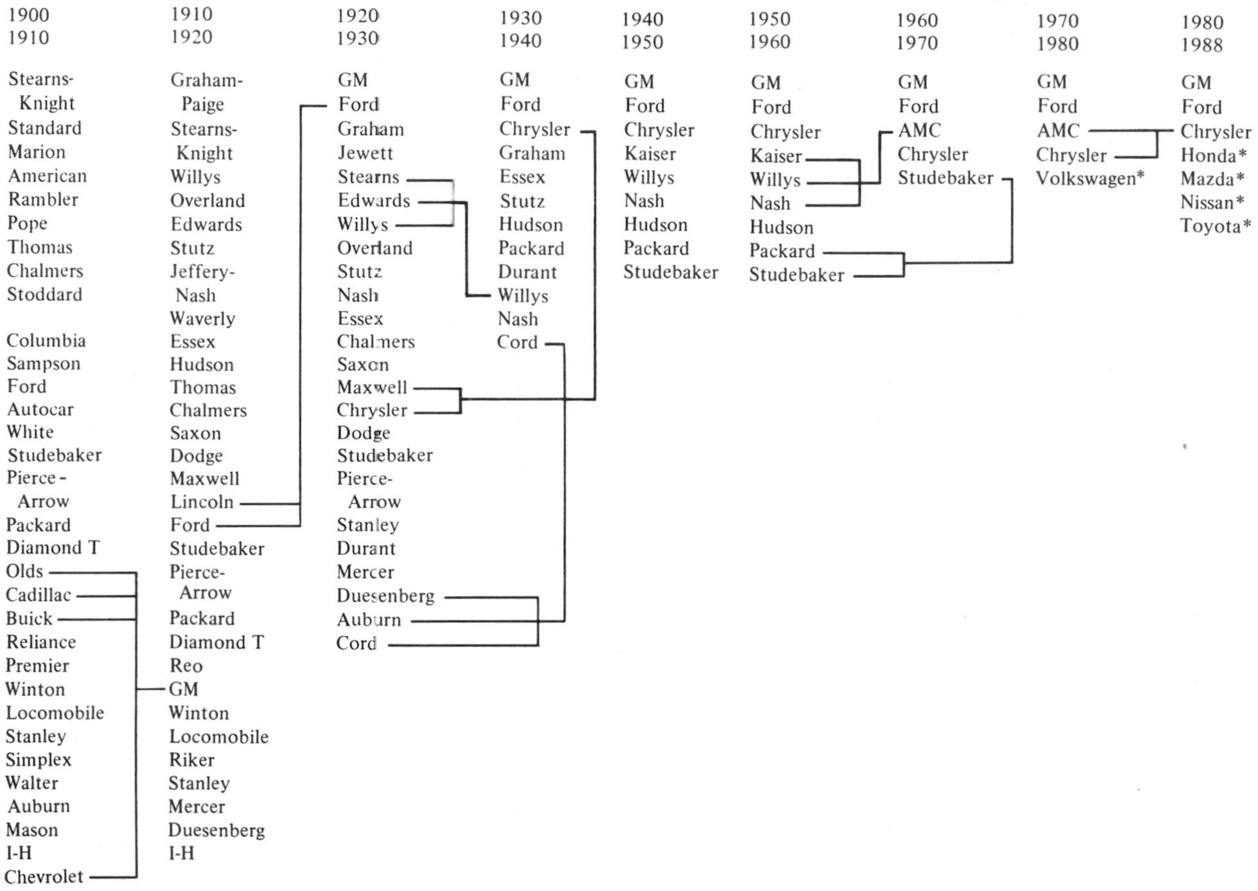

1900 1910	1910 1920	1920 1930	1930 1940	1940 1950	1950 1960	1960 1970	1970 1980	1980 1988
Stearns-Knight	Graham-Paige	GM	GM	GM	GM	GM	GM	GM
Standard	Stearns-Knight	Ford	Ford	Ford	Ford	Ford	Ford	Ford
Marion	Willys	Graham	Chrysler	Chrysler	Chrysler	AMC	AMC	Chrysler
American	Overland	Jewett	Graham	Kaiser	Kaiser	Chrysler	Chrysler	Honda*
Rambler	Edwards	Stearns	Essex	Willys	Willys	Studebaker	Volkswagen*	Mazda*
Pope	Willys	Edwards	Stutz	Nash	Nash			Nissan*
Thomas	Stutz	Willys	Hudson	Hudson	Hudson			Toyota*
Chalmers	Jeffery-Nash	Overland	Packard	Packard	Packard			
Stoddard	Waverly	Stutz	Durant	Studebaker	Studebaker			
		Nash	Willys					
Columbia	Essex	Essex	Nash					
Sampson	Hudson	Chalmers	Cord					
Ford	Thomas	Saxon						
Autocar	Chalmers	Maxwell						
White	Saxon	Chrysler						
Studebaker	Dodge	Dodge						
Pierce-Arrow	Maxwell	Studebaker						
Packard	Lincoln	Pierce-Arrow						
Diamond T	Ford	Stanley						
Olds	Studebaker	Durant						
Cadillac	Pierce-Arrow	Mercer						
Buick	Packard	Duesenberg						
Reliance	Diamond T	Auburn						
Premier	Reo	Cord						
Winton	GM							
Locomobile	Winton							
Stanley	Locomobile							
Simplex	Riker							
Walter	Stanley							
Auburn	Mercer							
Mason	Duesenberg							
I-H	I-H							
Chevrolet								

* U.S. plants opened by foreign-based producers.

102

successive "price reductions meant new enlargements of the market, and acceleration of mass production's larger economies, and greater aggregate profits. The company's firm grasp of this principle . . . was its unique element of strength, just as failure to grasp it had been one of the weaknesses of rival car makers. As profits per car had gone down and down, net earnings had gone up and up."[1] Not surprisingly, by 1921, Ford's Model T (which had remained largely unchanged for 19 years) accounted for more than 50 percent of the market.

The 1920s marked a shift of preeminence from Ford to General Motors —an amalgam of formerly independent firms (Chevrolet, Oldsmobile, Oakland, Cadillac, Buick, Fisher Body, Delco). GM adopted a two-pronged strategy. First, contrary to Ford's emphasis on a single model, GM offered a broad range of products to blanket all market segments. Its motto was "a car for every purse and purpose." Second, again contrary to Ford's strategy, GM decided to modify its cars each year with a combination of engineering advances, convenience improvements, and styling changes. GM felt that annual model changes, despite the sacrifice of cost savings, would stimulate replacement demand and increase sales—enough to compensate for the higher costs. This strategy catapulted the company into industry leadership, which it did not relinquish from 1931 on.

In the new era, the groundwork was also laid for the concentration that is the hallmark of today's auto industry. Figure 4-1 depicts the successive acquisitions and mergers that have produced the triopoly that still dominates domestic auto production in the United States.

A final observation: Starting in the mid-1950s, successive waves of imports have challenged the domestic oligopoly. By the mid-1970s, imports had captured more than 25 percent of the U.S. market and triggered repeated efforts by the Big Three—in collaboration with the U.A.W.—to obtain government protection from foreign competition. Today, the question of foreign competition is perhaps the prime public policy issue in this industry.

II.
INDUSTRY STRUCTURE

The most important structural features of the U.S. automobile industry are buyer demand and the nature of the product; the number of competing sellers and their relative size (concentration); the extent of economies of scale; and barriers to the entry of new competitors.

Demand and the Nature of the Product

The demand for new cars is influenced by a variety of factors. First, the demand for new cars in the United States is predominantly a replacement demand. The acquisition of a new car can be deferred, and this injects considerable volatility into the market.

Second, because an automobile involves a large outlay of funds, the demand for new cars is highly sensitive to macroeconomic conditions, including employment, income, and interest rates.

Third, an important determinant of demand, of course, is price. Although the aggregate demand for new cars is slightly price-elastic, the demand for a particular make of car is much more price-sensitive because of the general availability of close substitutes.

Fourth, a long-term shift in the composition of new-car demand has taken place, in favor of smaller cars. The share of small cars (compacts and subcompacts) rose, from 25 percent of all new-car sales in 1967 to 52.4 percent by 1984; over the same period, the share of large cars declined from 51 to 21.4 percent. This shift is partly explained by fuel shortages and the skyrocketing price of gasoline in the 1970s. Yet, the trend in demand toward small cars began well before the first oil embargo in 1973. Gasoline supplies and prices may have amplified this trend, but other factors have been exerting a long-run influence, such as smaller family size and the growing prevalence of multiple-car households, whose second car is generally smaller and more utilitarian in purpose.

Industry Concentration

Domestic automobile production is dominated by a tight triopoly. Because of growing import competition, domestic sales are less concentrated, but the impact of this competition is attenuated by the trend toward cross-national ownership positions and joint ventures between U.S. producers and their foreign rivals.

1. Concentration of Domestic Production. The manufacture of automobiles in the United States is, as Table 4-1 shows, highly concentrated. From a high of 88 firms in the early 1920s, the number of domestic producers dwindled to four by the mid-1970s.

General Motors is, and has long been, the largest firm in the industry, typically producing more cars than the remainder of the domestic industry combined. Ford accounts for approximately 25 percent of domestic production, and Chrysler for approximately 15 percent. (AMC—long a distant fourth—disappeared through acquisition by Chrysler in 1987. Volkswagen, which launched U.S. production operations in Pennsylvania in 1978, decided to abandon U.S. production ten years later.)

More recently the number of domestic producers has increased as foreign firms have built U.S. assembly plants. As Table 4-2 shows, established Japanese automakers have launched six new U.S. auto assembly operations. In addition, Toyota and General Motors have reopened GM's Fremont, California, facility and are operating it as New United Motors Manufacturing Inc. (NUMMI). These production facilities represent the addition of com-

Table 4-1 _____

U.S. Auto Production: Market Shares and Concentration, 1913–1987

Year	General Motors	Ford	Chrysler	Other U.S. Producers	Share of Top Three
1913	12.2%	39.5%	a	48.3%	
1923	20.2	46.0	1.9%	31.9	68.1%
1933	41.4	20.7	25.4	12.5	87.5
1946–1955	45.2	24.4	19.4	11.0	89.0
1956–1965	50.9	28.6	14.3	6.2	93.8
1966–1975	54.1	27.1	16.5	2.3	97.7
1976–1985	59.4	23.6	13.0	4.0	96.0
1986	55.1	22.5	16.6	5.8	94.2
1987	48.7	25.8	15.6	9.9	90.1

aChrysler was not yet in existence.

Sources: L. J. White, *The Automobile Industry Since 1945* (Cambridge, Mass: Harvard U.P., 1971), Appendix; L. J. White, "The Automobile Industry," in W. Adams (ed.), *The Structure of American Industry*, 6th ed. (New York: Macmillan, 1982), p. 147; *Ward's Automotive Yearbook.*

bined production capacity equivalent to that of Ford Motor Company. Yet, because most of these operations are joint ventures between American producers and their foreign rivals (or involve foreign firms in which U.S. producers hold sizable ownership stakes), they do not constitute the entry of independent new competitors.

Nevertheless, the Big Three collectively continue to dominate the industry. Moreover, they are extensively integrated not only horizontally, but also vertically and internationally. They produce a substantial proportion of the parts and components from which automobiles are assembled: GM produces 70 percent or more of the parts and components it uses; in-house parts production at Ford ranges from 50 to 60 percent; and Chrysler's internal supply of parts and components is on the order of 30 percent.

GM, Ford, and Chrysler are also extensively integrated internationally. For example, Ford is the largest auto producer in Australia; the second largest in Canada and England; the third largest manufacturer of autos in Brazil, Mexico, and Spain; and the fourth largest in West Germany. Similarly, GM and (to a lesser degree) Chrysler rank among the largest automobile producers in a number of countries around the world.

Finally, through a series of large acquisitions in recent years, the Big Three have also accentuated the conglomerate nature of their companies: General Motors expended $2.5 billion to acquire Electronic Data Systems (EDS) in 1984 and outbid Ford in 1985 to acquire Hughes Aircraft (a leading defense contractor) for $5 billion. Following its government bailout, Chrysler has acquired Gulfstream Aerospace ($636.5 million), E. F. Hutton's credit

Table 4-2
New Foreign-Owned U.S. Production Operations

Operation	Owner	Location	Production Start Date	Planned Capacity	1987 Production Volume
Honda of America	Honda Motor Co.	Marysville, OH	1982	360,000	324,064
Nissan Motor USA	Nissan Motor Co.	Smyrna, TN	1983	265,000	117,334
New United Motors Manufacturing Inc. (NUMMI)	50/50 GM–Toyota joint venture	Fremont, CA	1984	250,000	187,378
Mazda Motor USA	Mazda Motor Co. (Mazda 25% owned by Ford)	Flat Rock, MI	1987	240,000	4,200
Diamond-Star Motors Corp.	50/50 Chrysler–Mitsubishi joint venture	Bloomington, IL	1988	240,000	0
Toyota Motor USA	Toyota Motor Corp. (joint venture with GM in NUMMI)	Georgetown, KY	1988	200,000	0
Subaru–Isuzu Automotive	Fuji–Isuzu joint venture (Isuzu 39% owned by GM)	Lafayette, IN	1989	120,000	0

Source: U.S. General Accounting Office, Foreign Investment: Growing Japanese Presence in the U.S. Auto Industry; Automotive News, March 1988.

operations ($125 million), Bank America's consumer finance operations ($405 million), and Electrospace Systems ($367 million). Meanwhile, Ford has acquired First Nationwide Financial Corporation (the nation's ninth largest savings and loan association) for $493 million; New Holland farm equipment ($330 million); U.S. Leasing International ($513 million); and BDM International ($425 million), as well as investing $1.2 billion in the buyout of Hertz (the nation's largest rental car company and one of the biggest buyers of new cars).

2. Foreign Competition. Foreign-produced imports have steadily increased in competitive importance over recent decades. The import share of U.S. auto sales grew from 0.4 percent in the immediate post-World War II decade to 21.2 percent in the years 1976–1983. In 1987, imports accounted for 30 percent of new-car sales in the U.S. (The relative share of imports is somewhat overstated because of "captive" imports, brought into the U.S. by American producers; examples are Chrysler's importation of the Colt, Chevrolet's importation of the Spectrum and Sprint, and Pontiac's importation of the LeMans.) Nevertheless, foreign producers—led by the Japanese—have been a critical, if not the only, source of effective competition for the U.S. oligopoly in the post-World War II period. Their competitive success has been especially significant as a force for deconcentration of the U.S. automobile market. Thus, although GM, Ford, and Chrysler together accounted for 90 percent of U.S. production in 1987, import competition reduced their collective shares of sales to 68 percent on the U.S. market (representing individual firm shares of 37, 20, and 11 percent for GM, Ford, and Chrysler, respectively).

Initially, foreign producers focused their efforts on the low-price, small-car segment of the market, where they eventually won nearly half the field. Then, beginning in 1981, constrained by the number of cars they were allowed to import into the United States, the Japanese began to move upscale into the midsize region of the market—the traditional mainstay of the Big Three. Japanese and European producers also began to capture larger shares of the high-price luxury end of the market. As a result, the Big Three now confront greater foreign competition across the entire spectrum of the American market.

Needless to say, however, import quotas and the perennial threat of protectionism are jeopardizing the otherwise salutary effect that foreign competition has in eroding sales concentration in the U.S. auto market—a point to which we shall return in our public policy discussion.

3. Cross Ownership and Joint Ventures. Another significant feature of concentration in the industry is the increasingly intricate latticework of cross-ownership positions and joint ventures between U.S. and foreign automakers. This web of intercompany coordination is illustrated in Figure 4-2.

Figure 4-2

Cooperation between world auto manufacturers.

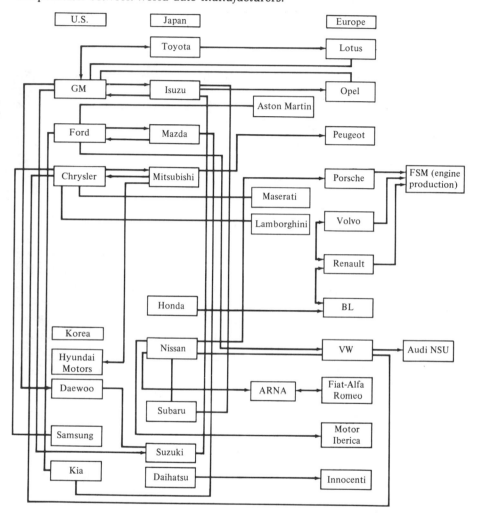

These arrangements—which are now becoming trilateral in nature, conjoining U.S., Japanese, and newly emerging Korean producers—are structurally significant because they expand interfirm coordination and cooperation and thus constrict autonomous, independent decision making. Given the important competitive role of imports, these associations between U.S. firms and their potential—or actual—foreign rivals are of particular concern.

The Question of Economies of Scale

To what extent is the observed level of concentration in U.S. automobile production dictated by efficiencies of large-scale operation? Are these gains and efficiencies of large scale in automobile manufacturing and assembly so great as to necessitate a triopoly structure?

In fact, economies of scale are not as extensive as is commonly assumed. For example, a team of manufacturing engineers estimates that minimum efficient scales of production can be achieved at annual output levels in the 200,000- 400,000-unit range.[2] Although large in an absolute sense, these production levels imply that a firm with a 3–6 percent share of U.S. auto production would be big enough to benefit from all significant economies of scale, or, conversely, that the industry could conceivably support 17 to 35 efficient producers (at 1987 production levels). Another industry expert, Lawrence J. White, suggests that the risks and vagaries of the market might require a viable firm to produce two distinct lines of automobiles, rather than one, thereby approximately doubling minimum efficient scale estimates.[3]

The record of actual plant output levels reinforces the conclusion that there are limits to scale economies in auto production. The Big Three assemble cars at multiple locations rather than concentrating all assembly in one or two giant plants: They produce 85 percent of their total output in plants with annual production volume of less than 300,000 units per year. Thus, it would appear that optimum assembly-plant scale lies between 200,000 and 300,000 units per year—a figure quite comparable with the foregoing minimum efficient scale estimates.

GM's persistent woes in the 1980s seem to indicate not only that economies of scale are limited, but that there are serious diseconomies of scale. Measured by annual dollar sales, GM is 1½ times bigger than its next largest rival, Ford, and larger than the three biggest Japanese automakers combined. But GM's size seems to be a liability, rather than an asset. It has the lowest productivity, and the highest per-car production costs, in the industry. Despite modernization investments of tens of billions of dollars in the 1980s, it still costs GM $250–$800 more to produce a car than Ford and Chrysler. By its own admission, GM has been forced to turn to joint ventures with smaller foreign rivals in a struggle to learn how to make cars economically. In addition, GM's "Saturn" project—a separate, stand-alone auto manufacturing operation that will have its own plants, procure its own materials and parts, build its own cars, and market them—seems designed to escape the infirmities of GM's bigness. Indeed, if the Saturn project makes economic sense, then GM's size does not—an increasingly common observation. "The basic question nagging this biggest, most diverse, and most integrated of car companies," *Business Week* concludes, "is whether [GM] is just too big to compete in today's fast-changing car market."[4] Perhaps GM's main operating divisions would be closer to optimum production scale if they were split off and operated independently.

Thus, there is a glaring divergence between optimal plant scale and the size of firms in the industry, a difference that cannot be explained solely on the basis of economies of scale in production at the plant level. Perhaps this divergence is dictated by economies of scale in marketing. Or perhaps it stems from noneconomic advantages of large firm size, such as enhanced capacity to influence government and public policy regarding antitrust (joint ventures); international trade (import quotas); safety and pollution controls; or, ultimately, the capacity to obtain government bailouts (a la Chrysler) because a giant firm is believed to be too big to allow to fail.

Barriers to Entry

Barriers to the entry of new competition (another important element of industry structure) are substantial in the automobile industry.

Costs to construct a new auto assembly plant, according to the Department of Transportation, would amount to more than $200 million.[5] Production of major components and parts would drive capital costs even higher for a new entrant. The combined construction costs for four basic types of facilities (engine plant, transmission plant, parts and components plant, and assembly plant) would range from $1.2 to $1.4 billion.

A new entrant must not only produce automobiles, but also sell them to consumers—another barrier to new competition. In 1986, the Big Three together spent $693 million advertising their automobiles; General Motors alone spent $285 million. With these levels of advertising by established firms, a newcomer would have to incur heavy expenses merely to announce its arrival.

Finally, in addition to producing and advertising its cars, a new entrant would have to assemble a dealer system for distribution and service. Given the extensive dealer systems developed by the Big Three firms, this would be a daunting (though not insuperable) task: GM, Ford, and Chrysler cars are sold through 15,585, 8,975, and 10,499 dealer franchises, respectively.

It is not surprising, therefore, that few new firms have commenced domestic production of automobiles since the early 1950s, and that these "new" producers are all established companies that have produced cars abroad and imported them into the U.S. for a number of years.

III.

INDUSTRY CONDUCT

Market behavior conforms to what would be expected in a tight-knit oligopoly. Strategic decisions with respect to both price and nonprice rivalry are marked by a notable degree of parallelism.

Pricing

As economic theory predicts, the general pricing pattern in automobiles is characterized by the recognition of mutual interdependence among a few large firms. The Big Three understand that their interest as a group is best served by avoiding serious price competition among themselves. *The Wall Street Journal* explains: "Auto makers can maximize profits because in the oligopolistic domestic auto industry the three major producers tend to copy each other's price moves. One auto executive notes that if one company lowered prices, the others would follow immediately. . . . As a result, price cuts wouldn't increase anybody's market share, and 'everybody would be worse off,' he says."[6]

General Motors is clearly the price leader in the industry. It initiates general rounds of price increases; it can, by refusing to follow, prevent either of its two main rivals from leading price alterations; and, finally, its price changes establish de facto price ceilings for Ford and Chrysler.

The prices actually adopted by the Big Three appear at times to represent a tacit bargain arrived at through a delicate process of communication and signaling. The machinations of the Big Three during the summer and fall of 1983, as they prepared for their 1984 model lines, provide an example of this process at work. General Motors led off by communicating its "preliminary," planned price increase of 2 percent. Chrysler followed, signaling its "tentative" consideration of a 1.4 percent price rise; and Ford communicated "expected" price increases of 2.3 percent. With the players' intentions revealed, GM then raised prices by an average of 2.4 percent—an increase matched shortly thereafter by Ford and Chrysler.

Parallelism and uniformity in pricing among the Big Three is strikingly —and at times, astonishingly—close. Although automobiles are highly differentiated products, and although a certain amount of price flexibility occurs at the retail level, there is, nonetheless, substantial price uniformity for comparable models offered by different manufacturers. This, in turn, limits price differentials up and down the chain of manufacturing and distribution.

In the small-car segment of the industry, which is populated by a larger number of competing producers, pricing behavior is distinctively different. There, foreign competitors occupy nearly 40 percent of the field; there is no recognized price leader; there is no rigid pattern of leadership–followership; and pricing exhibits the variability and unpredictability characteristic of a more competitive market.

This pricing behavior in the small-car segment underscores the key role that imports play in disciplining the pricing power of the domestic oligopoly. It also explains why government constraints on foreign competition enable the Big Three to boost prices substantially.

Nonprice Rivalry

With price competition largely eschewed, rivalry in the domestic automobile industry is channeled into nonprice areas. Most prominent among these are styling, model changes, and advertising. Yet, nonprice conduct, too, is marked by mutual oligopolistic interdependence and tacit collusion, both generally (in terms of the degree of product uniformity among producers) and specifically (in mutual restraint by the Big Three in entering new market segments).

1. Styling and Annual Model Changes. Product styling and annual model changes are the predominant mode of rivalry in the domestic industry. For the most part, these changes are cosmetic style variations rather than technological breakthroughs. From the industry's viewpoint, they have the virtue of stimulating the replacement demand for automobiles while avoiding the competitive uncertainty and possible "market disruption" that aggressive technological rivalry would entail. Once Alfred Sloan, Jr. (G.M.'s former board chairman) had taught the industry to avoid "radical" product innovation and what he called "the risk of untried experiment," styling became the principal arena for interfirm rivalry. Yet, as in the case of pricing, the result of leadership–followership and "protective styling imitation" is a surprising degree of uniformity in the offerings of the Big Three. "Historically," F. M. Scherer points out, "Detroit has offered Americans nothing like the diversity of technical approaches in Europe and Japan."[7]

2. Advertising. Advertising constitutes a second feature of nonprice rivalry in the automobile industry, with the Big Three ranked among the largest advertisers in the country. GM is the industry's largest advertiser, having spent $285 million advertising its passenger cars in 1986; Ford and Chrysler are the second and third largest advertisers in the field, respectively. But rates of advertising expenditures, calculated on a per-car basis, vary inversely with firm size. In particular, although the absolute amount of GM's expenditures exceeds that for any other firm, GM's advertising per car is far less than that for any other firm ($63 per car for GM versus $130 for Ford and $113 for Chrysler in 1986). This pattern reflects an important nonproduction economy of scale: Given GM's larger size, it can spend a larger total amount on advertising; yet, by spreading its expenditures over an even larger volume of sales, it can reduce its per-car rate of spending. In attempting to match GM, however, its rivals must spend proportionately more per car.

3. Mutual Interdependence and Oligopolistic Restraint: The Case of Small Cars. The historic resistance by the Big Three to the introduction of small cars is a poignant illustration of oligopolistic rationality in nonprice rivalry.[8]

At the conclusion of World War II, the small, lightweight, inexpensive automobile was seen as a prime means for expanding the postwar urban car market in a manner analogous to Henry Ford's Model T decades earlier. The United Auto Workers, for example, urged Detroit to build a small car, citing an opinion survey conducted by the Society of Automotive Engineers, which revealed that 60 percent of the public wanted the industry to produce a small car. In May 1945, General Motors and Ford disclosed that they were considering the production of small cars. The following year, Chrysler announced that "if the market exists and if other companies have a low-priced car, Chrysler will be ready with something competitive."

However, the Big Three did not seriously undertake to produce and market such a car until the 1970s, at least for the American market.[9] Attempts were made to meet successive import surges with the introduction of the "compact" car in the late 1950s and the "subcompacts" in the 1960s. But these efforts were, at best, halfhearted and dilatory. In 1962, for example, Ford canceled the planned introduction of its "Cardinal," which featured a front-mounted, four-cylinder engine and front-wheel drive—a compact car quite similar to the X-cars, the Escort, and Omni of the 1980s.

Lawrence White explains this antipathy to small cars in terms of oligopolistic firm behavior. General Motors, Ford, and Chrysler, he writes, each seemed to recognize that vigorous entry into small cars by any one of them would trigger entry into the field by the others. Further, each firm seemed to believe that the demand for small cars was not great enough to permit profits acceptable to the group if all of them should simultaneously decide to enter this part of the market. "Twice, one or two of the Big Three pulled back from plunging ahead with a small car when the market did not look large enough for all three. . . . A sizable niche might well have been carved out at the bottom of the market by a Big Three producer in 1950, or again, with a 'sub compact' in 1962 or 1963. Room-for-all considerations, however, appeared to rule this out." Reinforcing the "room-for-all" Weltanschaung was the apparent desire by each of the Big Three to protect group profits in large cars by withholding the small car as an inexpensive substitute. "In this behavior, the Big Three definitely recognized their mutual interdependence, since in the absence of retaliation by rivals a single firm contemplating the production of a small car should have expected to gain more profits from stealing the dissatisfied customers from other firms than he would lose from dissatisfied customers of his own large cars. . . . But the Big Three mutually contemplating a small car could only see lost profits from reduced sales of large cars."

Independents and foreign competitors, of course, were not immobilized by such considerations because they had no vested interests and no established positions to protect. For these reasons, they broke through the logjam of tacit restraint and forced the domestic oligopoly to confront the challenge of building small, lightweight, fuel-efficient automobiles. "In the absence of the press of competition from imports," White concludes, "it is likely that the Big Three might never have provided small cars to the market."

4. Interfirm Rivalry: Summary. Perhaps H. Ross Perot, founder of the EDS Corporation and erstwhile director of General Motors, has best summarized the industry's oligopolistic market behavior since World War II: "General Motors and the entire American automobile industry had a big respite from competition," Mr. Perot explains. "[I]t got so bad that [U.S. auto companies] tried to get divisions to compete with one another—Chevrolet compete with Pontiac, Oldsmobile with Buick, and so on. . . . Now we've got a whole generation of people who think that's what competition is. And I don't like that, and I say 'Fellows, that's intramural sports.' I said, 'You don't even tackle there, you just touch the guy. . . . You don't even play with pads. . . . Now the Japanese have showed up, and they're competing professionally.' . . . First board meeting . . . I gave 'em my immigrant's view of General Motors. And I said, 'You don't understand competition. . . .'"[10]

IV.
INDUSTRY PERFORMANCE

The nagging problems currently confronted by the industry are an outgrowth of the noncompetitive structure and noncompetitive conduct that have resulted in deficient performance.

Production Efficiency

Recent sizeable reductions in fixed costs and overhead expenses by the Big Three—triggered by foreign competition—attest to production inefficiencies built up in the era of stable, entrenched oligopoly. Bloated salaries and redundant white-collar positions, ineffective utilization of plant and equipment, and excessive vertical integration (in-house manufacture of parts and components) all combined to inflate production costs unnecessarily. So did excessive labor compensation—the result of what is perhaps most accurately described as vertical collusion, or "coalescence of power," between organized labor and management. On the one hand, the union has demanded wages far in excess of labor productivity gains; on the other hand, oligopoly in the product market has rendered the management of the Big Three firms quite compliant with union wage demands. Until the advent of foreign competition, higher labor costs could easily be passed on to buyers merely by raising car prices. Thus, although labor productivity in autos rose over the years 1967–1980, labor compensation in the industry rose five and one-half times faster. As a result, unit labor costs escalated sharply. (Recently, foreign competition seems to have moderated this cost–price spiral).

Comparative analyses of U.S. and Japanese production operations reveal that poor organization and management of manufacturing processes is a further source of inefficiency in the domestic industry. As GM chief executive Roger Smith aptly points out, the main reason for Japanese efficiency is not to be found in "exchange rates, differential tax burdens or other external factors . . . (but) management—of both people and work processes."[11]

Finally, production inefficiency in the domestic industry has been compounded by the bureaucratic morass (diseconomies) of excessive organizational size. As described by Fortune, "GM's mammoth bureaucracy—layer upon layer of managers, departments, and committees—(has) to approve, re-approve, and cross-approve the car divisions' every move."[12] This hardly promotes efficiency. Former GM president Elliot M. Estes put the matter bluntly: "Chevrolet is such a big monster that you twist its tail and nothing happens at the other end for months and months. It is so gigantic that there isn't any way to really run it. You just sort of try to keep track of it."[13]

Pricing and Profitability

Pricing and profitability constitute a second dimension of industry performance. Are automobile profits, and hence, prices, excessive? How have automobile prices behaved over the long run? Does the short-run behavior of auto prices dampen or aggravate cyclical fluctuations in the industry and the American economy generally?

1. Industry Profitability. Table 4-3 depicts profit rates for the auto industry and for all U.S. manufacturing corporations over the years 1947–1984. These data show that, historically, the industry's profit rates have been excessive when measured against those of all U.S. manufacturing corporations. They also show that, since the late 1970s, the fortunes of U.S. automakers have fluctuated dramatically. Chrysler faced imminent bankruptcy in 1979 and was saved only by a government bailout. Then, in 1980, the industry recorded a loss of more than $4 billion—a $9 billion swing in profits from the previous year and the worst one-year performance ever turned in by any U.S. industry. By 1983 the Big Three reaped record profits —in part due to efficiency gains, but in important part due to the pricing protection afforded by government import restraints. And in 1986 and 1987, reflecting GM's travails, Ford recorded absolute profits greater than those of GM, the first time in sixty years that Ford outearned its much larger rival.

2. Long-Run Price Behavior. The long-run record of automobile prices is one of sustained, sizeable price escalation. The average selling price of new cars in the U.S. quadrupled from 1967 to 1987, rising from $3,310 in 1967 to $13,255 in 1987. Put differently, new-car prices during this period were raised at an average annual rate 25 percent greater than the rate of inflation in the overall consumer price index.

Table 4-3
Profitability in the U.S. Auto Industry: Net Income After Taxes, Divided by Stockholders' Equity

	1947–1977	1980	1981	1982	1983	1984	1985	1986	1987
Big Three producers[a]	14.3%	−11.1%	−6.3%	−2.8%	31.3%	40.1%	24.3%	19.3%	18.6%
General Motors	19.5	−4.3	1.9	5.3	18.0	18.9	13.5	9.6	10.8
Ford	13.1	−18.0	−14.4	−10.8	24.7	29.5	20.5	22.1	24.9
Chrysler[b]	10.2	—	—	—	51.3	72.0	38.8	26.3	20.0
All U.S. manufacturing corporations	11.8	13.9	13.6	9.2	10.6	12.5	10.1	9.5	12.8

[a]Arithmetic average: GM and Ford only, 1980–82.
[b]1980–1982 data not meaningful owing to federally guaranteed loans and government stock-ownership program.

Sources: *Moody's Industrial Manual*, various years; U.S. Congress, Senate, Subcommittee on Antitrust, Committee on the Judiciary, *A Reorganization of the U.S. Automobile Industry*, Committee Print, 93rd Cong., 2nd sess., 1974, p. 234; *Economic Report of the President*, 1989.

One other observation is relevant: In spite of contentions to the contrary, the secular rise in new-car prices cannot be attributed to the costs of government safety and pollution regulations. According to the Bureau of Labor Statistics, these costs accounted for less than 12 percent of the total increase in automobile prices between 1975 and 1979.[14]

3. Cyclical Price Behavior. The cyclical behavior of auto prices is significant in two respects. First, automobile prices are rigid in a downward direction; they tend to be unresponsive to even large short-run declines in new-car sales. (In recent years, this tendency has been counteracted somewhat by the price rebates and subsidization of interest rates, sporadically instituted by auto manufacturers in periods of slack demand.) Second, new-car prices not only fail to decline in the face of large drops in demand and sales, but they behave in a highly perverse fashion; that is, they are often raised in the face of sales declines. Such downward price rigidity and perverse pricing exacerbate instability, not only in autos, but in the economy at large.

Dynamic Efficiency

Dynamic efficiency encompasses product innovation (the development and commercialization of new-product technology) and process innovation (the adoption over time of better, more effective production methods). The industry's performance record in these areas is notable in at least four respects.

First, the rate, breadth, and depth of product innovation were greatest in the era prior to World War II, when the field was populated by many independent producers. Competition was intense, and new people with new ideas could put their ideas (the bad along with the good) into commercial practice. The Big Three innovated new-product technology during this period but, owing to what Donald A. Moore has characterized as "competitive vigor born of necessity," the contributions of the independents far exceeded their market shares.

Second, with the demise of a vigorous independent sector, and with the consolidation of the industry into a tight oligopoly, the pace of genuine product innovation slackened. Innovations like front-wheel drive, disc brakes, fuel injection, utilitarian minivans and fuel-efficient subcompacts, and four-wheel steering languished in the hands of the Big Three. "Since competition within the industry was mild," David Halberstam explains, "there was no impulse to innovate; to the finance people, innovation not only was expensive but seemed unnecessary. . . . Why bother, after all? In America's rush to become a middle-class society, there was an almost insatiable demand for cars. It was impossible not to make money, and there was a conviction that no matter what the sales were this year, they would be even greater the next. So there was little stress on improving the cars. From 1949, when the automatic transmission was introduced, to the late seventies, the cars remained remarkably the same. What innovation there was came almost reluctantly."[15] It was a record that former GM executive John DeLorean calls "a quarter-century of technical hibernation" — an era when the U.S. industry "went on a two-decade marketing binge which generally offered up the same old product under the guise of something new and useful."[16]

Third, while the domestic oligopoly luxuriated in complacency and the cosmetic style game, foreign producers took the lead in aggressively exploiting the frontiers of automotive technology. According to veteran industry observer Brock Yates, they "continued to move ahead with fuel injection, disc brakes, rack and pinion steering, radial tires, quartz headlights, stalk-mounted windshield wiper and dimmer controls, ergonomically adjustable bucket seats, five-speed manual transmissions, high-efficiency overhead camshaft engines, independently sprung suspensions, advanced shock absorbers, and strict crash-worthiness standards."[17] This lead persists to the present day, with foreign producers commercializing such recent product innovations as four-wheel steering, electronically controlled active suspensions, multivalve engines, and ceramic engine componentry.

Fourth, with regard to *process* innovation, the domestic oligopoly's performance is hardly more enviable. Here, too, foreign firms — especially the Japanese — have exhibited far more entrepreneurship in seeking out and implementing improved manufacturing techniques. The proof, measured by labor productivity gains, is clearly evidenced in Table 4-4. "On the basis of our research and of what we saw in Japan," three industry analysts report, "we would conclude that, on balance, Japanese manufacturing systems keep their lines operational a higher percentage of time, make greater use of materials-handling equipment, process fewer defective parts, enjoy lower rates of worker absenteeism, and match workers better with their tasks than do most comparable systems in the United States." Also, "the Japanese

Table 4-4
Vehicles Produced per Worker: U.S. vs. Japanese Firms

	1960	1970	1983
General Motors[a]	8	8	11
Ford[b]	14	12	15
Chrysler[a]	11	11	16
Nissan	12	30	42
Toyota	15	38	58

[a]Worldwide.
[b]U.S.

Source: Michael A. Cusumano, *The Japanese Automobile Industry* (Cambridge, Mass.: Harvard University Press, 1985), pp. 187–88.

showed themselves to be doggedly persistent in their efforts to master operational detail. We had been half-prepared to find them using process technology far more advanced than anything available to their American counterparts. What we saw about us at every turn, however, was not newer technology but better management of the technology in place—not the exotic gimmickry of wide-eyed public expectation but a sober mastery of manufacturing."[18] In their devotion to production, and in their relentless willingness to experiment, the Japanese seem to have been far more astute students of Henry Ford than the chieftains of the U.S. industry, who succumbed to satisfaction with the status quo.

In the 1980s the Big Three have struggled to advance, both in product innovation as well as in production technology. They have progressed on both fronts—examples are the successful Ford Taurus program, GM's "Saturn" project, billions of dollars in cost reductions, and productivity gains on the factory floor. But the questions remain: Does high industry concentration almost inevitably retard, rather than promote, technological advance? At what cost to the economy; the society; and, eventually, to the firms themselves? And can the Big Three traverse the technological chasm they allowed foreign competitors to open up over the past two decades?

Social Efficiency

Social efficiency is the last dimension of industry performance we shall consider, albeit briefly. It measures how well the industry has served the public interest in such areas as pollution control, auto safety, and fuel efficiency.

1. Smog and Automotive Air Pollution. By the early 1960s, the typical American automobile spewed approximately one ton of pollutants per year into the nation's atmosphere, and motor vehicles accounted for an estimated 60 percent of all air pollution. Yet the industry confronted this fact with remarkable equanimity.

At first, the industry simply denied the existence of the problem—observation and its own internal research results to the contrary notwithstanding. "[W]aste vapors are dissipated in the atmosphere quickly and do not present an air-pollution problem," Ford Motor Company told Los Angeles County supervisors in 1953. "The fine automotive powerplants which modern-day engineers design do not 'smoke.'"[19]

Later, as automotive air pollution worsened, and as national concern about the problem increased, the automobile companies maneuvered to eliminate rivalry between themselves in developing and commercializing pollution-control technology. In an antitrust suit, filed in 1969 and not contested by the industry, the Justice Department found that domestic auto producers "conspired not to compete in research, development, manufacture, and installation of [pollution] control devices, and did all in their power to delay such research, development, manufacturing, and installation."[20]

When the government promulgated auto-emission standards in the 1970s, the industry insisted that the regulations were technologically impossible to meet—despite the fact that Honda and other foreign producers subsequently introduced redesigned engines that combined high performance with low exhaust emissions, without the need for costly, complicated catalytic converters. When the Big Three finally responded, however, they chose the catalytic converter as the centerpiece for their approach—an approach that the National Academy of Science characterized as "the most disadvantageous with respect to first cost, fuel economy, maintainability, and durability." Said the Academy: "It is unfortunate that the automobile industry did not seriously undertake such a [pollution control] program on its own volition until it was subjected to governmental pressure. A relatively modest investment, over the past decade, in developmental programs related to emission control could have precluded the crisis that now prevails in the industry and the nation. The current crash programs of the major manufacturers have turned out to be expensive and, in retrospect, not well planned."[21]

2. Automotive Safety. "In 1965," a Senate Committee reported, "49,000 persons lost their lives in highway accidents, 1,500,000 suffered disabling injuries, and an equal number suffered non-disabling injuries. Economic costs of highway accidents which can be tabulated for the same year aggregated $8.5 billion. Since the introduction of the automobile in the United States, more Americans have lost their lives from highway accidents than all the combat deaths suffered by America in all our wars."[22]

Although a variety of factors (road design, weather conditions, reckless and drunk driving) influence automobile safety, it is incontrovertible that the design of the automobile itself plays a major role in the carnage on the nation's roads and highways. Nevertheless, for a long time the industry seemed casually indifferent to the problem. Patents awarded to the auto companies in the 1920s and 1930s for such safety features as padded dashboards and collapsible steering wheels were shelved for decades, until their incorporation in automobiles was mandated by government decree. As automobiles became progressively more dangerous in design over the postwar period, the industry insisted that safety should be optional, supplied only in response to consumer demand and preference. Yet it steadfastly refused to make available the safety information essential to informed consumer decision making. The industry spent hundreds of millions of dollars extolling raw horsepower and rocket acceleration and then hid behind its slogan, "Safety don't sell"—despite evidence to the contrary.[23]

An explanation for the industry's lackluster performance, once again, may be rooted in oligopolistic interdependence among the Big Three. As former GM president Alfred Sloan once put it, "I feel that General Motors should not adopt safety glass for its cars. I can only see competition being forced into the same position. Our gain would be purely a temporary one and the net results would be that both competition and ourselves would have reduced the return on our capital and the public would have obtained still more value per dollar expended."[24]

Eventually, the protracted battles over safety produced results. The Big Three conceded the importance of safety belts and, in 1988, announced their intention to begin installing safety bags as standard equipment.

3. Automotive Fuel Consumption. The fuel economy of automobiles decisively affects the nation's petroleum consumption and thus significantly influences national dependence on geopolitically volatile foreign petroleum supplies.

In characteristic fashion, the industry considered neither the fuel efficiency of its products nor finite domestic petroleum supplies to be pressing concerns. It ignored warnings, even when sounded by responsible officials within the industry itself. Instead, the industry absolved itself of responsibility as it had done in pollution and safety matters. The general manager of GM's Buick division was asked in 1958 what steps his division was taking in the area of fuel efficiency. "Oh," he flippantly replied, "we're helping the gas companies, the same as our competitors."[25] Likewise, the domestic oligopoly seemed uninterested in engine innovations (including alternative power plants) capable of enhancing fuel economy. During Congressional hearings conducted in 1973, a parade of inventors, scientists, and engineers testified to the companies' indifference. "I was assured in the first meetings with the Big Four in Detroit that what they would like to do with [fuel-efficient engine design] is put it into a 20- or 30-year development program," said one. "I told them I would rather do it next year in Japan, and I meant that very seriously."[26]

As a consequence of the industry's nonchalant attitude, the fuel efficiency of U.S. automobiles steadily worsened from 1958 to 1973—primarily due to the bloated size and weight of the cars the industry produced in its race for styling supremacy. Ironically, this made the industry especially vulnerable to the flood of fuel-efficient imports that swamped the American market in the wake of periodic gasoline shortages and skyrocketing fuel prices. Indeed, as *Fortune* points out, had the government not imposed fuel economy standards on the industry, the auto companies "might have been even less prepared than they were for the . . . swing in customer preferences to small cars."[27]

V.
PUBLIC POLICY

In this final section we shall examine public policy toward the automobile industry in three major areas: antitrust; protection from foreign competition; and government efforts to regulate automotive air pollution, safety, and fuel economy.

Antitrust

The bulk of the antitrust suits in the industry have been tangential and peripheral in nature; they have never challenged the structurally rooted market power of the automobile oligopoly. In fact, the only structural antitrust case brought by the government against GM's automotive operations was filed forty years ago and was directed against the firm's GMAC new-car financing subsidiary.

Other antitrust cases have dealt with only isolated aspects of noncompetitive conduct in the industry. For example, the government charged GM and Ford with collusive pricing, but only in the fleet market for new cars sold to businesses and rental-car agencies. In another case, it charged the auto companies with unlawfully conspiring to eliminate competition, but only in the pollution-control field. Of late, the government has abandoned even these pusillanimous antitrust forays; instead it has encouraged the rash of joint ventures and cross-ownership arrangements between the domestic oligopoly and its major foreign rivals (such as GM–Toyota) which, as we have seen, pose serious anticompetitive problems. Moreover, in what might be considered "failing-company" antitrust, the government has engineered the Chrysler bailout, in part to prevent the automobile triopoly from degenerating into a duopoly.

Protection from Foreign Competition

As we have seen, in the post-World War II period a recognition of (and respect for) the mutual oligopolistic interdependence between the domestic auto companies became solidified. This, together with the protection afforded by formidable entry barriers, insulated the domestic industry from effective competition. Noncompetitive conduct, including tacit vertical collusion between management and organized labor and steady price–wage–price escalation, flourished in this cozy noncompetitive environment.

Initially dismissed as an anomaly, foreign competition eventually began to disturb this oligopolistic *bonhomie*, and this made it imperative for the domestic producers to obtain government protection from imports. Accordingly, starting in 1974, management and labor began to lobby for protection. Their efforts were crowned with success when, starting in 1981, the government persuaded the Japanese to accept voluntary import quotas. These "temporary" quotas, designed to give domestic producers "breathing space," were renewed in 1983 and formally expired in March 1985—only to be replaced by a quota system promulgated by the Japanese government. Since then, U.S. producers, led by Ford, have urged further reductions in Japanese imports in order to "offset" expanding Japanese auto production in U.S. assembly plants. In their continuing battle against imports, they have also charged foreign producers with "dumping" compact pickup trucks in the U.S. market—even as sales of their own compact pickup models increased sharply, and even as the Big Three themselves are procuring ever greater quantities of foreign-produced automotive parts.

By creating an artificial scarcity, the "voluntary" quotas have dramatically driven up the prices of Japanese cars. The rise in Japanese prices, in turn, has permitted domestic producers to push through sizable price boosts of their own. According to industry experts, 1983 new-car prices (both foreign and domestic) rose $800 to $1,000 as a direct consequence of import quotas; additional dealer markups on some Japanese models reportedly rose as much as $2,600. In the aggregate, "protection" from foreign competition is estimated to have cost American car buyers $15.7 billion in artificially inflated new-car prices.[28] Moreover, the quotas have effectively cartelized Japanese production by allocating—via government fiat—quota shares among Japanese competitors in the U.S. market. And, ironically, numerical restrictions impelled Japanese producers to upgrade their offerings and to invade the vast midsize region of the market, where they now pose a much greater threat to the domestic oligopoly.

Regulation: Safety, Pollution, and Fuel Economy

Have government's attempts to regulate automobile safety, pollution, and fuel consumption been too costly in comparison with the benefits obtained? Is it true, as the industry generally maintains, that "excessive" regulation "adds unnecessary costs for consumers, lowers profits, diverts manpower from research and development programs, and reduces productivity—all at a time when our resources are desperately needed to meet the stiff competition from abroad"?[29] Or is it a fact, as Henry Ford II has conceded, that "We wouldn't have had the kinds of safety built into automobiles that we have had unless there had been a Federal law. We wouldn't have had the fuel economy unless there had been a Federal law, and there wouldn't have been the emission control unless there had been a Federal law."[30]

Regulation of safety is prototypical of the problem. Responding to the "grim roll of Americans lost and maimed on the nation's highways," disturbed by "evidence of the automobile industry's chronic subordination of safe design to promotional styling," as well as the industry's "laxity in furnishing adequate notification to car owners of latent defects which had crept into the manufacturing process — defects frequently directly related to safety," Congress concluded in 1966 that "the promotion of motor vehicle safety through voluntary standards has largely failed. The unconditional imposition of mandatory standards at the earliest practicable date is the only course commensurate with the highway death and injury toll."[31] Congress therefore enacted the Motor Safety Act, which directed the Secretary of Commerce (and later, the Secretary of Transportation), in conjunction with what would become the National Highway Traffic Safety Administration (NHTSA), to research, promulgate, and enforce motor vehicle safety standards. The Act prohibits the sale of any vehicle not in conformity with these standards; it provides penalties in the form of fines; it provides for the recall and repair by the manufacturer of cars later determined to be unsafe in operation; and it mandates that producers maintain records and information necessary to determine compliance with the standards promulgated.

Air-pollution and fuel-economy regulations are based on a similar rationale — that is, the finding that voluntary industry efforts are inadequate for the task at hand. Nevertheless, some have argued that less direct forms of regulation — for example, "incentive-based" measures, featuring taxes or "fees" imposed on the sale of unsafe, polluting, gas-guzzling cars — would be preferable. Such proposals are attractive to economists who are congenitally sympathetic to market-oriented solutions. But is it realistic to assume that government would impose penalties, fines, or mass recalls if to do so would jeopardize the financial viability of a General Motors, a Ford, or a Chrysler? Would the government ever consider shutting down GM, for example, if the firm failed to meet emission standards, safety requirements, or fuel-economy regulations? Conversely, given their size and political influence, would not a threat by any of the Big Three to shut down almost inevitably compel government to grant delays, extensions, exemptions, and so on?[32] In short, whether direct or "incentive-based," regulatory policy is bedeviled by the same problem: the labor – industrial bigness complex that dominates the U.S. auto industry.

VI.

CONCLUSION

Our study of the American automobile oligopoly highlights the crucial effect of industry structure on corporate behavior and economic performance. It underscores the perennial public-policy dilemma of deciding whether (to borrow a phrase from former GM president Charles E. Wilson) what is good for GM is necessarily good for the country.

NOTES

1. Allan Nevins, *Ford: The Times, the Man, the Company* (New York: Scribner's, 1954), p. 493.

2. Eric J. Toder, *Trade Policy and the U.S. Automobile Industry* (New York: Praeger, 1978), p. 133.

3. Lawrence J. White, "The Automobile Industry," in Walter Adams (ed.), *The Structure of American Industry*, 6th ed. (New York: Macmillan, 1982).

4. *Business Week* (March 16, 1987), p. 110.

5. U.S. Department of Transportation, *The U.S. Automobile Industry, 1980* (Washington, D.C.: 1981), p. 66.

6. *The Wall Street Journal*, August 3, 1983, p. 1.

7. U.S. Congress, House, Subcommittee on Monopolies and Commercial Law, *Corporate Initiative: Hearings*, 97th Cong., 1st sess., 1982, pp. 40–41.

8. This account is drawn from Lawrence J. White, "The American Automobile Industry and the Small Car, 1945–70," *Journal of Industrial Economics* 20 (1972), p. 179; Brock Yates, *The Decline and Fall of the American Automobile Industry* (New York: Vintage, 1984), Chap. 3; and Paul Blumberg, "Snarling Cars," *The New Republic* (January 24, 1983).

9. A small, light-weight car developed by GM was marketed in Australia in 1948 by a GM subsidiary; Ford's light car appeared the same year, as the French Ford Vedette.

10. Interview, *The Washington Post*, July 7, 1985.

11. Quoted in *Business Month* (June 1988), p. 14.

12. *Fortune* (November 10, 1986), p. 57.

13. Quoted in J. Patrick Wright, *On a Clear Day You Can See General Motors* (Grosse Pointe, Mich.: Wright, 1979), p. 100.

14. U.S. Congress, House, Subcommittee on Economic Stabilization, *The Chrysler Corporation Financial Situation: Hearings*, part 1A, 96th Cong., 1st sess., 1979, p. 557.

15. David Halberstam, *The Reckoning* (New York: Morrow, 1986), pp. 244–45.

16. Wright, p. 4.

17. Yates, p. 149.

18. William J. Abernathy, Kim B. Clark, and Alan M. Kantrow, *Industrial Renaissance* (New York: Basic, 1983), pp. 76, 78.

19. See U.S. Congress, Senate, Subcommittee on Air and Water Pollution, *Air Pollution—1967: Hearings*, part 1, 90th Cong., 1st sess., 1967, p. 158. GM was sufficiently concerned about automotive air pollution to begin researching the problem at least as early as 1938. See "Smog Control Antitrust Case," *Congressional Record* (May 18, 1971), pp. 15626–27 (House ed.).

20. "Smog Control Antitrust Case," *Congressional Record* (May 18, 1971), p. 15627 (House ed.).

21. National Academy of Sciences, Report by the Committee on Motor Vehicle Emissions, February 12, 1973, reprinted in *Congressional Record* (February 28, 1973), pp. 5832, 5849 (Senate ed.).

22. U.S. Congress, Senate, Committee on Commerce, *Traffic Safety Act of 1966: Report*, 89th Cong., 2nd sess., 1966, pp. 2–3.

23. John Jerome found in his study of the industry that Ford was overwhelmed by the unexpectedly strong demand for safety options offered in some of its 1956 models. Jerome, *The Death of the Automobile* (New York: Norton, 1972), p. 273. Yet, Ford's president, Robert S. McNamara, canceled the safety package—perhaps, some suggest, because of pressure exerted by General Motors. See Lee Iacocca, *Iacocca* (New York: Bantam, 1984), p. 296.

24. U.S. Congress, Senate, Select Committee on Small Business, *Planning, Regulation, and Competition—Automobile Industry: Hearings,* 90th Cong., 2d sess., 1968, p. 967. For example, Ford remained silent after discovering (through its own internal testing) the dangerous design of GM's infamous Corvair; Ford's reticence seems, in part, to have been motivated by a desire to maintain cordial relations with its dominant rival. See Ed Cray, *Chrome Colossus* (New York: McGraw-Hill, 1980), p. 409.

25. John Keats, *The Insolent Chariots* (New York: Lippincott, 1958), p. 14. Only months before the first OPEC oil embargo of 1973, GM's chairman suggested more rapid licensing of nuclear power plants as a good means for dealing with the nation's energy problem. One month before the overthrow of the Shah in 1979, and the onset of the nation's second oil crisis in six years, GM took the position that auto "fuel-economy standards are not necessary and they are not good for America." See U.S. Congress, Senate, Committee on Commerce, *Automotive Research and Development and Fuel Economy: Hearings,* 93rd Cong., 1st sess., 1973, p. 564; Cray, p. 524.

26. *Automotive Research and Development Hearings,* p. 70.

27. *Fortune* (October 22, 1979), p. 48.

28. See Robert W. Crandall, "Import Quotas and the Automobile Industry: The Costs of Protectionism," *Brookings Review* (Summer 1984); *The New York Times,* April 8, 1984, sec. 3, p. 1; U.S. International Trade Commission, *A Review of Recent Developments in the U.S. Automobile Industry, Including an Assessment of the Japanese Voluntary Restraint Agreements* (Washington, D.C.: 1985).

29. U.S. Congress, House, Committee on Government Operations, *The Administration's Proposals to Help the U.S. Auto Industry: Hearings,* 97th Cong., 1st sess., 1981, p. 129.

30. Quoted in U.S. Congress, Senate, Subcommittee for Consumers, *Costs of Government Regulations to the Consumer: Hearings,* 95th Cong., 2d sess., 1978, p. 87.

31. *Traffic Safety of 1966: Report,* pp. 1–4.

32. On this problem generally, see Walter Adams and James W. Brock, "Corporate Power and Economic Sabotage," *Journal of Economic Issues,* 20 (December 1986), p. 919.

SUGGESTED READINGS

Books

Automotive News. *Market Data Book* (annual).

Cole, R. *The Japanese Automobile Industry: Model and Challenge for the Future?* Ann Arbor, Mich.: University of Michigan Press, 1981.

Crandall, R. W., et al. *Regulating the Automobile.* Washington, D.C.: Brookings Institution, 1986.

Cray, E. *Chrome Colossus.* New York: McGraw-Hill, 1980.

Cusumano, M. A. *The Japanese Automobile Industry.* Cambridge, Mass.: Harvard University Press, 1985.

Ford, H. *My Life and Work.* New York: Doubleday, 1926.

Halberstam, D. *The Reckoning.* New York: Morrow, 1986.

Lee, A. *Call Me Roger.* Chicago: Contemporary Books, 1988.

Levin, Doron F. *Irreconcilable Differences: Ross Perot versus General Motors.* Boston, Mass.: Little Brown & Co., 1989.

Nader, R. *Unsafe at Any Speed.* New York: Grossman, 1965.

National Academy of Engineering. *Competitive Status of the U.S. Auto Industry.* Washington, D.C.: National Academy Press, 1982.

Reich, R. B., and J. D. Donahue. *New Deals: The Chrysler Revival and the American System.* New York Times, 1985.

Report of MIT International Automobile Program. *The Future of the Automobile.* Cambridge, Mass.: MIT Press, 1984.

Sloan, A. P. *My Years with General Motors.* New York: Doubleday, 1965.

Ward's Automotive Yearbook (annual).

White, L. J. *The Automobile Industry Since 1945.* Cambridge, Mass.: Harvard University Press, 1971.

Wright, J. P. *On a Clear Day You Can See General Motors.* Grosse Pointe, Mich.: Wright, 1979.

Yates, B. *The Decline and Fall of the American Automobile Industry.* New York: Vintage, 1984.

Articles

Adams, W., and J. W. Brock. "Tacit Vertical Collusion and the Labor–Industrial Complex," *Nebraska Law Review* 62, Fall 1983.

Boyle, S. E., and T. F. Hogarty. "Pricing Behavior in the American Automobile Industry, 1957–71," *Journal of Industrial Economics* 24, December 1975.

Bussey, J. "Did U.S. Car Makers Err by Raising Prices When the Yen Rose?" *The Wall Street Journal,* April 18, 1988, p. 1.

Claybrook, J., and D. Bollier. "The Hidden Benefits of Regulation: Disclosing the Auto Safety Payoff," *Yale Journal on Regulation* 3, 1985.

Fisher, F. M., Z. Griliches, and C. Kaysen. "The Costs of Automobile Model Changes Since 1949," *Journal of Political Economy* 70, October 1962.

Flint, J. "Best Car Wins," *Forbes,* January 27, 1986.

Hampton, W., and J. Norman. "General Motors: What Went Wrong," *Business Week,* March 16, 1987.

Hoffer, G. "Auto Recalls and Sales," *Challenge* 26, October 1983.

Kwoka, J. E. "Market Power and Market Change in the U.S. Automobile Industry," *Journal of Industrial Economics* 32, January 1984.

Note, "Annual Style Change in the Automobile Industry as an Unfair Method of Competition," *Yale Law Journal* 80, January 1971.

CHAPTER 5

THE BEER INDUSTRY

Kenneth G. Elzinga

I.

INTRODUCTION

In 1620, as every youngster knows, the Pilgrims landed at Plymouth Rock. Less commonly known is that the Pilgrims set sail for Virginia, not Massachusetts. What led them to change their minds? One of the voyagers recorded the following entry in his diary: "Our victuals are being much spente, especially our beere." The voyage was cut short because of a shortage of "beere." One can only speculate about the effect on American history if the *Mayflower*'s beer had not run low. Speculation is not required, however, in ascertaining the structure and level of competition in the beer industry today. Economic analysis provides some answers.

Definition of the Industry

Beer is a potable product with four main ingredients.

1. Malt, which is a grain (usually barley) that has been allowed to germinate in water and is then dried.
2. Flavoring adjuncts, usually hops and corn or rice, which give beer its lightness and provide the starch that the enzymes in the malt convert to sugar.
3. Cultured yeast, which ferments the beverage and feeds on the sugar content of the malt to produce alcohol and carbonic acid.
4. Water, which acts as a solvent for the other ingredients.

Because the process of brewing (or boiling) is intrinsic to the making of beer, the industry often is called the brewing industry.

All beers are not the same. The white beverage (spiced with a little raspberry syrup) that is favored in Berlin; the warm, dark-colored drink served by the English publican; and the amber liquid kept at near-freezing temperatures in the cooler of the American convenience store are all beer. Generically, the term *beer* means any beverage brewed from a starch (or farinaceous) grain. Because the grain is made into a malt that becomes the main substance of the beverage, another term for beer is *malt liquor*, or malt beverage. In this study, the terms *beer, malt liquor*, and *malt beverage* are used interchangeably to include all such products as beer, ale, light beer, porter, stout, and malt liquor. The factor common to the beverages of this industry, and that which differentiates them from other alcoholic and nonalcoholic beverages, is the brewing by a process of fermentation applied to a basic grain ingredient.

Beer's unique production process is not, however, the key to defining it as a market. The concept of a market entails a group of firms (or conceivably one firm) supplying products that consumers, voting in the marketplace, find to be close substitutes for each other. Some avid drinkers of the product beer may not prefer to substitute, say, the product ale; but they would prefer to substitute milk even less. The cross-elasticity of demand is high between malt beverages, and the cross-elasticity of demand between beer and other alcoholic beverages, for most customers, is lower.[1] It is this fungibility characteristic that distinguishes malt beverages as a separate industry. The delineation is supported by the high cross-elasticity of supply between different types of malt beverages and the low cross-elasticity of supply between malt beverages and all other beverages, including wine, wine coolers, and distilled spirits.

Early History

Beer was a very common beverage in England in the 1600s and among the early settlers in America. In 1625, the first recorded public brewery was established in New Amsterdam (now New York City). Other commercial brewing followed, although considerable brewing was done in homes in seventeenth-century America. All the equipment that was needed at the time was a few vats, one for mashing, one for cooling, and one for fermenting. The resulting product would not be recognized (or consumed) as beer today. The process was very crude, the end result uncertain. Brewing was referred to as "an art and mystery."

Brewing was encouraged in early America. For example, the General Court of Massachusetts passed an act in 1789 to support the brewing of beer "as an important means of preserving the health of the citizens . . . and of preventing the pernicious effects of spiritous liquors." James Oglethorpe, trustee of the colony of Georgia, was even blunter: "Cheap beer is the only means to keep rum out."

Lager Beer: The Jumping-Off Point

The 1840s and 1850s were important decades in the growth of the industry. The product beer, as it is generally known today, was introduced in the 1840s with the brewing of lager beer.[2] Before lager beers, malt beverage consumption in America resembled English tastes — heavily oriented toward ale, porter, and stout. Lager beer represented the influence of German tastes and brewing skills. The influx of German immigrants provided not only skillful brewers but also eager customers for this type of beer. At the start of the decade in 1850, there were 431 brewers in the United States producing 750,000 barrels of beer.[3] By the end of that decade, 1,269 brewers produced more than a million barrels of beer — evidence of the bright future expected by many for this industry.

The latter half of the nineteenth century saw not only the successful introduction of lager beer in America but also the adoption of technological advances in production and marketing. Mechanical refrigeration greatly aided the production process as well as the storage of beer. Prior to this development, beer production was partly dependent on the amount of ice that could be cut from lakes and rivers in the winter. Cities such as St. Louis, which had underground caves where beer could be kept cool while aging, lost this (truly natural) advantage with the advent of mechanical refrigeration. Pasteurization, a process originally devised to preserve wine and beer, not milk, was adopted during this period. Beer no longer had to be kept cold; it could be shipped into warm climates and stored for a longer period of time without refermenting. Once beer was pasteurized, the way was opened for wide-scale bottling and the off-premise consumption of beer. In addition, developments in transportation enabled brewers to sell output beyond their local markets. The twentieth century saw the rise of the national brewer.

Prohibition

The twentieth century also saw the outlawing of beer sales. The temperance movement, which began by promoting voluntary moderation and abstention from hard liquors, veered toward a goal of universal compulsory abstention from all alcoholic beverages. The beer industry seemed blissfully ignorant of this. Many brewers thought (or hoped) the temperance movement would ban only liquor.

In 1919, 36 states ratified the Eighteenth Amendment to enact the national prohibition of alcoholic beverages. This led many brewers to close up shop; some produced products such as candy and ice cream. Anheuser–Busch and others built a profitable business selling malt syrup, which was used to make "home brew." Because a firm could not state the ultimate purpose of malt syrup, the product was marketed as an ingredient for making baked goods, such as cookies.

Prohibition lasted until April 1933, and the rapidity with which brewers reopened after repeal was amazing. By June 1933, 31 brewers were in operation; in another year, the number of brewers had risen to 756.

The Demand for Beer in the Post-World War II Period

Nationally, the market demand for beer began a slow decline in 1948 from a 1947 record sale of 87.2 million barrels. During this period, per capita consumption of beer fell from 18.5 gallons in 1947 to 15.0 gallons in 1958. It was not until 1959 that sales surpassed the 1947 total.

In the 1960s and 1970s total demand began to grow again at an average rate of better than 3 percent per year. The year 1965 marked the first year in which more than 100 million barrels were sold. Per capita consumption of beer increased from 1958's level of 15 gallons to a level of 24 gallons by the end of the seventies. The rightward shift in the demand curve for beer was the result of the increasing number of young people in the United States (the result of the post-World War II baby boom), the lowering of age requirements for drinking in many populous states, and the enhanced acceptability of beer among females. Moreover, the number of areas in the United States that were "dry" shrank considerably.

In the 1980s, the market demand for beer stabilized. Demographic patterns reversed themselves as the pool of young people (18–34 years of age) declined. States escalated their minimum age requirements for the purchase of alcoholic beverages to 21 years. Other factors that have cut into demand include the pursuit of physical fitness and the increasing concern with alcohol abuse, particularly drunk driving. In some states laws restraining the use of one-way containers may have reduced consumption.

The total market demand for beer exhibits seasonal fluctuations as a result of greater thirsts during hot weather. The demand for beer in the United States also varies from region to region. The mountain and west south central states show the highest per capita consumption; the east south central and Middle Atlantic states show the lowest. By states, the demand for beer differs considerably. Oklahoma and Utah had per capita consumption of 18 and 13 gallons in 1987, respectively, while Nevada leads all others with a per capita consumption of over 38 gallons. The Nevada figure is biased by beer-quaffing tourists. The highest per capita consumption by natives of a state probably occurs in Wisconsin.

Although economists are not able to measure price elasticity infallibly, statistical estimations indicate the market demand for beer to be inelastic — in the range of 0.7 to 0.9. However, brand attachment for most beer drinkers is not so strong as to make the demand for any particular malt beverage inelastic. Indeed, the demand for individual brands of beer appears to be quite elastic.[4] This elasticity places an important limitation on the market power of domestic brewers.

One indication of how responsive beer consumers are to price changes is provided in the records of a price discrimination case that is discussed later. Table 5-1 shows, for St. Louis on various dates, the percentage of beer sales

Table 5-1.

Percentage of the St. Louis Market Recorded by Anheuser–Busch

Brewer	December 1953	June 1954	March 1955	July 1956
Anheuser–Busch	12.5	16.6	39.3	21.0
Griesedieck Bros.	14.4	12.6	4.8	7.4
Falstaff	29.4	32.0	29.1	36.6.
Griesedieck Western	38.9	33.0	23.1	27.8
Others	4.8	5.8	3.9	7.2

Source: Taken from *Federal Trade Commission* v. *Anheuser–Busch*, 363 U.S. 536 at 541. Subsequent evidence indicated that factors in addition to price accounted for the Griesedieck Bros. drop in market share.

of Anheuser-Busch, three important rivals, and the remaining sellers. At the end of 1953, Anheuser-Busch's Budweiser brand was selling for 58 cents per case more than the three rivals and has 12.5 per cent of the sales. Early in 1954, Budweiser's price was cut 25 cents, and Anheuser-Busch's share increased. In June 1954, Anheuser-Busch reduced its price again, this time to the level of the three rivals, and became the largest selling beer in St. Louis. But after price increases by all sellers that left Budweiser at 30 cents more per case than its rivals, Anheuser-Busch's share dropped—evidence that consumers shift brands in response to price incentives.

There are many contemporary illustrations of the high elasticity of demand for individual brands of beer. When Stroh cut the price of its Schaefer brand in Ohio, this provoked a sizable increase in the quantity demanded. Heileman had a similar experience in other parts of the country with price reductions on its Carling Black Label brand. But when Heileman attempted (unsuccessfully) to raise the price of its Old Style brand in the Midwest (where in some cities it was the leading seller), many of its customers switched to rival brands.

II.

MARKET STRUCTURE

According to economic theory, when consumers face a monopolist (or tightly knit oligopoly), the price they pay is likely to be elevated. For this reason, the size distribution of brewing firms arrayed before consumers is of economic importance. Is the beer industry unconcentrated, with its customers courted by many firms, or is it concentrated, leaving beer drinkers with little choice?

In the post-World War II period, two contrary trends have been at work in the industry, one leading to increased concentration, the other in the opposite direction. On the one hand, there has been a marked decline in the number of brewers in the United States. At the same time, there has been an increase in the size of the market area that is potentially served by existing brewers.

The Decline in Numbers

The decline in the number of individual plants and independent companies in the brewing industry has been dramatic. In 1935, shortly after repeal, 750 brewing plants were operating in the United States. Since that time, the number of brewing plants has declined to a total of 67 in 1986. Table 5-2 shows the decline in the number of beer companies and plants. In the period shown, the number of companies dropped over 90 percent (although beer sales doubled). Few, if any, American industries have undergone a similar structural shakeup.

Along with the decline in the number of companies, there has been an increasing share of the market held by the largest brewers. As shown in Table 5-3, in 1947, the top five companies accounted for only 19 percent of the industry's barrelage; in 1987 their share was 88 percent. Another way of summarizing the distribution of firm size is to compute the Herfindahl index (also shown in Table 5-3). It is the sum of the individual sellers' market shares squared (its maximum value is 10,000, with one firm in the market). The rising Herfindahl also testifies to the industry's structural transformation. Whereas some industry observers speak of the big five (Anheuser–Busch, Miller, Stroh, Coors, and Heileman in 1987 order), one might refer to the big

Table 5-2. _____

Company and Plant Concentration, 1947–1986

Year	Independent Companies[a]	Separate Plants[a]
1947	404	465
1954	262	310
1958	211	252
1963	150	211
1967	124	153
1974	57	107
1978	44	96
1983	35	73
1986	33	67

[a]Excludes microbreweries of less than 10,000-barrel capacity.

Source: Adapted from *Breweries Authorized to Operate*, Department of the Treasury, Bureau of Alcohol, Tobacco, and Firearms (Washington, D.C.: U.S. Government Printing Office, various years); *Modern Brewery Age, Blue Book* (Stamford, Conn.: Modern Brewery Age Publishing Co., various years); and *The Brewing Industry*, Staff Report of the Federal Trade Commission, Bureau of Economics (Washington, D.C.: U.S. Government Printing Office, 1978).

Table 5-3.
Concentration of Sales by Top Brewers

Year	Five Largest	Ten Largest	Herfindahl Index
1947	19.0%	28.2%	140
1954	24.9	38.3	240
1958	28.5	45.2	310
1964	39.0	58.2	440
1968	47.6	63.2	690
1974	64.0	80.8	1080
1978	74.3	92.3	1292
1981	75.9	93.9	1614
1984	87.3	94.2	1938
1987	87.9	93.9	2280

Source: Adapted from A. Horowitz and I. Horowitz, "The Beer Industry," *Business Horizons*, 10:14 (1967), various issues of *Modern Brewery Age*, and Beer Marketer's Insights *1988 Beer Industry Update*.

two, since Anheuser–Busch and Miller in 1987 held over 60 percent of the national market.

The Widening of Markets

The decline in the number of brewing companies can be misleading. In the days of hundreds of brewing companies, most beer drinkers still faced an actual choice of only a few brewers. Most brewers were small, and the geographic area they served was severely limited. Beer is an expensive product to ship, relative to its value, and few brewers could afford to compete in the "home markets" of distant rivals.

Thus, at one time it was very meaningful to speak of local, regional, and national brewers. Of these, the local brewer who brewed for a small market, perhaps smaller than a single state and often only a single metropolitan area, was the most common. The regional brewer was multistate, but usually encompassed no more than two or three states. The national brewers, those selling in all (or almost all) states, were very few. In addition, it was uncommon for a firm to operate more than one plant.

Today, the terms *local, regional* and *national brewers* are less meaningful. The average geographic market served by one brewer from one plant has widened because of the economies of large-scale production and, to some extent, marketing. With the average-size brewing plant much larger today, the brewing company may extend itself geographically to maintain capacity operations.[5] The premier example of this is the Adolph Coors Company, which reaches customers on the Eastern seaboard from its single brewing plant in Colorado. But it does so at a significant transportation cost disadvantage.

A second factor extending the reach of large brewers to serve new geographic regions is their propensity to operate more than one plant. In 1959, the top 10 brewers operated 34 breweries. By 1987, they operated 43.

Size of the Market

Determining the degree of market concentration in brewing entails knowing how wide the geographic markets are for beer. If there is one market, a national one, then concentration statistics for the entire nation are relevant. But if brewing, like cement or milk, has regional markets, then delineating their boundaries is necessary before the industry's structure can be ascertained.

The federal courts have to solve this problem when deciding antimerger cases in the brewing industry. A couple of examples taken from these attempts indicate that to understand the supply and demand forces in this industry, one must look to a wide geographic market, but possibly not so wide as to include the entire country.

In evaluating the merger of the Joseph Schlitz Brewing Company with a California brewer and its stock control over another western brewer, a California district court, noting that freight rates were important in beer marketing, singled out an eight-western-state area as a separate geographic market.[6] The judge was impressed by the fact that, in 1963, 80 percent of the beer sold in this area was also produced there and 94 percent of the beer produced in the area that year was sold there. The Continental Divide was seen as a transportation barrier of sorts from outside the area, as evidenced by those brewers who, having plants both in the eight-state area and outside, generally supplied the eight-state area from their western plants only.

Given these figures, many economists would agree that if one wants to understand what determines the supply and demand for beer in this eight-state area, one might be able to ignore what is happening in the regions east of the Continental Divide. After all, a market, in its economic sense, should include only buyers and sellers who are important in explaining the supply-and-demand conditions in any one place. But even here the geographic area is not perfectly clear cut. Coors, located outside the eight-state area, was the leading seller of beer in the eight-state area in 1963, with 13.6 percent of the total sales. Any market area that overlooks this important seller neglects an important force on the supply side. By 1980, 38 percent of the beer consumed in the eight-western-state area was imported from outside.

In another case involving the merger of two brewers located in Wisconsin, the Antitrust Division asked an eminent economist at nearby Northwestern University to testify in support of the view that Wisconsin was a separate market for beer. The economics professor told the government lawyers that this position was economically untenable. Nevertheless, the lawyers persisted in this view without him and eventually persuaded the Supreme Court that

Wisconsin, by itself, is "a distinguishable and economically significant market for the sale of beer."[7]

Although Wisconsin was held to have been a separate market for legal purposes, to single it out as a market in the economic sense is to draw the market boundaries too narrowly. In 1978, brewers in the state of Wisconsin sold 21.3 million barrels of beer; that year, consumers in Wisconsin bought 4.8 million barrels of beer.

Because beer is also "imported" into Wisconsin from brewers in other states, obviously more than three-fourths of Wisconsin beer is "exported" for sale outside the state. To say that Wisconsin is a separate geographic market is to overlook the impact of over three-fourths of the production of beer in that state, not to mention the impact on the supply of beer coming into Wisconsin and competing with the "home" brewers. In 1961, the time of the antitrust contest, roughly 25 percent of the beer consumed in Wisconsin was not produced there.

Consequently, one cannot explain the price of beer in Wisconsin without looking at the supply-and-demand conditions in other states whose citizens consume the bulk of Wisconsin's beer production. In this case, the court erred by singling out Wisconsin as an economically meaningful market.

Despite the difficulties of ascertaining with numerical exactness the geographic scope of the brewing industry, brewing *is* a concentrated industry, more concentrated than the average food and tobacco industry.[8] In most states the forces that work to widen markets have been more than offset by the forces that increase concentration.

Reasons for the Decline in the Number of Brewers

What explains the precipitous drop in the number of brewing companies? In a sense, each brewer's demise is unique, but many have common characteristics. In this section, two possible explanations are considered: mergers and economies of scale. In a later section, the effect on the industry's structure of entry conditions, product differentiation, and the conglomerate nature of one leading brewer is assessed.

Mergers

A common explanation for an industry's oligopolization is a merger–acquisition trend among the industry's firms. In the period 1950–1983 there were about 170 horizontal mergers in the beer industry.[9] From this it might seem that mergers are the primary cause of the rising concentration in this industry. But corporate marriages between rival brewers do not explain the increase in concentration by the largest firms. It will prove instructive to review the merger track record of the top five brewers (as of this writing).

The first antimerger action by the Antitrust Division in the beer industry was taken in 1958 against the industry's leader, Anheuser–Busch.

Anheuser–Busch had purchased the Miami brewery of American Brewing Company. The government successfully argued that this merger would eliminate American Brewing as an independent brewer and end its rivalry with Anheuser–Busch in Florida. The final judgment called for Anheuser–Busch to sell this brewery and refrain from buying any other breweries without court approval for a period of five years. As a result of this action, Anheuser–Busch forsook any policy of acquiring rival brewers and instead began an extensive program of building large, efficient plants in Florida and at other locations. Anheuser–Busch deviated from its internal growth policy in 1980 when it purchased for $100 million the modern Baldwinsville, N.Y., brewing plant of the Schlitz Brewing Company. Schlitz's sales had declined so much that it did not need the brewery; the plant's capacity was so huge that only an industry leader could absorb its output.

The second largest brewer, Miller, purchased brewing plants in Texas and California in 1966 but acquired no other breweries until 1987, when Miller acquired a small family-run brewery in Wisconsin. In 1972 Miller acquired three brand names from a bankrupt brewer, and in 1974 it bought the rights for the domestic manufacturing and marketing of a prominent German beer. The latter acquisition was unsuccessfully challenged by a private antitrust plaintiff, Miller's only encounter with the antimerger law. The Miller Brewing Company itself, however, was the subject of a conglomerate acquisition by the Philip Morris tobacco company in 1970. The consequences of this merger are discussed in a later section.

The third-ranking firm, Stroh, acquired the F. M. Schaefer Brewing Company in 1980. This did not significantly affect its rank (it was then the seventh largest brewer). But in 1982, Stroh acquired the Joseph Schlitz Brewing Company, itself in a sales tailspin, and at the time the fourth largest brewer. This catapulted Stroh to number three in the industry. The Antitrust Division, in consenting to the merger, required Stroh to divest a brewery in the Southeast. Stroh complied by exchanging its Tampa plant for a brewery in St. Paul, Minnesota, owned by Pabst.

Fourth-ranked Coors has never acquired another brewer. Its stated policy has been to brew its beer only in one location, Golden, Colorado; but Coors does ship beer by tankers to Virginia, where it is bottled and canned for sale in the East.

The G. Heileman Brewing Company, the industry's fifth-ranking firm, is the product of over a dozen acquisitions from 1960 to the present, notably Wiedemann, Associated Brewing, the Blatz brand, Rainier, Carling, and portions of Pabst. In 1960, Heileman was only the nation's 31st ranking brewer. In 1987, Heileman itself was acquired by a large Australian brewer and holding corporation, Bond Corp. Holdings. Bond already owned the Pittsburgh Brewing Company. Adding its output to Heileman's would move Heileman to a number four rank.

In 1981, Heileman was a rejected suitor for Schlitz (just prior to the Stroh–Schlitz amalgamation), and in 1982 it was a rejected suitor for Pabst.

At that time, the Antitrust Division objected to both mergers. But Pabst and Heileman became substantially intertwined. Pabst, during this time frame, had purchased the Olympia Brewing Company (producer of the Olympia, Lone Star, and Hamm's brands) in a complex exchange that transferred its breweries in Georgia, Texas, and Oregon to rival Heileman, as well as the Lone Star, Red White and Blue, Blitz–Weinhard, and Burgermeister brands; it also entailed the obligation on Heileman's part to brew beer in the Southeast for Pabst at the former Pabst brewery in Perry, Georgia, that Heileman had acquired. Heileman was thwarted in a private antitrust suit from acquiring the remainder of Pabst. Most of the Pabst assets were acquired by the owner of Falstaff.

The Antitrust Division's determination to stop the Heileman–Schlitz merger indicated the limits to which expansion by merger could take place in the beer industry. Heileman–Schlitz would have resulted in a firm with 16 percent of the national market (Heileman had 7.6 percent in 1980; Schlitz, 8.5 percent). Heileman and Schlitz were the two runaway leaders in malt liquor sales (with about 67 percent of that market segment in 1980), and Schlitz's Old Milwaukee brand (one of the best-selling popular-price beers) was in head-to-head rivalry with a stable of Heileman's popular-price beers (such as Carling Black Label, Blatz, and Wiedemann). Independent rivalry in these segments would have been lost as a result of the merger. Strong rivalry in popular-price brands not only benefits consumers favoring that segment of the market but also those purchasing premium brands, since competition at the popular-price level places a downward drag on premium prices. In assessing what would have been the largest horizontal merger in the history of the brewing industry, the Antitrust Division quite properly said no.[10]

But most mergers in the beer industry have not involved firms of such stature. Generally, they represented the demise of an inefficient firm, which salvaged some remainder of its worth by selling out to another brewer. The acquiring brewer gained no market power but might have benefited by securing the barrelage to bring one plant to full capacity or gain access to an improved distribution network or new territory. Mergers such as these are not the cause of structural change; rather, they are the effect, as firms exit through the merger route. This type of merger should be allowed—even encouraged—for, in a roundabout way, easing the exit process facilitates entry of new firms into the industry. If exit is difficult, potential aspirants will be unlikely to enter any industry.

Mergers have made some imprint on the structure of the brewing industry. The present stature of Stroh and Heileman is the result in part of important mergers. But the trend to concentration would have occurred even if all mergers had been prohibited. Much of the increase in concentration in the seventies was due to the two leading firms, whose growth was virtually all internal. Indeed, the enforcement of the antimerger law against firms such as Pabst, Schlitz, Falstaff, and Anheuser–Busch was partly responsible for the emphasis on internal growth by most of the leading brewers. At this point, the application of the antimerger law can do little to stem the rising concentration or the demise of independent brewers. While it did prevent the combination of Heileman and Schlitz, one of the few mergers stopped by the Antitrust Division in recent years, the antitrust authorities recognized in the mid-1970s that mergers they once would have attacked do not merit challenge, even if the merger involves sizable regional sellers.[11] One must look to factors other than mergers to explain the industry's structural shakeup.

Economies of Scale

When discussing economies of scale, economists generally plot a smooth, continuous average-cost curve that is the envelope of a host of similarly curvaceous short-run average cost-curves, each one representing a different size plant. Economies of scale exist if large plants produce at lower unit costs than small ones. What is seldom mentioned in the discussion of these curves, however, is that great confidence cannot be attached to the location of any point on these cost curves, notwithstanding their precise, scientific appearance in the economics literature.

With this caveat firmly in mind, Figure 5-1 is a representation of economies of scale in the brewing industry. The figure illustrates the fairly sharp decline in long-run unit costs until a plant size of 1.25 million barrels per year of capacity is reached. Beyond this capacity, costs continue to decline, but less sharply, until a capacity of 4.5 million barrels (an enormous brewery) is attained. Here economies of large scale seem to be fully exploited.[12]

Table 5-4 shows one method (the survivor test) used by economists to

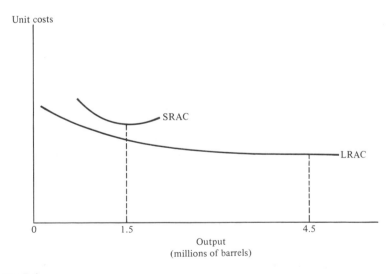

Figure 5-1 ⎯⎯⎯⎯⎯⎯⎯⎯⎯⎯⎯⎯⎯⎯⎯⎯⎯⎯⎯⎯⎯⎯⎯⎯⎯
Economies of scale in brewing.

Table 5-4.
Surviving Breweries by Capacity: 1959–1986

Listed Capacity Barrels (Thousands)	1959	1963	1967	1971	1975	1979	1983	1986
10–100	68	54	36	21	10	10	15	13
101–500	91	72	44	33	19	13	12	8
501–1000	30	33	35	32	13	8	2	3
1001–2000	18	17	18	21	13	11	13	10
2001–4000	8	10	10	12	12	13	9	10
4001+	2	3	4	7	15	20	23	23

Source: Compiled from plant capacity figures listed in the *Modern Brewery Age Blue Book* (Stamford, Conn.: Modern Brewery Age Publishing Co., various years); Charles W. Parker, "The Domestic Beer Industry" (1984) and industry trade sources. These figures do not include plants listed only on a company-consolidated basis (in the case of multiplant firms) or single-plant firms not reporting their capacity. Excludes microbreweries of less than 10,000 barrels capacity.

estimate the extent of economies of scale. This test, like all techniques for estimating economies of scale, is not without its difficulties.[13] As its name implies, the survivor test distinguishes those size plants that have survived over time. There has been a steady decline (dramatic in some cases) for breweries of under 2-million-barrel capacity and a large increase in breweries of 4 million barrels and above. That large brewing plants are not only surviving but growing in number is prima facie evidence of their lower unit costs. One can understand much better the concentration statistics in brewing after learning that the 17 plants of industry leaders Anheuser–Busch and Miller have an average capacity of 7 million barrels. Table 5-4 does not reflect the appearance of very small breweries—"microbreweries" or "boutique breweries," as they are called. In 1986 there were over 50 brewers of less than 10,000-barrel capacity. Most are new firms, and some are very small indeed, such as California's Buffalo Bill's Brewery, with a capacity of 450 barrels. Microbreweries receive much attention in the business press, in part because there has been so little new entry into the beer industry in the post-World War II period. Their owners, who often are also the managers and brewmasters, are portrayed as a new breed of entrepreneur in the beer industry. But the competitive significance of microbreweries is itself microscopic.

Figure 5-1 also includes a single short-run average-cost curve above the long-run average-cost curve. A long-run cost curve represents the envelope of different-sized plants, each of which uses the latest in capital equipment and production techniques. The curve standing by itself better portrays the situation of many breweries that have met (or will meet) their demise. These breweries were not only too small to exploit all the economies of scale, but their capital equipment was of such an outmoded vintage that their costs were elevated even more.

Some of the economies from larger operations come in the packaging of the beer. The newer bottling lines at the Anheuser–Busch Houston brewery have line speeds of 1,100 bottles per minute. Modern canning lines are even faster: 2,000 cans per minute. It takes a brewery of substantial size to utilize such equipment at capacity. Large plants also save on labor costs via the automation of brewing and warehousing and on capital costs as well. Construction cost per barrel is cut by about one-third for a 4.5-million-barrel plant rather than one of 1.5-million-barrel capacity.[14] However, no significant reduction in production costs was detected in a study of *multiplant* economies of scale.[15]

In a real sense, economies of scale relate not only to some finite productive capacity but also to management's ability to use the capacity efficiently. Shortly after the repeal of Prohibition in 1933, there was a flood of new entrants into the brewing industry, all expecting to be met by thirsty customers. However, the demand for beer was unexpectedly low after repeal. From a high of 750 brewers operating in 1935, almost 100 were quickly eliminated in but five years. Quite a few of these enterprises had operated before Prohibition, but many were under new management. Some were family-owned firms, and heredity had been cruel to the second or third generations, not endowing them with the brewing and/or managerial capabilities of their fathers or grandfathers. Competitive pressures, with no respect for nepotism, eliminated such breweries.[16]

A small brewer, producing a quality product and marketing it so as to keep transportation costs at a minimum, might survive in today's industry by finding a special niche for itself. This seems to be the status, by way of examples, of Wisconsin's Stevens Point Brewery, D. G. Yuengling & Son in Pennsylvania (the nation's oldest brewing firm still in business), and the pioneer microbrewery, San Francisco's Anchor Steam Brewery. However, such cases are the exceptions that prove the rules. In brewing—unlike many manufacturing industries where optimum-sized plants seem to be getting smaller—large, capital-intensive plants are necessary to exploit economies of scale and survive in the industry.[17] In markets where vigorous competitive pressures exist, firms that do not exploit economies of scale or operate with internal efficiency will not survive. This has been the fate of many brewers; they have exited from the industry because of inefficient plants, poor management, or both.

The Condition of Entry

The ease with which newcomers can enter an industry is a structural characteristics of great importance in ensuring competitive performance. If entry is easy, if potential rivals are lurking in the wings, so to speak, existing firms will be unable to raise prices significantly—lest they encourage an outbreak of new competition. On the other hand, if entry is barred, perhaps by a patent or government license, existing firms may be able to garner monopoly gains.

Entry into the beer industry is not hindered by the traditional barriers of patents and exclusive government grants. Key inputs are not controlled by existing firms. Nor are economies of scale so important that an efficient entrant would have to supply an enormous share of industry output. However, the sheer expense of entering the beer industry is considerable (although it would be less if profits were higher, thereby making credit easier to acquire). The price of constructing a modern 4–5 million-barrel brewery is some $250 million. And once the brewery is built, marketing the new brew also will be costly because entrants must introduce their products to consumers already smitten by vigorous advertising efforts.

A look at the record indicates the low probability of any entry threat to existing brewers from *de novo* aspirants. No top-ranking firm in the brewing industry has been a new entrant since World War II. This paucity of entry is explained by the relatively low profitability of the industry and the ominous fate of so many exiting firms. Moreover, the industry is risky because its plant facilities have few uses other than brewing beer. Finally, current demographic trends would not be encouraging to prospective entrants, especially given the abundance of existing brewing capacity. The eighties have been a decade of the market wringing excess capacity from the industry, not inviting new firms in. Miller alone has 10 million barrels of unutilized capacity sitting in Trenton, Ohio, at a new brewery it has yet to open.

The beer industry has been classed as one with moderate, although increasing, barriers to entry.[18] Presently, the most promising source of new competition is that of an established brewer moving into a new geographic market, the importation of foreign beer, or the introduction of new product lines by existing brewers. Beer imports to the United States, which come mostly from the Netherlands, Canada, Germany, and Mexico, have increased tenfold in the period 1970–1987. Imports (mostly in the superpremium category) now represent about 5 percent of domestic consumption, up from less than 1 percent in 1970. Imported beer no longer can be discounted as insignificant; in California, for example, a Mexican import was the sixth leading brand in 1987, with over 4 percent of the state's consumption.

Product Differentiation

When consumers find the product of one firm superior to others, the favored firm can raise its price somewhat without losing these customers. This phenomenon is called product differentiation. Three characteristics of product differentiation in the brewing industry bear mentioning at the outset. First, several studies indicate that, at least under blindfold test conditions, most beer drinkers cannot distinguish between brands of beer.[19] Second, more expensive brands do not cost proportionately more to brew and package. Third, considerable talent and resources are devoted to publicizing real or imagined differences in beers, with the hope of producing product differentiation. Notwithstanding all this, product differentiation in the beer industry has not led to individual brewers having market power to a degree that would be a concern of antitrust policy.

One indicator of the relative amount of advertising done by industries is the ratio of advertising expenditures to sales. For some companies in the soap, cosmetic, and drug industries, this ratio is greater than 10 percent. For the malt beverage industry, this ratio is notable but has modulated. In the years 1961–1965, this ratio was close to 7 percent; in 1976–1977, the figure fell below 4 percent; for 1981–1984, the latest dates for which data were available at this writing, the average was 5 percent.[20] This is less than the average of leading food and tobacco firms, and considerably less than is expended in such industries as soft drinks, candy, cigarettes, preserved fruits, and other alcoholic beverages.

There has been a significant escalation in beer advertising costs beginning in 1976–1977. For example, in 1977, Anheuser–Busch, Miller, Coors, and Stroh spent $1.46, $2.20, $.48, and $1.56 per barrel on media advertising, respectively. In 1986, the figures for these companies were $5.47, $7.73, $5.53, and $2.38.[21] One explanation given for this increase is that of a response to Miller's enormous promotional outlays following its affiliation with Philip Morris. One conclusion drawn is that increased advertising is responsible for the increased concentration. Douglas F. Greer, Willard F. Mueller, and others have stressed advertising, particularly television advertising, as a primary cause of increasing concentration in the industry.[22] But the facts do not permit any tidy explanations or conclusions about the consequences of advertising.

There is no hard-and-fast relationship between dollars spent on advertising and market share gained. Miller has long been a heavy advertiser; in the period 1967–1971, it generally spent twice as much per barrel as rival brewers. But Miller's market share did not expand then, nor did other firms feel compelled to emulate Miller's sizable promotional outlays. Schlitz spent more on advertising in 1975 and 1976 than either Anheuser–Busch or Miller, and yet the Schlitz brand had declining sales in that very time frame. Coors experienced expanding sales with very small advertising expenditures: In 1968–1974, during years of sizable growth, Coors spent only an average of $.17 per barrel on media advertising. Coors' growing use of media correlates with a declining share position in many states. Miller was not able to secure more than a toehold in the superpremium segment of the market (one would conjecture the most image-conscious), notwithstanding extraordinary advertising expenditures per barrel. In 1980 Miller High Life was the most heavily advertised brand of beer in the United States; in that year, its sales slowed down and have been declining every year since.

The amount spent on advertising beer is large, and this is not surprising.

There are millions of actual and potential beer drinkers a brewer wants to inform of the quality and availability of its product. New beer customers come of age and producers seek to inform them; old customers may forget and producers seek to remind them. Nevertheless, at some stage, massive advertising offers only inframarginal information and may have the effect of entrenching the industry leaders. Unfortunately, economic analysis does not provide a criterion for determining at what stage advertising becomes redundant and wasteful.

The product differentiation of premium beer is important to understand. This phenomenon began years ago when a few brewers decided to attempt to sell their beer nationally and added a price premium to offset incremental transportation costs that were encountered in shipping greater distances. To secure the higher price, the beer was promoted as superior in taste and quality, allegedly because of the brewing expertise found in their locations. At one time the premium price was absorbed by higher shipping costs; but the construction of efficient, regionally dispersed breweries by most of the large shippers now eliminates the transportation disadvantage. The premium image remains. With transportation costs equalized, and production costs generally lower, these firms can wage vigorous advertising (and price-cutting) campaigns in areas where regional and local brewers were once the largest sellers.

The national brewers also have two other advertising advantages: (1) none of their advertising is "wasted," whereas regional brewers do not always find media markets (especially in television) that coincide with their selling territories; and (2) their advertising investment is less likely to be lost when a customer moves to another part of the country.[23] Still, advertising presents no inevitable relationship between firm growth and promotion expenditures, and the concentration statistics for the industry cannot be explained facilely by current trends in promotional expenditures, since concentration also increased at a time of declining advertising-to-sales ratios.

Rising per capita income may also contribute to increasing concentration. Premium beer is what economists call a normal good, with a positive income elasticity. The brewers who came to be the major factors in the industry in the 1970s are, essentially, producers of premium brands. Popular-priced brands were once the leaders in their region. This has changed. Premium brands and premium-price light beer now occupy about two-thirds of the market. Imports and superpremiums now hold about 8–9 percent. The loser in the past two decades: popular-price beer, dropping from almost 60 percent in 1970 to less than 20 percent in 1981. In 1982 and 1983 the share of popular-price brands began to increase, at the expense of premiums. But by this time most of the leading popular brands were marketed by the top four brewers, for example, Stroh's Old Milwaukee and Schaefer brands, which have led the resurgence of popular-price beer, and Anheuser–Busch's Busch brand. Some popular-price beers for the first time now receive exposure through television advertising. Low-calorie beer, virtually nonexistent in

1970, by 1987 had gained close to 25 percent of the market, almost all of this being brewed by the top brewers and selling at premium prices. The downswing of Schlitz and Pabst in recent years is explained in part by their lack of success in the growing light-beer segment of the market.

The Philip Morris–Miller Affiliation

In the decade of the 1970s, the most dramatic single factor in the brewing industry's structural change was the rise of the Miller Brewing Company from the seventh to the second largest seller. Miller's ascent involved far more than a mere shuffling of rank among industry leaders. Its production capacity and marketing methods have added a new dimension to the industry that affected the industry's economic behavior throughout the 1980s.

The dates of two acquisitions are important in understanding the Miller phenomenon: 1970, when Miller's procurement by the Philip Morris Company was completed, and 1972, when Miller purchased the brand names of Meister Brau, Inc., a defunct Chicago brewing firm.

The 1970 date initiated the management takeover of Miller by Philip Morris personnel. The new management accomplished three master strokes with the Miller High Life brand. First, it was (in marketing parlance) repositioned to appeal to the blue-collar consumer, who may drink several beers a day. Previously the brand was directed at a group of consumers who rarely consumed more than one beer at a sitting. As one Miller advertising executive put it, the strategy was to ". . . take Miller High Life out of the champagne bucket and put it into the lunch bucket without spilling a drop."[24] The repositioning was effected by a very successful advertising campaign. Second, Miller improved the quality of its product; any of its beer not drunk within 120 days of its production was destroyed. Third, the company introduced a 7-oz. (pony) bottle that appealed both to infrequent beer drinkers with small capacities and drinkers who found that the beer remained colder in the small receptacle. These three events alone yielded Miller enormous growth.

But Miller's adroit use of amyloglucosidase[25] amplified even more the company's ascendancy. The virtually unnoticed Miller purchase of the three Meister Brau trademarks included one called Lite, a brand of low-calorie beer brewed by the amyloglucosidase process and once marketed locally by Meister Brau to upper-middle-class weight-conscious consumers. The Miller management became curious about the fact that Lite had once sold fairly well in Anderson, Indiana, a town with many blue-collar workers. In what is now a marketing classic, Miller zeroed in on "real" beer drinkers, claiming that its low-calorie beer allowed them to drink their beer with even less of a filled-up feeling. The upshot of this marketing campaign would be evident to any grocery or convenience-store shelf-stocker: Lite is the most popular new product in the history of the beer industry, and many brewers now have their own brand of light beer as competition. Miller failed in its legal campaign to reserve not only Lite but even the term *light* to itself; the courts left the generic word in the public domain and thereby allowed other brewers to use this term to describe their low-calorie emulations.

Miller's ascendancy has not been without its brickbats, which come generally in two forms. The first criticism is that Miller changed the *process* of beer rivalry, with the emphasis no longer on production economies but upon market segmentation and brand proliferation. If "beer is beer," then it is argued that consumers do not truly benefit by the product and packaging differentiation that is now common in the industry.

Some economists are concerned that brand proliferation, and the advertising dollars needed to sustain it, can erect barriers to entry to smaller firms, thereby lessening competition. The contrary argument has been made that Miller had to bear the financial burden of making its low-calorie beer palatable to consumers; having done this, Miller's rivals have been able to introduce their own light beers more easily.[26]

The second criticism of Miller stems from its conglomerate ownership and the allegation that Philip Morris's "deep pocket" provides unfair advantages to Miller vis-à-vis its rivals. For example, Professor Willard F. Mueller testified before a Senate committee that "Miller's expansion after 1970 was made possible by Philip Morris's financial backing and willingness to engage in deep and sustained subsidization of Miller's operations."[27] He cited Miller's media advertising budget and capital expansion program as evidence of this, arguing that Miller could not have raised such funds on its own. Mueller implicitly concluded that Philip Morris's behavior makes economic sense only if the upshot of its subsidization is a monopoly position for Miller (or shared monopoly with Anheuser–Busch) in the near future.

However, the matter of cross-subsidization is not simple to analyze. The detailed accounting records of the Miller subsidiary are not in the public domain. So it remains an open question whether, for example, the depreciation (instead of expensing) of Miller's advertising expenditure would reveal any sizable loss on the Miller operations. Moreover, even if Miller were a poor investment as a beer business, it is clear now, with almost two decades of experience, that Philip Morris cannot expect to recoup these alleged losses through Miller's monopoly power in the beer industry, given the sizable rivals still remaining, their intense rivalry with Miller, and the significant lead that Anheuser–Busch enjoys over Miller.

III.

CONDUCT

Pricing

Judging from the early records of the pre-Prohibition beer industry, life in the industry was very competitive. Entry was easy; producers were many.

Given these two characteristics, economic theory would predict a competitive industry, and the evidence bears this out.

In fact, the early beer industry offers a classic example of the predictions of price theory. Given the inelastic demand, brewers saw the obvious advantages of monopolizing the industry, raising prices, and gleaning high profits. Various types of loose and tight-knit cartels were seen as advantageous, but the difficulty of coordinating so many brewers and the lack of any barriers to entry prevented any of these efforts from being successful, at least for long. The degree of competition is evidenced by this turn-of-the-century plea from Adolphus Busch to Captain Pabst:

> I hope also to be able to demonstrate to you that by the present way competition is running we are only hurting each other in a real foolish way. The traveling agents . . . always endeavor to reduce prices and send such reports to their respective home offices as are generally not correct and only tend to bring forth competition that helps to ruin the profits . . . all large manufacturing interests are now working in harmony . . . and only the brewers are behind as usual; instead of combining their efforts and securing their own interest, they are fighting each other and running the profits down, so that the pleasures of managing a brewery have been diminished a good deal.[28]

In a free market economy, it is best that rival managers avoid any communications about prices. But if such letters are written, this is the sort of letter vigorous market rivalry should provoke.

The beer industry also escaped the horizontal mergers that transformed the structure of so many industries—such as steel, whiskey, petroleum, tobacco products, and farm equipment—during the first great merger movement. There were attempts, mostly by British businessmen, to combine the large brewers during this time. One sought the amalgamation of Pabst, Schlitz, Miller, Anheuser–Busch, and Lemp into one company, a feat that, had it been successful, may have greatly altered the structure and degree of competition in the industry. But the attempt failed, and brewing entered Prohibition with a competitive structure that responded with competitive pricing.

The Pricing Pattern

Beer is generally sold f.o.b. the brewery. Some brewers sell on a uniform f.o.b. mill basis, but most vary their prices at times to different customers to reflect localized competitive conditions or to test perceived changes in the marketplace. For example, in 1980 Stroh's prices differed in the contiguous states of Illinois, Kentucky, and Indiana, and its prices in Pennsylvania, a state with unusually vigorous price-cutting, were lower than in nearly all Midwestern states.

The present pattern of prices dates back to the turn of the century.

Premium beers generally will be priced just above the price level of popular-price beers, which in turn will be above local (or "price" or "shelf") beer. A more contemporary category is the superpremium, a beer selling at a price above premium. A number of major brewers market their own brand of superpremiums, and most imported beers fall in this price category.

The demarcation between local–popular–premium has become blurred in recent years, not only because of the introduction of the superpremium, but because the price differential between premium and popular-price brands has narrowed. At the same time, the distinction between local and popular beer on the basis of price has become murky because of pricing specials that regularly appear in either segment of the market. The demise of most local breweries has reduced the distinction further.

The pattern for beer price differentials is not attributable to some identifiable physical characteristic of the product. In the case of malt beverages, price differences are in part the result of customers' tastes and are thus subjective. Beer drinkers have not distinguished themselves by their ability to discern taste differences or brand identities when a beer's brand name is kept secret.

Price Discrimination

In 1955, the Federal Trade Commission (FTC) charged Anheuser–Busch with unlawful price discrimination. Anheuser–Busch had dropped the price of its premium brand to all buyers in the St. Louis area but did not make this reduction in any other areas. The FTC maintained this was price discrimination that would impair competition by diverting to Anheuser–Busch sales from regional brewers serving St. Louis.

The charge was brought under Section 2(a) of the Robinson–Patman Act. Proof of such a violation involves answering three questions:

1. Is there price discrimination?
2. If so, does the respondent have a defense?
3. If not, might the price discrimination lessen competition?

There was vigorous disagreement on the answer to each of these questions.

After the price cut, Anheuser–Busch's Budweiser brand beer was selling for less money per case in St. Louis than anywhere in the country, and this differential could not be explained fully by the lower transportation costs from the Anheuser–Busch brewery in St. Louis. Query: Is this automatically price discrimination?

The court of appeals said no, claiming price discrimination could not exist unless different prices were charged to *competing* purchasers. The court put it this way:

> Anheuser–Busch did not thereby discriminate among its local competitors in the St. Louis area. By its cuts, Anheuser–Busch employed the same means of competition against all of them. Moreover, it did not discriminate among

those who bought its beer in the St. Louis area; all could buy at the same price.[29]

The FTC and ultimately the Supreme Court disagreed with this interpretation. The Supreme Court said that price discrimination is "selling the same kind of goods cheaper to one purchaser than to another" and thereby overruled the court of appeals.[30]

A defense to a charge of price discrimination is to show that one's lower price was offered to meet the equally low price of a rival. Prior to the FTC complaint, Budweiser was selling at $2.93 per case in St. Louis; its three regional rivals were selling their beer at $2.35 per case. In two successive price cuts, Anheuser–Busch dropped its price to $2.35 per case. Query: Could not Anheuser–Busch argue that it was only meeting the equally low price of its rivals?

Anheuser–Busch tried, but the FTC categorically rejected this defense. Note what this implies: Anheuser–Busch went on record, so to speak, that its premium beer is the same product as popular-price beer—that is, "beer is beer." The FTC, however, argued that, at $2.35 a case, Anheuser–Busch "was selling more value than its competitors were. . . . [T]he consumer has proved . . . that [he] will pay more for Budweiser than . . . for many other beers."[31] This statement comes close to saying that Budweiser, because of its "superior public acceptance," must be priced higher than regional and local beers. After the Supreme Court ruled that Anheuser–Busch had priced in a discriminatory fashion, the court of appeals entertained the case a second time to decide whether competition might be lessened by the company's pricing practice. The FTC, arguing from the figures shown in Table 5-1, said that this practice would give Anheuser–Busch market power in St. Louis by increasing its market share.

The court of appeals disagreed, ruling that diversion of business did not prove competition in St. Louis was being lessened. The court's decision pointed out that Anheuser–Busch was not subsidizing St. Louis with revenues from other markets and that none of the rivals of Anheuser–Busch in St. Louis had felt so "pushed" as to lower their price in response to the Anheuser–Busch cut. The only result was that consumers of beer in St. Louis could buy Budweiser for less money, which the court opined is what competition is all about.

If the FTC had won its case and Anheuser–Busch had been barred from cutting prices in St. Louis, one might argue that competition would be increased, because companies would then be prevented from making selective price cuts to eliminate smaller rivals or to enforce price leadership. But there is another implication to consider. Barring selective price cuts may be the same as barring price competition. Anheuser–Busch could respond to the loss of sales in its own backyard by cutting its prices across the board all over the country. But, as one observer put it, "If a seller by law must lower all his prices or none, he will hesitate long to lower any."[32]

One unfortunate response to the pricing practices of the national brewers was the installation in a number of states of price-posting laws. Basically these laws provide that sellers must publicly post their wholesale prices, maintain them for some period of time, announce any price changes, and in some cases specify the retail price of the product as well. Although such legislation has the façade of protecting beer consumers against quick price increases, its impetus actually came from smaller brewers, who saw such laws as protection against competition from promotional price campaigns, and from wholesalers and retailers, who saw these as laws providing floors under their own price structure. Price posting of alcoholic beverages has met a checkered legal response, in some states (such as Missouri) passing legal scrutiny, in others (such as California) being struck down as violating federal antitrust law.

Questionable Payments

In the early 1970s some brewers and beer wholesalers used "questionable payments" (or "blackbagging") in marketing their beer to selected retail accounts. This is a pricing practice that, depending upon one's point of view, could be dubbed either a bribe or a price cut. For example, a brewer might offer, through its distributor, a thousand dollars to a restaurant chain if that company would sell only that brewer's beer on tap at its outlets. If the payment went to a restaurant employee to secure the business, it would be a bribe, but if it went into the restaurant's till, it would be (from an economic standpoint) like a price cut. One reason why brewers simply would not cut their prices openly would be to avoid Robinson–Patman Act vulnerability; another would be to conceal the price cut from rivals (who might match it) or other customers (who might demand it too). Price-posting laws themselves may have encouraged blackbagging.

Whatever the rationale, such payments may violate certain tax and beer marketing laws. Schlitz, for example, incurred a 747-count criminal indictment in 1978 for its questionable payments. In a 1984 consent decree Anheuser–Busch agreed to pay a $2 million penalty to resolve such allegations against it.

Price-Affirmation Laws

State price-affirmation laws constitute a potential impairment to the competitive pricing of beer. These statutes require a firm to sell its product within a state at a price no higher than is charged in specified nearby states. Several states required manufacturers of distilled spirits to notify the state alcoholic beverage authority of the prices they charge, and to "affirm" that lower prices for these products are not charged in the pertinent states. Some states embraced malt beverages within their affirmation requirements.

On the face of it, these state regulations might seem beneficial, at least for the residents of those states that have enacted them. But economic theory cautions about legislation that tampers with the nervous system of the marketplace: price. The consequence of these regulations is to reduce price competition and handicap sellers in testing the price sensitivity of products (not to mention the paperwork costs in compiling and submitting forms validating prices). Fortunately, the Supreme Court recently struck down one such law, and this decision, and those of other courts as well, has weakened if not nullified the economic consequences of such regulations.[33]

Marketing

Although all industries are subject to various federal and state laws that affect the marketing of the industry's product, the brewing industry faces an especially variegated pattern of laws and regulations concerning labeling, advertising, credit, container characteristics, alcoholic content, tax rates, and litter assessments.

For example, Michigan does not permit a beer label to show alcoholic content, while Minnesota requires an accurate statement of alcoholic content. In Indiana, advertising is strictly regulated; in Louisiana there are no such regulations. Some states require sales from the brewer to the wholesaler to retailer to be only on a cash basis, whereas other states allow credit. Some states stipulate both the maximum and minimum size of containers; Alabama, for example, permits no package beer containers larger than 16 ounces. States also have varying requirements on the maximum and minimum permissible alcoholic content; in some, alcoholic content is different for different types of outlets.

The governmental involvement in the beer industry also includes taxation. The federal tax alone on a barrel of beer is $9.00 and, in 1986, the Treasury Department coffers gathered $1.5 billion in beer taxes. The state taxes on beer vary substantially but average over $6.00 per barrel. In addition, brewers, wholesalers, and retail outlets pay federal, state, and sometimes local occupational taxes. Taxes represent the largest single-cost item in a glass of beer.

There is little forward integration by brewing firms into the marketing of beer. In England, the brewing industry has extensive holdings in the retailing of beer, owning more than half of all retail outlets, including about 80 percent of the public houses and hotels. But in the United States, brewers are prohibited by law from owning any retail outlets, which leaves the wholesale distribution of the product as the only legitimate forward vertical integration route. Even wholesaling is prohibited in some states. The retailing of beer is done through two general types of independent outlets: those for on-premise consumption and those for off-premise consumption.

Most brewers rely on independent distributors to channel their product to these retail outlets. In 1984, there were approximately 4,000 wholesalers of beer, the vast majority being independent merchant wholesalers. Some brewers own a portion of their wholesale channel. For example, Anheuser–Busch distributes about 75 percent of its beer through independent wholesalers; the remainder is marketed through branch offices in large metropolitan areas.

A brewer's keen financial interest in the distribution of its beer is self-evident: A disgruntled customer reads the brewer's name on the container, not the name of the wholesaler or retailer. Therefore, brewers negotiate contracts with wholesalers as to the marketing obligations of each party, but not all areas of concern to the brewer are open for negotiation. For example, the determination of resale prices is not a matter for private agreement because the antitrust laws limit the contractual opportunities of a brewer in this area. The antitrust laws potentially could make it difficult for a brewer to prevent what in economics is called the free-rider problem. An example would be a distributor who trans-ships dated beer to a territory that has long been served by a distributor who, by careful stock rotation, had given that brand a reputation for freshness. On the other hand, territorial exclusivity clauses give the distributor a reprieve from intrabrand competition.

Some large retail customers, notably chain stores, would prefer to purchase beer directly from brewers, eliminating the wholesale distributor. Or they want to bargain with different distributors of the same brand of beer (possibly purchasing from a price-cutting wholesaler in another area). But brewers almost unanimously market through a three-tier distribution system and support federal legislation that would immunize from antitrust attack a distributor's exclusive territorial limits. The beer industry has joined with the National Beer Wholesalers Association in championing legislation permitting exclusive territorial agreements similar to legislation secured earlier by the soft drink industry. Both the Department of Justice and the Federal Trade Commission have opposed this antitrust exemption.

While this legislation has not been adopted by Congress (as of this writing), most major brewers have proceeded with new wholesaler agreements that restrict a distributor's sales only to his own territory; a wholesaler who makes sales directly or indirectly to customers outside the assigned territory is subject to immediate termination. Clauses of this character earlier had been illegal *per se* under the antitrust laws. But they are now scrutinized more permissively under the rule of reason.

The beer wholesaler at one time distributed mainly kegs of beer for on-premise draught consumption. In 1935, only 30 percent of beer sales were packaged — that is, in bottles or cans suitable for on- or off-premise consumption. Since that time there has been a shift to packaged beer relative to draught; in 1986, 88 percent of beer sales were packaged. The popularity of the can and one-way bottle, the changing consumption habits of the male, the apparent loss of the "saloon habit" during Prohibition, and the preferences of the female mean that the beer distributor today will make more delivery trips to grocery and convenience stores than to the tavern.

This trend in beer marketing works to the disadvantage of the small brewer. When beer sales were primarily by the keg for on-premise consumption, the small brewer could survive by selling to taverns in the immediate area. But packaged beer sales are primarily for off-premise consumption, and the distribution of packaged beer increases the importance of product differentiation and brand emphasis.

Profits

If an industry is effectively monopolized, one might expect to see this reflected in its profits. This is not necessarily so, since (1) demand may not be sufficiently high to yield profits in spite of monopoly; (2) the monopolists may be inefficient; or (3) accounting records often are imperfect measures of economic costs and profits and may not show the monopoly gains. In spite of these difficulties, economists regularly look at profit data for some insight into an industry's performance.

On the whole, brewing firms have been less profitable than the average manufacturing firm in the post-World War II period. Profits in the industry were quite modest until 1967. During the three years 1968–1970, the industry's rate of return on net worth after taxes averaged 9.5 percent, as compared to the return for all manufacturing firms of 7.4 percent. However, in the five most recent years for which data are available, 1981–1985, the beer industry tallied a return of 2.1, 3.1, 9.7, 3.3, and 5.2 percent, respectively—generally below the average rate of return on net worth for all manufacturing firms.[34]

As one might expect from our discussion of economies of scale, the largest brewers have done better than the industry average. Beginning in 1964, the top four companies began to outperform the rest of the brewing industry in terms of profits. Prior to that time, the profit record of the top four brewers approximated that of the rest of the industry and was usually inferior to the firms ranked five through eight.[35]

Externalities

Externalities, or spillover effects, occur when transactions between parties (such as the simple sale of a product) have economic consequences on persons not part of the transaction. These spillover effects can be positive or negative and, to the extent that an industry manifests externalities—either in the production process or in the consumption of its product—the social performance of that industry is likely to be affected.

The beer industry is remarkably free of the two negative externalities in production commonly associated with manufacturing enterprises: air and water pollution. Brewing is a very "clean" industry (breweries must be more sanitary than hospitals, in fact), and brewing firms are often courted by areas seeking industry partly for this reason. The brewing industry performs well on this count.

The externality problems in brewing occur in the consumption of the product. True, there would be positive externalities for members of the Beer Can Collectors of America in finding along the roadside an empty can of Monticello beer (with its emblem of Mr. Jefferson's home) or Olde Frothingslosh (with its rather rotund female bathing beauty trademark). However, most citizens are able to restrain their enthusiasm for that proportion of the billions of beer cans and bottles that end up as litter—that is, negative externalities imposed on them though they neither sold nor bought the beer.

Although legislation banning or restricting the sale of beer containers is commonly proposed, only a few states and localities actually have passed such laws. The most restrictive of these laws is in effect in the college town of Oberlin, Ohio, which simply outlawed the sale or possession of beer in nonreturnable containers. The most well known of these laws is the Oregon "bottle bill," passed in 1971, which bans all cans with detachable pull tabs and places a compulsory 5-cent deposit on all beer and soft drink containers. Because retail stores particularly do not want to handle returned cans, this has drastically reduced the sale of beverages in this container and offers an inducement to the use of returnable containers or on-premise draught consumption. In Oregon and Vermont, mandatory deposit legislation apparently led to reductions of 60 and 80 percent, respectively, in roadside beverage container litter. However, the statewide (or local) approach cannot solve the problem (say, in Vermont) of customers going "over the line" (to New Hampshire) to avoid the deposit requirement and higher prices.

American brewers (with the exception of Coors) oppose all taxes and bans on containers, stressing instead voluntary action and other litter-recovery programs. The latter, if generously financed, could solve the litter problem, but partially at the expense of nonproducers and nonconsumers.

The economic question of where the liability for an externality should be placed depends on which party—the consumer, the producer, or a third party (or some combination of the three)—would be the most efficient at removing the externality. The evidence is not yet in on this complicated question.[36] A full discussion of the externality problem in brewing would require many pages and should include what is also a significant externality: the economic and noneconomic costs imposed by intoxication and alcoholism.

Competition

Increasing concentration at the national level and the unlikely entry of new rivals pose a threat to the future level of competition in the beer industry. As the industry becomes populated by fewer companies, and given the inelastic nature of demand, the potential for tacit or direct collusion is

enhanced. One study argues that high two-firm concentration ratios constitute a critical measure of market power.[37] Similarly, with high concentration,
the chances may be lessened that smaller firms will follow a truly independent
price and production strategy. The presence in an industry of only a few
sellers normally results in an increased danger of parallel business behavior.

However, the prospect of joint profit-maximizing behavior in the beer
industry is not worrisome for the near future. Thus far there is no evidence of
collusion in the industry. Even with the increased demand for beer in the
1960s and 1970s, competition forced the exit of marginal firms. Moreover,
Miller's increase in productive capacity (imitated by its rivals) overhangs the
industry and now provokes the large brewers to battle among themselves
instead of merely competing away market share from smaller firms. For
example, it was Coors whose share of the market declined in Anheuser–
Busch's recent California expansion, and it was Schlitz who lost considerable
business in Texas as Coors entered that state. This overhang of capacity,
barring collusion or government interference, should keep brewing firms
from exercising harmful market power in future years, notwithstanding the
relative increase in concentration that the industry has experienced.

One measure of an industry's rivalry is the extent of changes in market
share or turnover in the ranking of its sellers. The beer industry exhibits high
mobility in this regard. Schlitz, the nation's second-ranking firm in 1976 and
the "Beer That Made Milwaukee Famous," no longer is even brewed there.
Pabst was the third leading seller as recently as 1975, ahead of Miller, and
even the subject of Antitrust Division action. It became a shell of its former
self. In 1987 Schlitz and Pabst sold only 2.2 million barrels of premium beer.
A decade earlier, combined, they sold 30 million barrels.

Miller, number eight in 1968, rose in rank and has been number two
since 1977. But Miller, the darling of the industry in the 1970s, thus far has
experienced an absence of growth in the 1980s. Coors once "owned" Oklahoma and California, with 54 percent and 40 percent of the sales in these
states. In 1987, these percentages had slipped to 26 and 14 percent.

The one constant in all this has been Anheuser–Busch: number one
since 1957. Even more remarkable than its hold on number one has been its
relative growth. In the period 1970–1983, the company has averaged a
better than one-percentage-point annual increase in national market share,
its portion increasing every year since 1976. Several factors contribute to
Anheuser–Busch parlaying its leadership position into a powerful financial
posture relative to its competitors. All of its breweries are large, low-cost
facilities. In addition, most of its output is sold at premium and superpremium prices. Moreover, much of that output takes the form of only one
brand, purchased primarily in one package format (Budweiser in 12-ounce
cans). This means Anheuser–Busch does not often incur the cost of changing
brewing formulas or reconstituting packaging lines. Anheuser–Busch's pricing strategy builds on the firm's efficiencies in production. It endeavors to

have prices change only in line with production-cost changes and to build overall profits through volume gains. Currently Anheuser–Busch is the price leader in the industry.

Rivalry from foreign producers has never been a strong force in the beer industry. However, the amount of beer imported into the United States has been increasing and provides a modest source of rivalry to the high-priced brands. Presently, imported beer faces a tariff of approximately $1.86 per barrel. To preserve the present degree of competition, it is important that the threat of foreign rivalry be preserved. Consequently, the tariff on beer should be removed.

Increases in concentration in brewing are neither the result nor the cause of market power. The reasons, rather, are benign: the exploitation of scale economies and the demise of suboptimal capacity; new or superior products; changes in packaging and marketing methods; poor management on the part of some firms; and product differentiation, which, if not unambiguously benign, is at least outside the pale of traditional antitrust concern.

The statistics of the structure of the beer industry, the pricing and marketing conduct of its members, and the profits it has received do not mark it as a monopolized industry. Consumers are pursued by both price and nonprice competition. The changing fortunes of even major brewers indicate that this is no stodgy oligopoly, with firms adopting a live-and-let-live posture toward each other. The extent of exits from brewing in the last two decades indicates that this is hardly an industry in which the inefficient producer is protected from the chilling winds of competition.

NOTES

1. For certain individuals, this figure may be relatively high. Some Germans claim the reason Dinkelacker is such good beer is because it must compete with the fine wines also produced in the Stuttgart area.

2. Lager beer is aged (or "stored") to mellow. Also, it is bottom-fermented—that is, the yeast settles to the bottom during fermentation. The result is a lighter, more effervescent potation.

3. A barrel of beer contains 31 gallons, or 446 eight-ounce glasses (allowing for spillage), or almost 14 cases of 24 12-ounce bottles.

4. Thomas F. Hogarty and Kenneth G. Elzinga, "The Demand for Beer," *Review of Economics and Statistics*, 54 (May 1972), p. 197. Income elasticity is approximately 0.4.

5. Many brewers regularly ship distances of 300–500 miles. For example, one major brewer ships about 40 percent of its production 300 miles or more; but it ships less than 20 percent of its production more than 500 miles.

6. See *United States* v. *Jos. Schlitz*, 253 F.Supp. 129 (1966); aff'd. 385 U.S. 37 (1966). The states were California, Oregon, Washington, Nevada, Idaho, Montana, Utah, and Arizona.

7. *United States* v. *Pabst*, 384 U.S. 546 (1966) at 559.

8. John M. Connor, *The U.S. Food and Tobacco Manufacturing Industries*, U.S. Department of Agriculture Report No. 451 (March 1980), p. 11.

9. Victor J. Tremblay and Carol Horton Tremblay, "The Determinants of Horizontal Acquisitions: Evidence from the U.S. Brewing Industry," *Journal of Industrial Economics*, 37 (September 1988), p. 22.

10. For a contrary view, see A. J. Chalk, "Competition in the Brewing Industry: Does Further Concentration Imply Collusion?" *Managerial and Decision Economics*, 9 (March 1988), pp. 49–58.

11. Such as Carling and National, Heileman and Rainier, Olympia and Lone Star, General Brewing and Pearl, Olympia and Hamm, Heileman and Carling, and Stroh and F. M. Schaefer.

12. See Kenneth G. Elzinga, "The Restructuring of the U.S. Brewing Industry," *Industrial Organization Review*, 1 (1973), pp. 105–109 and the sources cited therein.

13. See William G. Shepherd, "What Does the Survivor Technique Show About Economies of Scale?" *Southern Economic Journal*, 34 (July 1967), p. 113.

14. *The Brewing Industry*, Staff Report of the Federal Trade Commission, Bureau of Economics (Washington, D.C.: U.S. Government Printing Office, 1978), pp. 48–49.

15. F. M. Scherer et al., *The Economics of Multi-Plant Operations: An International Comparisons Study* (Cambridge, Mass.: Harvard Univ. Press, 1975), pp. 334–335.

16. Alfred Marshall saw this phenomenon as one of the important factors limiting the growth and size of firms and an important determinant in the preservation of competition. See his *Principles of Economics*, C. W. Guillebaud, ed. (New York: Macmillan, 1961), pp. 315–317.

17. In 1951, the total number of employees in the beer industry was over 80,000; by 1985, the number had fallen by more than a half, yet industry production (in barrels) more than doubled. For evidence that the economy-of-scale phenomenon is not unique to the United States, see Anthony Cockerill, "Economies of Scale: Industrial Structure and Efficiency: The Brewing Industry in Nine Nations," in A. T. Jacquemin and H. W. DeJong (eds.), *Welfare Aspects of Industrial Markets* (Leiden: Martinus Nijhoff, 1977), pp. 273–301.

18. H. Michael Mann, "Seller Concentration, Barriers to Entry, and Rates of Return in Thirty Industries, 1950–1960," *Review of Economics and Statistics*, 48 (August 1966), p. 299.

19. For example, see J. Douglas McConnell, "An Experimental Examination of the Price–Quantity Relationship," *Journal of Business*, 41 (October 1968), p. 439; and Ralph I. Ellison and Kenneth P. Uhl, "Influence of Beer Brand Identification on Taste Perception," *Journal of Marketing Research*, (August 1964), p. 36.

20. As calculated from U.S. Department of the Treasury, *Corporation Source Book of Statistics of Income* (Washington, D.C.: U.S. Government Printing Office), various years; and 1987 *Brewers Almanac*, Table 28. The Treasury data include figures for the malt industry as well. Because the product malt is not as extensively advertised as beer, this understates somewhat the actual ratio for brewing.

21. Backer & Spielvogel Media Department and *1988 Beer Industry Update*.

22. Douglas F. Greer, "The Causes of Concentration in the Brewing Industry," *Quarterly Review of Economics and Business*, 21 (Winter 1981), p. 100; Greer, "Product Differentiation and Concentration in the Brewing Industry," *Journal of Industrial Economics*, 19 (July 1971), pp. 201–219; and John M. Connor, Richard T. Rogers, Bruce W. Marion, and Willard F. Mueller, *The Food Manufacturing Industries* (Lexington, Mass.: Lexington Books, 1985), pp. 244–259. William J. Lynk has criticized this hypothesis. See "Information, Advertising, and the Structure of the Market," *Journal of Business*, 54 (April 1981), pp. 271–303; and "Interpreting Rising Concentration:

The Case of Beer," *Journal of Business*, 57 (January 1984), pp. 43–55. See also the response of Victor J. Tremblay, "A Reappraisal of Interpreting Rising Concentration: The Case of Beer," *Journal of Business*, 58 (1985), pp. 419–431.

23. Yoram Peles, "Economies of Scale in Advertising Beer and Cigarettes," *Journal of Business*, 44 (January 1971), p. 32.

24. "John Murphy of Miller Is Adman of the Year," *Advertising Age* (January 9, 1978), p. 86.

25. This is a natural enzyme that reduces the amount of carbohydrates (and therefore calories) in beer. The enzyme was commercially available in 1964.

26. Lutz Isslieb, a General Brewing Company executive, stated, "It's no longer necessary to sell the idea of a light beer; the issue now is *which* light beer." *Modern Brewery Age* (April 21, 1980), p. 12.

27. See Mergers and Industrial Concentration, Hearings, U.S. Senate, Committee on the Judiciary, Subcommittee on Antitrust & Monopoly, 95th Cong., 2nd Sess., May 12, 1978, p. 99.

28. Thomas C. Cochran, *The Pabst Brewing Company* (New York: New York University Press, 1948), p. 151. (Letter of January 3, 1889).

29. *Anheuser–Busch, Inc.* v. *Federal Trade Commission*, 265 F.2d 677 (7th Cir. 1959) at 681.

30. *Federal Trade Commission* v. *Anheuser–Busch, Inc.*, 363 U.S. 536 (1960) at 549.

31. *In the matter of Anheuser–Busch*, FTC, Docket no. 6331, p. 19. Emphasis supplied.

32. F. M. Rowe, "Price Discrimination, Competition, and Confusion: Another Look at Robinson–Patman," *Yale Law Journal*, 60 (1951), p. 959.

33. See *Brown–Forman Distillers Corp.* v. *New York State Liquor Authority* 476 U.S. 573 (1986).

34. Compiled from U.S. Department of the Treasury, *Statistics of Income, Corporation Income Tax Returns* (Washington, D.C.: U.S. Government Printing Office, various years). The figures include the malt industry.

35. See FTC, *Report of the Federal Trade Commission on Rates of Return in Selected Manufacturing Industries, 1960–1969* (Washington, D.C.: U.S. Government Printing Office); FTC *Quarterly Financial Reports for Manufacturing Corps.* (Washington, D.C.: U.S. Government Printing Office, various years).

36. One study done at the University of Iowa's Division of Energy Engineering suggests that mandatory deposit legislation is not the economical way to correct negative externalities in beer consumption. Based on a cost–benefit study of one Iowa county's experience with such legislation, the conclusion was reached that the costs incurred by consumers and merchants of handling the returned beer containers would have allowed the purchase of road crews to clean 2,000 miles of road of *all* litter (the county has only 750 total miles of roadway). See Gustave J. Fink and Richard R. Dague, "The Iowa Beverage Containers Deposit Law," College of Engineering, University of Iowa (December 1979).

37. John E. Kwoka, "The Effect of Market Share Distribution on Industry Performance," *Review of Economics and Statistics*, 61 (February 1979), p. 101. This scenario does not fit the brewing industry. See William J. Lynk, "Interpreting Rising Concentration: The Case of Beer," *Journal of Business*, 57 (January 1984), pp. 43–55.

SUGGESTED READINGS

Books, Pamphlets, and Monographs

Baron, Stanley Wade. *Brewed in America*. Boston: Little, Brown and Company, 1962.

Beer Marketer's Insights — Beer Industry Update, West Nyack, N.Y., an annual.

Beer Marketer's Insights. West Nyack, N.Y., published 23 times per year.

Brewers Almanac. Washington, D.C.: The Beer Institute, an annual.

Connor, John M., Richard T. Rogers, Bruce W. Marion, and Willard F. Mueller. *The Food Manufacturing Industries*. Lexington, Mass.: Lexington Books, 1985.

Freidrich, Manfred, and Donald Bull. *The Register of United States Breweries 1876– 1976*. 2 vols. Stamford: Holly Press, 1976.

Modern Brewery Age: Blue Book. Stamford, Conn.: Modern Brewery Age Publishing Co., an annual.

Norman, Donald A. *Structural Change and Performance in the U.S. Brewing Industry*. Unpublished doctoral dissertation, UCLA, 1975.

Porter, John. *All About Beer*. Garden City, N.Y.: Doubleday, 1975.

Robertson, James D. *The Great American Beer Book*. New York: Warner Books, 1978.

Articles

Ackoff, Russell L, and James R. Emshoff. "Advertising Research at Anheuser–Busch, Inc. (1963–1968)." *Sloan Management Review*, 16 (Winter 1975).

———. "Advertising Research at Anheuser–Busch, Inc. (1968–74)." *Sloan Management Review*, 16 (Spring 1975).

Burck, Charles G. "While the Big Brewers Quaff, the Little Ones Thirst." *Fortune* (November 1972), pp. 103–107 ff.

Clements, Kenneth W., and Lester W. Johnson. "The Demand for Beer, Wine and Spirits: A Systemwide Analysis." *Journal of Business*, 56 (1983).

Cockerill, Anthony. "Economies of Scale: Industrial Structure and Efficiency: The Brewing Industry in Nine Nations," in A. T. Jacquemin and H. W. DeJong, eds. *Welfare Aspects of Industrial Markets*. Leiden: Martinus Nijhoff, 1977.

Elzinga, Kenneth G. "The Restructuring of the U.S. Brewing Industry." *Industrial Organization Review*, 1 (1973).

Greer, Douglas F. "Product Differentiation and Concentration in the Brewing Industry." *Journal of Industrial Economics*, 19 (July 1971).

———. "The Causes of Concentration in the Brewing Industry." *Quarterly Review of Economics and Business*, 21 (Winter 1981).

Hogarty, Thomas F., and Kenneth G. Elzinga. "The Demand for Beer." *Review of Economics and Statistics*, 54 (May 1972).

Horowitz, Ira, and Ann Horowitz. "Firms in a Declining Market: The Brewing Case." *Journal of Industrial Economics*, 13 (March 1965).

———. "The Beer Industry." *Business Horizons*, 10 (Spring 1967).

Lynk, William J. "Interpreting Rising Concentration: The Case Of Beer." *Journal of Business*, 57 (1984).

———. "The Price and Output of Beer Revisited." *Journal of Business*, 58 (1985).

McConnell, J. Douglas. "An Experimental Examination of the Price–Quality Relationship." *Journal of Business*, 41 (October 1968).

Modern Brewery Age. Stamford, Conn.: Modern Brewery Age Publishing Co., tabloid edition, 40 times a year.

Ornstein, Stanley. "Antitrust Policy and Market Forces as Determinants of Industry Structure: Case Histories in Beer and Distilled Spirits." *Antitrust Bulletin*, 26 (Summer 1981).

Ornstein, Stanley I., and Dominique M. Hanssens. "Alcohol Control Laws and the Consumption of Distilled Spirits and Beer." *Journal of Consumer Research*, 12 (September 1985).

Peles, Yoram. "Economies of Scale in Advertising Beer and Cigarettes." *Journal of Business*, 44 (January 1971).

Tremblay, Victor J. "A Reappraisal of Interpreting Rising Concentration: The Case of Beer," *Journal of Business*, 58 (1985).

Tremblay, Victor J., and Carol Horton Tremblay, "The Determinants of Horizontal Acquisitions: Evidence from the U.S. Brewing Industry." *Journal of Industrial Economics*, 27 (September 1988).

Government Publications

Connor, John M. *The U.S. Food and Tobacco Manufacturing Industries*, U.S. Dept. of Agriculture Report No. 451 (March 1980).

Mueller, Willard F. Testimony in *Hearings, Mergers and Industrial Concentration*, U.S. Senate, Committee on the Judiciary, Subcommittee on Antitrust & Monopoly, 95th Cong., 2nd Sess., May 12, 1978.

Staff Report of the Federal Trade Commission Bureau of Economics. *The Brewing Industry* (December 1978).

CHAPTER 6
THE COMPUTER INDUSTRY
Gerald W. Brock[1]

INTRODUCTION

The electronic digital computer was born out of the critical military requirements for computation during World War II and the early cold war. Prior to World War II, many efforts were underway to advance computation beyond the level attained by mechanical hand-operated calculators. Major centers of computation research included: (1) IBM's efforts to combine computational abilities with its established punch-card sorting and tabulating machines, (2) Bell Laboratories' efforts to apply its electrical relay expertise (developed for telephone switching devices) to fast computation machines, (3) Vannevar Bush's efforts at M.I.T. to develop analog computers for solving differential equations, (4) the British Government Code and Cypher School's development of various methods of coding messages for secure communication and of breaking codes used by others, and (5) the U.S. Navy Communications Security Group's development of similar capabilities to those of its British counterpart. None of these groups were seriously working on designs for electronic digital computers. However, John Atanasoff of Iowa State University designed a prototype digital computer in 1939 but never completed a working model.

When World War II began, the demand for fast computation accelerated. The most pressing need was for code-breaking capability. Because naval communications were normally transmitted by radio over large distances, they could be easily intercepted. Security of messages depended entirely on the coding system used, rather than on older methods of physically safeguarding the messages. Early in the war, the British code group developed a method of decoding messages intercepted from the German Navy's Enigma system by using mathematical techniques developed by mathematician and computer theorist Alan Turing together with electromechanical punch-card machinery to perform the data processing. However, in 1942, Germany began using an improved Enigma with a much larger number of possible keys along with other more secure coding machinery. Although the mathematical techniques developed by the British codebreakers remained applicable to the new codes, the greater complexity of the codes meant that either very long computation times were required to break a single code or a much faster data processing machine was required.

The critical importance of codebreaking inspired intensive efforts to develop faster computation on both sides of the Atlantic. The U.S. Naval Computing Machinery Laboratory grew from 20 to 1,100 people and produced large numbers of experimental computing machines using combinations of electromechanical and electronic parts. The British codebreaking group succeeded in producing an electronic digital machine known as the Colossus in 1943. The Colossus and its later versions built by both the British and American codebreaking groups were apparently the first electronic digital computers. Although the machines themselves remained a secret even long after the war's end, many of the wartime codebreakers became the early computer pioneers and transferred the knowledge gained on secret wartime projects into a variety of public computer designs in the postwar period.

In a parallel war effort, apparently uncoordinated with the Navy computation activities, J. Presper Eckert and John Mauchly of the University of Pennsylvania submitted a proposal to the Army for a large electronic digital computer in 1943. Although the project was opposed by leading figures in the wartime scientific community, who believed that it was infeasible to build a reliable computing machine out of vast numbers of unreliable vacuum tubes, the Army accepted the proposal. The project attracted the support of mathematician John von Neumann of Princeton, who was overseeing the computational work on the atomic bomb project and recognized the crucial importance of vastly improved computing capability for military projects. The Eckert–Mauchley machine, known as the ENIAC, was completed in late 1945 after the war's end. It was a monstrously large and unwieldy machine that was two stories tall, weighed thirty tons, and contained 18,000 vacuum tubes. However, it was by far the fastest computing machine in the world and was immediately set to work on complex calculations for atomic weapons.

In contrast to the super-secret codebreaking computers, the ENIAC was open to the public even before its completion. While the ENIAC was still under construction, von Neumann prepared a report setting out the design of an improved version, including the crucial concept of stored program control. The von Neumann report was openly published and was used as a guide in the construction of many early computers. In the immediate postwar period, the public availability of the working ENIAC and the scientific reports related to that project inspired many researchers to begin computer-related work. The early computer research was almost entirely funded by the military, either through military research grants to universities or through contracts to purchase specific computers for military purposes. The largest project in the late 1940s was the M.I.T. Whirlwind project, funded jointly by the Navy and Air Force. The ambitious Whirlwind project lasted several years and required very large amounts of funding, leading some observers at the time to conclude that it should be canceled, but it resulted in major advances in computer technology as well as the training of many key computer personnel.

The Whirlwind project provided initial impetus for the nation's first mammoth computer project — the SAGE air defense system. The SAGE plan was far beyond the level of then existing technology. It attempted to put together a network of computers with high reliability to respond practically instantaneously to air attack on the United States. The SAGE project drew on concepts developed in the M.I.T. Whirlwind project and converted those into massive contracts for computers and programming. The huge expenditures on SAGE played a critical role in moving both computer hardware and programming from an experimental to a commercial industry.

The heavy U.S. military expenditures on computers made the early U.S. computer industry practically synonymous with the world-wide computer industry. The U.S. policy of purchasing military equipment from private companies provided a ready market for computer entrepreneurs. The first computer company, Engineering Research Associates, was formed (with support from the Navy) by William Norris and other experts in the Navy codebreaking effort. That group eventually developed into the Control Data Corporation. The leadership for IBM's transformation from electromechanical to electronic technology also came from the Navy codebreaking group, while the early demand for computers came from defense orders. Eckert and Mauchly left the University of Pennsylvania to form a computer company that eventually became the Univac division of Sperry Rand. The Univac I, first delivered in 1951, is generally considered the first large-scale commercial computer. The first six models went to government agencies. Kenneth Olsen of M.I.T. contributed significantly to the Whirlwind and SAGE projects before founding Digital Equipment Corporation (now the second-ranked world-wide computer company) to commercialize the technology developed in those projects. The first major software company, System Development Corporation, was formed to write programs for the SAGE air defense system. The spectacular advances in U.S. computer technology, fueled by seemingly unlimited military demand and a large base of technologically innovative entrepreneurs, left the rest of the world far behind by the 1960s and led to concerns in other countries about U.S. technological dominance.[2]

II.

STRUCTURE

Barriers to Entry

A useful computer system requires (1) a central processing unit and memory, (2) data storage and input–output equipment, (3) programs (software) to control the sequence of instructions, and (4) individual user familiarity with the knowledge necessary to solve the user's problems with the computer system. The four major components can be provided as a complete package by the computer manufacturer or can be provided by any combination of the computer manufacturer, other independent companies, and the user's own resources. However, the inputs to a computer system must be totally compatible. Software or disk drives for one type of computer will not necessarily work on another, nor can an expert at using one type of computer immediately transfer that expertise to using another type. In addition, the inputs are highly complementary. The value of a computer system is enhanced by an increase in the amount of software, input–output equipment, and individual experts available for that particular computer system.

Two distinct kinds of opportunities for entry have occurred in the computer industry. The first kind of opportunity occurs when advancing technology and reductions in the price of computing make it economically feasible to apply computer technology to a new market segment. In the computer industry, the sustained rapid technological progress has continually opened up new areas for the use of computers, and consequently, new opportunities for entry without direct competition against established companies. The established companies are not necessarily the quickest to recognize a new potential market and to tailor a product to that market. A continual theme of computer industry history is the computer engineer who perceives a new market opportunity, fails to convince his company to pursue the opportunity, and then resigns to form a new company devoted to satisfying that market segment. Spectacular successes by new entrants who pioneered new market segments include Kenneth Olsen's Digital Equipment Corporation (minicomputers), William Norris's Control Data Corporation (supercomputers), Seymour Cray's Cray Research (supercomputers), and Stephen Jobs' Apple Computer (low-cost microcomputers for individual use).

The barriers to entry into a new market segment vary with the segment but overall have been relatively low. Because there is little competition from existing computer manufacturers in such market niches, the main entry problem is to assemble a complete package of hardware and software at a price that the customer finds reasonable for the proposed application. In some cases, such a package can be created from existing components available on an open market and entry merely requires the expertise of a small group of people who have an innovative way of packaging the components to attract new customers. In most cases, the entrant adds some innovation to the existing components—either in hardware or software—to produce a package that could not be assembled entirely from open-market components. In some cases, the entrant requires large amounts of research and development to produce a highly innovative product, such as the supercomputers developed by Control Data and Cray Research. Although heavy research burdens for several years prior to delivery of a product would normally constitute a high barrier to entry, the computer industry barriers have been reduced by government demand for the highest-capacity computers. The Control Data 6600 development was financed by advance payments from Lawrence Livermore Laboratories, and many other supercomputer projects were financed by the government either through research and development projects or advance payments for a working machine. However, the Cray supercomputer project was financed privately, and even though the first Cray-1 went to Los Alamos, it was only paid for after a working machine was in place.[3]

The second opportunity for entry consists of ordinary competition with existing firms. This is the typical situation for standard barriers-to-entry analyses. The distinguishing factor in the computer industry is the requirement that all components of a computer system be fully compatible and the absence of widely accepted industry standards. A potential entrant has a choice of attempting to offer a complete system and thereby gain freedom to set standards among components in any desired manner or of attempting to offer only pieces of another manufacturer's system. Barriers to entry for complete systems in established markets are extremely high because of the need to assemble a complete system, write a large library of software, and convince customers to pay the high costs of switching from their current supplier to the new entrant. Switching among suppliers often means modifying existing programs and retraining or replacing personnel. Consequently, a new entrant's incompatible system would have to offer great advantages over the existing supplier's system in order to make entry viable.

Barriers to entry are far lower for individual system components. An innovation in one particular component may lead to a viable entry product either by selling the improved component to an established system manufacturer for resale under that brand name or by direct marketing to end users. The ability to enter with piece-part competition for individual components sold directly to end users constrains the pricing practices of the systems manufacturer. If entry to all combinations of piece parts is easy, then the system must be priced so that no combination of entry prices can undercut the manufacturer's price. This situation is analogous to the theory developed for multiproduct firms and consideration of the conditions under which entry is possible in "contestable" markets.[4] Many of the competitive strategies in computer systems have been related to preventing easy entry into piece parts and thereby preserving freedom for the systems manufacturer to price the various components of a system in order to extract the maximum profit.

Capital availability has varied with general stock market conditions but generally has not been a significant barrier to entry in the computer industry. In fact, stock market enthusiasm for new computer companies has been a positive spur to new entry. Many small groups of engineers or programmers have been induced by the lure of stock market wealth to break away from an established company and form a new one. In the late 1960s, vast profits to early stockholders in Control Data and Digital Equipment fueled a speculative bubble in new computer-company stocks. Even startup companies with very poor business prospects received high valuations in the stock market. Around 1970, the availability of funds for new computer companies began to diminish as general money conditions tightened, investor disillusionment with high-technology companies set in, and IBM's aggressive tactics created doubt about the viability of IBM competitors. By the end of the 1970s, capital again became freely available to new computer companies. Helped by a reduction in capital-gains tax rates and the emerging new market segment of microcomputers, money flowed rapidly into new computer companies. The success of Apple Computer's public offering inspired venture capitalists to invest in new computer-related companies. Increasing public fascination with high technology also contributed to a flood of venture capital into computer-related companies. According to one estimate, half of all venture capital placed in the early 1980s went into new computer-related companies.[5]

The segment with the highest economies of scale is software. Once software is written, it can be duplicated practically for free. In many industries, high economies of scale imply high barriers to entry. But in the computer industry, rapid technological progress prevents the economies of scale in software from forming a barrier to entry. Continually changing machines and continual new ideas for improved software have allowed a steady stream of successful new software companies. For many applications, a small team of programmers or even a single individual can produce a marketable product, leading to frequent entry by those who believe they can improve on the software their company is currently purchasing.

Concentration

Although IBM was not the first computer company, it became the world's dominant computer company in the 1950s and has retained that position ever since. IBM used its established base of punch-card accounting machines as a method of entry into the commercial computer market. Its small-scale Model 650, introduced in 1954, formed a natural upgrade from punched-card accounting machines. The 650 became the first mass-produced computer and clearly established the commercial viability of computing technology at a time when the main demand was still for specialized military and scientific computers. IBM dramatically expanded its research capability in the early 1950s and positioned itself to lead the development of improved generations of computers. Although IBM's first large-scale computers were delivered after the Univac I and were considered inferior to the Univac I, IBM was quicker than Univac to introduce new models. By the late 1950s IBM was the leading computer manufacturer for commercial, scientific, and military computers.

Throughout the 1950s, IBM's success in military contracts overshadowed its commercial computer business, but IBM successfully transferred the technology developed for the military into commercially successful machines.

In 1955, IBM received $10 million in revenue from its 650 and 700 series of commercial computers, while receiving eight times that amount from the B-52 bombing/navigation computer and the SAGE air defense computers. IBM's revenue from SAGE computers peaked at $122 million in 1957 and remained near $100 million per year for the next two years. But while the specialized military sales remained roughly constant in the late 1950s, IBM's introduction of improved commercial computers accelerated the demand so fast that the revenues from the commercial products grew from one-eighth of the military products to approximately equal to that of military products between 1955 and 1959 and continued to grow far faster than military computers in later years.[6]

By the late 1950s, IBM had attained a United States market share in commercial general-purpose computers (excluding specialized military computers) of approximately 75 percent. IBM's market share in the 1960s and early 1970s has been a source of great controversy because of the antitrust suits filed against IBM and the antitrust significance of market shares. The Department of Justice defined a mainframe or general-purpose market consisting of IBM's competitors for full-line general-purpose machines. That market excluded companies that provided only software or specialized computers. It included only a small number of companies, showed no new entry after 1960, and showed IBM with a steady market share in the 65–75 percent range. IBM maintained that the proper market was a broadly defined electronic data processing market that included all forms of computer-related products, from full-systems suppliers to small software companies to AT&T's electronic telephone switching machines. By that measure, there was a vast amount of continuous entry in the industry, rapidly increasing the number of competitors and bringing IBM's market share down to approximately 35 percent. The issue was not fully settled in an antitrust sense because the Justice Department suit was dropped prior to a court decision, but both measures provide some information in an economic sense. There is no single right definition of the market for economics, but rather a range of potential definitions, each of which is useful for analyzing a particular problem. The very broad market defined by IBM included many products that are not directly substitutable, but it has value in showing the relative size of various companies in related products.[7]

One reason for the large difference in market shares depending on how the market is defined is that most new entrants have entered new segments of the expanding computer-related field rather than entering into direct competition with IBM. IBM commercial customers of the 1960s frequently still have IBM products because IBM has remained competitive, and there are large costs to switching systems suppliers. The greater competition for new segments of the market has caused much lower IBM domination of those areas. Consequently, it is possible to define a meaningful mainframe market in which IBM's share has only slowly declined and still remains above 60 percent. But it is also useful to look at shares of more broadly defined markets in order to gain a more complete picture of the competition in the computer industry.

Table 6-1 shows market shares for an extremely broadly defined market —the world-wide information systems market, including computer systems, work stations, word processors, peripherals, software, data communications equipment, and various services. According to estimates of Arthur D. Little, the world-wide information systems market in 1987 had total revenues of $255 billion. The products in that market are not fully substitutable in either the product or geographic sense. Most of the Japanese company production was sold in Japan, and much of the European company production was sold in Europe, but the markets are not geographically distinct because IBM sold world-wide. By this very expansive definition of both the product and geographic market, IBM had about 20 percent of the world-wide market. It is by far the largest company, with revenues about five times the size of its closest rival, Digital Equipment Corporation. Third-ranked is Unisys, formed by the merger of early industry participants Sperry Rand and Burroughs. The fourth-, fifth-, and sixth-ranked companies are Japanese, representing a rapidly growing, technologically progressive Japanese industry that is becoming a major challenge to American dominance of computer technology. The seventh-ranked company is the largest European producer, the West Germany-based Siemens AG. Using this market definition, the largest 4 companies had 31 percent of the market; the largest 8 had 41 percent; and the largest 100 had 82 percent.[8] This is a moderate level of concentration for the expansive market, but concentration would be much higher in more narrowly defined markets. While IBM remains by far the largest information systems

Table 6-1 _____
Revenue Shares for World-Wide Information Systems

Company	1987 IS Revenue (Millions of Dollars)	Share (Percent)
IBM	50,486	19.8
Digital Equipment	10,391	4.1
Unisys	8,742	3.4
Fujitsu Ltd.	8,740	3.4
NEC Corp.	8,231	3.2
Hitachi Ltd.	6,274	2.5
Siemens AG	5,703	2.2
NCR Corp.	5,076	2.0

Total World-Wide Information Systems Revenue: $255 billion

Source: Computed from revenue figures in "The Datamation 100," *Datamation* (June 15, 1988), pp. 14–29.

company, the rise of new market segments and of the Japanese computer industry has greatly reduced IBM's world-wide dominance in computers from the commanding position that it held in the 1960s.

Table 6-2 shows market shares for the mainframe market, a much more narrowly defined market than the information systems of Table 6-1. The mainframe market of Table 6-2 is similar to the Justice Department's mainframe market defined in its antitrust case, but the Table 6-2 mainframe revenues exclude some peripheral products that were in the Justice Department market. The first column of Table 6-2 shows the mainframe revenue shares of the largest U.S.-based companies as a percentage of all mainframe revenues of U.S.-based companies. It is an approximation to a mainframe market limited geographically to the United States. The second column of Table 6-2 shows the mainframe revenue shares of the largest world-wide mainframe producers as a percentage of all world-wide mainframe revenues. These shares represent market shares for a narrowly defined product market (mainframe computers) but an expansively defined geographic market (world-wide). IBM retains a dominant market share (76.6 percent) of mainframe revenues from U.S.-based companies and a substantial share (43.3 percent) of mainframe revenues of all companies. The first number overstates IBM's dominance because foreign producers provide competition in the U.S. domestic market. The second number understates IBM's dominance in the U.S. domestic market because many of the foreign companies focus primarily on their respective domestic markets.

Table 6-2
Revenue Shares for Mainframe Computers

Company	1987 Share of U.S.-Based Companies (Percent)	1987 Share of World-Wide Revenues (Percent)
IBM (U.S.)	76.6	43.4
Fujitsu (Japan)		12.9
NEC (Japan)		11.9
Hitachi (Japan)		7.2
Unisys (U.S.)	9.8	5.5
Groupe Bull (France)		3.7
Amdahl (U.S.)	6.3	3.6
Siemens AG (Germany)		2.7
STC PLC (England)		2.3
Control Data (U.S.)	3.5	2.0

Source: Computed from revenue figures in "The Datamation 100," *Datamation* (June 15, 1988), pp. 42–94.

III.
CONDUCT

The early computer industry pattern was the development of full-scale systems and support from a single manufacturer for each customer. IBM was the premier developer and practitioner of this strategy, and because of its success, other manufacturers imitated it. The strategy was dictated by the fact that information was scarce in the early industry. Computers were complex, specialized machines that required a great deal of machine-specific knowledge. Capable professionals who were experienced with IBM equipment could not easily program a different machine or even evaluate its capabilities. The decision to purchase a company's machine was a decision to establish a long-term relationship with the company; it included a commitment by the customer to invest in personnel and software specialized to that type of machine and an expectation that the manufacturer would provide adequate support for the existing machine and would provide improved products in the future.

The undeveloped and rapidly growing computer industry of the 1960s allowed IBM to satisfy its customers' needs and to gain a great deal of market power by concentrating on total solutions. The IBM salesmen were renowned for their knowledge of a customer's business, and, in addition to selling, frequently acted as consultants about potential applications and necessary equipment. Close relationships were developed between technical and managerial personnel in each customer location and the IBM personnel. IBM systems engineers and salesmen were often key sources of information for evaluating the performance of their customers' personnel, and they assisted in recruitment efforts. Once an IBM system was ordered, vast amounts of support services (such as education and consulting) were provided free to the customer. IBM's approach is clearly stated in this excerpt from a report to the IBM Management Committee:

> The basic concept revolves around an in-depth planning session for each account initially involving only IBM personnel. The purpose will be to look at the account power structure and decision-making process, designing a data processing system as if we were board chairman, and developing an open item list with individual IBM responsibilities of all things necessary to sell the resultant system.[9]

As part of the account-control process, IBM emphasized leasing rather than selling. Leasing allowed IBM continued interaction with the customer and reduced the customer's risk when accepting a very expensive piece of capital equipment. IBM sold itself as the knowledgeable party that could provide a limited-risk solution to the customer's business problems for a fixed price per month. Considering the limited information possessed by top management regarding how to translate specific business problems into requirements for arithmetic speed and storage capacity, the IBM total-solution approach was very effective in attracting customers. It also limited competitive inroads, because the customer who was dependent upon IBM advice and assistance lacked the ability to fully evaluate the alternative solutions offered by other manufacturers.

The early machines were designed for particular market segments and were generally incompatible with each other even within a particular manufacturer's offerings. In the early 1960s IBM began an ambitious effort to develop a line of compatible machines covering all aspects of the computer market. The machines were designed with a single basic architecture and were designed to provide a high degree of interchangeability of peripheral equipment and programs. The new line was announced in 1964 as the System/360, and initial deliveries began in 1965. The System/360 was a spectacular success despite difficulties in achieving all of the original design goals. IBM has continued to use the basic architecture of the System/360 in its later machines so that even with massive changes in computer technology, the new machines appear to the user as a compatible evolution from the System/360.

The System/360 prices were based on value-of-service prices for the hardware pieces and on free provision of software and support services. Despite massive resources invested in the development of IBM's complex operating system for the System/360, no separate charge was made for the operating system, language compilers, utility programs, or even for many kinds of application software provided by IBM. The availability of a large library of free software was a major selling point for IBM and also encouraged users to try to develop new applications that would increase the demand for hardware capacity.

Once a customer made a decision to purchase a System/360, there was no further competition for the individual pieces of hardware. A Control Data disk drive, for example, could not be substituted for an IBM disk drive because only the IBM disk drive would work with the IBM system. Consequently, IBM used a value-of-service price policy for the individual pieces of hardware in order to maximize its revenue. A fast tape drive could be priced far above the price of a slow tape drive because the customer received much greater value from the fast tape drive, even if the manufacturing cost of the fast tape drive was only slightly higher than that of the slow tape drive. All pieces of hardware were priced far above their manufacturing cost in order to cover costs of services and software provided free and to provide a substantial profit margin. This pricing system was very effective in extracting profit from IBM's control of the market as long as IBM could prevent competition for individual pieces of hardware, but it left IBM vulnerable to competition if competitors could develop compatible pieces that could be substituted for individual system components.

The vast demand for the System/360, along with IBM's pricing strategies, caused several firms to begin the development of compatible replacement tape and disk drives. The replacements were known as plug-compatible competition because the competitors claimed that a user could simply unplug the IBM unit, plug in the replacement unit, and continue operating as if the entire system were provided by IBM. The first plug-compatible competition began in November 1967 with tape drive replacements; this was followed by the entry of other competitors with both tape and disk drive replacements in 1968. The Memorex replacement for IBM's popular 2311 disk drive rented for $500 per month per drive and also had slightly better performance than IBM's drive, which rented for $590 per month. At the time Memorex deliveries began, IBM had 19,000 of that type of disk drive installed and 10,500 on order. Because of its own large demand backlog and the limited manufacturing capacity of the new entrants into the market, IBM considered the new companies to be no serious threat when its first study of their capabilities was made. IBM's 1968 study concluded that it was "too early to forecast effect" of the competition, that "IBM strategy [was] sound over [the] plan period," and recommended improved products for later years.[10]

The absence of IBM reaction to the initial plug-compatible competition spurred the entry of many companies with a broad line of products. High initial profits and a booming stock market created great paper wealth for the pioneers of direct competition with IBM systems. Manufacturing capacity rapidly increased, and the competitors moved from the long-established products into the newer, more technologically advanced ones—those on which IBM counted for future revenue growth.

As the competition grew, IBM responded with three basic strategies. The first strategy was based on changing interface standards and tying equipment such as disk controllers and memory to the central processing unit. The second strategy was the development of a term-lease plan in which discounts over the basic monthly rental were given for one- or two-year lease commitments. From the time when an IBM product was installed, the competitors needed some time to reverse engineer a product that would be competitive with the IBM product; the competing company could then receive full rental until a replacement IBM product was introduced. With monthly rental, customers could accept a new product from IBM, then replace it with a competitive product as soon as the competitive product was ready. With the fixed-term plan, the customer either had to retain the IBM product for the full term (and therefore reduce the effective life of the competitive product) or pay the higher monthly rental rate in order to preserve flexibility.

Although changing interface standards and the fixed-term plan slowed the plug-compatible competition, they did not stop it. IBM's ability to control the evolution of the market was further reduced in 1970 when Gene Amdahl, a key IBM designer since IBM's early computer days and a prime architect of the System/360, left IBM to form Amdahl Corporation. Amdahl's goal was to develop a plug-compatible CPU. With Amdahl's CPU, it became possible to put together an IBM-like system with the only actual IBM components being the software provided free by IBM. The system would consist of the plug-compatible CPU connected to plug-compatible peripherals running on the IBM operating system and would run applications software created for IBM systems without any changes. Consequently, IBM's third strategy was to accept the greater competitiveness of the market and respond with overall lower prices and a closer alignment of prices to the costs of producing the various products, including separate charges for some software and services previously bundled into the price of the machines. An IBM analysis of tape-drive competition concluded:

> Due to the increased amount of competition, it is our belief that the concept of functional pricing is no longer the most suitable way to price in the magnetic-tape area. Apparently, manufacturing costs of high- and low-performance drives do not differ substantially and competition has concentrated in the higher-performance area and priced their drives very competitively . . . a continuation of this policy would contribute to future losses.[11]

The plug-compatible competition brought about a major change in IBM's strategy and in the overall competitive strategy in the industry. Greater competitive pressure forced faster product cycles and brought prices closer to costs. The wide variety of choices in the IBM world made it more difficult for other full-line manufacturers to maintain their separate standards and operating systems. The IBM standards began to take on the role of de facto industry standards even without formal acceptance by the established standards groups. IBM's ability to control the standards was weakened by the fact that customers now had the ability to shift to other sources of IBM-compatible equipment if they did not like IBM's new products.[12]

Of particular importance in the changing industry strategies was Amdahl's surprising difficulty in raising capital for his plug-compatible computer. Given Amdahl's reputation and the normal stock market excitement about new computer ventures, capital should have been abundantly available. However, the timing of his venture, just after many computer companies had suffered large drops in stock market value and after IBM had become very aggressive about protecting its market share, made capital difficult to raise. In order to proceed, Amdahl sold a large interest in his company to Japan's Fujitsu Corporation, including a technology exchange by which Fujitsu obtained full access to Amdahl's technology. At that time, Japan had a substantial internal computer industry protected by trade barriers and was struggling to develop computers that would be fully competitive on the world market. Soon after the Amdahl agreement, Fujitsu and Hitachi announced a joint series of IBM-compatible computers spanning the full performance range. Fujitsu and Hitachi later broke their partnership, and each began marketing IBM-compatible computers. By combining the IBM standards for compatibility with Japan's leading-edge components technology, Fujitsu and Hitachi became fully competitive with IBM.[13]

The movement toward a more open IBM world in which many companies produced products compatible with IBM standards was confirmed by the explosion in the very low end segment of individual computers in the 1980s. Semiconductor innovator Intel developed the first microprocessor (an entire central processing unit on a single silicon chip) in 1971. That initial microprocessor was of very limited capacity and suitable only for calculators. Continued component advances during the 1970s resulted in the development of microprocessors of moderate power and also of very inexpensive semiconductor memory over the next several years. Several companies began packaging kits of components that hobbyists could put together to build a primitive home computer. The personal-computer market was transformed from an experimental niche to a major market by Apple Computer's introduction of its line of inexpensive machines along with software and peripherals. A key event in the development of the market was the introduction of the program VisiCalc, an electronic spreadsheet program that greatly simplified routine financial calculations. The combination of VisiCalc with the Apple produced an inexpensive package with substantial commercial value and purchases accelerated.

The initial rapid growth of the personal-computer segment occurred without any IBM product in that segment. The personal-computer segment of the market threatened a repeat of the minicomputer segment, in which IBM had failed to respond to DEC's initial products and then found a major market developing with little IBM influence. Full development of IBM proprietary personal products and software would have taken considerable time and then would have had to break into a market established by others. Instead, IBM developed a product with an open architecture that could easily be used with software and peripherals developed by others. IBM's initial personal computer, introduced in 1981, was largely constructed from components and software purchased from others. The IBM PC quickly became an industry standard, with sales of $500 million in 1982 and of $2.6 billion in 1983. The IBM PC had several technical advantages over the Apple. Furthermore, the IBM name and support helped many corporations to purchase large numbers of the machines with the expectation that they could be more easily integrated into corporate data processing procedures than could the Apple. IBM introduced an improved version of the PC (the PC-XT) with much better disk storage capacity in 1983 and introduced a higher-capacity version (the PC-AT) with a new microprocessor chip in 1984.

IBM's open architecture allowed it to make a fast beginning in the personal-computer market but also provided many opportunities for competitors. Software and upgrade components for the IBM PC and then entire clone systems developed a thriving market. Even individuals without special training could buy parts from mail-order houses and upgrade or modify their computers. Some clone makers developed major product lines with their own brand identity. Among the most successful of these was Compaq Computer Corporation, which doubled its sales from $625 million in 1986 to $1.2

billion in 1987. Others concentrated on low price with no brand identity, often putting together clone systems in neighborhood stores from the cheapest selection of parts available on the world-wide market.[14] The intense competition in the IBM clone market and the resulting price declines cut dramatically into IBM's control of its personal-computer family; IBM's share of the IBM-compatible personal-computer market dropped to 42 percent in 1986 and to 27 percent in 1987, according to estimates by International Data Corporation.[15]

In 1987, IBM introduced a new line of personal computers, the Personal System/2, with four models ranging in price from $1,700 to over $10,000. The PS/2 introduced a number of technological improvements but also included a more proprietary architecture. Many industry observers interpreted the PS/2 as an attempt by IBM to gain more of its traditional control over its products and avoid the intense competition experienced by its personal computers from multitudes of component assemblers. Although it is too early to fully evaluate the success of the PS/2, it is unlikely to reestablish IBM's proprietary control. There is now a large and highly competitive clone industry as well as general customer acceptance of IBM-compatible but non-IBM-manufactured products. The initial reaction of the clone makers to the PS/2 was to continue producing the clones of the older IBM models at lower and lower prices. If the PS/2 is able to establish new industry standards, it is likely that the clone makers will adapt to those standards and continue in business.

To summarize, IBM's strategy of total account control floundered on the twin problems of increasing customer sophistication and successful selective entry by competitors into overpriced IBM products. The strategy has been successfully changed into one based on traditional competitive criteria—technological innovation and low-cost manufacturing—along with emphasis on the advantages of dealing with a widely diversified IBM, which can provide a solution for any computer problem. Although IBM retains some market power in the mainframe market, the highly competitive minicomputer and microcomputer market segments, together with extensive competition from Japanese producers, have greatly reduced IBM's dominance of the world-wide data processing market.

IV.
PERFORMANCE

The three basic economic measures of performance are allocative efficiency, technical efficiency, and dynamic efficiency. Allocative efficiency refers to how well the price system allocates goods to supply user desires. It is high if prices are close to marginal costs and progressively lower as prices depart from marginal costs. Technical efficiency refers to how close the actual costs of production are to the lowest possible costs of production, considering the product mix to be produced. Dynamic efficiency refers to the rate of technological progress compared with the optimal rate.

Because of the unprecedented level of technological progress in the computer industry, only dynamic efficiency is important as a measure of progress. Allocative and technical efficiency problems typically result in losses equal to a small percentage of the value of an industry's output. The dynamic efficiency has been so high in computers that it totally dominates any issues of allocative or technical efficiency.

A large number of studies of the rate of technical progress in computers has been done. Although the methods and results vary somewhat, they show a sustained real price decrease of between 20 and 27 percent per year between 1958 and 1985.[16] This is an unprecedented rate of sustained innovation and means that, even at the conservative estimate of 20 percent per year, computer prices have declined by a factor of 400 times over the past 30 years. In other words, a unit of computer capacity that cost $400,000 thirty years ago could be purchased for $1,000 today. In fact, that is a common experience for personal computers—thousand-dollar personal computers that are purchased for home use or by the hundreds for employee desks in large corporations have similar power to a major system costing hundreds of thousands of dollars in the early commercial computing days. The modern systems not only cost far less but are much more reliable and dramatically easier to use. The $400,000 system of the late 1950s would have required a substantial crew of experts in maintenance, programming, and operations to get the work from it that an individual with minimal training can now obtain from a personal computer.

The sustained price declines in computers have resulted in computers spreading throughout U.S. society. From the initial demand for critical military needs and for producing scientific computations that could not be performed with older methods, computers have now replaced vast numbers of older technologies that initially were not seen as competitive with computers. Even the office typewriter is now obsolete, displaced by the ubiquitous word processing system. The newer functions have a lower economic value per unit of computer capacity required, but as computer prices decline, it is economical to computerize more and more functions. The conventional wisdom among computer experts is that the next major area of computer expansion is into artificial intelligence. Much research has been done over many years on artificial intelligence systems, but the vast amounts of computing capacity required for useful systems have generally made them uneconomic. Declines in the price of computing, along with improvements in programs available, are expected to bring artificial intelligence applications into widespread use over the next several years.

The most sophisticated and extensive artificial intelligence application currently under active discussion is the computer plan for the proposed

Strategic Defense Initiative. The SDI plans envision a computer network capable of processing large numbers of signals, distinguishing decoys from warheads, and giving commands to launch defensive measures in the optimal manner. Because of the expected extremely short time intervals between detection of an attack and launch of defensive measures, most of the decision making of the system would be preprogrammed into the computer controllers. The proposed system would require a major leap forward in computer technology, similar to the leap required during the 1950s when the SAGE air defense program was planned while computers were still in the experimental stage. One of the major controversies related to the SDI program is whether it is possible to develop computers and software capable of meeting the planned requirements.

The rapid technological progress of the computer industry has had a major beneficial effect on the overall economy. Kenneth Flamm estimates that technological progress in computers has resulted in an overall economic benefit of between 0.3 and 0.8 percent of GNP per year, accounting for a substantial percentage of the total productivity improvement in the economy. Flamm also estimates that the social rate of return to research and development in the computer industry has been between 50 and 70 percent, with private benefits much lower because of the difficulty of capturing the total benefits.[17] Flamm's estimate of the social rate of return suggests that despite the high rate of research and technological progress in the computer industry, the industry is still underinvesting in research relative to the social optimum (that is, the position where a dollar spent on research generates the same benefits as a dollar invested in another use). Thus it is possible that even though the technical progress in the computer industry has been extraordinary, it could be even higher with a socially optimal rate of research.

V.

PUBLIC POLICY ISSUES

The critical role played by computers in the economy and in the military has raised several policy issues. Among these are antitrust policy, technology policy, and the definition of intellectual property rights.

Antitrust

IBM's dominance of the industry has made it a natural target of antitrust suits. Control Data filed the first important suit, based on its allegation that IBM's losses on the 360/91 (a system competitive with Control Data's 6600 supercomputer) were evidence of predatory pricing. After several years of pretrial proceedings, Control Data and IBM reached an out-of-court settlement, which included a substantial payment by IBM to Control Data.

Soon after the Control Data private suit was filed, the Department of Justice filed a major antitrust suit against IBM, seeking the dismemberment of the company. The suit was filed on the last day of the Johnson Administration (January 1969), went through pretrial proceedings during the Nixon Administration, went through a massive trial during the Ford and Carter Administrations, and was finally dropped by the Reagan Administration. As the suit was being prepared in 1968, the computer industry appeared to be an obvious candidate for antitrust action by all the standard measures; one firm dominated the industry, barriers to entry were high, and there was evidence of conduct designed to maintain a monopolistic position. In retrospect, 1968 marked the high point of IBM's dominance of the industry. The extraordinary success of the System/360, then at its peak, provided a set of standards that was a natural target for fringe competitors. The heavy user investment in software for the System/360, which had tied customers to IBM, also restricted IBM's freedom to change the standards and allowed other companies to design products to replace the IBM models. By the time the suit was dropped in 1982, the industry had become substantially more competitive, and IBM had modified many of the practices complained of in the suit.

IBM's efforts to protect its peripheral market from plug-compatible peripheral companies provoked strenuous protests from the companies involved and led to a series of private antitrust actions. Telex won an initial victory in district court in 1973 and was awarded what was then the largest antitrust damages ever, a payment from IBM to Telex of $260 million. Telex's victory inspired other peripherals makers to file their own suits. However, Telex's victory was reversed by the appeals court. Eventually, all of the peripherals cases were either settled out of court with nominal payments or were carried forward to trials that ended with victories for IBM.

Technology Policy

Computers have been recognized from the beginning as having important national-interest characteristics. Despite Britain's wartime development of prototype computers, massive postwar U.S. military support for computer development produced a commanding lead in U.S. computer technology. Although early military support included generous grants to universities for general computer technology development, most of the military support was in the form of purchases of specific products for specified needs rather than general technology development. However, the military support sometimes included research and development contracts for the desired products, and it also included a willingness to make advance payments for promising but undeveloped products from new companies. As the computer industry matured, military support was reduced and became more tightly focused on purchasing specific functioning products through a rigorous competitive bidding process.

The U.S. technological lead made other developed countries uneasy about their dependence on foreign technology. By the late 1960s, Japan and the major European countries had developed national programs to promote computer technology. The European model consisted of choosing a national champion, a particular firm that would be favored with various advantages within the country and would be expected to develop advanced technology with little domestic competition. The Japanese model consisted of cooperative basic technology research to be shared among highly competitive Japanese firms.[18]

The European national champions were not so successful as had been hoped and are not major players in the world computer market. However, the Japanese model has been very successful, and many observers are worried about eventual Japanese dominance of the U.S. computer market. Japan's previous successes in dominating various electronics fields gives some credence to expectations that the Japanese producers will be vigorous competitors with U.S. companies in the world-wide computer market.

The Japanese successes and the critical importance of the computer industry have led to considerations of the need for a U.S. technology policy. In particular, the successful Japanese combination of cooperative basic research with competitive producers has attractive economic properties. Basic research is the most difficult to capture by one firm, and therefore economic theory predicts that too little of it will be done if each firm simply follows its own economic interest. Cooperative arrangements among private companies or publicly sponsored basic research are more likely to approach the socially optimal amount of basic research than total reliance on independent decisions by each firm.

The general military buildup of the 1980s, together with the specific plans for the Strategic Defense Initiative, have focused renewed attention on the military significance of computers. It is unlikely that the U.S. would allow itself to become dependent upon foreign technology for such a critical military technology as computers. Military support for computer technology has been increasing and could expand dramatically in the future. Many policy questions remain to be answered on the relationships among international trade policy, public support for basic computer research, and military requirements for advanced technology.

Copyright Protection for Programs

A third kind of major policy issue is the extent of copyright protection for programs. Copyright law has distinguished between ideas (not protected by copyright) and the form in which the ideas are expressed (protected by copyright). When a violation of copyright is alleged, the established method to prove copying is to show that the alleged infringer had access to the original work and that a substantial similarity exists between the original and the alleged copy.

Application of copyright law to programs led to the conclusion that the idea or concept behind a program may not be protected by copyright, but that the actual code may be. It is well established that copyright protection applies to programs and that direct copying of the instructions is illegal. However, programmers frequently prepare programs designed to be competitive and compatible with copyrighted programs. If a company is sensitive to copyright issues, it may even attempt to prevent its programmers from ever seeing the copyrighted code so that even if there is a substantial similarity between the original and the alleged copy, it will be impossible to show that the programmer had access to the original work.

Recent decisions and court cases have suggested a more expansive definition of copyright protection, with potentially farreaching implications for the computer industry. In the case of *Whelan Associates* v. *Jaslow Dental Laboratory*, the court held that a program that performed the same function as a copyrighted program, but that was written in a different source language for a different computer than the copyrighted program, infringed the copyright. Encouraged by that case and others that have suggested an expansive reading of software programming protection, Lotus Development Corporation has filed suit against producers of programs very similar to Lotus's popular and profitable 1-2-3 spreadsheet package for infringing its copyright to the "look and feel" of Lotus 1-2-3. The challenged programs use different internal code but are explicitly designed to look like Lotus 1-2-3 to users and to run existing user-created Lotus files. While the competitive programs contain all of the functions of one particular release of Lotus 1-2-3, they also contain additional features not included in the Lotus program.

The Lotus lawsuit has attracted wide attention because if Lotus is successful, many standard practices in the computer industry will be endangered. A common method of software development is to take a piece of popular software, improve it with added features while retaining enough similarity of user controls that users of the original software can easily adapt to the new, and then to market the new program as an improved version of the old. It is that practice that is at issue in the Lotus lawsuit; if the look and feel of a program are protected, then efforts to produce a high degree of user compatibility with existing software may violate the copyright.

A further potential result of the current software litigation is a challenge to the concept of clone computers. A clone computer requires compatibility of the BIOS program that controls input and output. IBM's BIOS is a copyrighted program, and clone makers produce a BIOS with different code that performs exactly the same functions in order to ensure compatibility of the computers. If copyright protection extends to the look and feel of a program rather than merely the actual language in which the program is expressed, then it would be a reasonable implication that a BIOS program that performs exactly the same functions as the IBM BIOS violates IBM's copyright. If that interpretation were adopted, then fully compatible computers could not be produced because their BIOS programs would violate IBM's copyright.[19]

The extent of copyright protection will have a major effect on the future direction of the computer industry. If copyright protection is defined expansively, market power will increase for both hardware and software producers as basic concepts become off limits to imitators. New legislation may be necessary to tailor copyright law to the special conditions of the computer industry.

NOTES

1. The author is currently Chief of the Common Carrier Bureau of the Federal Communications Commission. The views expressed in this chapter are those of the author alone and do not necessarily represent the views of the commission.

2. For a detailed account of early computer development with extensive references to the literature, see Kenneth Flamm, *Creating the Computer: Government, Industry, and High Technology* (Washington, D.C.: The Brookings Institution, 1988).

3. Kenneth Flamm, *Targeting the Computer: Government Support and International Competition* (Washington, D.C.: The Brookings Institution, 1987), p. 81.

4. The theory of contestable markets is a generalization of the theory of perfect competition. A contestable market is one for which there are no barriers to entry or exit. Even if there are economies of scale and complex multiproduct cost functions, a contestable market will impose a severe price discipline upon the incumbent firms. For a full development of the theory, see W. J. Baumol, J. C. Panzar, and R. D. Willig, *Contestable Markets and the Theory of Industry Structure* (New York: Harcourt Brace Jovanovich, Inc., 1982).

5. John Verity, "Start-up Fever Is Spreading," *Datamation* (September 1982), p. 180.

6. IBM's revenues from each product for each year through 1970 were provided in a court-ordered census of the industry for the *Control Data* v. *IBM* litigation. Although the data were originally collected under strict nondisclosure requirements, they were introduced several years later into the trial record of *California Computer Products* v. *IBM* and became a matter of public record.

7. For an extensive discussion of the antitrust issues from the perspective of IBM, see F. M. Fisher, J. J. McGowan, and J. E. Greenwood, *Folded, Spindled, and Mutilated: Economic Analysis and U.S.* v. *IBM* (Cambridge, Mass.: MIT Press, 1983); for the same issues from the perspective of the Department of Justice, see Richard T. DeLamarter, *Big Blue: IBM's Use and Abuse of Power* (New York: Dodd, Mead & Company, 1986).

8. "The Datamation 100," *Datamation* (June 15, 1988).

9. IBM, "Management Committee Minutes," January 6, 1972, released in *Telex* v. *IBM* as Plantiff's Exhibit 387-066.

10. IBM, "Management Committee Minutes and Charts," July 15, 1968, *Telex* v. *IBM*, Plaintiff's Exhibit 384-035.

11. IBM, "Phase II Forecast, Aspen I, Monarch," June 15, 1970, *Telex* v. *IBM*, Plaintiff's Exhibit 272, p. 9.

12. For detailed discussions of the plug-compatible competition with sharply contrasting interpretations, see Fisher; DeLamarter; and Gerald W. Brock, *The U.S. Computer Industry* (Cambridge, Mass.: Ballinger, 1975).

13. Flamm, *Creating the Computer*, p. 195.

14. *PC Magazine* (which describes itself as "the independent guide to IBM-standard

personal computing") provides a detailed account of products available for computers compatible with the IBM PC family.

15. John Burgess, "Revolutionary PS/2 Line Is Here to Stay, IBM Insists," *The Washington Post*, August 25, 1988, pp. B1, B6.

16. For discussion of various performance studies, see Flamm, *Targeting the Computer*, Chapter 2 and Appendix A.

17. Flamm, pp. 32–39.

18. Flamm, Chapter 5.

19. Bill Machrone, "Taking the Stand: The Look-and-Feel Issue Examined"; Winn L. Rosch, "The Copyright Law on Trial"; Bill Machrone, "Roots: The Evolution of Innovation"; Jim Seymour, "Who Owns the Standards?"; Jared Taylor, "You Be the Judge"; all in *PC Magazine* (May 26, 1987).

SUGGESTED READINGS

Books

Brock, Gerald W. *The U.S. Computer Industry: A Study of Market Power*. Cambridge, Mass.: Ballinger Publishing Company, 1975.

DeLamarter, Richard T. *Big Blue: IBM's Use and Abuse of Power*. New York: Dodd, Mead & Company, 1986.

Dorfman, Nancy S. *Innovation and Market Structure: Lessons from the Computer and Semiconductor Industries*. Cambridge, Mass.: Ballinger Publishing Company, 1987.

Fisher, Franklin M., John J. McGowan, and Joen E. Greenwood. *Folded, Spindled, and Mutilated: Economic Analysis and U.S. v. IBM*. Cambridge, Mass.: MIT Press, 1983.

Flamm, Kenneth. *Targeting the Computer: Government Support and International Competition*. Washington, D.C.: The Brookings Institution, 1987.

Flamm, Kenneth. *Creating the Computer: Government, Industry and High Technology*. Washington, D.C.: The Brookings Institution, 1988.

Periodicals

Datamation. Magazine that provides extensive coverage of companies, products, and competitive issues in the computer industry.

Computerworld. Weekly newspaper that covers the industry in great detail.

PC Magazine. Magazine that provides extensive coverage of products compatible with the IBM PC family of computers.

CHAPTER 7

THE MOTION PICTURE ENTERTAINMENT INDUSTRY

Barry R. Litman

As the motion picture industry approaches its centennial celebration in 1989, the world of entertainment has changed significantly from that bygone era when George Eastman applied for his patent for celluloid film and William Kennedy Laurie Dickson first demonstrated to his boss, Thomas Edison, that he had invented a motion picture camera that would fulfill the master inventor's dream of "doing for the eye what the phonograph does for the ear."

On the eve of the twenty-first century, motion pictures still hold forth as one of America's most treasured art forms, but theater attendance has gradually given way to other home entertainment media such as television, cable, and the videocassette recorder. Yet, the movie itself has never been stronger, now the centerpiece content form driving a series of exhibition "windows" so intertwined that traditional industry boundaries are blurred, and it is now proper to refer to this broadened industry landscape as encompassing a motion picture "entertainment" industry.

I.

INTRODUCTION

Early History[1]

Shortly after receiving his patent for the motion picture camera and its viewing machine, Edison introduced motion pictures to an unbelieving public in 1894. These early peep-hole viewing machines (kinetoscopes), with their continually rotating 50-foot strips of celluloid film, proved to be an instantaneous success and were easily added novelties to a curio hall or penny arcade. Yet, the novelty of motion pictures could not sustain a growing industry.

By failing to protect his patents abroad, Edison invited in a series of foreign inventors, who soon foresaw the wisdom of a more sophisticated projector system using the same stop-action technique of the kinetoscope. In 1896, Edison belatedly caught up with the European and new American

183

inventors when he introduced a new projector called the vitascope. The projector meant that a crowd of people could simultaneously view a single strip of film, thus reducing the capital investment of the parlor operator. Each of the rival projector manufacturers produced its own films. Without standardization of equipment and given that cameras were not freely licensed, machines and films were tied to each other, forcing parlor operators either to choose one incompatible projector system over another or to purchase all the different systems.

Once again, the public grew weary of this novelty act and attendance faltered until more sophisticated movies could be developed. By the early 1900s, "stories" of approximately 15-minute duration (so-called one-reelers) soon became the industry standard. Essentially, the movie industry had passed across that imaginary line from being merely a novelty to being an art form.

The arrival of the nickelodeon theater in 1905 provided the movie industry with its first opportunity to stand on its own as an entertainment industry. The nickelodeon was not really a theater in its modern sense; rather, it was a converted storefront with 100 chairs and a projector and screen. Nevertheless, the motion picture program, consisting of four or five consecutive one-reelers, often emphasizing different genres, would soon overshadow its vaudevillian counterparts.

These fundamental changes in the industry brought forth corresponding new business practices. The emergence of the film exchange and the conversion of the industry from purchase to *leasing* of motion pictures was a critical factor in maintaining the rapid turnover of film product — a factor thought critical to continually lure the customer back to the nickelodeon and to establish a loyal clientele. The exchange functioned as a intermediary by purchasing the films itself and then sharing the cost burden among its clients through a sophisticated library rental system. Later on, as one-reelers gave way to two-reelers and eventually feature films, and the nickelodeon was replaced by first-class and then deluxe movie theaters, rising costs would have to be met by lengthened runs and higher admission prices.

Thus, the development of motion pictures as a mass medium involved a series of cycles, each with some driving force that would further cultivate a mass audience with the movie-going habit. Each new invention and each improvement in content and in the luxuriousness of the exhibition hall would propel the industry through a ratchet-type effect to a new higher equilibrium level.

Search for Market Power

Concomitant with the development of motion pictures as mass medium was the attempt by a small group of companies to acquire monopoly power. As is typical of most fledgling industries, the original power brokers were enthroned through manipulation of the patent process. As alluded to previously, Edison and a small group of inventors tried to dominate the market by exploiting their patents on cameras, projectors, film, and other integrated components. Because of the simplicity of the film content, these manufacturers (and a group of bootleggers) were initially able to supply the burgeoning industry with all its film product needs. However, as filmmaking (the production stage) became more complex, it grew beyond the scope of many of the original producers. Eventually, a small, specialized group of skilled artisans successfully entered and competed with the equipment manufacturers in the production of films and helped to fill the demand from the nickelodeons for enough product to maintain a daily turnover pattern. Essentially, partial vertical disintegration of the industry was taking place into four largely separate strata: manufacture of equipment, production of film product, distribution of product via local exchanges, and exhibition of product at nickelodeons.

When the Supreme Court sanctioned both the Edison and Biograph camera patents, a cycle of costly patent infringement suits cropped up, which threatened the stability of the industry. Eventually, a truce was called in 1909 between the major patent holders, and a collusive agreement was forged to collectively monopolize the industry. The Motion Picture Patents Company was a trustlike patent-pooling arrangement between the holders of the 16 key motion picture patents, including Edison, Biograph, Armat, and Eastman–Kodak. The major domestic and foreign producers of that era were also members, but they didn't explicitly share in the royalties accruing from the patents. Each producer was exclusive to the trust and had to pay a royalty of ½ cent per foot of completed film. Eastman–Kodak, the exclusive supplier of film stock to the producer members, collected this royalty. The leading exchanges also were exclusively licensed, and they purchased film product at prices ranging from 9 to 13 cents per foot. The exchanges then leased films at market prices to nickelodeon operators, who also signed exclusive contracts with the trust. Their contracts mandated their purchase of trust-sanctioned projectors plus a two-dollar weekly royalty payment for the use of the trust-produced films. Therefore, by cornering the market on equipment and offering top-quality producers, the trust believed that their product was indispensible and that they could monopolize the industry and exclude independents at all access points.

Troubles arose for the trust when they were unable to prevent maverick exchanges and nickelodeons from dealing with independents for additional needed supply of product. This instability could only be eliminated by exerting greater control over the distribution stage; hence, the General Film subsidiary was established to acquire or drive out of business all licensed exchanges. Once this was achieved, the trust had vertical monopoly control over every stage of production save exhibition and was able to dominate the industry during its first few years of existence. However, a series of mutually reinforcing events would soon cause its demise.

First, the trust was unable to enforce its court-ordered injunctions against patent infringers using bootlegged equipment. These elusive independents quickly fled from the grasp of the U.S. marshalls and private company security guards to the sunny Los Angeles area—just a few miles from the Mexican border. Second, William Fox, one of the few remaining independent exchange operators, filed an antitrust suit against the trust, which was soon joined by the Department of Justice[2] and eventually ended the Trust, although many commentators feel that it merely formalized an internal decaying process already in the terminal stage.

Internal bickering among the trust members over the failure of Edison and Biograph to share royalties more equitably, and the shifting around of many producers and directors from one company to another and to independents, further destabilized the industry. More crucially, because of an inflexible standard of using single reels coupled with daily turnover, the trust was slow to adapt to changing consumer tastes for motion pictures. When the independents introduced the feature films and simultaneously capitalized on the drawing power of box office stars by publicizing their names and paying them higher salaries, the trust could not meet this competitive challenge and fell by the wayside.

With the rise of feature films, a new distribution organization was needed to handle such a different species of film. Under the leadership of Adolph Zukor, head of Famous Players, an exclusive alliance was formed in 1914 with an association of state's-rights distributors (known as Paramount) to distribute feature films. Within two years, Zukor assumed control and soon merged his Famous Players company with Paramount. Zukor's feature films were superior to the competition, and with his acquisition of famous stars like Mary Pickford and Douglas Fairbanks, he was able to charge high fees and license his films in blocks—by tying the star films to lesser films on an all-or-nothing basis. Thus the production–distribution stage had the upper hand with quality product, and the exhibitors had to accept the terms or suffer the loss of this popular fare.

When the terms became too dear, the 100 largest first-run exhibitors formed their own organization, called First National Exhibitors Circuit, and integrated backward into production in an attempt to supply their own needs and thereby circumvent the power of the Zukor organization. Zukor realized that even quality films had to have first-run access to earn high box office dollars, and after failing to form a joint alliance with First National, he reluctantly acquired a string of theaters in order to guarantee access for his films. The merger race was now on, as all the large companies in each stage of production sought merger partners to guarantee either an assured supply of films or access at reasonable terms. By 1925, there was only a handful of giant vertically integrated firms left in the industry.

The arrival of sound occurred in the mid-twenties at precisely that point in time when something new and exciting was once again needed to stimulate movie attendance. Silents had reached their zenith of artistic achievement.

The industry seemed listless and now was forced to compete with the burgeoning mass medium of radio. As a series of competing and incompatible technologies sought marketplace approval, Western Electric finally joined with Warner Brothers to introduce the first "talkies" in late 1926. Within a year, buoyed by the phenomenal success of *The Jazz Singer*, Western Electric severed its exclusive ties to Warner Brothers and sought industry-wide approval and exclusive use of its sound-on-film technology. The remaining major distributors/exhibitors soon signed exclusive arrangements with Western Electric to use its equipment in both the filming and exhibition of motion pictures.

Once again, the tendency of the industry toward oligopolistic consensus was manifest, this time with the invention of sound being the catalytic agent. Yet, even with the propulsion that sound gave to new companies like Warner Brothers and RCA, they still could not be viable without a chain of theaters providing an assured point of access for their films and were forced to integrate into the exhibition stage.

While the Depression of the early thirties did dampen the box office revival induced by sound, the industry was not as severely impacted as many large smokestack industries. Nevertheless, the industry did attempt to improve its popularity by appealing to more salacious themes as well as introducing the double feature. Most importantly, the industry crafted a Code of Fair Competition under the National Industrial Recovery Act of 1933 to protect itself against the ravages of unbridled competition. The code regulated various trade practices and was administered by the Motion Picture Producers and Distributors of America, the industry trade association. Such trade practices as block booking, blind selling, time clearances, zoning, and admission price discrimination, which severely disadvantaged independent theater owners, were now legally sanctioned and enforceable in a court of law.[3] Within two years, the National Industrial Recovery Act was declared illegal and the code was discontinued; but the lesson of the beneficence of mutual cooperation had already been taught. The industry would now follow a tacit form of shared monopoly[4] rather than the explicit form; in the long run, the results would be indistinguishable.

The Paramount Case

During the late 1930s, the five fully integrated firms ("the majors") set upon a deliberate course of action to eliminate the remaining independents within the industry. Since none of the majors, individually, possessed enough first-run theaters (the cream of the business) or produced enough A-quality feature films to be self-sufficient, *they needed each other.* Acting in concert, they had enough first-run theaters to provide a nationwide exhibition showcase for their films, and their combined production efforts (in association with three minor distributors)[5] were sufficient to fill an entire year's schedule of films. Achieving near 100 percent self-sufficiency severely restricted the freedom of independent producers, distributors, and exhibitors from access at any point along the vertical chain.

It is instructive to examine this tacit cartel in greater detail to understand the vertical nature of this industry and how vertical integration can be utilized as an anticompetitive tool to form an impenetrable barrier to entry and to coalesce monopoly power.[6] The Big Five were fully integrated across the three critical strata and were the primary producer/distributors of A-quality films. They were aligned with the Little Three and some other minor independents who acceded to the stiff distribution fees demanded by the majors for access to the system.These companies collectively provided the lower-quality, lower-budgeted B films destined to fill the lower half of the double bill. Collectively, the Big Five, Little Three, and aligned independents could supply virtually 100 percent of the program fare for an entire year's playbill at the exhibition stage. During this period, they released three-fourths of the total number of non-Western films and earned a comparable percentage of industry rentals.

At the exhibition level, the Big Five either wholly owned or had significant financial interests in only 3,137 out of 18,076 U.S. theaters, or 17.35 percent; yet, in the more significant first-run market, they collectively operated 70 percent of all first-run theaters in the 92 cities with 100,000 or more population and 60 percent in cities between 25,000 and 100,000 in size.

The price-fixing conspiracy had both horizontal and vertical aspects, spanning the distribution and exhibition levels. Theaters were categorized according to their status in the temporal distribution scheme and assigned territorial and time clearance to protect their status and earning power. Distributors, furthermore, fixed minimum admission prices for films according to their run. While none of these practices in isolation is anticompetitive, when the distributor conspirators *uniformly* and unchangeably determined these designations and *arbitrarily* gave favorable terms to the vertically owned majors, this system of distribution became rigged. Hence, with high admission prices and excessive temporal and geographic clearances, the bulk of film revenues would be guaranteed for the first-run theaters controlled by the majors, thereby injuring the independents, who had in many cases been unfairly relegated to second-run or lower status. In cities where majors faced each other in direct competition or where independents had a strong theater position, the majors would pool their theaters together, affiliate with the independents, and jointly maximize profits.

When these practices were buttressed by a film-licensing process that also favored the large theater owners (through chainwide negotiations of master and formula deals and franchise agreements) at the expense of the independent exhibitors, who when given a chance to show A films were continually forced to block book, the exclusionary aspects of the conspiracy were vividly demonstrated. The inevitable effect of these practices in the context of a vertical market structure was almost total regimentation of the industry and denial of access to nonaligned independents.

This pattern of vertical organization was attacked by the Antitrust Division of the Justice Department beginning in 1938. The ultimate outcome of the decade-long case was that the courts ordered vertical divestiture of the exhibition level from the production–distribution level and furthermore required that theaters that were illegally acquired or that were used as part of the conspiracy be sold off by the newly reconfigured exhibition circuits. The divestiture process was fashioned through a series of consent decrees negotiated with each company on an individual basis. For the most part, the divested chains of theaters could not acquire new theaters without specific approval of the courts, and none of the affected parties could reintegrate (either forward or backward). Furthermore, competitive bidding was suggested (but not mandated) as a way of further insuring that decentralization of power and open access would prevail in the exhibition level.

While divestiture did not totally eliminate monopoly power in the film industry, this case became a prototype for the restructuring of an industry under the antitrust laws. The language of *Paramount* with respect to vertical integration still is the cornerstone for prosecution of vertical accumulations of power:

> First, it runs afoul of the Sherman Act if it was a calculated scheme to gain control over an appreciable segment of the market and to restrain or suppress competition, rather than an expansion to meet legitimate business needs. . . . Second, a vertically integrated enterprise . . . will constitute monopoly . . . provided a power to exclude competition is coupled with a purpose or intent to do so.[7]

Aftermath of Paramount

The dismantling of the vertical monopoly in the motion picture industry should have provided a laboratory setting to assess the impacts of antitrust structural remedies, but alas, the arrival of television at precisely the same point in time confounds the analysis. Nevertheless, some industry changes can be directly attributed to the breakup.[8]

With vertical disintegration and the end of block booking and franchising, assured access to theaters was no longer guaranteed; *films would have to compete according to their intrinsic quality.* This naturally opened up the market for independent producers and distributors, whose products would now be judged according to merit rather than parentage. Many new independent producers entered the scene and, paradoxically, they were now welcomed with open arms by the major and minor distributors. The majors had decided to reduce their risks by cutting back on their in-house productions, which correspondingly meant the end of the studio system of star exploitation. Given their excess studio capacity and their need to obtain economies of scale in distribution, they courted the favor of the independent production sector —the same group of people they had sought to eliminate only a few years before.

For the Little Three distributors, the opening up of the exhibition market meant that they could upgrade their product line and thus compete head to head with the majors; no longer were they relegated to the subservient role of producing B films. Within a few short years, their status as distributors became comparable to that of the Big Five. Allied Artists (formerly Monogram) and Republic, two independent producer/distributors who had weathered the cartel years, also became more prominent after divestiture. Surprisingly, the distribution level that would soon become the new center of power and profits for the industry invited only sporadic entry. This is generally explainable by the fact that the arrival of television cut box office demand by an estimated one-third to one-half and eliminated the low-budget B film (which was similar to the free television program) from the marketplace. Given such adverse market conditions and the need to achieve economies of scale of two or three films distributed per month, new entry was not feasible.

The most striking changes occurred at the exhibition level. As part of their divestiture plans, many of the divorced circuits exceeded the requirements of the consent decrees by ridding themselves of marginal theaters, especially in small towns. Since such a large share of their remaining holdings were first-run theaters, they remained in a relatively advantageous position. Some 20 percent of the second-run theaters of independents had their classifications improved after divestiture, but the most significant change was the elimination of the third-run (and lower-run) theaters due primarily to the loss of B films and the emergence of drive-ins. Thus, divestiture meant the removal of the umbrella that artificially had been propping up many inefficient-sized theaters. The inevitable result of such theater upgrading was higher average admission prices for the movie-going public; yet this was counterbalanced by a general improvement in the quality and diversity of films distributed. While pictures were supposed to be equally available to all local theaters, the chain organizations still ran the show, owing to their deep pockets, superior efficiency, and negotiating prowess.

Impact of Television

The initial reaction of the motion picture industry to the fledgling television industry was one of ridicule. Early television programs were compared to the B films of the 1940 era. Nevertheless, as TV penetration increased and Americans stayed at home rather than attending movies, the motion picture industry soon understood the enormity of the situation.

Its initial strategy was to boycott the television industry by refusing to permit its creative personnel (primarily actors) from appearing in television programs and refusing to produce television series or license films for television exhibition. It also sought to counter the inroads of television by introducing a number of product innovations, including Cinerama, three-dimension movies, and big-budgeted films with lavish production values.[9]

After recognizing the revenue-generating capability of television production, Warner Brothers became the first major distributor to break the boycott in 1955 by agreeing to produce a weekly series. Shortly thereafter, the remainder of the large distributors decided to hitch their wagons to the rising star of television rather than retain their purity in producing films. They also realized that television networks (and later television stations) could become subsidiary markets for licensing theatrical films, once those films had reached the saturation level of theatrical exhibition. In other words, the new television markets could now replace the third- and lower-run theatrical markets that had been lost. The temporal price-discrimination pattern that had worked so well when only theaters were involved could now accommodate the new television technology. Therefore, what had begun in the late 1940s as a major confrontation between two entertainment media took on a pattern of stability, mutual interdependence, and economic symbiosis within a short span of 10–15 years.[10] This stable business relationship continues to exist, and in fact has been extended to the newest technologies of cable and videocassette recorders—all of which have been folded into the distribution price-discrimination process.

II.
MARKET STRUCTURE

Because of the various subsidiary markets and the historical pattern of vertical integration, the structure of the motion picture entertainment industry is extremely complex. The focus will be placed on the distribution and exhibition levels, since the production level is so closely interwoven with distribution and is largely competitive.

Distribution

The distribution stage still remains under control of a handful of major companies, although a few names have changed since the *Paramount* divestiture.[11] In terms of the majors, RKO has left the scene; in 1983, MGM took over distribution for United Artists and eight years later acquired the company completely. Monogram became Allied Artists and was recently purchased by Lorimar, which in turn is in the final stages of being acquired by Warner Brothers.[12] Another independent, Embassy, was sold in 1985 to Columbia and then resold that same year to Dino DeLaurentis; it is currently in financial reorganization. American International was sold to Filmways in 1979, and its name was changed to Orion in 1980. Another key player in the distribution realm is Tri-Star. Formed in 1983 as a joint venture of Columbia, HBO, and CBS, it was purchased late in 1987 (including its theater circuit) by Columbia and folded into the new Columbia Entertainment Division.[13] Finally, the latent Disney studio was reorganized in the mid-1980s, shed its exclusive family-entertainment label (G rating), and has now established itself in the top rung of industry companies.

The market shares of the leading motion picture distributors are given in Table 7-1. While the familiar majors still remain, their stranglehold on industry power has diminished in recent years[14] due to the entry of significant newcomers like Tri-Star and the intensified competition posed by Disney, Orion, and a few independents, such as Cannon and New World. The four-firm concentration level has fallen from 68 percent in 1982 to 57 percent in 1987, while the Herfindahl–Hirschman Index has declined correspondingly from .16 to .11. This still indicates considerable oligopoly market power, but, interestingly, market shares and industry leadership seem very volatile, often influenced by having one or two box office smashes in any given year. Thus,

Table 7-1

Market Shares for North American Film Distributors,[a] 1982–87

Company	1987	1986	1985	1984	1983	1982
Columbia	4	9	10	16	14	10
20th–Fox	9	8	11	10	21	14
MGM–UA	4	4	9	7	10	11
Paramount	20	22	10	21	14	14
Universal	8	9	16	8	13	30
Warners	13	12	18	19	17	10
Disney	14	10	3	4	3	4
Orion	10	7	5	5	4	3
Tri-Star	5	7	10	5	—	—
Embassy	—	—	1	<.5	1	1
Atlantic	na	1	1	1	.5	<.5
Cannon	na	2	2	1	<.5	<.5
New World	na	3	1	1	1	1
DeLaurentis (Embassy)	1	3	—	—	—	—
All others	12	3	13	2	1.5	2
CR$_4$	57%	53%	55%	66%	66%	68%
CR$_8$	83%	84%	79%	91%	96%	96%
H-H	.11	.11	.11	.13	.14	.16
CR$_6$-Majors	58%	64%	74%	81%	89%	89%
Instability[b]		21%	49%	37%	40%	39%

[a]Market Shares = Percentage of annual film rentals to distributors.

[b]Instability $= \sum_{i=1}^{N} S_i^t - S_i^{t-1}$

Source: *Variety*, annual editions.

for the last three and one-half years, Paramount has performed most consistently, being the clear-cut industry leader three times; yet, as of August 1988, Disney/Buena Vista, with a 22 percent market share, had a 7 percent lead over Paramount. Nevertheless, with Columbia's acquisition of Tri-Star and the financial problems of DeLaurentis and Cannon, the early 1988 market-share figures suggest the competitive flurry may have bottomed out.

Barriers to Entry

It is not surprising that the distribution level is highly concentrated. This is a characteristic common to all the mass media and is largely explained by the economies of scale that accompany national distribution of entertainment product. To service the 22,300 North American movie screens and take advantage of the foreign market potential, a distributor must have a vast worldwide network of offices. Furthermore, if other subsidiary markets, like pay cable, commercial television, and home video, are to be tapped, additional bureaucratic layers must be established. Focusing on domestic distribution of motion pictures, a major company needs somewhere between 20–30 regional offices and a sizable number of salespeople and marketers. It also is necessary to have a full lineup of features released throughout the year so that these offices can work at full capacity. Yet, the number of releases may be misleading, since it does not always correspond to the relative success of the distributor. In 1987, Disney and Paramount had the smallest number of releases of the top nine distributors but the largest market shares, while Tri-Star and Cannon had exactly the opposite situation. At any one time, it often is preferable to employ one's work force on a relatively small number of good prospects (those currently in release and those on the horizon) than to waste one's efforts on films that may last only a few weeks.

While some critics would argue that ownership of studios and back lots is an albatross around the necks of the major distributors and merely drives up their overhead costs, there may still be some strategic nonpecuniary advantage (in scheduling time and having creative experts on hand) that accrues to those so situated, especially during a production boom.

Since cost efficiencies dictate large size, there must be a corresponding level of demand to justify such a large enterprise and to use the capacity most efficiently. Here is where product ideas, differentiation, and managerial skill play such an important role. The studio chief and his top lieutenants must consistently make correct decisions concerning their product composition. This is unlike a modern industrial enterprise, where automobiles or steel are turned out in large quantities over long manufacturing runs; rather, each film is hand-crafted with a very short product life and only occasional opportunities for reuse of the creative inputs. In fact, the motion picture differs from episodic television series in this key creative dimension. The successful studio requires a continual stream of new ideas, since the product and consumers' tastes change so often; the matching of tastes and product is made more complicated by the nearly two-year lead time required to produce and release a new film. Therefore, it should not be surprising that one witnesses a revolving-door policy for studio production chiefs.

Given the escalating production and advertising costs of recent years, the average release by a major distributor runs nearly $20 million in negative costs plus at least half that amount to give it a national day-and-date launch. Understanding these economic risks and the fact that the major distributors have a portfolio of such projects at different stages in the two-year cycle, the distributors and their corporate parents tend to act rather conservatively. They seek to minimize their financial risks in whatever way is available; hence, like their television counterparts, they often seek some formula. This formula may take the form of employing bankable movie stars, top directors, and writers who at some point have touched the magic of a box office smash or else laying off the risk through coproduction with foreign investors.[15] Alternatively, they may repeat ideas, themes, or characters that worked well in the past, thus generating the ever-present sequel.[16] This risk-averse philosophy is not new; it simply has replaced the assured theatrical access in operation during the heyday of the trust and the cartel.

Vertical Integration and Conglomerateness

Part of the risk can also be reduced if the distributors have vertical integration or deep corporate pockets. While the *Paramount* decrees forbade reintegration between the distribution and exhibition levels, as time has passed, the original companies have been resold or absorbed into larger conglomerate corporations. Furthermore, entry has occurred at both levels, thus introducing new companies that are not covered by the original decrees. Most importantly, given the degree of competition from other subsidiary exhibition markets, the antitrust-tolerant Department of Justice has not opposed reintegration by the original *Paramount* defendants during the 1980s.

There currently exists a significant and growing degree of forward integration by the leading distributors into the exhibition realm. The advantages of vertical integration are numerous. They clearly give the distributor greater control over admission prices, release patterns, and the avoidance of anti-blind-bidding statutes. Most importantly, they permit all of the box office dollars to remain with the distributor without worrying about sharing them with exhibitors. While Disney has concentrated on theme parks, Twentieth-Century Fox has eschewed theater ownership in favor of TV stations and its new Fox Broadcasting Network, and MGM–United Artists has been too busy with corporate takeovers and reorganizations to concentrate on this activity, most of the other major companies have obtained a foothold in domestic and international theaters. Most of the key acquisitions have occurred in the last two years. For example, in 1986, MCA acquired a 50 percent interest in

Cineplex—Odeon, the second largest theater circuit in North America, which has grown by over a thousand theaters in the last several years since acquiring Plitt and other medium-sized circuits. Gulf and Western has approximately 470 domestic and 433 Canadian theaters, making it the fifth largest chain in North America. It also is a partner with MCA in the 76 screen circuit in Europe, known as Cinema International Corporation.[17] In late 1987, Columbia Entertainment obtained full ownership control of Tri-Star, including its circuit of 310 theaters (the former Loews circuit). In early 1988, the Loews subsidiary acquired the USA circuit, thereby adding another 317 theaters to Columbia's holdings and making it the sixth largest circuit in North America.

Meanwhile, Cannon, which had a 525-screen circuit in Europe (with a very strong position in the United Kingdom), bought the domestic Commonwealth circuit (number 9) in 1986, with its 432 screens, and has a pending offer to acquire the 157-screen French Pathé circuit. By bailing out Cannon with a large loan in 1987, Warner Brothers allegedly has established new ties to the Cannon theaters, and given its pending partnership with Gulf and Western,[18] it soon could become a major theater owner.

Most interesting is the position of the industry leader, United Artists Theater Circuit. Not only has it aggressively sought merger partners and embraced new construction programs within the theater exhibition level, but it is controlled by Telecommunications, Inc. (TCI), which is by far the leading multiple-system cable operator. TCI recently bought stock in Blockbuster video stores, an industry leader in videocassette sales with a projected 600-store chain by the end of 1988.[19] Given this dominant position across so many exhibition windows, and with partial ownership of such cable networks as Turner Broadcasting Systems (CNN, WTBS, TNT), Black Entertainment Network, Cable Value Network, Tempo, and American Movie Classics (100 percent control), we may be witnessing a vertical chain of control never even dreamed of by the *Paramount* conspirators.

In terms of conglomerateness, the motion picture companies are no longer independent companies but rather subsidiaries of major communications corporations or other conglomerates. To the extent that these major distributors can rely on the resources of their parent corporations for production loans or capital expansion, this further enhances the barriers to entry in the industry and widens the historic gap between the majors and independents.

Table 7-2 gives a brief synopsis of each parent company, its market ranking according to *Business Week*, and the percentage of its 1987 revenues that came from filmed entertainment—a category broad enough to include film-related revenues earned in the broadcasting and home video markets. Columbia, Disney, and Paramount are subsidiaries of very large corporate giants and consequently account for a rather small percentage of the parent company's operations. Twentieth-Century Fox, Warner Brothers, and Universal are divisions of large media conglomerates, albeit somewhat smaller

Table 7-2
1987 Diversification Ratios and Profitability for Selected Film Distributors

Parent Corporation (Distributor)	Business Week Ranking[b]	Parent $ Sales	Distributor $ Revenues (Millions of Dollars)	Distributor $ Profits	Sales Margin[c]	Diversification %[a]
PURE/SEMI-CONGLOMERATES						
Coca-Cola (Columbia)	17	7658.3	$1066.0	$ 28.1	2.64%	13.92
Walt Disney (Disney)	45	2876.8	875.6	130.6	14.92	30.44
Gulf and Western (Paramount)	104	4681.1	1829.6	297.3	16.25	39.08
MEDIA CONGLOMERATES						
News Corporation (20th-Century Fox)	NA	3503.4	914.6	113.0	12.36	26.11
Warner Communications (Warner Brothers)	125	3403.6	1355.7	176.4	13.01	39.83
MCA (Universal)	170	2589.6	1330.3	162.9	12.25	51.37
OTHER						
Lorimar-Telepictures (Lorimar)	625	766.2	574.0	−46.0	−8.01	74.90
MGM–UA	811	479.0	479.0	−88.6	−11.27	100.00
Weighted Averages					8.86%	43.62

[a]Diversification % = Distributor revenues/parent corporation sales
[b]Ranking according to market valuation of stock
[c]Margin = filmed entertainment profits (after taxes)/entertainment revenues

Sources: *Business Week*, April 15, 1988; *Channels*, June 1988.

than the pure conglomerates associated with the first grouping of distributors. Nevertheless, these are still enormously large corporations with annual sales in the $2.6–3.5 billion range. The motion picture distributors in this grouping account for a higher percentage of total corporation sales, ranging from 26 to 51 percent. The final grouping consists of Lorimar–Telepictures and MGM–United Artists. These corporations are considerably smaller than the first two groupings, with annual sales of approximately three-quarters of a billion dollars. Correspondingly, their film entertainment divisions account for a very high percentage of the parent's sales. Of course, the remainder of distributors would rank further down the list and would neither be very large in absolute terms nor very diversified. In terms of major theater circuits, United Artists Communications is ranked number 406 in *Business Week's* list, while TCI, a majority stockholder in this company, is ranked number 121.

Exhibition

To understand the degree of concentration in the exhibition stage, one should first differentiate between national and local markets. One commonality across both geographical delineations is the overwhelming prevalence of chain ownership. Just as chain ownership has permeated the grocery, drug, and department store industries, so it has throughout the mass media. The days of the stand-alone theater owner, cable system, newspaper, or television station are fast diminishing. Chain ownership yields some efficiencies in spreading managerial (such as motion picture booking) and legal expertise, as well as advertising and marketing costs, across a large number of outlets; yet it has the potential for creating barriers to entry and enhancing market power.

The national concentration indices given in Table 7-3 indicate a moderate degree of concentration in theater ownership,[20] but the recent trend is definitely on the rise. Since December 1983, the four-firm concentration index has increased by 9 points, while the eight-firm index has correspondingly risen by nearly 12 points. The current industry leaders, United Artists and American Multi-Cinema, both have more than doubled their theater holdings over these scant number of years. United Artists has, in fact, risen from second place to first by adding some 1,260 screens, while AMC leaped over long-time industry leader General Cinema by adding nearly 800 screens. It should be noted that such expansion of circuit size is not limited to only the acquisition route; a net of some 4,400 (23.3 percent) new screens have also been built. Restricting ourselves to only the top four firms, collectively these companies have added about 2,800 new screens (82.5 percent), nearly four times the industry average for new builds. The unmistakable evidence points to the existence of a merger wave being driven largely by the industry leaders. The theater circuits originally divested in *Paramount* have been absorbed by other equally large circuits.

The Structure of American Industry

Table 7-3

Number of Screens for Top U.S. Theater Circuits, 1983–1988

		May 1988				December 1983	
Rank	Company	Number of Screens	%	Rank	Company	Number of Screens	%
1	United Artists	2,264	9.8	1	General Cinema	1,050	5.6
2	AMC	1,528	6.6	2	United Artists	1,005	5.3
3	General Cinema	1,358	5.9	3	AMC	736	3.9
4	Cineplex Odeon	1,047	4.5	4	Plitt	605	3.2
5	Carmike	675	2.9	5	Martin	431	2.3
6	Loews	627	2.7	6	Commonwealth	362	1.9
7	Hoyts	507	2.2	7	Mann	315	1.7
8	Mann	447	1.9	8	Redstone	302	1.6
Total U.S. Screens		23,200				18,884	
CR$_4$		26.7%				18.0%	
CR$_8$		36.4%				25.5%	
H-H		.024				.011	

Source: *Variety*, annual editions.

Yet it would be wrong to examine only national concentration, since movie theaters are local retail outlets. Is the local degree of concentration better or worse than at the national level? The Detroit market is fairly typical of what is happening in metropolitan areas throughout the country. In Detroit, four chains collectively control 71% of the 255 screens in the greater metropolitan area. AMC is the largest circuit in Detroit, with 86 screens, while National Amusement is second, with 44 screens. Hence, the top two circuits themselves account for slightly more than half of all screens! The average number of screens per site in Detroit is 4.32, with the average for the four chains at 5.48. This reflects the national trend to downsize theaters into multiscreen auditoria. It is a significant change from the deluxe theaters built in the 1920s and the willingness of owners to bank their entire business on a single feature.

III.

CONDUCT

The process of product pricing and revenue sharing has altered very little since the *Paramount* restructuring. At the exhibition level, theaters will either bid for upcoming features or individually negotiate the contract. The *Paramount* decrees require that motion pictures should be contracted picture by picture at the *local* rather than chain level so that all theaters have an equal opportunity for obtaining product. The contract generally has standard provisions with respect to admission prices, beginning date, length of run, minimum guarantee, dollar advance, terms for extended runs and early cancellation and, most critically, the rental terms. Rental terms refers to the percentage split of box office dollars between the exhibitor and distributor. The industry standard is a 90–10 split in favor of the distributor *after the house expenses are deducted.* This small profit margin for theater owners demonstrates the relative bargaining power of the distributors vis-a-vis the exhibitors.

It is important to understand the flow of money in the theatrical motion picture industry. Starting with box office gross and subtracting house overhead expenses and the theater's share yields gross rentals to the distributor. From these rentals, the domestic distribution fee (usually standardized at 35 percent) and all of the distribution expenses (advertising, print duplication) are deducted, leaving gross profits for the producer. From profits are subtracted the production loan and interest payments, yielding net producer profits. Net profits are then split among all the profit participants, which include financial investors and deferred payments to actors and directors and the major motion picture distributors themselves, if they have financed the production loan or guaranteed a bank loan. Any residual profits remain with the producer. Thus, the major distributors have achieved some industry consensus and standardization in terms of the exhibition contract, the split of box office dollars, distribution fees, and profit sharing. This cooperation also spills over into their subsidiary markets through a sophisticated price-discrimination plan.

Price Discrimination

With the arrival of television and the subsequent development of the other subsidiary markets, the theatrical tiering system of runs and clearances was replaced by the sequencing of subsidiary markets, or exhibition "windows." In economic terms, both systems represent forms of second-degree price discrimination — charging different prices to classes of customers who place different utility valuation on obtaining the product. In the case of motion pictures, these groups cluster according to the value they place on the time dimension. The avid moviegoers who absolutely must be the first to see newly released theatrical films are willing to pay the highest price per individual ticket.[21] Those who receive less utility from attending movies may be prepared to wait until the second theatrical run or until the movies appear in the video stores or on pay cable, where the prices per *household* are significantly lower. Those with even less interest may wait several years for the movies to make their way to network or local television, which impose no direct programming charge.

Such a price-discrimination plan works to maximize profits for the distributors who have rights across all these windows only if the preponderance of major distributors follow approximately the same time sequencing, and there is no significant leakage or resale between the windows. This does not mean that a person or household can only participate in a single window. Frequently people will enjoy repeat viewing of motion pictures across time as the picture makes its way through the various windows. The goal of this price discrimination is to establish the optimal sequencing of windows so as to skim the consumer surplus from each succeeding market as the movie journeys from the highest consumer surplus window (theatrical movies) to pay cable and eventually to commercial television. For the windows that stand toward the end of the line, not only will the distributor receive a very small average price per film but only a minuscule price per household or per viewer.[22]

Exhibition Conduct

The process of downsizing average theater size and building multiple-screen auditoria illustrates a different profit-maximization approach by the theater owners. This permits a more cost-efficient utilization of seat capacity than was possible in the old single-auditorium deluxe theaters. With, say, six to eight screens per site, a theater owner can manage a portfolio of different pictures and is fairly certain that at least one or two of the screens will have a hit, while the others will do moderate business until their run is over. In this way, average load factors can be increased compared to the hit-and-miss strategy associated with having a single screen.

The multiple-screen concept is tied in with the shopping-mall phenomenon.[23] The movie theater complex is an integral part of the modern shopping mall, since it generates a lot of foot traffic for other store owners. For this reason, the recent construction boom in movie theaters is more a shopping-mall phenomenon than it is related to fundamental industry economics. If one only looked at theaters as an isolated business, given the stagnant demand for admissions due to the VCR and pay-cable alternatives, one could not explain the addition of nearly 1,000 new screens per year. In short, theater construction is only justified as part of the profit-maximizing calculus of building a successful shopping mall. It shouldn't be surprising to thus find mall entrepreneurs cross-subsidizing such theaters through favorable leasing provisions or low-interest loans.

The theater concession stand also fits into this traffic flow analysis and multiple-theater concept. Since the theater retains 100 percent of all concession revenues (which have an extremely high markup), yet only makes about 10 percent excess profits from box office gross, any strategy that maintains a high load factor can be very profitable. By having multiple screens in operation at staggered starting times and centrally locating the concession stand in the lobby, the theater can operate this aspect of its business at near capacity, although the peak times about 10 minutes before each new showing cannot be totally avoided.

The theaters can further minimize their excess seat capacity by negotiating escape clauses in their booking contracts that permit shortened runs for unpopular films and, correspondingly, lengthened runs, additional screens, and moveovers (to a larger auditorium) for films that prove unexpectedly popular. The prices that local theaters charge for performances at comparable times tend to be very similar, and most theaters follow a price-discrimination pattern of discounting for off-peak time periods (such as matinees, twilight, midnight, and occasionally certain weekdays like Tuesdays) and for customers with elastic demands (such as children and senior citizens). Once again, this brings more customers into the theaters, sells more popcorn, and, since the theaters usually have unlimited numbers of showings per day and split the box office dollars with the distributor, it is still profitable to show a movie with only a couple of dozen patrons in the theater. Seldom will a theater charge differential prices based on the perceived quality or popularity of the individual film.

The local exhibitors have sought to countervail the power of the distributors who, either explicitly through open bidding or implicitly through the grapevine, continually desire exhibitors to bid against each other for exclusive rights. The local theater owners would band together and split the forthcoming product among themselves according to a preconceived plan. In this way, the distributor could only negotiate with a single theater, and such a bilateral monopoly would even up the negotiation process for the theater owners. The courts originally permitted such an obvious price fixing/territorial allocation plan provided distributors were not involved and nonaligned independents were still free to enter negotiations for any film. In April 1977, the Department of Justice reversed its position and announced that all splits were per se illegal and would be prosecuted. This triggered a renewed series of legal proceedings, but the overall pattern of decisions points toward the discontinuance of this attempt at price coordination.

Therefore, both distributors and exhibitors alike have practiced cooperative conduct strategies aimed at countervailing the oligopoly strength of the other side. At this juncture, the distributors seem to have the upper hand because of their control over the product and the proliferation of subsidiary markets for reaching their American and worldwide customers. These subsidiary markets will now be analyzed in greater detail to illustrate their similarities and differences from the traditional theatrical marketplace.

The Television Network Market

In the market for regularly scheduled prime-time programs, the major movie distributors have maintained an extraordinary presence, collectively averaging in excess of 40 percent since the mid-1960s, with Universal being the dominant supplier over the entire span of time. The networks themselves produce a small percentage of their prime-time programming needs, concentrating primarily on news, sports, and specials rather than entertainment series.[24] The remainder of prime-time series are produced by independent production houses, many of which have market shares comparable to the major film distributors. *The major movie companies have no economic advantage in this programming area* because of a well-developed rental market for inputs, minimal economies of scale, and easy entry.[25]

Given such competitive conditions, the supply industry has been unable to countervail the coordinated monopsony power of the three networks. The networks understand that their bargaining advantage is greatest in the initial developmental stages, when the quality of the scripts and pilot are unknown and the future success of the program is uncertain. At this stage, venture capital is scarce because of the financial risk. Once a show becomes a hit and its true value is known, however, it can command a high price on the open market.

To prevent competitive bidding for hits, the networks have developed a series of parallel steps in the buying process that, if commonly followed, will bind series to long-term option contracts prior to knowledge being available regarding their ratings. This will enhance the networks' position relative to their suppliers. The triopoly structure of the networks acts as a bottleneck, which narrows down the number of potential sources of access. The profit-maximizing incentive for oligopolists to coordinate their behavior inhibits the emergence of significant internetwork competition for programming. The uncertainty over quality, large number of competing producers, and scarcity of venture capital make the producers unable to resist this network power.

Historically, theatrical movies represented a different species of network programming because specific knowledge existed about their value in the theatrical market. The known quality of theatrical movies not only reduced the uncertainty and risk to the networks, but also enabled the movie companies to demand prices reflecting the marginal worth of their movies. The major movie companies also had more bargaining power because of a more dominant position in the movie industry as producer–distributors than as television series suppliers, as well as the fact that the sale of network television rights was only a secondary consideration to the movie companies, yet a life-and-death decision for the series suppliers. Given such circumstances, the networks were unable to refrain from intense bidding wars for exclusive rights to these movies.

Movie distributors have received high and increasing prices for their films since the early sixties. The prices for theatrical movies have always been two to three times higher (for a standard length of time) than the prices of regularly scheduled programs of comparable quality. Movie prices started to rise because of increasing network demand (more movie nights) and internetwork rivalry for theatrical movies. The average price of a theatrical movie rose from $100,000 for two network runs in 1961 to around $800,000 by the end of 1967.

Around 1966 and 1967, the networks attempted to neutralize the power of the movie distributors by producing their own made-for-television movies (a substitute product), and ABC and CBS entered directly into motion picture production. This vertical integration into the production sphere resulted in some 80 theatrical movies during 1967–1971 and 40 to 50 percent of their yearly requirements of made-for-television movies. The effect of such a large foreclosure of product was devastating and sent a clear message that, hereafter, movie licensing fees would be stabilized.[26]

Private and public antitrust litigation ensued.[27] The motion picture distributors charged that the television networks were in violation of the *Paramount* decrees since they had set up a fully integrated market chain through network distribution, ownership, and affiliation with broadcast exhibition outlets and now production of theatrical movies. These lawsuits had been filed shortly after the FCC had reduced the ability of the networks to coventure programming with outside packagers (another form of vertical integration) and had forced the networks to abandon one hour of prime-time programming to the open airwaves to independent sources of supply.

The case ended with a consent decree that basically ratified the FCC's rules and limited the ability of the networks to produce in-house television series. Paradoxically, the decrees did not forbid the networks from producing theatrical movies or from broadcasting them on their own network after the theatrical run.[28] While ABC and CBS had left the theatrical production industry in 1972 because of the lawsuits as well as an inferior product, all three networks reentered this arena in the late 1970s and early 1980s.

In 1978, the networks once again tried to stabilize the prices of theatrical films (now at roughly $2 million per film) by purchasing television rights before the theatrical movie was released and, often, before filming was completed. The strategy was to obtain commitments by the movie producers at an early stage in the production process when the quality was uncertain, the risk high, and the television value indeterminate. In this way, the networks sought to bind themselves to specific producers and thereby reduce internetwork competition over theatrical movies. It was, of course, a risk for the networks because they would be wedded to the flops along with the hits, but it was a risk that had been shown to be acceptable and profitable with regularly scheduled programming. By the mid-1980s, the entire point became largely moot as the television networks severely reduced their reliance on theatrical movies since they had been pushed further back in line behind other exhibition windows, and the plummeting television ratings of these shopworn movies no longer justified such high license prices.

The Pay Television Market

The development of the pay television market and role of motion picture distribution are rooted in the scarcity of space in the electromagnetic spectrum, which created a natural limitation on the number of available very high frequency (VHF) stations in any local market. Given the overwhelming economic incentive to share programming expenses through networking, and the necessity for networks to have local affiliates to transmit their programs, there was room for only three national TV networks.[29] With only three network signals and the incentive (imposed by advertising sponsorship) to maximize ratings by seeking the lowest common denominator of programming, minority-taste programming went unfulfilled even though public broadcasting sought to fill the void.

Proponents of pay TV argued that direct consumer payment would make programming more sensitive to viewers' preferences than the current advertiser-supported system of free television.[30] The zero-priced television system is inconsistent with an efficient allocation of resources among program types, since it does not provide information concerning *intensity of consumer demand.* With pay TV, this efficiency can be cured as viewers express their strength of program preferences through a pricing system. With the development of cable television during the 1960s, a collection mechanism was now in place for excluding free riders — the basic market-failure problem associated with over-the-air broadcasting.

After intense lobbying by broadcast interests not to permit pay TV to gain a foothold, the issue was resolved with a series of FCC rules, which permitted pay TV to exist but restricted its programming to those types that were unavailable from commercial broadcasting. The most important program area permitted was that of recent theatrical movies for the time interval between their theatrical run and their appearance on network television.

In 1972, Home Box Office initiated a pay-cable program service consisting of recent uncut, uninterrupted movies, Las Vegas night club acts, and special sporting events. This channel (package) of programming was sold on a monthly subscription basis for about $7 to those areas already wired for cable. Yet the nationwide development of this alternative form of television would not come until the expensive system of microwave transmission was replaced in 1975 by the new cost-effective satellite-to-dish transmission system and until the U.S. Court of Appeals, in 1977, declared null and void all programming limitations imposed by the FCC on pay-cable networks. This Magna Carta for pay-cable networking meant that they could become full-fledged competitors to the three commercial networks and is generally credited with triggering what has come to be known as the cable revolution, with 54 percent penetration of all U.S. households.

Such movie-driven premium networks as the Movie Channel, Showtime, and Cinemax soon joined HBO, the industry leader, to exploit this new pay-cable market.[31] In recent years, several specialty networks have entered by differentiating their product in other dimensions (such as Disney, Playboy, American Film Classics) rather than offering a full range of motion pictures and entertainment specials.

In the development years of the late 1970s, the pay-cable networks decided on a conscious policy of *nonexclusive* licensing of theatrical movies.

The strategy was for each network to present a full movie package, including all the box office hits, to overcome viewers' hesitancy in paying for a product that formerly was provided free of charge (albeit with commercials). This meant that for the movie component of the pay-cable schedule, usually 80–85 percent of the total schedule, all the pay networks were virtually identical, since the motion picture distributors would license everyone at approximately the same time. At the cable system level, the local cable monopolist would generally license only a single pay network to avoid programming redundancy; frequently, the local cable system was a part of a nationwide chain (multiple-system operators), which in turn was a subsidiary of one of the top pay-cable networks. As is true for all such vertical arrangements, there was the incentive for self-preference, and the same linkage that had occurred in motion picture distribution/exhibition began to surface in the pay-cable industry. Competition for exclusive access to smaller cable systems would necessarily then turn on nonproduct dimensions such as marketing or the percentage split of the consumer's monthly payment between the network and the local system.

Ironically, in these pre-VCR days, in a few markets, consumers expressed a willingness to buy a multiple number of redundant networks in order to gain more viewing flexibility. Soon most cable systems began offering multiple networks, which meant that there would be competition for local patronage even in vertically integrated systems. HBO set up a sister service, Cinemax, to try to capture the extra business, but the genie could not be put back in the bottle and *product competition* became a new reality. Product competition/differentiation meant having exclusive rights for a period of time to certain movies and, of course, not sharing your entertainment or sports specials. While at first the networks continued licensing box office hits on a nonexclusive basis while less successful movies and all-time classics were licensed exclusively, by 1981, exclusive rights were also obtained for the former category of movies. Throughout this period, HBO and Cinemax collectively dominated this market, with a combined market share of nearly 60 percent, over twice that of Showtime. HBO used its monopsony power to reduce the license prices to the motion picture distributors, paying on a flat rental, take-it-or-leave-it basis rather than the customary per-subscriber method.

In April 1980, a new and potentially explosive element was introduced into the pay-cable industry. Getty Oil, a partner in the ESPN cable network, announced a joint venture with four of the major motion picture distributors (Fox, Universal, Paramount, and Columbia) to establish a new programming network known as Premiere. The Premiere network was scheduled to begin operations on January 1, 1981, and would offer 12–15 films a month, primarily those of the movie distributor partners. The key provisions in this venture were the exclusivity clause, which permitted Premiere to withhold the theatrical films of these four companies for a period of nine months from the other pay-cable networks, and the formula for setting the license prices. The Premiere network felt that only through such a product-differentiation plan could it possibly compete with HBO and Showtime.

After the Justice Department filed a civil antitrust suit against the Premiere principals in August 1980, alleging price fixing and a concerted refusal to deal, the Premiere network soon folded. However, HBO had learned an important lesson; lacking an assured source of films, it was vulnerable to such an "end around" as Premiere. It decided to become vertically integrated through ownership and long-term contracts to avoid future problems. It established a theatrical film subsidiary called Silver Screens, joined CBS and Columbia in launching a new mini-major production/distribution company called Tri-Star, and signed long-term exclusive contracts for the full line of theatrical films of Columbia, Orion, and CBS.

To counteract this move, in 1983, the owners of Showtime and the Movie Channel, in conjunction with Warner Brothers, Universal, and Paramount, announced a new joint venture under which the number 2 and number 3 pay-cable networks would be merged. While the principals claimed that these networks would continue to be run separately and that the motion picture distributors would continue to license their theatrical films on a nonexclusive basis, the Justice Department believed that such an amalgamation at the production stage would increase the likelihood of coordinated behavior, with the possibility of price squeezes on nonintegrated downstream competitors.[32] Upon the withdrawal of the motion picture companies, Showtime and the Movie Channel were permitted to merge. Within months, the Spotlight network folded, and the newly combined Showtime–the Movie Channel signed a five-year exclusive pact with Paramount Pictures.

Since the execution of the merger, many other exclusive arrangements have taken place. For example, Showtime–TMC locked up Atlantic, Cannon, DeLaurentis, and Touchstone. As original contracts expire, there has been considerable shifting around as well. The main point is that while some large studios have *not* signed these agreements and prefer to negotiate picture by picture for either exclusive or nonexclusive rights, a significant share of the movie supply industry has been committed to this form of vertical tying arrangement, and this severely restricts a potential new pay-cable distributor from gaining access to a sufficient number of box office hits in order to offer a competitive service to HBO and the other giants. Thus, the pay-cable networks have followed the practice of exclusive dealing, first initiated by the commercial networks, but on a much grander scale and have now become an indispensible window for theatrical motion pictures.

The Videocassette Market

Of even greater importance to the motion picture industry than cable has been the videocassette revolution of the past five years. VCR penetration, at over 60 percent, now exceeds cable penetration by nearly 10 percent and has even surpassed the theatrical box office in revenues generated.[33] The main reason for the popularity of the VCR is its versatility; it permits viewers to time-shift programming to escape the temporal tyranny dictated by the networks and local stations; it allows playback of home video photography made by compatible portable video cameras; and finally, it allows consumers to access, through purchase or lease, a wide array of prerecorded videocassettes. Thus, the VCR significantly improves consumer sovereignty and provides the diversity of programming that is absent from commercial television.

The key difference among the VCR, television, and cable markets is that in VCRs, *the majors act as distributors themselves,* while in the latter two markets, they rely upon specialized distributors like CBS, HBO, Viewers Choice, and others. In fact, VCR distribution is very similar to that of magazines, paperback books, and records. The market shares for VCR distributors are given in Table 7-4. It is clear that the major theatrical distributors have transferred

Table 7-4

Market Shares for VCR Distributors
(Calculated from Annual Dollar Sales)

Distributor	1987	1986	1985	1984[d]	1983[d]
CBS/Fox[a]	10.0%	13.7%	13.5%	18.6%	18.2%
Vestron[b]	6.4	8.0	10.4	10.0	6.0
RCA/Columbia	7.8	9.2	10.1	8.5	12.9
MGM/UA	4.3	7.5	9.0	6.5	10.0
Warner	9.1	8.5	8.3	9.0	10.0
Paramount	12.8	11.0	8.3	10.5	12.0
MCA	5.3	7.1	7.0	8.5	8.1
Disney	8.9	8.2	6.2	6.7	5.3
Thorn	n.a.	n.a.	6.2	5.0	5.0
Embassy	n.a.	3.4	3.6	4.5	4.1
Media	n.a.	3.4	3.2	1.8	—
New World	3.0	2.4	2.4	—	—
Karl–Lorimar	4.7	3.4	2.4	2.1	—
IVE[c]	1.4	1.8	2.4	1.2	—
Prism	1.0	1.2	1.2	1.1	—
Western	n.a.	n.a.	1.0	—	—
Maljack	n.a.	n.a.	—	.6	—
Continental	n.a.	n.a.	—	.3	—
HBO/Cannon	6.6	6.4	6.2	n.a.	n.a.
Heron	5.5	—	—	—	—
Nelson	3.7	—	—	—	—
Cinema Group	1.0	—	—	—	—
All Others	8.5	4.8	—	5.1	8.4
CR$_4$	40.8	42.4	43.0	48.1	53.1

[a]Includes Key Video and Playhouse.
[b]Includes Lightning Video.
[c]Includes Family Home Entertainment, USA Monterey.
[d]Some data are missing, unreported, or not available (n.a.).

Source: Videoweek, annual editions, various years.

their power into this market. While this market is still driven by feature films, their dominance in VCR software is much smaller than in the traditional theatrical market.[34] This is explained by the persistence of a strong group of independent distributors who specialize in nonmovie types of videos such as the how-to genre (such as "Jane Fonda's New Workout"), music videos, children's, pornographic, and educational. The independents have also distributed B-quality movies that purposely have a short theatrical run (sometimes none at all) in order to move more quickly through the VCR and other subsidiary markets. It is the insatiable appetite of these subsidiary markets for product that has caused the growth of the independent production industry and led to a record number of movie releases since 1986.

It should be noted that these market shares are based on sales of cassettes rather than rentals, even though rentals account for the vast majority of consumer transactions. This is due to the first-sale copyright provision, which permits distributors to collect copyright payments only the first time a cassette is sold, not every time it is rented. Thus retail establishments will pay the wholesale price for theatrical movie cassettes but need not share revenues from renting. To capture some of this producer's surplus, the movie distributors charge very high wholesale prices for their cassettes, and the retailers mark them up by their customary margins to yield extremely high retail prices, which scare away consumer sales and further encourage the rental market. Occasionally, the wholesale price will be lowered after the first 90 days in order to stimulate the sell-through consumer market.

One interesting difference between the prerecorded videocassette industry and the other subsidiary markets is the partial integration of the cassette distributors into the manufacturing (for example, duplication) stage but not into the wholesale or retail stages. Because of high capital costs, long-term contracts, and vertical integration, the tape-duplication stage is very concentrated, with a four-firm concentration index fluctuating between 71–94 percent since 1984 and the merger between the number 1 and number 3 firms within the last year, giving industry leader VCA–Technicolor a market share of 40–47 percent.[35] Until CBS–Fox (number 3) merged with VCA–Technicolor, it and Bell&Howell–Columbia–Paramount (number 2) were the only two vertically integrated firms and accounted for roughly a third to a half of the industry's market. Most of the other distributors have long-term exclusive contracts with duplicators, making new significant entry very difficult. On the other hand, the retail stage is extremely competitive, with large discount department chains like K-Mart and Sears in competition with grocery chains and individually owned specialty shops. The availability of videocassette movies is now as plentiful as cigarettes and bread.

The International Market

Historically, the second most important window has been the international market, which is the aggregation of some 80 or more trading partners of the United States. Going as far back as World War I, the American film distributors have dominated this world market for film, later extended to television and most recently to videocassettes.[36] In fact, the American control has been so pervasive that charges of media imperialism have been leveled.

The reason why the American motion picture distributors have been so powerful rests primarily on the relative size and strength of the American market compared to those of other countries. American motion picture and television producers can largely recoup their production costs from the domestic market alone and, given the public-goods nature of the mass media and the fact that the greatest expense is the first-copy production cost, distribution prices to foreign lands only need cover the incremental expenses. This pricing practice is often mislabeled as dumping. Since prices are based primarily on the strength of a country's demand, providing they cover the incremental costs of distribution, the richer and more populous countries pay higher prices for the same video product. For example, a theatrical movie distributed in France would yield $30,000–40,000 in rentals; $60,000 or more in Japan, and only $3,500–4,000 in Norway or Denmark.[37]

The leading American film distributors have bolstered their economic advantage by developing the most far-flung distribution networks throughout the world–comparable to their extensive domestic networks. This also includes significant ownership of foreign theaters! Furthermore, with government protection under the Webb–Pomerene Act of 1918, the major movie distributors had a formal export cartel in place for nearly forty years, which acted as the sole export sales agent for its members. The Motion Picture Export Association set general export price levels for each country; they also set terms of trade and guaranteed the smooth functioning of the distribution process.

The protectionist response of foreign countries to American dominance has been the erection of trade barriers, including import quotas, tariffs, strict licensing procedures, limitations of the percentage of screen time for imported films (and TV programs), and the freezing of local currencies from leaving the country. Additionally, foreign governments have provided encouragement to indigenous producers through formal subsidies, production prizes, tax breaks, or loans at favorable (or zero) interest rates.

The American response to such foreign government tactics has been to qualify as an indigenous producer within the countries, thereby escaping the penalties associated with being importers while enjoying the benefits afforded local companies. This is one reason why Hollywood has experienced runaway production over the last 10–20 years and why the so-called foreign coproduction has become more prevalent; the other reasons include the attractiveness and mystique of foreign locales and the cheaper costs in filming abroad.

One interesting example of cultural and economic dependency is Canada, which recently instituted comprehensive reforms in its content rules. Yet a more fundamental structural problem exists in the Canadian film industry.

Canadian motion picture distribution is controlled by the eight largest U.S. distributors, which collectively account for two-thirds of all rentals, while some 75 Canadian distributors split the remaining one-third of the business.[38] There are two large theater chains in Canada, Famous Players and Cineplex Odeon, which control 40 percent of all screens, yet collect 55 percent of box office dollars due to their overwhelmingly first-run status and strategic locations in the most populated provinces. Famous Players is wholly owned by Paramount, while Cineplex Odeon is jointly owned by MCA and a Canadian firm.

The eight major American distributors are exclusively licensed with one or the other of the large chains and are permitted to establish franchises covering their entire line of product and block-booking arrangements. Furthermore, they are given preferential access through committed playing time. As a result, the independent distributors (mainly Canadian) are at the mercy of the circuits and must fight for scraps of leftover time. Because of this vertical structure, Pendakur concludes that the perception that Canadian films are of low quality becomes a self-fulfilling prophesy. The system dooms them to failure.

IV.
PERFORMANCE

If an industry has a concentrated market structure and if it attempts to coordinate pricing behavior as well as having significant barriers to entry and an inelastic demand, the end results should be high prices for the consumer and excess profits for the industry. To assess the excess-profits issue, it is necessary to choose a time period of sufficient duration to insure that the industry in question is indeed in the long run; disaggregate product lines from corporate annual reports that approximate the industry segments under examination; and compare the rate of return for this period to industries with comparable products, risks, and capital–labor ratios.

In a study by Veronis and Suhler, which separated motion picture entertainment from the other product lines of these corporations, the average operating income margin (on sales) for 49 companies from 1982 to 1986 was 10.12 percent, while the cash-flow margin was 11.26 percent.[39] For the 344 companies occupying all ten communication industry segments, the corresponding margins were 14.16 percent and 17.92 percent, respectively.

It seems that the motion picture distributors have not been able to exert as significant a market control in their own industry segment as have some other communication distribution companies; yet compared to a broader grouping of leisure and service companies throughout the economy, they do relatively well. This failure is undoubtedly due to the vast degree of product differentiation accompanying motion picture product, the unpredictability of consumer tastes, and the instability of market shares from one year to the next. This is compounded by the fact that industry leadership rotates among the top firms, and market shares are more evenly dispersed than in other industries with comparable concentration ratios. It may also reflect the fact that there is now a plethora of different media available for consumers to obtain their entertainment product.

What about the impact of this market structure on the public? One way to answer this is to examine inflationary trends in motion picture admission prices compared to other products and services in the economy at large. Using 1967 as a common base year, indoor admission prices have risen by 209 percent over the twenty-year period, while the CPI category of entertainment services and products has increased by 174.1 percent, and the category of "all goods and services" has risen by 228.4 percent. Since 1980, admission-price inflation has risen at less than half the rate of these categories. This evidence is thus consistent with the profitability data and implies that the full force of the concentrated market structure is not inflicting unusual pain on consumers' pocketbooks.

Technological Progress

Given the creative nature of the motion picture product, it is not surprising to see technological progress surfacing only in the exhibition sphere. The rapid development of such subsidiary markets as pay cable, pay-per-view, satellite dishes, and especially home video attests to the speed of diffusion of these new technologies and the added programming flexibility they provide for consumers. The willingness of the distributors to embrace these new markets and fold them into their sequential distribution plan clearly demonstrates the lesson they have learned from the boycott days of the early television industry.

The multiplicity of exhibition markets has also spurred the production side of the industry, especially small independents, to release record numbers of theatrical films. These shoestring films, of dubious quality, critically depend on presales to the subsidiary markets to finance their undertakings. The theaters themselves have only lost a small percentage of their equilibrium demand to the new technologies and have not yet made a price- or quality-competitive response. If the erosion of patronage becomes more pronounced or unfavorable demographics (such as the aging of the population) plague the industry, theaters may need to rethink their spartanlike furnishings in favor of a more unique viewing experience. While more competition means even greater financial risk in the future, the fundamental undying truth is that this motion picture industry, and especially the production and distribution sectors, seem impervious to whatever technical marvels the twenty-first century brings forth.

Diversity

Because the motion picture industry produces cultural products, a critical question is whether concentration of control over the production–distribution business affects product diversity to the American people. A variety of studies of other mass media have all concluded that such control adversely impacts on product diversity—the amount and kinds of program choices available to consumers. Absent the spur of competition, oligopoly firms tend to lead a quiet, imitative life rather than engage in costly product experimentation and new ideas.

Given the strong oligopoly control of the leading distributors and recalling their conglomerate ties, the incentive may be to stress the bottom line rather than worry about the impact on motion pictures as an art or cultural form. This would mean the constant search for formulaic content that reduces risks for a motion picture as it winds through all the subsidiary markets. This might mean a reliance on sequels that have a built-in recognition factor or extravagant spectacles with universal themes and international stars who appeal to international audiences.[40] In either case, the end result is homogenization of content.

In recent studies, both Dominick and Litman and Kohl[41] have documented the strong correlation between concentration of control and lack of content diversity. Dominick studied nearly 1,900 films that were released over the twenty-year period spanning 1964–83. He correlated a Herfindahl–Hirschman index of market-share concentration with a similar index measuring concentration of content into fewer film categories and discovered the significant relationship. Similarly, Litman and Kohl studied some 700 films released during the 1980s and concluded that "almost every variable which represents some known factor or conveys information that reduces uncertainty seems to be correlated with financial success." Thus, not only are the filmmakers seeking some secret formula for reducing risks, but the audience has also become conditioned to seek *familiarity* in their choice of movie entertainment.

V.
CONCLUSIONS

The American people's love affair with motion pictures has lasted for nearly a century since that eventful day when Edison first introduced the kinetoscope to a skeptical audience. While production budgets have skyrocketed since the days of the one-reelers and the space-age and computer technologies have opened up many new points of competitive access, the motion picture industry remains a cherished institution on the American landscape, as venerable as the automobile. The basic structure of this industry was forged in the 1920s and continues largely intact except for the growth of subsidiary markets to replace the traditional system of theatrical runs. The concentration of market power, which had its roots in economies of scale and a vertically interlocking, self-sufficient system of arrangements, was decimated by the *Paramount* consent decrees but has regrouped and refocused at the distribution stage. Throughout all of the technological innovations, truly remarkable have been the resilience and adaptive capability of the industry. As theater circuits seek new horizontal and vertical merger partners under the laissez-faire attitude of the antitrust authorities, the historic dangers of expanding market control may resurface. In this regard, most dangerous and hence most important is the kind of multimedia acquisition strategy of companies like TCI, which seek dominance across multiple exhibition markets. Constant antitrust vigilance is required lest the type of vertical market control (which originally was confined to the motion picture industry alone) spread across the entire entertainment landscape, extinguishing the competitive fires that have brought so many benefits to consumers in recent years.

NOTES

1. The sources for our discussion of the industry's history are A. R. Fulton, *Motion Pictures: The Development of an Art from Silent Films to the Age of Television* (Norman, OK: University of Oklahoma Press, 1960); and the contributions by Tino Balio, Russell Merritt, Jeanne Allen Thomas, Robert Anderson, and Douglas Gomery in Tino Balio (ed.), *The American Film Industry*, rev. ed. (Madison: University of Wisconsin Press, 1985).

2. *U.S.* v. *Motion Picture Patents Co.*, 225 Federal Reporter 800 (1915). The salient issue was whether legally granted patents could be cross-licensed in such a fashion to regiment an entire industry. The Court ruled that the patent system did not supercede the antitrust laws; what might be legal for a single patent holder could not be done collectively "by combining in a vertical pattern and excluding non-members from access to trade."

3. Block booking is the forced licensing of a package of feature films, tying high- and low-quality films together and offering them on an all-or-nothing basis.

   Blind selling is the licensing of a film prior to its being available for commercial preview to the theaters.

   Zoning is the geographical area of exclusivity afforded a local theater.
Time clearance is the temporal period of exclusivity granted a certain run of a feature film.

   Price discrimination means charging different prices for a film depending on the classification of the theater into different runs. Theater classification depends on the number of seats, location, and interior splendor. For more detail, see Balio, *The American Film Industry* (Madison: University of Wisconsin Press, 1976 and 1985), 1985 ed., Part III.

4. For the export market, the Webb–Pomerene Act permitted the industry to establish an export cartel known as the Motion Picture Export Association (MPEA), which could establish common policies and negotiate on behalf of its members. The

MPEA continues to dominate the world markets, even though the Webb–Pomerene Act was finally repealed about a decade ago.

5. The five majors were Twentieth-Century Fox, Loews, RKO, Paramount, and Warner Brothers. The three minor distributors were United Artists, Columbia, and Universal. None of the latter companies officially owned theaters, although United Artists had interlocking directorships with a major chain.

6. This section draws largely on *U.S.* v. *Paramount Pictures*, 334 U.S. 131 (1948).

7. *U.S.* v. *Paramount*, at 174.

8. The best accounts of these impacts are in Michael Conant, "The Impact of the *Paramount* Decrees," in Balio (1976), Chapter 16, and "The *Paramount* Decrees Reconsidered," in Balio (1985), Chapter 20. This section draws heavily on these articles.

9. Balio (1985), Part IV introduction.

10. Barry R. Litman, "Decision Making in the Film Industry: The Influence of the TV Market," *Journal of Communication*, 32 (Summer 1982), pp. 33–52.

11. For a good overall account of the various mergers, see Conant, "The Decrees Reconsidered," (1985); Thomas Guback, "The Theatrical Film" in Benjamin Compaine, *Who Owns the Media? Concentration of Ownership in the Mass Communications Industry*, 2nd ed. (White Plains, NY: Knowledge Industries, 1982), Chapter 5; and end-of-year roundups in *Variety*, annual editions, January, various years.

12. *Multichannel News* (May 16, 1988), p. 1, and (June 20, 1988), p. 40.

13. *Variety* (January 15, 1988).

14. According to Table 7-1, the aggregate market share of the Big 6 *Paramount* majors and minors has fallen from 89 percent in 1982 to 58 percent in 1987.

15. Gorham Kindem, "Hollywood's Movie Star System: An Historical Overview," in Gorham Kindem (ed.), *The American Movie Industry: The Business of Motion Pictures* (Carbondale, IL: Southern Illinois University Press, 1982), Chapter 4.

16. Thomas Simonet, "Conglomerate and Content Remakes, Sequels and Series in the New Hollywood," in Bruce A. Austin, *Current Research in Film: Audiences, Economics and Law*, Volume 3 (Norwood, NJ: Ablex, 1987), Chapter 10.

17. Thomas Guback, "The Evolution of the Motion Picture Theater Business in the 1980s," *Jounral of Communications* 37 (Spring 1987), pp. 60–77.

18. *Variety* (August 10, 1988), p. 1, and (September 14, 1988), p. 1.

19. *Satellite Times* (July 27, 1988), p. 10.

20. Regrettably, the number of screens rather than box office admissions is the only available measure of assessing market shares.

21. David Waterman, "Prerecorded Home Video and the Distribution of Theatrical Feature Films," in Eli Noam (ed.), *Video Media Competition: Regulation, Economics and Technology* (New York: Columbia University Press, 1985), Chapter 7. If the movie theaters were to vary their prices according to how long the film had been at the particular location, a certain group would undoubtedly pay premium prices to see certain highly publicized movies their first night or opening week.

22. If a theatrical movie is licensed to the commercial TV networks for, say, $3 million for two runs and it attracts, say, 15 million households on its first showing and 12 on its second, this translates to only 11 cents per household and about 4 cents per person. In the syndication industry, such a film, licensed nationally as part of a package of, say, 20 films, and given 6 repeat showings over a 3-year period, would

bring in even lower net revenues to the distributor on a per-household or per-viewer basis.

23. This section draws heavily on Guback, 1985.

24. The networks are prohibited by the FCC's "Financial Interest and Syndication Rules" from coventuring prime-time programs with outside sources and are under consent decrees from producing themselves more than two and one-half hours of prime-time programming per week.

25. Bruce Owen, Jack H. Beebe, and Willard G. Manning, *Television Economics* (Lexington, MA: Lexington Books, 1974), Chapter 2.

26. Crandall argues that such network entry correspondingly improved competition in the theatrical exhibition market by bringing in a breath of fresh air to this highly concentrated industry. "The Post-War Performance of the Motion Picture Industry," *Antitrust Bulletin* 20 (Spring 1975), pp. 49–87.

27. *Columbia Pictures* v. *ABC and CBS*, U.S. District Court, Southern District of New York, 1972; *U.S.* v. *CBS, NBC, and ABC*, U.S. District Court, Central District of California, 1974.

28. For more detail on these decrees, see FCC Network Inquiry Special Staff, *An Analysis of Television Program Production, Acquisition and Distribution* (Washington, D.C.: GPO, 1980), Chapter 8.

29. In fact, the DuMont network realized this economic fact in 1955 and exited from the scene, greatly fortifying ABC, with whom it had been fighting for the limited number of affiliates. In 1986, with the greater viability of UHF signals transmitted by cable, Fox Broadcasting established itself as the fourth network, although it broadcasts only two nights per week.

30. This section comes largely from Barry R. Litman and Suzannah Eun, "The Emerging Oligopoly of Pay TV in the USA," *Telecommunication Policy*, 5 (June 1981), pp. 121–35.

31. A corollary market of advertiser-supported cable networks, such as USA, ESPN, CNN, MTV, and so on, and several superstations emerged and was packaged together by local cable systems and sold as "basic" cable service. The premium channels just mentioned have always been sold separately (a la carte).

32. Lawrence White, "Antitrust and Video Markets: The Merger of Showtime and the Movie Channel," in E. Noam, *Video Media Competition* (New York: Columbia University Press, 1985), Chapter 11.

33. See comparisons in annual *Variety* editions each January.

34. If one defined the market narrowly as theatrical videos, their control would be approximately equal to that of the theatrical movie market. However, just as movies on television must compete with other entertainment and information programming, so must videocassette recordings.

35. *Videoweek* (January 1988).

36. This section draws heavily on Thomas Guback, "Hollywood's International Market," in Balio (1985), Chapter 17.

37. *Variety* (October 12, 1988), p. 168.

38. This section draws on Manjunath Pendakur, "Cultural Dependency in Canada's Feature Film Industry," in Kindem, Chapter 17.

39. Veronis, Suhler, and Associates, *Fifth Annual Communications Industry Report* (New York: VS&A, 1987). Another good source for financial information is Harold L.

Vogel, *Entertainment Industry Economics: A Guide for Financial Analysis* (Cambridge: Cambridge University Press, 1987), especially Chapters 2–4.

40. Joseph D. Phillips, "Film Conglomerate Blockbusters: International Appeal and Product Homogenization," in Kindem, Chapter 15.

41. Joseph Dominick, "Film Economics and Film Content: 1964–83," in Austin, Chapter 9; Barry R. Litman and Linda Kohl, "Decision Making in the Motion Picture Industry: A Reassessment," unpublished paper, Michigan State University, Department of Telecommunication, Summer 1988.

SUGGESTED READINGS

Books

Balio, T. *The American Film Industry*, 1st and 2nd eds. Madison: University of Wisconsin Press, 1976, 85.

Compaine, B. M. *Who Owns the Media? Concentration of Ownership in the Mass Communications Industry*, 2nd ed. White Plains, NY: Knowledge Industries, 1982.

Fulton, A. R. *Motion Pictures: The Development of an Art from Silent Films to the Age of Television*. Norman, OK: University of Oklahoma Press, 1960.

Gregory, M. *Making Films Your Business*. New York: Schocken Books, 1979.

Guback, T. *The International Film Industry: Western Europe and American Since 1945*. Bloomington, IN: Indiana University Press, 1969.

Hampton, B. *History of the American Film Industry from Its Beginnings to 1931*. New York: Dover, 1970.

Kindem, G. *The American Movie Industry: The Business of Motion Pictures*. Carbondale, IL: Southern Illinois University Press, 1985.

Noam, E. *Video Media Competition*. New York: Columbia University Press, 1985.

Vogel, H. L. *Entertainment Industry Economics: A Guide for Financial Analysis*. Cambridge: Cambridge University Press, 1986.

Articles

Crandall, R. W. "The Post-War Performance of the Motion Picture Industry." *The Antitrust Bulletin*, 20, Spring 1975.

Hellman, H., and M. Soramaki. "Economic Concentration in the Videocassette Industry: A Cultural Comparison." *Journal of Communication*, 35, Summer 1985.

Litman, B. R. "Decision Making in the Film Industry: The Influence of the TV Market." *Journal of Communication*, 32, Summer 1982.

———. "The Economics of the Television Market for Theatrical Movies." *Journal of Communication*, 29, Autumn 1979.

——— and S. Eun. "The Emerging Oligopoly of Pay TV in the USA." *Telecommunication Policy*, 5, June 1981.

Government Publications

U.S. v. *CBS, NBC and ABC*, U.S. District Court, Central District of California (1974).

U.S. v. *Motion Picture Patents Company*, 225 Federal Register 800 (1915).

U.S. v. *Paramount Pictures*, 334 U.S. 131 (1948).

U.S. v. *Western Electric and AT&T*, Modified Final Judgment, U.S. District Court for District of Columbia (August 24, 1982).

Chapter 8

The Airline Industry

William G. Shepherd

Across the terrain of American industry, the airline industry stands out as a leading, sharply debated experiment in deregulation.

From 1938 to 1977, the airline sector was jointly controlled by about eight major airlines, whose power was protected and lightly regulated by the Civil Aeronautics Board. During 1977–84 the CAB's controls were removed and effective competition set in, bringing dramatic changes. But U.S. officials failed to protect the fledgling competition. By 1983 the airlines were beginning to quell price competition, and after 1985 the largest airlines were permitted to merge, creating even higher concentration than existed before 1978.

Since 1985, deregulation's aftermath has therefore *not* provided effective competition. Sharp debate continues about the industry's performance and deregulation's impact on it.[1] Some optimistic observers declare the industry to be highly competitive, efficient, and innovative.[2] Others agree that much of the sector's structure and behavior are still monopolistic, in fact increasingly so and with no relief in sight.[3]

This chapter surveys the industry, the issues, and the evidence. Section II defines airline markets and summarizes their structure. The determinants of structure are appraised in Section III, and then Section IV reviews the airlines' behavior. Section V assesses the industry's performance, and Section VI considers policy changes to promote competition.

I.

INTRODUCTION

Brief History to 1975

Airlines have had a colorful history. During the 1920s and until 1938, air travel grew from a group of hedge-hopping daredevils into a new industry dominated by about six trunk airlines.[4] There was much politicking and chicanery in this period, including political infighting for the government subsidies given for carrying air mail.

By 1938 the biggest airlines saw the advantages of being regulated in a way that would minimize competition while applying only gentle constraints. Regulation was created: The industry's structure was frozen, and the Civil Aeronautics Board was created both to preside over it and to promote its growth. During roughly 1938–70, the CAB adopted a booster role, applying little restraint on prices and permitting little new competition. The structure was monopolistic: 90 percent of city-pair routes, with 59 percent of all passenger miles, were actual or virtual monopolies.

Virtually no entry was permitted into the scheduled-airlines part of the industry during 1938–75, while the number of trunklines shrank from 16 to 11. Shifts of airlines into each others' routes were only gradually permitted, under close CAB controls, despite turbulent growth and massive shifts in traffic patterns among city pairs. By 1970 most routes had two or three airlines, but few routes had more than that, and many routes had just one dominant airline. The scheduled airlines functioned largely as a market-rigging cartel, agreeing on fares (which were usually identical) and then submitting them to the CAB for approval and enforcement. The CAB supposedly prevented fares from being too high, but in practice the CAB largely rubber-stamped the proposed fares. These price ceilings became concerted price *floors*, which minimized cutting.

The airlines' urge to compete was channeled to nonprice items, such as decor, personnel, meals, and scheduling more flights. To illustrate, the three airlines on the Chicago–Denver route could not depart from the $177 one-way coach-class fare. But they could each schedule more flights ("every hour, on the hour"); or make their meals fancier; or ensure that all of their cabin attendants were pretty, young, single, Caucasian women; or widen the seats and brighten the planes' decoration. As a result of this nonprice competition, the airlines' cost tended to rise above the efficient levels, making it necessary to set higher fares.

Moreover, the airlines were a soft touch for their workers' unions. As a quasi-cartel, the airlines could afford higher pay rates, and by yielding to pay demands the airlines avoided strikes and enhanced the loyalty of their workers. The outcome converted some of the airlines' cartel profits into higher workers' pay, further inflating airline costs.

CAB regulation, therefore, inflated costs.[5] Flying was dignified and smooth, though often running behind schedule. Service quality was much higher than it has been under deregulation. But ticket prices were inefficiently high and unnaturally uniform, and flying was affordable mainly to the well-to-do and to business travelers on expense accounts. Only a small minority of the populace traveled by air. The CAB had helped to prevent flexible, competitive price cutting to expand the market.

By 1975 the momentum for change had grown, as part of the wider deregulation movement.[6] The need to deregulate the airlines had become a staple topic at economics conferences. Theorists predicted strict competitive results.[7] Both free-market Republicans and consumer-oriented Democrats backed deregulation because it offered to improve consumer choice, efficiency, and managerial incentives and to "get the government out of the marketplace." Even some leading airlines began to see more gains for themselves from competing in an unfettered market rather than using the CAB as a shield against competition.

The Main Changes Since 1975

The first loosening of airline controls came during 1977. Modest amounts of entry and price cutting were permitted. Alfred E. Kahn, the new CAB head, then launched a successful crusade to eliminate regulation altogether. He pressed for the Airline Deregulation Act of 1978, which provided for free entry by 1980 and unfettered pricing by 1983, but actual decontrol was largely complete by 1981.

The larger airlines adjusted their routes, and some regional airlines (USAir, Delta) expanded into nationwide operation. Hub-and-spoke patterns developed, with each airline routing most of its traffic through one or two airports. Jet aircraft largely disappeared from hundreds of smaller airports, but new commuter airlines sent smaller planes to fill many of the gaps.

There was rapid entry by new, maverick airlines such as People Express, Southwest Airlines, and World Airways, which cut fares steeply while offering "no-frills" service. Those price cuts are demonstrated in Table 8-1, which compares them with fare changes in similar routes during 1980–84. Yet few of the newcomers got firmly established, some succumbed within a few years, and virtually all had passed from the scene by 1986. The broad average of airline fares per mile continued the decline that had been in progress since 1962, as Figure 8-1 shows. The decline reflected deregulation and other changes, such as new aircraft types and the changing composition of flight traffic. But after 1986 fares began to rise. By 1989, they had increased some 20 percent.

Route shifts by the older airlines were numerous, and they responded sharply to the new discount airlines. Although standard fares were sharply raised, fare discounts spread to over 75 percent of tickets by 1983. Competition became effective in much of the sector, especially on high-density routes that attracted five or more strong rivals.

Deregulation seemed to promise economic gains in the form of greater productivity, lower fares, and more consumer choice. Much of the industry showed the flexibility and variety normally associated with effective competition.

The Sector Now

The airline sector consists of three main interacting parts. The airports and flight-control systems are the infrastructure; the reservations systems are

Table 8-1

Performance of Markets Entered by People Express or Southwest with Otherwise Similar Markets (First Quarter 1980 and 1984)

Market	Distance	1980 Passengers	1980 Fare	Percentage Change in Fare	Percentage Change in Passengers
New York–Buffalo[a]	282	100,832	$48	−25%	179%
Boston–Philadelphia	281	100,590	$52	53%	2%
New York–Norfolk[a]	284	51,800	$48	−30%	264%
Chicago–Columbus	284	50,460	$48	103%	12%
Dallas–Little Rock[b]	303	23,650	$59	−17%	123%
Atlanta–Mobile	303	17,340	$56	56%	−8%
Albuquerque–Phoenix[b]	329	23,550	$61	−27%	160%
Columbus–Washington, D.C.	322	25,420	$53	96%	−18%
El Paso–Phoenix[b]	346	11,110	$74	−41%	178%
St. Louis–Tulsa	351	12,100	$60	83%	−20%
Houston–Tulsa[b]	453	38,930	$74	−23%	83%
Philadelphia–Detroit	453	40,880	$65	53%	−7%

[a]Market entered by People Express; data include all New York City metropolitan airports.
[b]Market entered by Southwest.
Source: Leonard W. Weiss and Michael W. Klass, *Regulatory Reform: What Actually Happened*, New York: (Little, Brown & Co., 1986), p. 59.

the medium for selecting and ticketing most flights; and the airlines' handling of airplanes provides the actual physical transport of people and baggage. There are auxiliary operations, such as nonscheduled flights, private planes, and the transport of packages and overnight mail, but they are outside the focus of this chapter.

Many of the largest airports are shown in Table 8-2. Their positions have shifted in recent years, reflecting different growth rates in regions and major cities, but Chicago, Atlanta, Dallas–Fort Worth, Denver and St. Louis are likely to continue as leaders. Table 8-1 also shows the shares of the largest airlines in the traffic at these larger airports.

The main airlines are listed in Table 8-3 by size of revenues. There have been some shifts in recent years, notably the rise of merger-active Texas Air, which bought Eastern and Continental (which itself had acquired Frontier and People Express) during 1984–87. The largest airlines have nationwide operations, while the second-echelon airlines (such as US Air and Delta) are more focused by regions.

These firms are the survivors from the old airlines and the many newcomers that entered during the heyday of deregulation between 1978–85. Most of the newcomers failed or were taken over by the major airlines. The carnage was severe, as some 50 airlines disappeared.

Figure 8-1

The trend in airline fares per mile, in constant 1967 values (cents per mile).

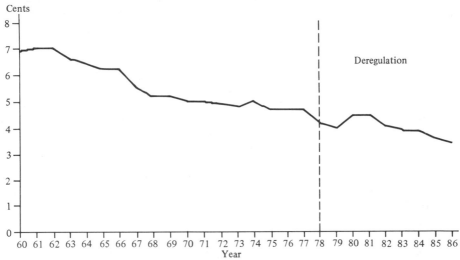

Source: Congressional Budget Office, *Policies for the Deregulated Airline Industry.* Washington DC: U.S. Government Printing Office, 1988, p. 6.

Scores of regional feeder lines also preexisted or were created during 1978–85. These local-service or commuter lines often flew small propeller-driven craft among the smaller airports, on more flexible schedules. They too have mostly been absorbed or formally tied to specific large airlines, as subordinate feeder lines.

Before deregulation, roughly six airlines dominated the industry. Deregulation brought a flood of new airlines, in a range of styles and regions. After 1984, this onrush was reversed by mergers and linkages. In 1987, the eight leading airlines controlled 92 percent of traffic, compared to just 80 percent in 1978 (see Table 8-3).

The industry's traffic ranges from huge volume among the largest cities down to thin trickles among the hundreds of smaller cities. Trunk lines carry heavy volumes between such major centers as New York, Chicago, Los Angeles, and Atlanta. There is also sizable traffic between major airports and lesser cities, such as Chicago–Des Moines or Boston–Albany. Finally, there are hundreds of low-volume routes between outlying airports, such as Des Moines–Kansas City. This complex traffic map is dominated by *hub-and-spoke* patterns. Most long flights go to a hub and require a transfer to another flight in order to reach the final destination.

Computer reservations systems were developed after 1975, and by 1981 United's Apollo system handled 41 percent and American's Sabre system claimed 39 percent of all computerized reservations; by 1986, the relevant percentages were 46 and 31. A few other airlines have developed similar systems, but they have much smaller shares of the market.

Table 8-2
Airport Size and Carrier Hub Operations, 1985–1987

Airport	Average Daily Departures[a]	Carriers Operating Hubs (Percentage Share of Departures in Parentheses)
Chicago O'Hare	814	United (41), American (24)[a]
Atlanta	778	Delta (46), Eastern (42)[a]
Dallas/Ft. Worth	577	American (52), Delta (29)[a]
Denver	487	United (30),[a] Continental (57)[b]
St. Louis	399	TWA (82)[b]
Minneapolis/St. Paul	307	Northwest (82)[b]
Pittsburgh	300	USAir (83)[b]
Phoenix	278	America West (35)[a]
Houston	232	Continental (72)[b]
Memphis	214	Northwest (87)[b]
Detroit	166	Northwest (65)[b]
Charlotte	164	Piedmont (67)[a]
Salt Lake City	158	Delta (75)[b]
Houston—Hobby	157	Southwest (52)[a]
Dallas—Love Field	132	Southwest (84)[a]

[a] As of 1985.
[b] As of 1987.

Note: A carrier is considered to operate a hub if it has more than 50 flights a day at that airport, and it is not located on either the east or west coast.
Source: Adapted from Congressional Budget Office, *Policies for the Deregulated Airline Industry*. Washington, D.C.: U.S. Government Printing Office, July 1988, p. 35; and *Consumer Reports*, "The Big Trouble with Air Travel," June 1988, pp. 362–7.

All these parts combine in carrying massive volumes of traffic within the U.S. and to other countries. Several thousand flights occur in the U.S. each day, totaling over 400 million passenger trips a year.

II.
MARKET STRUCTURE

Now we address the underlying economic nature of this industry. What are its true markets, and how competitive are they? Does monopoly in some parts affect competition in others?

Defining the Markets

In order to assess competition and its effects in a market, we must first *define the market*.[8] Markets are defined along two dimensions: *product* features

Table 8-3
Structure of the Domestic Airline Industry (in Percentages of Revenue Passenger Miles)

	1978	Percent of Revenue Passenger Miles	1983	Percent of Revenue Passenger Miles	1987	Percent of Revenue Passenger Miles
	Carrier		Carrier		Carrier	
1.	United	21.1	United	18.7	Texas Air	20.3
					Continental	10.2
					Eastern	10.1
2.	American	13.5	American	13.8	United	17.3
3.	Delta	12.0	Eastern	11.	American	15.4
4.	Eastern	11.1	Delta	11.1	Delta	13.0
5.	TWA	9.4	TWA	7.1	USAir	8.9
					USAir	4.0
					Piedmont	3.5
					PSA	1.4
6.	Western	5.0	Republic	4.2	Northwest (and Republic)	7.9
7.	Continental	4.5	Northwest	4.2	TWA	6.4
8.	Braniff	3.8	Western	3.9	Southwest	2.5
9.	National	3.6	Continental	3.5	America West	1.8
10.	Northwest	2.6	Pan Am	3.3	Pan Am	1.6
11.	USAir	2.2	Southwest	1.7	Braniff (New)	1.0
12.	Frontier	2.0	Frontier	1.7	Alaska	0.9
	Top Four	57.7	Top Four	54.7	Top Four	66.0
	Top Eight	80.4	Top Eight	74.1	Top Eight	91.7
	Top Twelve	90.8	Top Twelve	84.3	Top Twelve	97.0

Note: Northwest was on strike for part of 1978. Data for 1987 reflect mergers of American with Air California and USAir with Piedmont and PSA, even though operations were not affected for the entire year.

Source: Congressional Budget Office, Policies for the Deregulated Airline Industry. (Washington, D.C.: U.S. Government Printing Office, July 1988), p. 15.

and *geographic* areas. In the airline sector, product features are relatively simple, while geographic features are complex and debatable.

1. Product Substitutability. Airline travel is highly distinct from its alternatives in most cases. It is so much faster than bus, train, or automobile travel over distances above 150 miles that they are no substitute for it: That is, they are not in the market with airline services. For some short-range travelers the choice may be close; for example, driving or taking the Amtrak shuttle between New York and Washington, D.C., takes about as long as flying. A few executives may have the option of using their company jets, but for the vast majority of travelers there is no close (or even remote) substitute for using a scheduled airline.

2. Geographic Substitutability. This is a more complicated matter. The whole area of the U.S. is clearly not one big market. For instance, if you need to go from Miami to New York, a flight from Seattle to Chicago is useless, and even a closely parallel flight from Tampa to Philadelphia is virtually valueless for most flyers. On the other hand, some city-pair routes overlap others quite closely, either in whole or in part. For example, the New York–Denver route is overlapped by New York–Chicago–Denver, New York–Pittsburgh–Denver, New York–St. Louis–Denver, and even New York–Dallas–Denver (as illustrated in Figure 8-2). Your travel agent's screen may in fact display such alternative flights, which take about the same time and cost similar amounts; they may be quite close economic substitutes in service (getting from New York to Denver) and price.

In general, some of the main trunk routes have a degree of substitution by alternative routes, but most of the lesser city-pair routes do not. One can also think of major hub airports as being local markets of their own in some

Figure 8-2 _____

An example of alternative routes: New York to Denver and related routes.

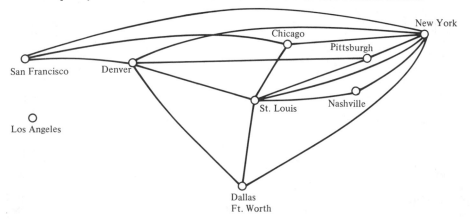

degree because they control access along their spoke routes, into and out of the hub airport.

Economic experts have therefore come to hold a complex view in defining markets within the industry. There are many shadings of market edges, and for some parts of the sector no clear markets can be agreed on. But many city pairs are pretty clear markets. And many hub cities can be regarded as meaningful markets or as cores of regional air-travel markets.

Structure and Degrees of Competition

The degree of competition in any market depends primarily on the lifetime elasticity of demand (or, to put it less formally, on the structure of that market and the behavior of the firms that operate in it).

1. Dominance of Many Routes and Hubs. In this complex industry, the evidence is mixed. Some markets are dominated by one airline, as Table 8-2 showed for major hub cities. Trunk routes tend to have low concentration, especially if parallel routings are considered. Lesser routes often have high concentration, and numerous spoke routes are virtual monopolies.

Concentration in the industry as a whole understates the degree of market power wielded by the major airlines. Each major realizes that it must confront other majors on many routes across the country. It understands that fighting its rivals on any one route is irrational because this would trigger retaliation on some other route. Fare cutting is contagious; if it breaks out on one route, it is likely to spread to others. Hence, where nationwide concentration is high, the recognition of mutual interdependence by rival carriers increases the incentives to avoid price cutting and other "aggressive" behavior.

Restrictions on Entry. During 1978–83, some economists maintained that airplanes are "capital with wings"—that airlines could send planes instantly into any route where a dominant carrier is making excess profit. Therefore, it was said, high market shares don't matter because potential entry is a formidable safeguard against monopolistic conduct. (This is the theory of "contestable" markets, according to which entry is "ultra-free.")[9]

But are airline markets open to ultra-free entry? No, the facts do not support the theory.[10] First, consider entry into the industry by creating an entirely new airline company. That kind of entry requires substantial funds and skills, months or years to build reputation and attract staff, and resources to withstand the retaliation of existing airlines. Virtually none of the entrants of 1978–85 has survived the fare wars and merger movement. Entry into the sector has, in fact, been virtually closed since about 1984.

Second, what about entry into individual markets? Can't the existing airlines merely move their planes about to undercut locally dominant positions? This is possible theoretically but not feasible practically. One obstacle is the bottleneck role of boarding gates and time slots. These are extremely scarce at the main airports and generally controlled by the dominant airlines, so that access to potential entrants is prevented by sheer physical blockage. Moreover, new entry is usually met by sharp retaliation. As a rule, it takes months to develop profitable repeat-business clientele for new routes. But rivals' fare cuts can be activated in a matter of minutes, to levels at or below the entrant's prices. The footholds can disappear before they are created.

Control of Reservations Systems

Computer reservations systems have become a strong factor in the competitive situation because they can inject bias into passengers' choices and can turn very high profits. As noted earlier, the systems owned by United and American have jointly dominated U.S. ticketing in the 1980s (although United sold part of its interest in Apollo in 1987) (see Table 8-4). They have had both of these effects.[11]

Both United and American candidly used strong bias in their reservations systems during 1977–84 (on the reasoning that "We created the systems, so we should get the advantage"), so as to get agents to favor their flights. This bias used the dominance in one crucial market (for reservations systems services) in order to increase monopoly in a related market (airlines traffic). The effects were powerful, probably shifting billions of dollars in traffic revenue to American and United.[12]

After other airlines protested strongly, the CAB in 1984 forced United

Table 8-4

Shares of Computer Reservations Systems Revenues in 1986, by Major City Markets

	Sabre (American)	Covia (United)	SystemOne (Texas Air)	PARS (Northwest, TWA)	DATAS (Delta)
New York	61.3%	12.0%	11.6%	13.5%	1.7%
Los Angeles	41.4	39.4	1.7	14.3	3.4
Chicago	41.8	50.5	1.7	2.7	3.2
San Francisco	39.4	42.3	1.5	14.6	2.1
Boston	61.3	13.9	9.9	10.9	4.0
Dallas	85.4	2.9	0.2	7.3	4.1
Washington	56.7	27.6	7.8	7.0	0.9
Atlanta	24.1	27.2	27.1	0.0	21.6
Miami	41.8	5.2	44.8	2.0	6.2
Detroit	55.4	36.0	0.3	2.4	6.0
TOTAL U.S.	45.5%	31.0%	8.6%	10.8%	4.0%

Source: *The Wall Street Jounral*, August 19, 1988, p. 13.

and American to reduce the bias. Some bias probably remains, though it is milder. Its effects are accentuated by concentration in hub cities. In any event, during the crucial years of industry reorganization, bias made new entry more difficult.

Also, since 1984 United and American have been content to extract maximum revenues from the systems. Their uniform $1.85 fee for each reservation yielded them a very large flow of revenues and net profits, drawn from their competitors. These reservations probably have little relation to cost, and they reap very high rates of return. Therefore, they continue to inject a cost disadvantage for the lesser airlines, while enhancing United's and American's profits.

Taken together, the industry's concentration, hubbing, entry barriers, and reservations systems have reduced competition. The industry is now a complex, tight oligopoly, with high dominance in many markets, but mingled with competition on some major routes. Most of the industry is not effectively competitive.

III.

DETERMINANTS OF THE INDUSTRY'S STRUCTURE

Why has the existing structure of the airline industry developed as it has? Are there large economies of scale, making it inevitable that only a few big airlines will survive? Or have mergers merely raised concentration? Have artificial conditions induced higher concentration and entry barriers?

Costs and the Economies of Scale

When they were regulated, airlines seemed to many observers to be unsuitable for open competition. Competition would be unstable and destructive, it was said, because a few large airlines could exploit the economies of scale to drive out others.

1. Economies of Scale. By 1970, research showed that the economies of scale in operating airline systems were pretty much exhausted at a relatively small scale: There was no technological advantage to very large size. Indeed, the emergence of many smaller regional commuter airlines since 1977 showed the great variety that can exist, as airlines focus on various regions and levels of service. The pre-1975 emphasis on ever-larger jet aircraft has given way to smaller aircraft flying shorter routes on the hub-and-spoke pattern. This sort of diversity could go much further, with a variety of airlines flying a range of aircraft sizes and offering a mix of service quality. In short, the industry was and is inherently competitive. There is ample room for a considerable number of efficient airlines to coexist and compete effectively.

2. Economies of Scope. There are significant *economies of scope*, which is a recent term for the familiar network effects. When an airline has established a hub airport with a number of routes extending out, it can often add new routes at relatively low cost. Those economies of network expansion encourage the airline to expand onto those routes, often by cutting air fares down toward the level of the marginal costs in order to attract passengers.

3. Costs. In the general structure of costs, only about 20 percent of total costs are linked to specific passengers. The remaining costs are overhead costs (in maintaining aircraft fleets, ground facilities, staff, central operations, advertising, and so on). The low ratio of direct costs to overhead costs had encouraged the earlier claim that competition would be self-destructive.

Discounting could indeed be sharp, but it could be procompetitive, not self-destructive. Vigorous competition usually involves flexible pricing and discounting, even to deep levels, as rivals interact in the process. The low ratio of direct to overhead costs would simply widen the range of discounting, without necessarily making competition self-destructive.

Mergers and Affiliations

Mergers have strongly shaped the current industry structure. The initial burst of competition brought in scores of new airlines, small and medium-sized. But the dominant airlines were able to buy up scores of their smaller rivals or link with them at favorable terms, which removed any danger that the lesser airlines would rise to challenge the large ones.

Then after 1985 the larger airlines proceeded to consummate a series of major mergers.[13] Approval of these mergers by the Department of Transportation was a major policy failure. As a result, the industry is now a tight oligopoly of about six airlines, which interact and manage the competition in the industry as a whole and occupy a position of dominance in scores of hub cities as well as in smaller airports.

Mergers did not cause all of this concentration, but they were deliberately designed to increase market shares and control, and that has occurred. And they have brought disorder and inefficiency to some of the merging airlines.[14] The resulting rise in unjustified monopoly power could easily have been prevented.

Artificial Conditions Favoring Larger Airlines

Other factors favoring the largest carriers include airport gates and time slots, advertising, mileage bonus programs, and computer reservations systems.

1. Gates and Slots. Loading gates and time slots for takeoffs and landings are bottlenecks at many airports. Those who hold them can fly, while others

Table 8-5
Major Airline Mergers, 1985–1987

	Share of Total Industry Revenue Passenger Miles, 1986	
Texas Air	20.1%	
Eastern		9.6
Continental		5.4
People Express		3.3
Frontier		1.2
New York Air		0.6
United	15.7	
American	13.5	
Delta	11.9	
Delta		8.8
Western		3.1
Northwest	9.4	
Northwest		6.6
Republic		2.8
TWA	81	
TWA		7.2
Ozark		0.9
USAir	7.2	
USAir		3.0
Piedmont		2.8
PSA		1.4
Pan American	5.7	

Source: Air Transport Association.

can't. They were largely retained by the airlines holding them before deregulation and thus have tended to entrench the older, larger airlines. Indeed, one purpose of many mergers has been to acquire gates and slots (which have both a strategic and cash value).

The scarcity of gates and slots has been aggravated by the proliferation of hubs and spokes. When all lines are attempting to extend routes, gates and slots become the crucial bottleneck that blocks many of them out. In some airports, the crowding occurs only at peak times, such as 8 A.M. and 5 P.M. In those cases, pricing or other incentives (or simple reassignments) could be used to spread traffic out over the day. That would ease the blockage on competition caused by the scarcity of gates and slots.

But numerous other airports, including many of those that are most critical to competition in the industry, are congested throughout the day. No simple spreading of flights will suffice. Competition may require a more open scheme to permit airlines to compete among themselves for the fixed volume of gates and slots. The only other solution would be to reduce the volume of nonairline traffic, such as small private craft. But that is politically extremely difficult, because the private, small-plane group includes influential business executives and local fliers.

2. *Advertising.* Larger airlines have lower per-unit costs of advertising because they can spread their advertising costs over larger volume. Smaller airlines may simply be unable to fund the cost of saturation advertising, which is necessary in order to survive as a major competitor. Thus advertising tends to raise barriers to entry and to reduce competition in this industry.

This kind of advertising is not clearly a social economy of scale. It does not save on real resources that are necessary for production. It is largely strategic, and a shifting of customers among airlines gives no net gain in economic efficiency. Therefore, advertising tends to limit competition while not improving efficiency.

3. *Mileage Bonus Programs.* The larger airlines have established mileage-plus and frequent-flyer bonus programs, which let frequent flyers win free flights and other benefits by piling up mileage with individual airlines. These are popular with business travelers, who often reap the bonuses for them-selves by sticking with one airline for their business flights. It is a powerful marketing tool, which favors the larger airlines: Flyers accumulate mileage faster on airlines that can take them to a wider range of cities. Regional and small airlines simply cannot match the benefits, even though some of them have tried to band together to pool mileage for their own programs.

Moreover, the bonus schemes help exclude new airlines from entering, because existing large-volume flyers are already tied to the established air-lines. Therefore, all existing airlines tend to have an interest in keeping the programs going. The airlines are conscious of this power and manipulate the programs so as to yield maximum advantage at the least cost in bonuses.

4. *Computer Reservations Systems.* Although the direct anticompetitive effects of these systems may have been reduced since 1984, some remain. To the extent that they persist, competition is likely to remain ineffective in much of the industry.

IV.

BEHAVIOR

Within the setting of the oligopoly-and-dominance structure, the airlines have a wide range of choice in the way they behave toward each other and toward possible new entrants. They could fight fiercely, in sustained pricing fare wars, which give the main results of effective competition. Or, at the other extreme, they could embrace quiet, cooperative coexistence, with a careful avoidance of price wars and a reliance on common pricing patterns that embody mutual cooperation. That semicartel behavior was common during the pre-1978 regulation era.

Deregulation at first unleashed a flood of competitive tactics, with route shifts, price discounting, variations in service quality, and severe mutual harms. The subsequent concentration of the structure has encouraged cooperation, with common pricing patterns minimizing the danger of fare wars. The upshot is a reversion to the costly, pre-1978 nonprice competition.

Matching Behavior

In a tight oligopoly, prices tend to be rigid. The few firms tend to match each other's prices quickly, hold them for long intervals, and then change them quickly, with a minimum of continuous flexibility and uncertainty.[15] This rigid behavior reduces the danger that prices will get out of control as a competitive weapon.

Since 1985, the leading airlines have settled into this sort of rigid behavior. They have all adopted the same basic structure of fare discounts, with "supersavers" and "maxsavers." The discounts are fixed, with uniform restrictions about advance payments and nonrefundability. As a further example of lockstep behavior, there are very few fare discounts on one-way flights. Because all maverick airlines (such as World Airways, People Express, and Florida Air) have been eliminated, there is little danger of active price cutting.

Moreover, fare changes tend to be done in clusters, not in an ongoing process. One airline announces fare increases of, say, 5 percent on average, with sharp variations among routes. Typically, other airlines promptly match those fare changes on the affected routes, confining the extent of the cuts as much as possible. The process is a classic illustration of tacit collusion under tight oligopoly.

It was cemented in 1987 when Continental Airlines, which has been the one remaining maverick low-cost, lower-fare airline, explicitly shifted to leading in fare *increases*. This was widely recognized at the time as the end of the industry's open competitive period. In March 1988, Continental again led the rises, which were matched by all large airlines on the same day. The *New York Times* noted that "In general, the major airlines have decided to compete not by cutting fares but by increasing service. They now promote convenient departure times and frequency of service, as well as improvements in food and a better handling of baggage."[16]

That precisely describes the muffled, wasteful competition that occurred under CAB regulation *before* 1977. But now there is no CAB to provide some degree of public restraint. And the degree of concentration is now greater than it was then.

Price Discrimination: Anticompetitive and Procompetitive

Price discrimination is the setting of different price–cost ratios on identical or related products. Prices then reflect *demand* conditions rather than just *costs*. In the airlines industry, such discrimination can be extreme. The business passenger paying a full coach fare of $475 may be seated next to someone who is paying only $192 on a supersaver or maxsaver discount ticket.

Price discrimination can be procompetitive when it is done sporadically by firms with small market shares. Indeed, discounting is often the very lifeblood of effective competition, a vital method for small firms to raise their market shares, eating into the market power of their larger rivals. When local stores hold sales or offer discounts on weekly specials, their flexible pricing is driving competition forward.

But the opposite is true when dominant firms apply rigid, systematic price discrimination. Discounting then becomes a system to suppress competition, by cutting prices selectively against smaller rivals. Instead of helping smaller firms to increase pressure on larger firms, price discrimination becomes a technique for systematically reducing competition and maximizing monopoly profits.

Airline price discounts are a mix that includes many anticompetitive cases. The discounts are confined within rigid categories, under tight restrictions that the airlines jointly follow. The airlines carefully monitor and adjust the number of discounted tickets for each flight, but the types of discounts are fixed, and they rigidly segment buyers into fare groups based on their demand.

Business flyers, who need last-minute flexibility in their reservations, rarely benefit from discount fares. The discount restrictions usually lock you in weeks in advance; you must stay over a Saturday night (which few business flyers do); and there are severe penalties for changing the ticket. Therefore, most business passengers must pay the full coach or first-class fare. Only "discretionary" flyers get the discounts, and even they must acquiesce in tight restrictions that bar any change in schedule. These restrictions have little or no basis in costs.

Airline pricing behavior has virtually ceased to be a competitive weapon and has become instead a complex process by which an airline tries to maximize the revenue it extracts from its customers. Thus each large airline has perhaps a hundred or more pricing staff members working on "yield management." Their assignment is to maximize the revenue from each flight by repeatedly adjusting the number of seats offered on discounts.[17] As the day of the flight approaches, the pricing choices may change hourly, as the yield manager tries to fill every seat but still charge each customer the maximum that he or she is willing to pay. As an American Airlines manager notes, "You don't want to sell a seat to a guy for $69 when he's willing to pay

$400." This process approaches the extreme case of perfect price discrimination, in which the seller extracts all of each buyer's consumer surplus.

This is anticompetitive. The system milks the customers for maximum revenue, within a fixed pricing structure, and it makes entry difficult.

Predatory Actions

The prevalence of pricing rigidity indicates that market power is high in the industry, especially where discrimination is reinforced by extreme instances of anticompetitive pricing actions, directed against specific airlines. This has enabled large airlines to eliminate small rivals from the market by setting extremely low prices on key routes.[18]

Predatory pricing is a hotly debated topic, but it has been used (and used successfully) in specific instances. Because no legal action was brought to penalize this tactic, the larger airlines may be ready to repeat it in the future. That prospect tends automatically to discourage price cutting by smaller carriers or new entrants.

Other Strategic Actions

The handling of computer reservations systems by United and American, with bias and monopoly pricing, has further reduced competition.

The development of hub-and-spoke patterns has also reduced competition, on balance. It has created a series of local dominant firms or duopolies at most of the important airports, and fares have gone up in line with market positions. The rush to create hubs has widened the reach of local monopoly, helping to discourage price-cutting behavior. Against this, there are some gains. To an extent, hubbing permits passengers to connect more smoothly between same-carrier flights in the airport, as contrasted with changes between airlines. Gates are closer, and baggage is handled directly. But the monopoly effects are strong, and the net efficiency gains may be small.

In a larger perspective, hubbing may discourage vigorous competition. Each airline knows that if it cuts prices to invade another carrier's hub, it can expect selective retaliation at its own hub. Since this hurts the profits of both sides, there is reluctance to initiate the price cutting. Hence a pattern of live-and-let-live has emerged, with each airline protecting its spheres of influence.

Finally, entry behavior reflects the recent fading of competition. Entry into new routes has dwindled, and the formation of wholly new airline companies has stopped entirely. The initial free-wheeling entrepreneurialism under deregulation has given way to a cautious avoidance of provocative actions. As it has become clear that few airline markets (if any) are "contestable," the willingness to punish entry has become bolder. Unless the basic setting changes sharply, entry is likely to remain minimal.

V.

PERFORMANCE

For a few years, deregulation replaced a state-reinforced cartel with active competition, and it yielded notable gains: Ticket prices rose less rapidly, with benefits to passengers that have been estimated at some $6 billion per year in 1977 dollars.[19] The volume of air travel rose more rapidly, and air travel became accessible to more segments of the population. Airline load factors went up, from 56 percent in 1977 to 62 percent in the mid-1980s. Airline profits were normal during 1978–1988, suggesting that the airlines were not extracting large monopoly gains from their customers. Finally, the rate of airplane crashes has declined since 1977, so that flying appears to be safer.

But closer inspection suggests that the net benefits may have been marginal or even negative and that the recent rise of market power may be eroding the initial gains achieved under deregulation.

Trends of Prices and Service Quality

There are estimates that ticket prices (in cents per passenger mile) were reduced by about 30 percent after deregulation, compared with the levels that *otherwise* might have prevailed.[20] Fuel prices rose sharply during 1978–81, reflecting the rise in oil prices from about $14 to over $30 per barrel. Other input prices rose too, including average wages and the cost of new aircraft. When these rises are allowed for statistically, relative fares appear to show a significant fall.

This decline in real fares has been advanced as a strong indicator of deregulation's success. But it is not conclusive and may in fact be wrong, for three reasons. First, fares were already declining in real terms before deregulation. No decline occurred between 1977 and 1979. Second, the reduction in competition after 1986 has probably reversed some of the earlier competitive effect, leading toward higher fares. Indeed, specific fares have gone up quickly and sharply during 1986–89, after mergers that created dominance on specific routes.[21] As a further indicator, the severe fall in oil prices during 1986–87 (from $30 to $15 per barrel) resulted in few cuts in ticket prices.

Third, and perhaps most important, while prices may have fallen relatively, so has the quality of service, perhaps even more sharply. Service quality includes such elements as the time interval taken by the flight (including time spent at the airport checking in), the risk of missing flights, the risk of lateness or loss of baggage, the crowding in lines and in the plane itself, and the general quality of the travel experience.

Service has deteriorated in virtually every dimension. Most longer flights now require two separate legs, with a transfer at a hub. That lengthens the time involved, it doubles the number of landings and takeoffs (which causes anxiety for some travelers), and it increases the passenger's burden in making connections. The risk of missing connections is raised, as is the risk that baggage will not make the connection. Because planes now have a higher load factor, passengers must arrive at least an hour ahead of flight time to allow for long baggage check-in lines, and baggage retrieval at crowded carousels takes longer than before.

Inside the plane, there is more crowding. With most seats filled, space is more cramped. The size and spacing of the seats have commonly been reduced. Meal service is slower and less attentive. Generally, the level of amenity has descended toward that of bus travel. Also, the frequency of flight cancellations for reasons of profit has risen.

Most discounts can be obtained only by conforming to narrow restrictions, as noted earlier. The traveler's freedom of choice has therefore declined, as many passengers are required to lock in their plans weeks or months ahead, with no chance of refunding the ticket if conditions change. These hidden economic costs to passengers are hard to estimate, but they are real.

Airline Profits

Despite the turbulence of competitive changes, airline profit rates on invested capital were actually as high during 1978–87 (6.4 percent) as they were in the decade before 1978. Moreover, by 1987–88 the reduction of competition was leading to higher airline profits. Future profit rates are likely to remain high and stable as long as the industry's structure and behavior are not changed.

Efficiency

A major benefit of reregulation was to remove the incentives under regulation to let costs rise. By shifting from nonprice competition, deregulation offered the possibility of removing excess airline costs that appeared to make airline prices about 50 percent higher than necessary.

In fact, load factors have risen significantly, and most airlines have trimmed their labor force to operate leaner than before. But part of their savings has come from eliminating employee unions and cutting wage rates. That may have been inevitable, because wages had been unusually high during the era of regulation, when airlines could pass labor costs on to their customers. Yet the wage cutting is merely a transfer of money out of workers' pockets, rather than a real deduction in the resources used. Therefore, it is primarily a matter of distribution and fairness, rather than of allocation and efficiency.

Innovation

Innovation can occur as *product* changes (new products, services, or methods of organizing production) or *process* innovations (which lower the costs of producing the same goods).

Before 1978, airline innovations of both types were reasonably rapid. New aircraft types were adopted without delay, and nonprice competition developed a variety of service amenities (meals, decor, and so on). Computer reservations systems began to be developed.

Deregulation brought a burst of innovations, particularly with the introduction of no-frills service at very low prices. People Express, World Airways, and Air Florida led this innovation, but it has now been abandoned. At the upper end, a number of new airlines offered executive-quality luxury service at higher fares. Computer reservations systems were improved rapidly. New fare discounts were developed, from extremely low "peanuts" fares to off-peak discounts. Most of them were offered without tight restrictions.

Meanwhile few innovations toward better service were made; rather, service quality was generally reduced. New aircraft types were adopted about as fast as before, with one exception. Small commuter-type aircraft were introduced on many new small-city routes, to fill the gap left as large airlines withdrew large aircraft from those routes.

All of these innovations were important in the early deregulation years of 1978–83, when competition and new entry were strongest. Since then innovations have been less rapid, and no-frills service has disappeared. The slowing of innovation probably reflects the rise of market power, with its well-known disincentives for rapid innovation.

Small-Airport Service

Deregulation always raises the spectre that small cities and towns will lose vital service (as in loss of train and bus service, telephone service, and mail service). That can happen, and there were strong fears that airline deregulation would eliminate flights to small airports. In the event, full-size jet aircraft were withdrawn from many smaller airports. But new, small-craft commuter lines emerged to provide service in most cases. Some cases of severe service losses have occurred, but the whole group of smaller airports has probably gained in flight frequency since 1978. However, fares are higher; those on small-city routes have risen roughly 30 to 50 percent compared to those on the major routes. Moreover, the small aircraft feel less safe and comfortable, and hence they inflict a perceived loss of service quality.

Safety

Statistically speaking, airline travel is safe, and since 1978 it has grown safer. There are greater risks in driving a car, riding a bike, cooking a meal, or crossing a moderately busy street. Yet the carnage caused by actual airplane crashes is so terrifying that safety is an extremely sensitive question about airline performance.

During 1978–88 the fatality rates per volume of flying declined by one-third or more. But since 1978 there have been rising frequencies of near-misses and errors in the flight-guidance system, leading to calls to reregulate the airlines so as to improve safety. Deregulation is accused of inducing airlines to skimp on maintenance, under the pressure of competition.

Yet this line of reasoning is not conclusive. The main causes of any risk lie outside the airlines themselves. One major factor was the firing of all striking air controllers in 1981, followed by a rigid refusal to hire any of them back later. Another cause is the Reagan administration's decisions about funding the FAA. Meager budgets have restrained both the FAA's staffing and its ability to expand and upgrade the technology of the flight-control system.

In sum, as of 1989, safety does not appear to be a growing problem. In any event, airline safety has little to do with deregulation.

Performance Taken as a Whole

By 1978, most of the airline industry was ripe for deregulation. Deregulation brought effective competition to much of the industry for several years, with flexible pricing and route strategies. It reduced relative real prices, but the extent of the reduction is debatable. Hub-and-spoke patterns emerged, with single airlines dominating the traffic in many cities and on many routes. Computer reservations systems and mileage bonus programs then accentuated the anticompetitive effects of the hubbing. Finally, a wave of mergers during 1986–87 removed all maverick airlines and locked the industry into an oligopoly structure with elements of regional monopoly.

VI.
PUBLIC POLICY

Deregulation was appropriate and effective, but it elevated antitrust to critical importance as the sole protector of the fledgling competition. Instead, antitrust protection was fumbled and withdrawn, permitting dominance and control to develop in much of the industry. The whole experience offers important lessons about public policy choices.

What Worked in Deregulation

1. Deregulation Was Not Premature. Deregulation worked (briefly) because it removed all of the CAB's control only *after* competition was already effective during 1980–84. The great danger is premature deregulation, which frees a dominant firm from restraints before competition has become effective. When that happens, the dominant firm can often use its advantages and resources to quell its rivals and many entrants. In this case, deregulation quickly brought an upswelling of competition—due in part to route shifting, the expansion of the smaller regional airlines, and the entry of newly formed airlines. The larger firms were initially unable to control the process, and so route entry and fare cutting became turbulent and powerful.

2. A Series of Careful Steps.   Moreover, CAB controls were removed in a series of steps, with continuous attention to the results. The process could have been stopped or modified at any point if monopoly was emerging. Care was taken to make sure that competition was effective in most parts of the industry by the time all restrictions ended.

3. Opening Entry Wide.   Fully open entry was established as soon as possible, so as to stimulate new firms with fresh and experimental approaches.

Evidently, deregulation works when competitive pressures are already bursting at the seams. That is most likely to occur when there are many firms already in a complex set of interrelated markets, with strong incentives to penetrate each others' areas.

What Hasn't Worked

1. Contestability.   Relying on ultra-free entry (or contestability) has failed to limit the dominant airlines at their hubs and on monopolized routes. High market shares have bred high fares on many routes, despite the early promises that the fear of instantaneous entry would prevent monopoly behavior. Moreover, entry of whole new airlines has been virtually blocked by existing airlines' strategies and controls over airport gates and time slots, the computer reservations systems, mileage bonus programs, and pricing tactics.

2. Permitting Mergers.   The Department of Transportation's "abysmal dereliction" permitted a reconcentration of the industry.[22] The result has been a tight oligopoly, with large elements of dominance. Maverick low-price airlines have been eliminated, taken over, or subordinated as affiliates of the largest airlines.

3. Controls Over Gates and Slots.   The scarcity of gates and time slots at crowded airports, and their control by the larger airlines, have raised important barriers to entry and increased monopoly power.

4. Price Discrimination and Unfair Competition.   The hardening of systematic price discrimination has both reflected and intensified the monopoly elements. Moreover, consistently severe pricing retaliation has helped to drive maverick airlines (such as World Airways, Air Florida, and People Express) from the market. This behavior could have been prevented by antitrust actions, but it continues to be permitted. As in the case of mergers, the Reagan administration's laxity in antitrust enforcement took effect just when the transfer to vigorous antitrust supervision was critical.

5. Scarcity of Air Controllers. The firing of striking air controllers in 1981 (plus the apparent lifetime prohibition on rehiring any of them) further reduced the system's capacity. This sharpened the controls and exclusions that the leading carriers enforced.

Needed Policy Changes

The sector's competitiveness and performance could be markedly improved by certain reforms, even though some elements of monopoly seem firmly entrenched.

1. Gates and Slots. Expanding the main airport's capacity to handle flights is widely favored. But it is not easy, because it requires large capital investments, which take many years to complete. There is also neighborhood resistance to the consequent increase in noise levels.

Better pricing and allocation might quickly relieve some of the pressure. Much private small-plane activity is of marginal value and could be moved out of those airports onto small nearby fields by applying direct regulations. Currently, small executive and pleasure aircraft pay a few dollars for landings, which delay hundreds of airlines passengers. Raising the fees would reflect true costs and discourage the wasteful use of these critical resources.

Gate capacity is largely controlled by the large airlines, especially at their hub airports. They either block entry or charge monopoly prices for renting it to rivals. A bidding system might correct this, by allocating gates to airlines offering the lowest fares. Precisely because open access could increase entry and competition, the dominant carriers will continue to oppose it.

2. Flexible Pricing Without Anticompetitive Extremes. The rigid system of discounts gives an illusion of flexibility and bargains without providing truly competitive pricing. This pricing system could be subjected to antitrust attack by prosecuting leading airlines, which systematically match the discount structures of their rivals. The Antitrust Division could also adopt a strict policy to prevent systematic retaliation by the majors against price-cutting small airlines.[23]

3. Bonus Plans and Reservations Systems. Mileage-based discounts for frequent flyers should also be prohibited. They are strictly a marketing device to tie flyers to the large airlines, making the survival of smaller airlines or entrants more difficult.

Finally, the major airlines should be required to divest their computer reservation systems, as Kahn and others have urged. These systems, plus commission overrides (under-the-counter rebates), continue to tilt travel agents toward the larger airlines.

Raising infrastructures capacity, making pricing more flexible, and eliminating biases toward the larger airlines could reestablish competition in the industry. They will take time and sophistication to apply. Above all, they will require an antitrust policy that is aimed at exorcising monopoly elements in this industry rather than permitting them to become further entrenched.

NOTES _____

1. The debates are intense for three special reasons. First, everyone who has taken a flight feels that they are something of an expert from this first-hand experience.

Second, there has been unusually thorough research on this industry, both under regulation (mostly seeking to show how harmful it was) and deregulation (mostly seeking to show that deregulation has been a great success).

Third, some of the main actors in the 1977–84 deregulation drama were articulate, energetic writers, who have continued tirelessly to publicize and defend their achievements. Alfred E. Kahn and Elizabeth E. Bailey, in particular, led the CAB into its own abolition, and they still urge that deregulation has been a "clear success."

2. Kahn and Bailey are among the most enthusiastic, though they do note rising problems since 1984. See especially the summary in Kahn's "Surprises of Airline Deregulation," *American Economic Review*, 78 (May 1988), pp. 316–22. Michael E. Levine, John R. Meyer, Clinton V. Oster, Theodore E. Keeler, Daniel P. Kaplan, Steven Morrison, Clifford Winston, and Thomas G. Moore are among those also leaning strongly in favor of deregulation.

During the height of the deregulation debate, most of the deregulation advocates speculated that *if* the airlines did not collude with each other, then efficient allocation of resources would result. They also predicted that the threat of entry would prevent airlines from exercising any market dominance. The whole deregulatory experiment therefore turned on whether the airlines would compete strongly and face powerful entry. The actual outcome was, roughly: (1) vigorous competition and attempted entry during 1978–83; and then (2) a shift toward collusion and wholesale exit during 1984–88.

3. These critics are not as close to the mainstream of economic research, but they raise important points, particularly about monopolistic changes since 1984. The business press itself has raised disturbing points, in many stories in *The Wall Street Journal, Business Week*, and *The New York Times*, some of which are noted in this chapter. Major skeptics also include Melvin A. Brenner, F. Spencer, F. Cassell, and a variety of people associated with consumer groups, such as *Consumer Reports*.

4. For a good review of the industry's history, see Richard E. Caves, *Air Transport and Its Regulators* (Harvard University Press, 1962); William A. Jordan, *Airline Regulation in America: Effects and Imperfections* (Johns Hopkins University Press, 1970); and Elizabeth E. Bailey, David R. Graham, and Daniel P. Kaplan, *Deregulating the Airlines* (MIT Press, 1985), which covers the deregulation steps thoroughly.

5. Two kinds of research suggested that costs were raised by 30 to 50 percent on many routes as an effect of CAB regulation. First, costs on *intrastate* routes in Texas and California, which were not regulated by the CAB, were compared with costs on *interstate* routes, which the CAB did regulate. The costs of flights on intrastate routes were lower by roughly 30 percent on average; see especially Jordan, op. cit.

Second, statistical analysis was used to factor out the sources of cost levels, including regulatory effects. The net effect of regulation was shown to raise costs by about 30 to 50 percent on typical routes; see Theodore E. Keeler, "Airline Regulation and Market Performance," *Bell Journal of Economics*, 3 (Autumn 1972), pp. 399–424.

6. It was partly inspired by a series of studies encouraged by George Stigler at the University of Chicago. They uniformly found that regulation was meaningless or harmful in whatever sector it was applied. Earlier research on the transport sector had already begun the attack on rigid regulation; see John R. Meyer et al., *The Economics of Competition in the Transportation Industries* (Cambridge, Mass.: Harvard University Press, 1959).

7. See Richard Schmalensee, "Comparative Static Properties of Regulated Airline Oligopolies," *Bell Journal of Economics*, 8 (Autumn 1977), pp. 565–76; John C. Panzar, "Equilibrium and Welfare in Unregulated Airline Markets," *American Economic Review*, 69 (May 1979), pp. 92–95; Elizabeth E. Bailey, "Contestability and the Design of Regulatory and Antitrust Policy," *American Economic Review*, 71 (May 1981), pp. 178–83; and Bailey and John C. Panzar, "The Contestability of Airline Markets During the Transition to Deregulation," *Law and Contemporary Problems* (Winter 1981), pp. 125–45.

8. On the methods for defining markets, see W. G. Shepherd, *The Economics of Industrial Organization*, 3d ed. (New York: Prentice-Hall, 1990).

9. The best sources on it are William J. Baumol, John C. Panzar, and Robert D. Willig, *Contestable Markets and the Theory of Industry Structure* (New York: Harcourt Brace Jovanovich, 1982); Bailey and Panzar; and Elizabeth E. Bailey and William J. Baumol, "Deregulation and the Theory of Contestable Markets," *Yale Journal on Regulation*, 1 (1984), pp. 111–37. For a critique of the concept and its relevance to airline markets, see William G. Shepherd, "'Contestability' versus Competition," *American Economic Review*, 74 (September 1984), pp. 572–87.

10. Indeed, the contestability proponents admitted later that airline markets are not contestable; see Bailey and Baumol. The lack of contestability is now universally agreed on.

11. Bias is possible because the flight desirability hinges on departure times, the number of plane changes, the fare charged, the time interval between departure and arrival, and other features. It is easy to slant the computer's priorities for listings, so that they favor one airline over another. See the CAB's analysis of the problem in its *Report to Congress on Computer Reservations Systems*, Washington, D.C., 1983. See also the criticism of bias in Meyer and Oster, pp. 131–33; and Bailey, Graham, and Kaplan, at pages 187–90.

12. As Meyer and Oster note, "A bias that diverts only one passenger per month with a $200 round-trip flight for each SABRE computer terminal would gain American Airlines, and cost American's competitors, $120 million per year." Since marginal costs per passenger are low, the shifted revenues are virtually all net profit.

13. To some extent, the mergers merely reflected the damage to smaller airlines inflicted by the pricing policies, control of hubs, and other market strategies of the largest airlines.

14. Thus in 1988 Northwest Airlines was "still struggling to solve its service problems," caused by the merger with Republic Airlines in 1986. And Texas Air, after its buyouts of Eastern Airlines, Continental, Frontier, and People Express, was still

"struggling to integrate all of its parts into a smooth-running whole." *The New York Times*, "How to Beat the Mega-Carriers," April 12, 1988, p. D1.

15.   See William J. Fellner, *Competition Among the Few* (New York: Knopf, 1949); and John M. Blair, *Industrial Concentration* (New York: Harcourt Brace), 1972.

16.   *The New York Times*, "Air Fares Rise for Many Travelers as Big Carriers Dominate Market," March 15, 1988, pp. A1 and D8.

17.   For example, American's yield managers "monitor and adjust the fare mixes on 1,600 daily flights as well as 538,000 future flights involving nearly 50 million passengers. Their work is hectic: a fare's average life span is two weeks, and industry wide about 200,000 fares change daily." *The New York Times*, "The Art of Devising Air Fares," March 4, 1987, p. D1. The managers repeatedly adjust the number of seats on each plane that are available at the various discounts.

18.   For example, in June 1984 People Express entered the Newark–Minneapolis route, at fares of $99 on weekdays and $79 on evenings and weekends. Previously the lowest fare had been $149, and the standard coach fare was $263. Northwest, the dominant firm, promptly cut its fares to $95 and $75, for service that was much better (in seating, meals, baggage handling, and so on). Therefore, Northwest was undercutting People's fare "very substantially," as Kahn notes (1985, p. 13).

Desperately, People cut further, to $79 and $59; Northwest matched those cuts. Eventually People disappeared, bought by Texas Air; Northwest merged with Republic and held over 80 percent of traffic into Minneapolis; its fares rose sharply.

19.   The figure is controversial because it compares actual prices with those that might have occurred under certain assumed conditions. See Morrison and Winston; Melvin A. Brenner, "Airline Deregulation—a Case Study in Public Policy Failure" and "Rejoinder to Comments by Alfred Kahn," *Transportation Law Journal*, 16, No. 2 (1988), pp. 179–228 and pp. 253–62, respectively.

20.   See Morrison and Winston; Bailey, Graham, and Kaplan; and Meyer and Oster.

21.   For instance, *The Wall Street Journal*, "Finding the Best Air-Travel Deal Gets Harder as Restrictions Grow," March 31, 1986, p. 21; *The Wall Street Journal*, "After the Mergers: Air Fares Rise, but Era of Bargain Rates Isn't Over," February 2, 1987, p. 25; *The New York Times*, "Fares Rise as Airlines Merge," September 9, 1987, p. A1; and *The New York Times*, "Air Fares Rise for Many Travelers as Big Carriers Dominate Market," March 15, 1988, p. A1.

22.   The phrase is Alfred E. Kahn's, in "Airline Deregulation—a Mixed Bag, but a Clear Success Nevertheless," *Transportation Law Journal*, 16, No. 2 (1988), pp. 229–252.

23.   For the basis for such an approach, see W. G. Shepherd, "Assessing 'Predatory' Actions by Market Shares and Selectivity," *Antitrust Bulletin*, 31 (Spring 1986), pp. 1–28.

SUGGESTED READINGS

Books

Bailey, Elizabeth E., David R. Graham, and Daniel P. Kaplan, *Deregulating the Airlines*. Cambridge, Mass.: MIT Press, 1985.

Baumol, William J., John C. Panzar, and Robert D. Willig, *Contestable Markets and the Theory of Industry Structure*. New York: Harcourt Brace Jovanovich, 1982.

Brenner, Melvin A., James O. Leet, and Elihu Schott, *Airline Deregulation*. Westport, Conn.: Eno Foundation for Transportation, Inc., 1985.

Caves, Richard E., *Air Transport and Its Regulators: An Industry Study*. Cambridge, Mass.: Harvard University Press, 1962.

Douglas, G. W., and James C. Miller III, *Economic Regulation of Domestic Air Transport: Theory and Policy*. Washington, D.C.: Brookings Institution, 1974.

Jordan, William A., *Airline Regulation in America: Effects and Imperfections*. Baltimore: Johns Hopkins University Press, 1970.

Kahn, Alfred E., *Economics of Regulation*, 2 volumes. New York: Wiley & Sons, 1971.

Meyer, John R., and Clinton V. Oster, Jr., *Deregulation and the Future of Intercity Passenger Travel*. Cambridge, Mass.: MIT Press, 1987

Morrison, Steven, and Clifford Winston, *The Economic Effects of Airline Deregulation*. Washington, D.C.: Brookings Institution, 1986.

Shepherd, William G., *Public Policies Toward Business*, 7th ed., Homewood, Ill.: Richard D. Irwin, 1985.

Spencer, F., and F. Cassell, *Eight Years of U.S. Airline Deregulation*. Evanston, Ill.: Transportation Center of Northwestern University, 1987.

Articles

Bailey, Elizabeth E., and William J. Baumol, "Deregulation and the Theory of Contestable Markets," *Yale Journal on Regulation*, 1 (1984), pp. 111–37.

Brenner, Melvin A., "Airline Deregulation—A Case Study in Public Policy Failure," *Transportation Law Journal*, 16 No. 2 (1988), pp. 179–228; and his "Rejoinder to Comments by Alfred Kahn, *ibid.*, pp. 253–62.

Butter, Richard V. and John H. Huston, "The Effects of Fortress Hubs on Airline Fares and Service," *The Logistics and Transportation Review*, 24 (September 1988).

Consumer Reports, "The Big Trouble with Air Travel," June 1988, pp. 362–67.

Kahn, Alfred E., "Airline Deregulation—A Mixed Bag, But a Clear Success Nevertheless," *Transportation Law Journal*, 16 No. 2 (1988), pp. 229–252.

Kahn, Alfred E., "Surprises of Airline Deregulation," *American Economic Review*, 78 (May 1988), pp. 316–22.

Kaplan, Daniel P., "The Changing Airline Industry," *Regulatory Reform: What Actually Happened*. (Leonard W. Weiss and Michael W. Klass, eds.). Boston: Little, Brown and Company, 1986.

Keeler, Theodore E., "Airline Regulation and Market Performance," *Bell Journal of Economics*, 3 (Autumn 1972), pp. 399–424.

Levine, Michael E., "Airline Competition in Deregulated Markets: Theory, Firm Strategy, and Public Policy," *Yale Journal on Regulation*, 4 (Spring 1987), pp. 393–494.

Government and Other Reports

Air Transport Association of American, *Air Transport—Annual Reports of the US Scheduled Airline Industry*. Washington, D.C.: 1975–87.

U.S. Civil Aeronautics Board, *Report to Congress on Airline Computer Reservations Systems*. Washington, D.C.: Civil Aeronautics Board, 1983.

U.S. Civil Aeronautics Board, *Report to Congress on Implementation of the Provisions of the Airline Deregulation Act of 1978*. Washington, D.C.: Civil Aeronautics Board, January 31, 1984.

U.S. Department of Transportation, *Reports on Airline Service, Fares, Traffic and Safety*. Washington, D.C.: Department of Transportation, periodical.

Chapter 9

The Telecommunications Industry

Manley R. Irwin

I.

INTRODUCTION

For decades, U.S. telecommunication policy rested on the simple premise that telephony constituted a natural monopoly. Competition, it was believed, duplicated investment, raised cost, inflated rates, and compromised the affordability of service to the subscriber public. Competitive rivalry was the equivalent of economic waste.

The natural monopoly assumption was the basis of both state and federal regulatory systems. Regulatory jurisdiction between states and the Federal Communications Commission (FCC) was divided, costs allocated, rates assigned, profits monitored, investment approved, and reasonable telephone service assured. Few questioned the workability of the public utility principle as a substitute for the energy of a competitive marketplace.

But regulatory harmony began to disintegrate in the 1960s. Although state PUCs (public utility commissions) and telephone companies resisted any change from the status quo, the Federal Communications Commission encouraged selective market access. AT&T and the Bell System companies resisted entry through price cuts, rate changes, and manipulation of the regulatory and judicial review process. The FCC found itself mired in interminable cost and pricing proceedings, investigations, and inquiries that stretched from months to years. Administration gridlock ensued—AT&T versus the FCC and the FCC versus state commissions. Congress remained impotent as hearings droned on endlessly.

In 1974, antitrust action superceded regulation. The Department of Justice filed suit charging that AT&T (American Telephone and Telegraph) had blocked competitive entry into the customer equipment market, that it had denied access to the intercity telephone market, and that it had foreclosed rivalry in equipment manufacturing. As the Justice case gained momentum, regulation was relegated to the role of spectator.

In 1982, AT&T and the Department of Justice ended their antitrust dispute. In the largest reshuffling of corporate assets in U.S. commercial history, AT&T agreed to divest ownership of 22 Bell operating companies (BOCs), which were subsequently reorganized into seven regional holding companies. Antitrust restructured the industry fundamentally. A new telecommunication era commenced in 1984.

Today, regulation is experiencing an institutional renaissance. State commissions retain control over telephone service and investment. Most of them tend to resist market entry and to ban telephone resellers; generally, they seek a return to the operating premise of natural monopoly. In the meantime, federal regulation is struggling to determine the future markets of the Bell operating companies. Indeed, the Federal Communications Commission, state commissions, the Department of Justice, the Department of Commerce, and the Department of Defense encourage the Bell operating companies to diversify into competitive markets — a move resisted by Judge Greene of the U.S. District Court, which has jurisdiction of the divestiture decree.

The result is a renewed jurisdictional struggle between federal regulation and federal antitrust. And once again Congress has entered the fray — threatening to introduce legislation that transfers the courts' jurisdiction back to the Federal Communications Commission. In four short years, regulation, as a policy institution, has staged a remarkable comeback. Although there is some validity to the cycle theory of history, clearly no one predicted that the antitrust cycle would be so short. But first, what is the origin of telephony in the United States and what is the industry structure in the post-divestiture world?

II.

MARKET STRUCTURE

History

In telecommunications, the institution of private monopoly and public oversight is due in part to historical accident, in part to entrepreneurial genius. Telecommunications cannot be separated from the original telephone patent. Once cleared by the U.S. Supreme Count in 1876, the Boston Bell Patent Association found itself in the telephone business after the Western Union Telephone Company turned down an offer to purchase the patent for $100,000. After realizing its blunder, Western Union started its own telephone operation, and from 1877 to 1879 the fledgling Bell Company battled Telegraph's colossus for customers, revenues, rights of way, and line interconnection.[1] When Western Union retreated to telegraphy in 1879, the industry marked that year as its Magna Carta. The U.S. telecommunication market was effectively cartelized—one giant, dominating telegraph service—while Bell was left alone to develop telephone service.

The Bell Telephone Company was off and running as a corporate entity. Local franchises were issued in exchange for shareholder equity; a long-distance company was established in 1885, known as American Telephone and Telegraph Company (AT&T); a manufacturer, Western Electric, was acquired in 1882. Within a decade of the basic patent grant the components of what was later to be known as the Bell System were set in place. The organizational genius behind the telephone company was an ex-Post Office employee, Theodore N. Vail.

Competition in telephone service and equipment commenced in earnest shortly after the expiration of the telephone patents in 1894. Bell occupied the densely populated centers, while independent telephone companies sprouted in rural areas. Non-Western Electric plants sprang up to supply the needs of new telephone companies. Predictably, as competition spread, telephone rates fell, productivity jumped, and phone service expanded accordingly.

Despite a 50 percent penetration by the independents in 1908, the Bell System remained dominant in the industry. The company occupied local sites, enjoyed a long-distance monopoly, and hooked its toll facilities to its own local companies exclusively. AT&T denied non-Bell companies access to the Bell long-distance network, thus isolating the independents geographically. AT&T assigned patents only to Bell System companies. Western Electric refused to sell equipment to independent telephone companies. A telephone patent was thus transformed into a corporate monopoly.

At the turn of the century AT&T—its organization, market size, and vertical integration—was exposed, if not vulnerable, to the charge of monopoly power. It was then that Theodore Vail, in 1907 Bell's chief executive officer, declared unequivocally that competition in telephone service was tantamount to industrial warfare. Diversity, entry, rivalry, he asserted, violated quality, service, scale economies, and the principle of universal telephone service. Telephony, Vail argued, was a natural monopoly.

Unlike his contemporaries, Vail realized that the proclamation of monopoly privilege was hardly a sufficient policy prescription. Borrowing a concept from the railroad industry, Vail advocated regulatory oversight—private ownership subject to public regulation.[2] Bell's chairman thus set in place an institution that was to serve as a unique response to the dilemma posed by natural monopoly.

Vail lobbied for regulation at the state level in 1907 and 1908. Two years later, the Mann–Elkins Amendment to the Interstate Commerce Act extended federal jurisdiction over interstate telephone service. The Communications Act in 1934, which created the FCC, merely formalized what Vail had begun 27 years earlier.

At the time, the bargain struck between the telephone company and the public appeared eminently workable. In return for an exclusive franchise, the telephone company consented to submit its rates, earnings, and services to public scrutiny and examination. Regulation would sanction a monopoly and at the same time protect consumers from excessive rates, exorbitant profits, and indifferent service.

From AT&T's point of view, government regulation possessed still another virtue. It could serve to hold the antitrust statutes at bay. Under regulation, AT&T could afford to relax its policies, permit toll interconnection to telephone companies, and sell telephone equipment to non-Bell carriers. Under regulation, the Bell System was free to evolve into the world's largest corporation.

The industry prospered in the Roaring 20s, weathered the Great Depression, and mobilized for World War II. But after Truman's election in 1948, Bell's structure, service, and monopoly came under antitrust attack. The Department of Justice alleged that Bell's telephone monopoly had also foreclosed competition in the manufacturing of equipment.[3] The government proposed to divest Western Electric from AT&T, to split Western into three separate corporate entities, and to force the Bell operating companies to buy equipment on the open market. Once again, vertical integration became a controversial policy question.

A 1956 consent decree with the Department of Justice ended the '49 antitrust suit. In return for a promise by AT&T to make available its past patents on a royalty-free basis, and a commitment to confine itself to regulated communication services only, the Department of Justice dropped its suit. The result reaffirmed the basic structure of the Bell System and was hailed as a masterful exercise in management perspicacity.

1956 represented a high-water mark for regulation as well. Not only did the decree draw a sharp line between telecommunications and nontelecommunications services, but it also imposed a demarcation between regulated and nonregulated activities. Now that AT&T agreed to confine itself to regulated activities, regulation could concentrate its energy on telephone rates and telephone service.[4]

A fundamental industry policy held that telephone subscribers could not attach equipment to the public dial-up network. "Foreign" attachments, according to AT&T, would compromise the quality and integrity of the dial-up network, and no regulator dared tamper with such a national asset.

A second practice, an extension of AT&T's structure, combined local telephone service and long-distance service under common ownership. Clearly, competition in local exchange service, namely, digging up streets for rival cable companies, seemed ludicrous. And the notion of competition in toll telephone service was thought to violate the concept of scale economies.

A third policy, also an extension of the Bell structure, accepted the common ownership of equipment-manufacturing and telephone service. Telephone companies did not entertain competitive bids in buying the bulk of their equipment. Presumably, the operating companies bought telephone products from their supplier on the basis of cost, price, and technical quality.

On the other hand, 1956 witnessed the erosion of industry policy and structure. The FCC began to relax its customer attachment policy to the network in 1968, encouraged the entry of firms into intercity toll services in 1969, and at least questioned whether the integration of utility and supplier yielded low cost and technical innovation.

State commissions regarded such a regulatory reassessment as outright heresy, and the telephone industry treated any policy that married competition to the concept of monopoly with contempt and ridicule. Predictably, AT&T mounted vigorous opposition to any change in longstanding telecommunication policy, tariffs, and practices.

Once the FCC encouraged selective entry into telecommunications, the commission found itself confounded by AT&T's reaction to market rivalry. When, for example, the commission declared that users could attach their own equipment to the telephone network, AT&T, alleging network harm, filed tariffs requiring a protective device for the subscriber equipment.[5] The FCC pushed for a certification program to eliminate the device and thus triggered a debate over telephone technical standards. Indeed, by the time regulatory due process had run its course, the commission found that controversy over the direct attachment of equipment had consumed ten years. In the meantime, so-called interconnect firms selling customer equipment began filing private antitrust suits.

The commission's move to let private microwave and satellite carriers into the long-haul transmission market was even more controversial. AT&T responded to entry by dropping rates by 80 percent.[6] As the FCC searched for appropriate pricing and costing standards, regulatory due process consumed 18 years.

Similar battles were waged with respect to the procurement of carrier equipment. The FCC launched an investigation of the purchasing practices of the Bell operating companies in the mid-'60s. But the FCC appeared unable or unwilling to choose a policy cure to Bell's vertical integration. The commission rejected competitive bidding; rejected the price-comparison studies of Western Electric; rejected buying quotas; rejected treating carrier suppliers as public utilities; rejected disallowing of equipment prices to the Bell operating companies; and rejected structural separation between Western Electric and AT&T.[7] The only conclusion the FCC reached after 16 years of investigation was that AT&T's equipment market was closed to competitors of Western Electric.

In 1974 a Department of Justice complaint charged that AT&T, among other actions, had precluded entry in all of three markets, and the Department of Justice sought a fundamental corporate restructuring of the Bell System. Antitrust action now superceded regulatory inaction.

In 1982 AT&T reached a settlement with the Department of Justice.[8] Known as the modified final judgment (MFJ), AT&T agreed to divest its 22 operating companies and sever the link between the exchange and toll market and between local service and manufacturing (Figure 9-1). AT&T retained Bell Laboratory and Western Electric (later renamed AT&T Network Systems) and was permitted to diversify outside of telecommunications, thus softening a barrier imposed by the 1956 consent decree.

The 22 Bell operating companies were reorganized into 7 major holding companies and assigned service in some 161 LATAs (regional calling areas). Under the MFJ the operating companies were precluded from diversifying into intercity telephone service; manufacturing equipment; and such services as electronic mail, data processing, and information retrieval.

The decree, to take effect in 1984, represented a massive restructuring of corporate investment. AT&T's $148-billion assets were reduced to $39 billion; its revenues dropped from $65 to $33 billion; and its net income was cut from $7.3 billion to $1.4 billion (1984). Eight hundred thousand employees were reassigned. The breakup ushered in a new market structure and presumably altered corporate conduct and performance.

Figure 9-1
The Bell System, old and new.

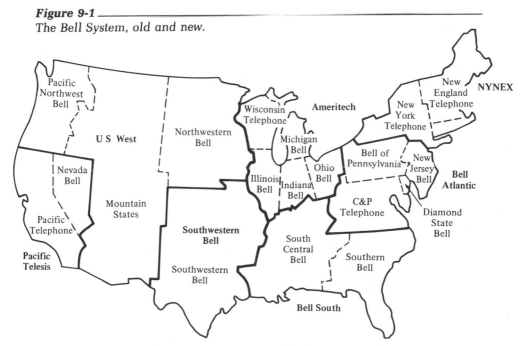

Source: Harry M. Shooshan III, *Disconnecting Bell: The Impact of the AT&T Divestiture.* New York: Pergamon, 1984, p. 1.

Current Market Structure

Today, in a post-divestiture environment, three markets are now discernible. These include

1. Interexchange or toll telephone service.
2. Exchange service market (intrastate telephone service).
3. Equipment manufacturing.

A brief note on each follows. In the predivestiture world, AT&T accounted for upwards of 90 percent of interexchange service, some 80 percent of local exchange service, and between 70 and 80 percent of U.S. telecommunication equipment manufacturing. In a post-divestiture world, market share has shifted, depending on barriers to market entry, capital requirements, economies of scale, and regulatory policy.

AT&T's market share (Table 9-1) in message toll telephone service has eroded from 90 to 80.2 percent in 1986; in 1987, it stands at 72 percent.[9] Although AT&T's market share is still predominant, other carriers offer message toll switched service, 800 service, and WATS (Wide Area Telephone Service) as rival services. In addition, the interexchange carriers offer wideband data services, private networks, and packet switching as part of their service portfolio.

Capital costs serve either as an invitation or as a deterrent to market entry. In the U.S. there are four nationwide fiber optic networks (Table 9-2), some 30 satellite carriers, dozens of value-added carriers, and some 520 regional toll carriers and resellers. At the same time, the interexchange market is undergoing consolidation. GTE's Sprint, for example, sold out to United Telecommunications. To the extent that interexchange telecommunications remain a capital-intensive industry, startup costs pose as one barrier to the entry process.

1. Interexchange Submarkets. Value-added carriers, sellers, resellers, "smart" buildings, teleports, regional microwave, and fiber optic networks all serve segments of the toll or interexchange market. Entry by value-added

Table 9-1
Market Shares of Interexchange Carriers

	AT&T	MCI (IBM)	USS	Other
1983	90.0%	5.0%	4.0%	1.0%
1984	88.0	5.9	4.8	1.3
1985	85.8	7.6	5.2	1.4
1986	80.2	10.6	6.6	2.6

Source: Walter Bolter, Bethesda Research Institute, "Policy Issues Facing the U.S. Telecommunications Industry in the 1980s and Future Prospects," *Communications Policy Research Conference*, United Kingdom, July 1987, p. 8.

Table 9-2
U.S. Long-Distance Fiber Optic Networks

Network	Planned Miles	Miles in Service (11/86)
US Sprint	23,000	6,500
AT&T	10,280	5,200
MCI	7,000	5,000
National Telecommunications Network	11,951	6,983
Regional Networks	9,126	2,480
TOTAL	61,357	26,163

Source: Peter Huber, "The Geodesic Network: 1987 Report on Competition in the Telephone Industry," Antitrust Division, U.S. Department of Justice, Washington, D.C., 1987, p. 3.2.

networks and resellers is facilitated by the ability of firms to lease telecommunications facilities rather than construct telecommunications investment de novo.

Another submarket, private corporate networks, has grown dramatically since 1984 and consists of leased circuits for intracompany relay of voice, data, video, and facsimile messages. By 1987, U.S. firms spent some $16 billion on related equipment for such corporate networks.[10]

When corporations sell network capacity to commercial users, such resale constitutes still another form of market rivalry. (Figure 9-2). Here firms provide in-house network services not only to sell excess capacity to commercial users but employ the network to link up with customers and suppliers. Customers as competitors are by no means small companies. They include IBM, Westinghouse, Merrill Lynch, General Electric, and Texas Air. The fact that AT&T recently lost part of its Holiday Inn account to the General Motors network suggests the potential of user resale as a market force.[11]

The buying side of toll or long-distance service similarly exhibits an uneven distribution. Professor John Wenders, a student of the telephone industry, notes user concentration in certain voice markets.

1. 10 percent of the residence customers account for approximately half of all interstate messages.
2. 10 percent of the business locations account for approximately three-quarters of all business interstate-message telephone service (MTS) revenues, and 1 percent of the business locations account for approximately 40 percent of all business interstate MTS revenues.
3. 10 percent of all the interstate WATS locations account for approximately 60 percent of all interstate WATS revenues.[12]

2. Intraexchange Market. The Intra-LATA or intraexchange market (within states) is inhabited by the Bell operating and independent telephone companies. Here market entry is under state PUC (pubic utility commission)

Figure 9-2
Network Strategies

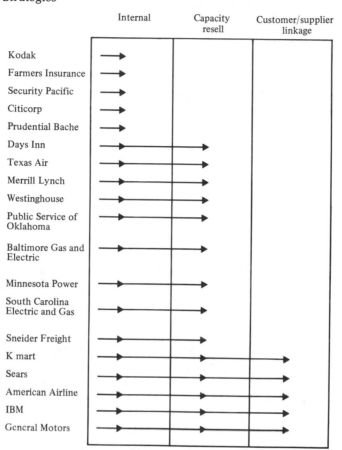

Source: Manley R. Irwin and Michael J. Merenda, "Private Networks and Corporate Strategy: The US/Pacific Basin Interdependence," Pacific *Cooperation and Information Technology Conference*, Vancouver, British Columbia, Canada, September 1988, p. 16.

control. Most PUCs, fearing that competition will threaten the price of local exchange service, are reluctant to solicit or encourage market access. True, technology in the long run holds the promise of new services in basic exchange services; but regulatory policy remains a key constraint to a policy of open access. Today, the local loop is generally regarded as a telephone-company monopoly.

On the other hand, the Bell operating companies are apprehensive that interexchange carriers will circumvent the investment of the BOC facilities and connect directly to their corporate customers. In telecommunications this form of rivalry is known as bypass. Here state and federal agencies agree that bypass can pose a threat to local service rates.

3. Telecommunication Equipment. The dynamics of entry and exit are

Table 9-3
U.S. PBX Market Shares (1985)

Firm	Estimated Share
AT&T	25.1%
Northern Telecom	19.1
Rolm	15.0
Mitel	8.2
NEC	7.6
GTE	4.0
Siemens	3.8
Others	17.2

Source: NTIA, *Assessing the Effects of Changing the AT&T Antitrust Consent Decree*, February 4, 1987, p. 30.

manifest in telecommunication manufacturing as well. Driven by technological change, domestic entry, and foreign competition, customer-owned premise equipment (CPE), PBX market share, has changed dramatically since 1980, when AT&T dominated the industry (Table 9-3).

In central office equipment, on the other hand, domestic consolidation and foreign market entry are very much in evidence. GTE has merged its central office operations with AT&T, and ITT has dropped out of the U.S. market altogether. On the other hand, the Bell operating companies now purchase switching equipment from AT&T, Northern Telecom, Ericsson, Siemens, NEC, CIT-Alcatel and U.K.'s Plessey (formerly Stromberg Carlson).

The capital cost of developing central office systems, particularly digital switching, has mushroomed over time. In the 1960s ITT spent some $40–50 million developing a new generation switch.[13] In the 1970s a new digital switch required a billion-dollar investment as well as $300 million annually to update software feature packages.[14] Such costs apparently account for a shakeout and consolidation in the central office equipment market not only in the U.S. but in overseas markets as well.

Predictably, divestiture has altered the buying practices of the Bell operating company in switching, fiber optics, and transmission hardware. From 1983 to 1985 the BOCs have shifted more and more of their purchase of hardware away from AT&T network systems (Table 9-4).

Table 9-4
Bell Network Procurement — Percentage Purchased from Foreign Firms

	'83	'84	'85
Switching	6%	18%	29%
Fiber optics	35	23	40
Transmission	5	3	23

Source: NTIA, *Trade Report: Assessing the Effects of Changing the AT&T Antitrust Consent Decree*, February 4, 1987, p. 32.

In addition, private corporations are emerging as an important source for equipment purchases. In 1987 some 40 percent of all telecommunication products and hardware were bought by corporations for private networks.[15] Given the concentrated bias in toll usage noted previously, such networks constitute a potential challenge to toll and local carriers alike.

III.
MARKET CONDUCT

Market conduct is inseparable from market structure. When regulatory entry barriers are eased, new firms challenge the price and nonprice policies of incumbent carriers. Indeed, market conduct develops its own dynamic counterpoint. The new entrant reduces prices and introduces new service features. The incumbent firm finds it essential to improve on that price offering. The process then commences another round. This dynamism is evident in the interexchange services market as well as the telecommunications equipment and hardware market, and it shows some potential of occurring in the monopoly exchange market.

Interexchange Services

Interexchange or interstate toll service includes public switched service; message toll telephone; and private-line service such as WATS, leased lines, and 800 service. Prior to divestiture, AT&T accounted for the bulk of these various switched toll services within the U.S. Today, post-divestiture, new entrants are soliciting customers through rate discounts. AT&T has responded with similar tariff reductions. As the other common carriers gain equal access, market entry invariably leads to subsequent rounds of price reductions to the subscribing public.

Price rivalry is particularly noteworthy in the corporate leased services market. AT&T, before divestiture, essentially dominated 800 service, WATS service, and private lines or dedicated circuits to business and government. Since 1984, other toll companies have become a presence in these segments. When rivals introduced bulk price cuts for leased services, AT&T filed discounts of equipment and hardware by up to 40 percent—price reductions that have precipitated the charge of discrimination by both competitive carriers and equipment manufacturers.[16]

Nonprice rivalry—in the form of features, software packages, packet switching, and data transmission rates—reveal a similar counterpoint between entrant and incumbent firm.

Exchange Services

Although the Bell operating companies' local exchanges are generally insulated from direct market competition, a muted form of price and nonprice rivalry is discernible nevertheless. Customer-owned PBXs compete with the Centrex service of the Bell operating companies. Prior to the AT&T breakup, Centrex was regarded as an obsolete telecommunication service. Indeed, AT&T, through rate increases, attempted to phase out this service in favor of PBX equipment. But post-divestiture, the Bell operating companies have introduced digital central-office switches embedded with software features. Stated differently, the Bell operating companies have rejuvenated Centrex features. Centrex has turned out to be a "treasure in the attic."[17] There is little doubt that market competition is responsible for the discovery of that treasure.

Some 30 percent of BOC revenues are derived from local access prices that are charged to interexchange carriers for using local facilities. But economists are quick to point out that a price to one firm (the BOC) constitutes a cost to another (the interexchange carrier). As a means of reducing that cost, business users consider circumventing local loops by employing satellite, cable, microwave, or fiber optics to their ultimate destination. Competitive substitutes are invariably an extension of the search for market efficiency.

Naturally, the Bell operating companies oppose alternatives to their telecommunication investment. But the carriers do more than fight bypass. They have responded through rate cuts and by pushing the adoption of fiber optics, digital microwave, and digital central office systems.[18] As in other markets, potential entrants activate a price and nonprice response from incumbent carriers.

Telecommunications Equipment

Finally, entry into telecommunications manufacturing carries both a domestic and a foreign dimension. As firms entered the V-SAT (very-small-aperture terminal) market, the T-1 multiplex market, and the digital microwave market, AT&T has responded by acquiring a V-SAT manufacturer and has added outside equipment to its in-house multiplexing product line.[19]

As corporate telecommunications networks multiply, the mix of equipment output is adjusted accordingly. As noted, users themselves become innovators and sell excess capacity to customers. Market competition is thus generated from a new and unexpected quarter of the market as corporate networks add to the dynamism of a post-divestiture environment.

IV. _____
MARKET PERFORMANCE

The transition from regulation to the incentives of market competition is bound to show up in economic performance. The differences are striking. Under regulation, a firm is driven by rate-base economics, a system whereby the total revenues of the firm must cover a carrier's operating expenses, taxes, maintenance, salaries, depreciation, as well as a return on capital investment. Rate-base regulation is essentially an exercise in cost plus. The more the firm spends on capital equipment, the higher the absolute level of profits. Given a fixed ceiling on investment return, there is little incentive for the firm to reduce its costs or investment. In fact, there is always a perverse tendency to gold-plate investment and to impose administrative expenses that can be passed forward to the consuming public — given the assumption that usage (that is, demand) is largely price-inelastic.

Of course, regulation is designed to serve as a surrogate for market competition, that is, to reduce costs and to reach levels of attainable efficiency. And commissions do endeavor to probe the debt, cost, price, earnings, and investment of firms under their jurisdiction. While that effort is invariably frustrating, commissions pride themselves at least in reducing a firm's depreciation expense by stretching equipment life to sometimes as long as forty years. In the commissions' view, lower depreciation expenses result in reduced telephone rates to the subscribing public.

The problem is that this short-run depreciation goal conflicts with the long-run goal of the modern telephone plant. Carriers are saddled with obsolete equipment as market forces produce new generations of telecommunications equipment, hardware, and products. In an era of technological change and global competition, market entry serves as a benchmark that measures the performance of the carrier and regulator alike.

Consider recent (post-divestiture) developments in choice, price, cost, and innovation as indices of market performance.

Choice

Consumers and business choices continue to expand and multiply in submarkets of the telecommunications industry. In interexchange services subscribers enjoy options on rates, features, quality, and accessibility. Business choices include private ownership, leased facilities, or combinations of both. Private-line features and software enhancements become available as satellite and fiber optic carriers customize features to customer requirements.

The mirror image of service choice is reflected in the diversity of communications equipment. Manufacturing choice is solicited by the Bell operating companies, by AT&T, by residential subscribers, and by business users. If nothing else, competitive entry has ushered in an unprecedented era of telecommunication options.

Prices

Competitive access has also reduced telecommunication prices. Message toll service, for example, has declined some 40 percent since 1984. Private-line rates have fallen by equivalent amounts.

Equipment prices also reflect competitive pressure. Prices have declined in satellite terminals, facsimile equipment, and fiber optics. In three years, PBX prices have fallen from $1,000 to $300 per line.[20] And since the 1980s central office equipment prices have dropped from $1,000 per line to $200 per line.[21]

On the other hand, basic exchange rates have increased by 8.7 percent annually since 1984, leading some consumer advocates to allege that the benefit of the AT&T breakup has proven a mirage to the local subscriber. An FCC study indicates, however, that local exchange rates were rising by 6 percent annually five years *prior* to divestiture.[22] Today, local exchange rates are increasing by 2.5 percent annually, suggesting that predictions of an explosion in rates have been misplaced. If nothing else, market entry tends to reduce price discrimination—even when price–cost disparities have occurred with the blessing of regulatory authorities.

Cost

Market entry places a premium on a firm's productivity and long-term efficiency. Since divestiture, AT&T, the Bell operating companies, and manufacturers have undertaken an excruciating exercise in cost reduction and containment. AT&T has reduced expenses, cut personnel, and contracted management decision levels. The company has offered to reduce its message toll telephone rates if its local-access charges can be cut. (The charge is paid to the local operating companies for toll termination or origination.) Indeed, there is some debate as to whether limiting regulation to prices rather than profits will give the local carriers an incentive to reduce local exchange plant, equipment, and administrative expenditures.[23]

The Bell operating companies have found themselves under some pressure to reduce operating expenses and access charges in order to prevent business users and interstate carriers from bypassing their local facilities. Though each company possesses a state franchise, Bell operating company cost efficiencies are not totally insulated from the consequences of interstate rivalry.

Similarly, competitive entry in equipment manufacturing has lifted productivity and placed a premium on economic performance. Since divestiture, AT&T has shut down six plants (on grounds of obsolescence or excess capacity), reduced manufacturing expenses, and moved plants overseas. When product gaps occur in AT&T's product line, the company has turned to outside OEM suppliers.

On the other hand, U.S. telecommunications trade balance has moved from a surplus to a post-divestiture $2 billion deficit. Operating companies and business users are apparently buying products irrespective of source, domestic or offshore. Yet when the FCC contemplated regulating or limiting access to the U.S. equipment market, the NYNEX operating company opposed that oversight with the observation that the FCC action "would result in increased prices and therefore adversely impact telephone rates."[24] And Ameritech commented that the commission's procurement regulation would "result in less competition, fewer choices and higher prices for telephone service."[25] AT&T has observed that a post-divestiture environment has "prompted new entry and spurred precisely the increased competition and dramatic benefits for consumers that the department (Department of Justice) predicted."[26]

To repeat, performance and market entry are inseparable in theory and in fact; the carriers now give testimony to that linkage.

Innovation

Perhaps in no other area has a post-divestiture environment acquitted itself so well as in innovation. Competition has spurred the introduction of new services, new products, new hardware, and new features. Toll telephone usage has not only doubled since 1984, but telephone plant equipment has been upgraded with fiber optic, digital switches, satellite relay, and broad-band transmissions facilities—to say nothing of cellular radio and data networking. The effect of market entry on research, innovation, and investment in the industry has prompted global emulation as well—liberalization, privatization, and competitive entry.

V.
PUBLIC POLICY

Today, U.S. telecommunication policy is struggling between the reality of international competition and a balance between domestic regulation and antitrust. Consider the international side of the equation.

International Development

First, the world is connected by an information infrastructure of cables, fiber optics, satellites, digital switching, and terminals. This infrastructure—in the Atlantic, Pacific, and Caribbean basins—is translated into lower cost, reduced prices, and new services available on a global scale. Voice and data transmission are readily accessible. Dialing London is as common as dialing Los Angeles.

Second, global networks are evolving into an explicit competitive strategy. Nissan, for example, employs satellites to link computer-aided design and computer-aided manufacturing operations with the Far East, North America, and Europe.[27] General Electric, General Motors, IBM, and AT&T employ telecommunications networks as a strategic response in all three continents. Corporate networks are moving from an internal response to an external link, from a domestic move to an international connection.

Third, the velocity of information exchange eases the mobility of capital investment. In the process, telecommunication networks have intensified regional rivalry within the United States. Citicorp's satellite, for example, permitted the firm to bypass the interest-rate ceiling of credit cards in New York and to employ Sioux Falls, South Dakota, as a means of circumventing New York's regulatory authority.[28] Networks enable firms not only to vote with their feet but to vote with electronic bit streams as well.

A similar competitive intensity can be detected internationally. The U.S. tax on interest payments to foreign bank holders precipitated the European Money Market, a "stateless" cache of billions linked by terminals, communications, and data bases, which is beyond national jurisdictional control.[29] A $15-billion, fourteen-day global run on Chicago's Continental Illinois deposits, sparked by a rumor on the Japanese money market, resulted in the bank's "nationalization" by the U.S. government.[30] In April 1987, interest on long-term U.S. bonds rose 30 percent because the Japanese insurance companies elected not to buy U.S. government debt. The U.S. stock market crash of October 1987 sent ripple effects around the world, from Hong Kong to Singapore, from New York to London. International markets are increasingly linked by telecommunications, and information is transmitted at 1.5 million miles per hour.

A nation's tax, savings, investment, and regulatory policies are today monitored, if not measured, by international equity, bond, futures, and foreign exchange rates. Global competition acts to circumscribe absolute power of the nation-state. And where does U.S. telecommunication policy stand in this era of global information and international competition? The answer is that policy is simultaneously undergoing federalization, jurisdictional in-fighting, and efforts to decide whether regional telephone companies can diversify into competitive markets.

Domestic Policy

1. Federalization of Telecommunications. First, over time the state commissions are losing their regulatory clout. Indeed, individual state agencies are in an ironic position of driving the federal preemption process. The following pattern is discernible. A firm attempts to enter a state regional market. The state PUCs reject entry on grounds that competition will raise telephone rates. The firm then turns to the FCC and seeks jurisdictional preemption by the commission. The FCC obliges. The case goes into the courts and the appeals court upholds federal authority. This process, ongoing for the past thirty years, shows little sign of attenuation. Over time, telecommunications policy in the United States is becoming federalized and concentrated in Washington, D.C.[31]

2. Jurisdictional Warfare. Second, once the locus of regulation shifts to the nation's capital, a jurisdictional fight breaks out among federal agencies.

The policy struggle seldom turns on the economic performance of regulation versus competition. Rather, the issue is procedural—which agency should attain authority over price, cost, investment, procurement, or carrier diversification. The FCC, for example, seeks to monitor BOC foreign equipment purchases, a policy opposed by Commerce and the State Department. The Department of Defense, under a mandate of national security,[32] attempts to monitor equipment exports, remote satellite sensing, and foreign rocket boosters. State and the Transportation Department quarrel over control of satellite exports. The Department of Commerce assaults the FCC's attempt to move into foreign affairs but invites the commission to preempt the antitrust role of the federal courts. The FCC advises the BOCs to ignore Judge Greene's restrictions on corporate diversification—all done under a mandate of the public interest and national security. In short, regulation abhors a vacuum.

3. *Monopoly Diversification.* Third, after eighty years of regulation in interexchange services, exchange service, and equipment production, U.S. policy is now prepared to overlook the antitrust issue of market structure and conduct. Today, the policy issue focuses on Bell Operating Company diversification. The 1982 modified final judgment assigned the BOCs a local monopoly franchise and permitted restricted diversification into interexchange services, manufacturing, and information services.

Now the Department of Justice, the NTIA, the FCC, and the White House seek to encourage monopoly firm diversification into competitive markets. What is to prevent cross-subsidization and predatory pricing between monopoly and competitive markets? The answer, according to the Department of Justice, is state and federal utility regulation. And how will such regulation be accomplished? Through cost-accounting bookkeeping techniques, through new regulatory tools, and through a renewed commitment by state and federal agencies to protect the public interest.[33] The problem is that antitrust intervened in the U.S. telecommunications market precisely because of the institutional failure of public utility regulation to deal effectively with these aspects of monopoly conduct.

VI.
CONCLUSION

After four years of a post-divestiture experience in telecommunications, federal policy is now prepared to return to the public-utility principle of benign surveillance. The causes of the industry's massive restructuring are all but forgotten; the conduct of firms occupying monopoly and competitive markets simultaneously is all but ignored; the gridlock of regulatory due process is recalled only by the participants—now retired and collecting their annuities.

The question remains whether telecommunications policy must be condemned to repeat the errors of the past. Are we destined to resurrect institutions whose performances have been found wanting? Are the policy options so ambiguous as to inhibit clear and unequivocal choice? That is the current status of U.S. telecommunications policy. Santayana once observed that each generation prefers to undertake its own folly; Bismarck remarked that he preferred to learn from the mistakes of others. As it stands now, it appears that U.S. telecommunications policy is about to take the advice of the philosopher rather than abide by the counsel of a statesman.

NOTES

1. Robert Cono, *A Streak of Luck* (New York: Simon and Schuster, 1978), pp. 82–83.

2. Annette Frey, "The Public Must Be Served," part 59, *Bell Telephone Magazine* (March–June, 1975), p. 5.

3. *United States* v. *Western Electric,* Civil Action No. 17-49 (DNJ 1949).

4. U.S. Congress, House, *Consent Decree Program of the Department of Justice,* Hearings Before the Antitrust Subcommittee (Subcommittee No. 5), Committee on the Judiciary, 85th Congress, 2nd Session, Part 2, Vol. 1, American Telephone and Telegraph, p. 38.

5. Alvin Von Auw, *Heritage and Destiny* (New York: Praeger, 1983), p. 163.

6. Federal Communications Commission, *Report of the Telephone and Telegraph Committees of the Federal Communications Commission in the Domestic Telegraph Investigation,* Docket 14650, April 29, 1966, p. 205.

7. Manley R. Irwin and Michael J. Merenda, "Should the FCC Regulate Telecommunication Manufacturing Again?" *International Telecommunications Society,* Seventh Annual Conference, M.I.T., Cambridge, MA, June 29, 1988.

8. *United States* v. *Am. Tel. & Tel. Co.,* 551 F Supp. 131 C.D.D.C. 1982.

9. "Aggressive and Flexible Strategy Termed Key to MCI's Success," *Journal of Commerce* (August 10, 1988), p. 4B; Anita Taff, "Washington Update," *Network World* (June 27, 1988), p. 11.

10. "A Scramble for Global Networks," *Business Week* (March 21, 1988), p. 140.

11. Kathleen Healy, "Thank You for Using Westinghouse," *Forbes* (November 30, 1987), p. 212.

12. John Wenders, "The Economic Theory of Regulation and the U.S. Telecommunications Industry," *Telecommunications Policy* (March 1988), p. 20.

13. "Telecommunications Equipment: Even a Growth Industry Can Have Structural Problems," *OECD Observer* (November 1982), p. 16.

14. "The Competition Besieging ITT in Telecommunications," *Business Week* (July 4, 1983), p. 47.

15. "Telecommunications: Rewiring the World," *The Economist* (October 17, 1987), p. 16.

16. Lawrence Gasman, "The ByPass Connection," *High Technology* (May 1986), p. 22.

17. Gary Kern, "PBX vs. Centrex," *Network World* (November 2, 1987), p. 34.

18. "The Rewiring of America," *Business Week* (September 15, 1986), p. 192.

19. John T. Mulqueen, "AT&T: Clever OEM or 'Sugar Daddy' of the Industry," *Data Communication* (March 1988), p. 103.

20. "Why AT&T Isn't Clicking," *Business Week* (May 19, 1986), p. 90.

21. *NTIA Trade Report, Assessing the Effects of Changing the AT&T Antitrust Consent Decree,* Department of Commerce, February 4, 1987, p. 21.

22. James Lande and Peyton Wynns, *Primer and Source Book on Telephone Price Indexes and Rate Levels,* Industry Analysis Division, Common Carrier Bureau, FCC (April 1987), p. 53. See also "Princes and Pumpkins at the Digital Switching-Hour," *The Economist* (August 29, 1987), p. 74.

23. Charles Mason, "Washington Wages War over FCC's Price-Cap Plan," *Telephony* (August 1, 1988), p. 12.

24. Before the Federal Communications Commission, "In the Matter of Regulatory Policies and International Telecommunications," Docket 86-494, *Comments of Nynex Corporation,* April 17, 1987, p. 12.

25. Ibid., *Comments of the Ameritech Operating Companies,* April 17, 1987, p. 6.

26. *U.S.* v. *Western Electric,* Civ. Action No. 82-0192, U.S. District Court, District of Columbia, *AT&T's Comment on the Report and Recommendations of the United States,* pp. 82–83.

27. Ian Rodger, "Nissan to Link Up World Production," *Financial Times* (July 29, 1988), p. 5; Karyl Scott, "Toyota to Link U.S. and Japan Facilities via T-1," *Network World* (August 24, 1987), p. 4; "A Scramble for Global Networks," *Business Week* (March 21, 1988), p. 140.

28. "Citicorp Transfer of Credit Card Center to South Dakota Has July Target Date," *The Wall Street Journal,* March 20, 1980, p. 4.

29. "Clash Over Stateless Cash," *Time* (November 5, 1979), p. 82. See also Peter Riddell, "London Markets Poised if U.S. Restricts Trading," *Financial Times* (February 9, 1980), p. 6.

30. Jack Anderson, "Is Your Bank Account Safe?" *Parade Magazine* (September 20, 1987), p. 14.

31. Manley R. Irwin, *Telecommunications America: Markets Without Boundaries* (Westport, Conn.: Greenwood Press, 1984), p. 118.

32. See National Academy of Science, Committee on Science, Engineering and Public Policy, *Balancing the National Interest* (Washington, D.C.: National Academy Press, 1987.)

33. Manley R. Irwin, "National Security and Information Technology: The New Regulatory Option?" *Government Information Quarterly* (Fall 1987).

SUGGESTED READINGS

Brock, Gerald. *The Telecommunications Industry: The Dynamics of Market Structure.* Cambridge, Mass.: Harvard University Press, 1981.

Coll, Steve. *The Deal of the Century: The Breakup of the Bell System.* New York: Antheneum, 1986.

Henck, Fred, and Bernard Strassburg. *A Slippery Slope: The Long Road to the Breakup of AT&T.* Westport, Conn.: Greenwood Press, 1988.

Huber, Peter. *The Geodesic Network.* 1987 Report on Competition in the Telephone Industry, Antitrust Division, U.S. Department of Justice, 1987.

Irwin, Manley R. *Competitive Freedom vs. National Security Regulation.* Westport, Conn.: Greenwood Press, 1989.

Temin, Peter. *The Fall of the Bell System.* New York: Cambridge University Press, 1987.

Von Auw, Alvin. *Heritage and Destiny.* New York: Praeger, 1983.

CHAPTER 10

THE BANKING INDUSTRY

Arnold A. Heggestad

I.

INTRODUCTION

The banking industry, or more precisely, the depository financial services industry, plays a critical role in the American economy. It has a pervasive influence because virtually every other sector of the economy must rely on its services. Households, government units, and business firms hold deposit balances in these institutions, as either transaction deposits or time and savings deposits.

Transaction deposits, which are primarily demand deposits, constitute the primary component of the money supply of the economy. Without the payments system, the economy could not function. The transactions and savings deposits that are entrusted to financial institutions are in turn loaned to others in the economy. They serve as the primary sources of credit for investment and for consumption by households, government, and business.

The critical importance of financial services to the economy has led to extensive regulation. The major thrust of regulation has been to promote industry "soundness." The safety of deposits is guaranteed through government-provided deposit insurance. Soundness is also protected by comprehensive financial regulations that limit the risk exposure of the industry. Despite regulation, widespread failures of large commercial banks and savings and loan institutions have placed a tremendous burden on the regulatory and insurance system in the past few years.

There are still other regulations that are intended to direct credit to certain sectors of society and to protect consumers from exploitation and unfair practices. Finally, competition is controlled through restrictions on entry and consolidations.

The past decade has been a major transition period for the industry. Longstanding limits on pricing, on asset management, and on geographic expansion have been reduced or eliminated. Deregulation has changed the products that financial intermediaries may legally offer and has substantially increased the degree of competition in banking markets. Banks are now able to compete for deposits with virtually no price limitations.[1] They are free to offer a wide range of new products. Their geographic limitations have also been lifted, but to a lesser degree. Increased competition is the order of the day.

Deregulation has also permitted much new entry. Other financial services firms have begun to offer deposits and loans services in direct competition with the regulated depository institutions. These firms have experienced significant growth because they are not constrained by the regulations imposed on depository institutions.

Three key public-policy issues now face the depository financial services industry. First, can the industry be deregulated further without leading to an increase in the overall concentration of financial resources, with adverse economic and political consequences? Second, would further deregulation expose the industry to excessive risk? Third, what role do market forces play in promoting competition within markets, in promoting efficiency in the provision of financial services, and in controlling the risk exposure of individual firms?

This chapter addresses these broad issues. The emphasis will be on commercial banking, because of its size and importance to all sectors of the economy. However, the conclusions about commercial banks will be relevant for other types of depository institutions as well.

Financial Services Sector

Financial markets play a critical role in the functioning of the market economy. Every element of the commercial society, from individuals to giant corporations, needs to have access to the payments mechanism in order to conduct economic activity. In addition, most need access to financial markets so that they can separate the timing of their spending decisions from the receipt of their income.[2] Individuals and businesses seldom receive their income at a rate that coincides with their need to purchase services.

Most individuals need access to financial markets, as both borrowers and lenders, at different times in their lives. So do commercial enterprises. The farmer must be able to purchase land, equipment, seed, and fertilizer and hire workers before the crops are harvested and sold. The manufacturing firm must invest in plant, equipment, and inventory of raw materials and finished goods before it can begin to sell its product. Consequently, the business firm must rely on financial markets as a source of short- and long-term funding. Similarly, at times it will have excess funds and will desire to earn a competitive return on these funds.

State and local governments also rely on financial markets. They are often required to provide basic public services prior to receiving tax revenues. They must borrow against future tax revenues on these occasions.

Conversely, they will on occasion have excess funds as revenues exceed current expenditures.

Individuals, business, and government must rely on financial markets to meet these basic credit needs as well as transaction balances. Because their requirements are very heterogeneous, there are many different types of financial instruments available. They vary in such critical parameters as maturity, risk, return, liquidity, and size.

The primary supplier of financial instruments to all but the largest corporations are financial intermediaries. Financial intermediaries simultaneously raise funds in credit markets and use the proceeds to advance credit to borrowers.

Figure 10-1 illustrates the process by which borrowers and savers may interact in the financial markets. Each relationship depicts cash flowing from a lender to the borrower in exchange for a financial asset passing from the borrower to the lender. Cash flows to the right in the diagram. Financial assets flow to the left. Typical financial assets include loan contracts, bonds, stocks, and commercial paper. The Federal Reserve is incorporated in the diagram as it may be a net supplier or user of cash, depending on current monetary policy. Flows may be direct or through a financial intermediary.

Borrowers and lenders may deal directly with each other. Financial

Figure 10-1_____
Financial markets' flow of funds.

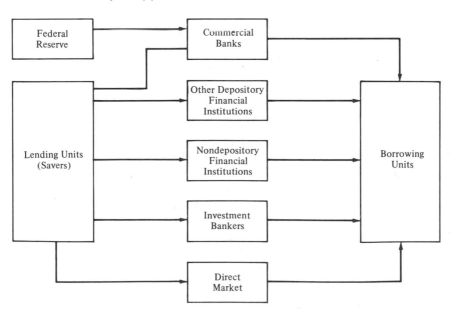

intermediaries range from investment banks to commercial banks. Private placement of loans or stock are examples of these types of transactions. However, because of the specialized nature of the needs of borrowers and lenders, transaction costs are very high. To reduce transaction costs, specialized financial intermediaries have been developed to serve these markets.[3]

Investment bankers facilitate the direct flow of financial assets. An organization wishing to raise funds may issue financial instruments, such as bonds or stock. The investment banker will purchase the instruments or guarantee a price. In turn, the investment banker will sell these instruments to final investors. As an intermediary, investment bankers take the initial risk. Their profit is derived from the differential between the price they pay for the securities and the price they receive on the open market when they sell to the final investors. In addition, as market makers in the secondary market, they provide liquidity to permit initial purchasers of the securities to reverse their positions.

Financial institutions provide a more complex service. Rather than facilitating the sale of assets, they create new financial products to fulfill the needs of borrowers and lenders. When their financial assets (deposits) are sold in the market, they typically have more liquidity and less risk than the underlying or supporting assets. A saver no longer needs to find a borrower with the exact risk, maturity, and liquidity characteristics he or she needs. Instead, the saver purchases a financial asset at an intermediary, that is, he or she makes a deposit. In turn, the financial intermediary pools the funds of many savers and lends money (provides capital) to borrowers.

Financial intermediaries may be divided into two major categories. Commercial banks and other depository institutions are able to offer risk-free deposits because of government insurance. In turn, they are subject to substantial regulation of their business and financial activities and their competitive environment. The major forms of depository institutions are commercial banks, savings banks, savings and loan associations, and credit unions.

Nondepository financial intermediaries, including pension funds, consumer finance companies, and mutual funds, offer competing products but do not have government-protected deposits as a source of funds. Although this places them at a disadvantage, it is at least partially offset by the absence of regulation.

The share of total financial activity held by nondeposit institutions has been growing in the past decade because these companies have begun to offer deposit-type services in direct competition with commercial banks (Table 10-1).

In this chapter, the discussion will stress depository institutions, because public-policy issues are focused on these firms. However, it will not ignore the nondepository institutions, because their rapid growth has brought about

Table 10-1
Shares of Total Credit Market Debt Claims, Five-Year Moving Averages, 1965–1984, Percent

Year-End	Commercial Banks	Depository Institutions	Insurance and Pension Funds	Other Financial	Non-financial
1965	26.38%	15.72%	20.15%	4.10%	33.64%
1970	27.88	16.00	18.99	4.55	32.58
1975	29.26	16.88	16.71	4.99	32.16
1980	27.26	17.45	17.65	5.21	32.44
1981	26.94	16.98	17.88	5.66	32.53
1982	26.56	16.30	18.14	6.11	32.89
1983	26.09	15.89	18.25	6.35	33.42
1984	25.56	15.63	18.21	6.66	33.95

Source of basic data: Board of Governors of the Federal Reserve System, *Flow of Funds Accounts, Assets and Liabilities Outstanding,* selected volumes.

much of the pressure for deregulation in recent years. Further, their continued growth and prosperity raise the critical issue facing the financial services industry: How much can the industry be deregulated to bring about the benefits of the free market, without risking financial chaos? If we do not deregulate depository institutions, can they survive under the new competitive pressures?

Depository Institutions

The depository institutions differ primarily in the types of financial products they offer. Table 10-2 illustrates the products offered by commercial banks and the change in the nature of these products over time, as evidenced in the sources of funds and in their investment portfolios.

1. Commercial Banks. The commercial bank may be thought of as a firm that produces various forms of credit. In its production process, its "inputs" are the funds entrusted to it by its depositors, as well as labor and equipment.

A broad array of deposit services is offered in order to obtain funds at lowest costs. Retail deposits include demand and other transactions deposits, savings deposits, time deposits, money market accounts, and NOW accounts. Each product offers a different combination of services and returns. Because all deposits under $100,000 are fully insured by the Federal Deposit Insurance Corporation (FDIC), most commercial banks' liabilities have no risk of default.

The availability of demand-deposit accounts to commercial banks has been sharply curtailed. In 1950, 70 percent of all funds available for commercial banks came from demand-deposit balances. By 1987, the demand-deposit

Table 10-2

Assets and Liabilities of All U.S. Commercial Banks, 1950–1987, in Billions of Dollars

Assets	1950	1960	1970	1987
Cash assets	$ 40.4	$ 52.2	$ 94.0	$ 353.2
Securities				
U.S. government	62.3	61.1	59.3	310.2
State and Local Government	8.2	17.6	67.9	119.0
Loans (total)	53.2	120.5	300.4	1810.7
Commercial and industrial	22.0	43.4	113.4	586.6
Real estate	13.7	28.8	73.3	591.2
Individuals	10.2	26.5	66.3	330.7
Other	7.3	21.8	47.4	302.2
Other assets	6.4	9.3	59.9	354.6
Total assets	170.5	260.7	581.5	2,947.7
Liabilities and equities				
Deposits	156.1	230.5	485.5	2,294.8
Demand	118.8	156.8	249.0	450.3
Time and Savings	37.3	73.7	236.5	1,844.5
Other liabilities	2.7	9.1	52.8	434.9
Capital	11.7	21.1	43.2	177.4
Total liabilities and equity	170.5	260.7	581.5	2,947.7

Source: Board of Governors of the Federal Reserve System, *Federal Reserve Bulletin* (Washington, D.C., selected issues).

share had fallen to 15 percent. Whereas the industry's assets had grown at an annual rate of 12.1 percent since 1951, its demand deposits had grown by only 5.3 percent. Therefore, it was forced to seek other sources of funds to finance its growth. For example, time deposits provide higher returns but require larger minimum balances and a definite time commitment by the depositor. The money market deposit account, which has become very popular, pays rates tied to an index of money market rates on instruments such as Treasury Bills.

In addition to retail deposit markets, many commercial banks have been forced to raise funds in the wholesale financial markets. They borrow in the money markets by issuing large, negotiable certificates of deposit. These accounts are not insured for amounts exceeding $100,000 and may generally be sold in secondary markets. Commercial banks also rely on the federal funds market, the Eurodollar market, and the commercial paper market. Commercial banks have been forced to utilize nondeposit sources of funds to finance their growth. In 1987, over 15 percent of their funds came from nondeposit sources. This compares with under 2 percent in 1950.

The output side of the commercial bank, or any intermediary, is its asset portfolio. The primary "output" of the commercial bank is its loan portfolio.

Other assets are held to complement the loan portfolio, either by providing liquidity or diversification to the entire portfolio. Approximately 55 percent of commercial bank funds are loaned to private borrowers, including individuals and small and large business firms. Business firms borrow to finance the purchase of fixed assets and to provide working capital. Individuals borrow for many reasons, most often to purchase real estate or consumer durables such as automobiles. Automobile purchase credit constitutes over 30 percent of all consumer credit extended by commercial banks. Credit cards constitute an additional 20 percent.

There are significant variations in loan portfolios among commercial banks. Differences are related primarily to the demand for loans in the market area and to the bank's strategic plans. Retail-oriented banks hold proportionally more consumer and mortgage loans. Wholesale-oriented banks concentrate more on commercial and industrial loans or on loans to other financial institutions.

The proportion of total loans to assets has not changed significantly over time. However, the financial characteristics of loans have changed dramatically as a result of the changes in deposit sources and interest-rate volatility in the economy.[4] Virtually all commercial and industrial loans are now made at interest rates that are tied to a prime rate that varies with money-market conditions. When the prime rate increases, borrowers pay more, and when rates fall, borrowers pay less. Because most short-term deposit rates are also effectively indexed, the variable-rate loan locks in a spread (or differential) between the borrowing and lending rate. If properly constructed, the spread will not change, irrespective of the level of interest rates. The bank can thus partially insulate itself from the risk of interest-rate fluctuations.

The risk of interest-rate fluctuations is now borne by the borrower. If interest rates, which are closely tied to inflation, increase at a rate faster than the borrowers' income, there will be a higher probability of default. This has happened to several industries, including energy and agriculture. It has also happened to several foreign governments, causing widespread failures of financial institutions or requiring the U.S. Government to step in and, with massive support, protect the banking sector.

A similar type of variable-rate instrument has become very common in the mortgage markets. The fixed-rate 30-year mortgage, which was the standard for the past 50 years on residential property, has been replaced by an adjustable-rate mortgage. Homeowners, rather than the lending institutions, now bear the risk of high interest rates. Just as in the case of variable-rate commercial loans, high-interest-rate periods have led to greater defaults.

2. Thrift Institutions. In recent years, as their investment powers have been widened, thrift institutions have become virtually indistinguishable from commercial banks. This has important implications for the degree of competition in local banking markets as the pool of potential suppliers of credit and deposit services has widened.

Savings bank and savings and loan associations have similar portfolios. Although they tend to differ in the states in which they operate, and in their primary regulatory authorities, the portfolios of both types of institutions are dominated by mortgage loans. The major source of their funds is consumer deposits.

The nature of savings institutions has changed dramatically in recent years. Their portfolio historically consisted of over 65 percent of total assets in fixed-rate mortgages. Since the mid-1970s, deregulation and disintermediation shortened the maturity of their deposit base, which was used to fund the mortgages. S&Ls found themselves in the position of holding long-term fixed-rate assets with revenues that did not change over the interest-rate cycle. However, their liabilities were interest-sensitive. If the rate increased, their costs increased; if rates fell, their costs fell.

The late 1970s were a period of steeply rising interest rates. As thrifts were forced to substitute high-cost funds for low-cost deposits, the cost of their inputs increased. However, their revenues did not increase correspondingly as holders of mortgages continued to pay the low rates negotiated at an earlier period. The net effect was to place the industry in severe financial stress. In 1981, the return on equity for the industry was −.74. Losses at that rate would erode its capital base in a very short period of time.

Regulatory agencies and the Congress attempted to deal with this problem. One major approach was to broaden the powers of S&Ls, so that they could offer loans with yields that are more sensitive to interest-rate changes, such as consumer and commercial loans. As this process has continued, the S&Ls have begun to compete directly with commercial banks.

Use of the increased lending powers along with an "energy recession" in the southwestern U.S. have led to an even greater thrift crisis in the past two years. Loan losses on commercial real estate and losses on direct investments are staggering. By 1988, it was commonly estimated that the liability of the Federal Savings and Loan Insurance Corporation (FSLIC) to pay off insured depositors from failed institutions exceeded $100 billion. This figure is far beyond the resources of the FSLIC and will require additional funds in the future. Congress's reaction to this major problem will have an important impact on the future of the financial services industry.

3. Credit Unions. The remaining type of depository institution is credit unions, which are chartered to provide consumer savings deposits to their members. In turn, they make consumer loans to finance automobile purchases, home improvements, and other consumer purchases to their members. Although deregulation has broadened their ability to offer a wider range of deposits and loans, their basic nature has not changed over the past decade. They generally play a less important role than the other depository institutions, because they are constrained by their cooperative form of organization and by the requirement that their members must have a common bond.

The Regulatory Environment

Depository financial institutions are heavily regulated. First, banking and other forms of commerce are separated by law. Commercial banks cannot own nonfinancial firms, and nonfinancial firms cannot own commercial banks. Second, the Glass–Steagall Act prohibits commercial banks from participating in most investment banking activities. They cannot underwrite securities for customers or make markets in most financial securities. Third, state and federal law limits the extent to which banks may expand geographically. Finally, bank portfolio investment activity is also constrained to control risk.

The commercial banking industry is subject to an extensive degree of regulation from several government agencies. Thus, a state-chartered bank that belongs to the Federal Reserve is directly regulated by the state chartering agency and by the Federal Reserve System. In addition, if it has set up a bank holding company, the holding company is regulated by the Federal Reserve.[5] The Federal Reserve is the primary regulator of all bank holding companies. All banks must also meet the insurance requirements of the FDIC.

A state-chartered bank that does not belong to the Federal Reserve may evade regulation by the Federal Reserve unless it has a holding company. However, it then becomes directly regulated by the Federal Deposit Insurance agency, along with the state agency.

National banks avoid state control, but they come under the domain of the Comptroller of the Currency and the Federal Reserve, the latter through their holding companies, which are required to be members of the Federal Reserve.

The regulatory control of these various agencies is extensive. They set broad portfolio requirements for liquidity, diversification, and leverage. They periodically perform direct audits or examinations on the companies that are under their direct regulatory control. They regulate expansion activity, that is, branching or obtaining new charters. They also control merger activity. Finally, they monitor compliance with consumer-protection laws.

Periodically, federal and state task forces have investigated the possibility of reorganizing the regulatory agencies to reduce the overlap in the present system. Proposed reorganization has generally been stymied by the industry and by the regulatory agencies—especially the state regulatory agencies, which have consistently opposed changes in the status quo.

Deregulation has become a major force in the industry, although the pendulum may be swinging the other way. At issue is the proper role of commercial banks in the new financial environment. Are commercial banks unique in financial markets, as they have been considered for the past two hundred years, or are they simply another alternative provider of financial services that should not have the regulatory attention they currently receive?

On this issue, Gerald Corrigan, currently the president of the Federal

Reserve Bank in New York, has made some thoughtful observations. He argues that commercial banks provide three unique services, which makes them substantially different from other financial firms.[6] Of course, the same arguments apply to other depository institutions.

The first, and most important, is that they provide a transaction account, payable at par throughout the economy. By use of the banking system, an individual can transfer purchasing power instantaneously (through wire transfer) to any other individual. A portion of the liabilities of commercial banks, therefore, constitutes the money supply of the U.S. Corrigan argues, correctly, that the economy could not function without this service.

Second, commercial banks provide backup liquidity for the remainder of the financial markets. Many financial markets rely on the commercial banking industry to provide liquidity in the event of a financial crisis. For example, the commercial paper market is supported by lines of credit at commercial banks. Without this support, Corrigan argues, many markets could not function efficiently.

Finally, commercial banks offer safe consumer deposits throughout the society. This allows savers to defer consumption and earn a return on their savings. Corrigan argues that without risk-free deposits, the economy would lose a great deal of its current stability.

Thus, the discussion of regulation of banking raises several questions. First, is any regulation necessary? Without a doubt, the answer is yes. Second, have we overregulated to protect against failures? The answer is again yes. The overlap in regulation and regulatory agencies is expensive and too restrictive. The other questions are less obvious: How much can we deregulate without destroying the essentially unique character of the banking system? At what level of regulation can the banking industry survive in a competitive world? The answers to the latter questions will be debated through the remainder of this century and beyond.

II.
STRUCTURE OF THE INDUSTRY

The U.S. banking structure is characterized by a large number of banks. Banks in the United States have been limited to operating within one state. Additionally, in many states, banks are limited to operating within restricted geographic areas, such as a county or perhaps a metropolitan area. However, geographic deregulation, as well as the growth of nonbank competitors, have significantly increased the options available to consumers in the past decade.

The unusual skewed structure of the U.S. banking industry is described in Table 10-3. There is a very large number of commercial banks—over 14,500. Most banks, however, are very small. Over 70 percent have assets under $50 million. A deposit base of $50 million is generally considered necessary to achieve the benefits of scale economies. Thus, 70 percent of the

Table 10-3
Asset Size Distribution of U.S. Commercial Banking Organizations (December 31, 1982)

Size Class (Millions of $)	Number of Organizations	Percent of Banks	Percentage of Total U.S. Commercial Bank Assets
0–5	428	3.4	0.1
5–10	1,405	11.5	0.5
10–25	3,837	31.3	3.3
25–100	4,968	40.5	12.0
100–250	923	7.5	6.9
250–500	246	2.0	4.3
500–1000	170	1.4	5.9
1000–5000	225	1.8	25.3
5000+	56	0.5	41.8

Source: Board of Govenors, Federal Reserve System. Banks reporting zero deposits, such as nondeposit trust companies, are eliminated.

banks (10,000 in number) are smaller than the estimated minimal optimal size. These 10,000 banks, however, hold less than 16 percent of the total deposits of the commercial banking system. In contrast to the large number of very small banks, there are a few quite large banks. The largest 356 banks, which make up 2.5 percent of the banks in the U.S., hold 55 percent of all the deposits in the banking system.

To some extent these firms operate in different submarkets. The largest banks serve a different set of customers than the smaller banks. However, this is not always true. Many large banks also compete for small-business customers, which are the primary customers of the small community banks. There has been considerable concern about the future of the small financial institutions in a highly deregulated environment. Most observers have argued that the vast majority of small institutions will do very well in serving specialized customers in local markets. Those institutions that cannot survive in this environment will generally be acquired by larger firms.

Overall Concentration

The concentration of deposits of the largest banks in the United States has increased since 1970 (see Table 10-4). In 1970, the top 100 banking organizations had 50 percent of the assets in the system. That number had increased to 62 percent by 1987. Since none of the change occurred in the largest institutions, it appears that the increase in concentration reflects consolidations among the regional interstate banking organizations.

The large U.S. banking firms are not big relative to larger banks in other countries. In many other countries, banking is concentrated in the hands of only a few banks. In 1957, 270 of the largest 500 banks in the world were

Table 10-4

Shares of Domestic Commercial Banking Assets Held by Largest Banking Organizations, Percent

Year	Top 5	Top 10	Top 25	Top 50	Top 100
1970	14.0	21.4	32.8	41.1	50.4
1971	13.4	20.5	31.7	40.1	49.5
1972	13.5	20.7	31.8	40.3	50.3
1973	13.3	20.9	32.4	41.1	51.2
1974	14.2	22.2	33.9	42.3	52.3
1075	13.7	21.3	32.6	41.1	50.8
1976	13.4	20.8	31.7	40.2	49.9
1977	13.5	21.0	32.0	40.5	50.2
1978	13.4	21.1	32.4	41.1	50.8
1979	13.4	21.3	32.6	41.5	51.2
1980	13.5	21.6	33.1	41.6	51.4
1981	13.2	21.1	33.1	41.6	51.7
1982	13.4	21.8	34.2	43.0	53.6
1983	13.1	21.0	33.8	43.2	54.3
1984	13.0	20.3	33.1	43.5	55.0
1985	12.8	20.4	33.2	45.8	57.9
1986	12.7	20.2	34.1	47.3	60.4
1987	12.6	19.9	34.7	48.3	61.6

Source: Board of Governors, Federal Reserve System.

American; by 1967, that number had fallen to 187; and by 1986, it further declined to 95. As shown in Table 10-5, only one of the ten largest banks is American. In contrast, seven are Japanese and two are French. Since U.S. banks are absolutely smaller than their foreign rivals, they present inviting acquisition targets for large European and Japanese banks. The number of such takeovers is becoming large enough to warrant public concern.

Overall concentration of deposits in the U.S. is below most other major countries (Table 10-6). Since 1960, concentration has not changed dramatically in any major country. This is most surprising, given the dynamic nature of financial markets during the period.

State Structures

The diffuse structure of banking nationally may not reflect the situation within the smaller geographic areas in which banks actually operate.

Under the U.S. dual-banking concept, each state is free to determine how its banks may expand geographically within the state. States may choose a statewide branching system or a limited branching network. For example, banks may be allowed to branch throughout the state, or only within their own county, or only into contiguous counties. In some states branching is prohibited altogether, but the number of such states is declining to the vanishing point.

Table 10-5
Leading Banking Organizations in the World

Rank	Name of Organization	Country	Total Assets (Millions of $) 12/31/86
1	Dai-Ichi Kangyo Bank Ltd., Tokyo	Japan	239,580
2	Fuji Bank, Ltd., Tokyo	Japan	212,441
3	Sumitomo Bank Ltd., Osaka	Japan	205,126
4	Mitsubishi Bank Ltd., Tokyo	Japan	203,806
5	Sanwa Bank Ltd., Osaka	Japan	191,362
6	Norinchukin Bank, Tokyo	Japan	161,569
7	Industrial Bank of Japan, Ltd., Tokyo	Japan	160,837
8	Credit Agricole Mutuel, Paris	France	156,382
9	Citibank NA, New York	United States	145,892
10	Banque Nationale de Paris	France	143,685

Source: *American Banker*, 1988 Yearbook.

All of the states in the high-concentration ranges are states that permit statewide branching. Conversely, the bulk of the states that are least concentrated permit only unit banking.[7] The range of concentration in states is quite substantial. Many states are highly concentrated, with the largest five banks holding as much as 95 percent of total deposits within the state. The increases in concentration have generally come in states such as Virginia, Texas, and Florida, which have liberalized their state branching laws. Thus, the increase reflects not a change in the competitive situation as much as it reflects a change in the branching laws. Recent merger activity in many states is likely to further increase aggregate state concentration levels.

Just as state laws limit geographic expansion within the state, federal legislation prevents banks from operating branches or banking subsidiaries in more than one state, unless the state specifically permits interstate banking. Most states have passed legislation that permits some form of interstate banking within their borders. There is considerable variation in approach.

Table 10-6
Five Firm Concentration Ratios, 1930–1980

	Canada	France	Germany	Japan	U.K.	U.S.
1930	84	41	44	22	70	9
1950	80	66	—	31	84	13
1960	83	65	24	26	83	15
1970	85	57	24	21	85	16
1980	80	81	24	22	68	18

Source: Herbert Baer and Elizabeth Pongracic, "The Development of Banking Structure Histories in Five Countries," unpublished paper, Federal Reserve Bank of Chicago, 1984.

Some states, such as Maine and Alaska, have opened their states to any bank from any other state. Others, such as South Dakota and Delaware, permit limited-service interstate banks such as a credit card business. States such as New York have passed reciprocal arrangements in which they will grant charters in New York to banks from any states that permit New York banks to enter their state. Finally, most states, led by New England and the Southeast, have established regional interstate banking compacts that allow banks from neighboring states to enter on a reciprocal basis. The general intent of the regional concepts is to allow banks to grow by merger from within the region but to restrict entry by acquisition by large money-center banks.

Local Concentration

The most important dimension of banking market structure is neither the national nor the state level of concentration. Concentration is most relevant in terms of its impact on the performance at the local market level. Banking is generally characterized as a local market industry.

Banks offer many products to different types of consumers. Depending on the size and type of the transaction, the geographic market for the bank product will differ considerably.[8] The market for consumer-demand deposits, where convenience is the most important factor, may be as small as a neighborhood or a section of a city. Conversely, the market for large commercial loans will cover the entire nation. The bulk of commercial banking operations, however, including financial services sold to most households and small businesses, is limited to a fairly small geographic area.

Banking markets have been approximated in most studies of bank performance, and in most merger cases, by a Standard Metropolitan Statistical Area (SMSA), or by a rural county, or by some combination of counties.[9] This may not be entirely appropriate. As Talley notes, "The bank regulatory agencies, the Department of Justice, and the courts frequently employ SMSA's and counties as approximations for banking markets, partly because deposit data on an office basis are readily available for these geographic areas."[10] If one recognizes these limitations, the SMSA will serve as a quite reasonable approximation.

The control of banking deposits by the largest banks in most metropolitan areas is highly concentrated. It is even higher in rural areas. Concentration levels for all U.S. metropolitan areas are presented in Table 10-7.

Two measures of concentration are given. The four-firm concentration ratio (CR4) indicates the share of deposits held by the largest four banks in the market. The second, and most precise, measure is the Hirschman–Herfindahl Index (HHI)[11] and its corresponding-numbers equivalent. The maximum HHI is 10,000, if one firm had 100 percent of the market. The HHI takes into consideration the relative size of all firms in the market, as

Table 10-7

Concentration Levels in Metropolitan Areas, 1982

Number of Banking Organizations in SMSA	Number of SMSAs	Average CR4 (%)	Average HHI
101 or more	7	54.4	1,103
61–100	7	52.0	907
41–60	14	58.4	1,257
31–40	15	64.8	1,483
26–30	16	67.5	1,602
21–25	22	61.1	1,320
18–20	26	68.1	1,708
15–17	32	69.9	1,615
12–14	44	74.0	1,908
9–11	60	80.7	2,163
6–8	57	89.1	2,732
5 or less	18	97.9	3,459

Source: Jim Burke, "Antitrust Laws, Justice Department Guidelines, and the Limits of Concentration in Local Banking Markets," *Staff Study*, Federal Reserve Board, 1983.

well as the number of firms. Consequently, it provides an index of concentration that is less subject to error.

An analysis of metropolitan area markets (as of 1982) reveals the following: First, even though most banking is retail-oriented, few markets have large numbers of banks. Only 52 out of 318 metropolitan areas have more than 25 banking organizations. Second, even those markets with a relatively large number of banks have high concentration levels. The seven markets with more than 100 banks have an average concentration ratio of 54.4 percent and an HHI of 1,103. This corresponds to a numbers equivalent of 9.1. On average, these markets are as competitive as a market would be with nine banks of equal size.

Concentration levels have been used as proxy for monopoly power in banking markets, and there have been numerous studies of the impact of market structure on performance in banking markets. The preponderance of evidence finds the existence of a statistical link between concentration and market performance.[12] Market performance is defined as profitability, prices relative to costs, and the provision of services to consumers. Although statistically significant, the economic effect of concentration on performance is relatively small.

Two major trends that have taken place in the industry make this approach questionable for structural analysis in the future. First, the granting of new powers to thrift institutions makes these institutions very comparable to commercial banks. If thrift deposits are included in the deposit base, concentration levels will change. Ignoring their presence disturbs the meaning of bank deposit concentration. The same concentration of bank deposits will have a different effect, depending on the strength of thrift institutions in the market. In addition, there has been a substantial increase in the intensity of competition from nonbank financial institutions in many, if not all, local markets. To the extent that nonbank competition varies across markets, it cannot be ignored when comparing and measuring market structures. For example, many banks have opened loan production offices (LPOs) in major markets across the country. Through their LPOs, they could be major competitors in the loan market by funding their loans from other nondeposit sources. Deposit concentration measures totally ignore their presence.

The second factor that undermines the importance of deposit concentration as a predictor of performance is the deregulation of deposits. In the pre-1984 regulated world, with low-rate ceilings on deposits, managers basically treated deposits as outside their control and invested these deposits to maximize profits. Deposits were an exogenous force, at least in the short run. Deposits consequently represented lending capacity and were the appropriate measure of market power. However, with deregulated deposit markets, a bank may increase its deposit size at will by raising rates above the market rate. Consequently, even a bank with a small level of deposits in a market can quickly become a dominant lending force, if it perceives profitable lending opportunities that are not being met in the market. It can simply outbid other financial institutions for the market deposits.

Economies of Scale

Economies of scale in the operation of financial intermediaries have been the subject of many studies.[13] The consensus appears to be that the minimum efficient scale (where the average-cost curve is at its lowest point) is in the range of $50 million in deposits. Indeed, average costs may well increase in banks with deposits above $50 million. Even if this estimate is too low by a factor of 10, it would still be possible to have viable competition in smaller cities and far less concentration than is found in the larger ones.

Several studies have also considered the possibility of economies of scope—cost advantages related to diversification of products—but there is no evidence that they are economically significant.

Given the absence of significant scale economies, and given the fact that bank mergers have not brought great benefits to shareholders of acquiring banks (as reflected in stock prices), why is there such a strong desire to grow among financial institutions?

Mergers and Acquisitions

The banking industry has gone through a major merger movement in recent years. The number and average size of acquisitions are increasing each year (see Figure 10-2). In 1985, over $50 billion in assets were acquired. This contrasts with an average annual value of acquisitions of less than $10 billion throughout the 1960s and 1970s.

The Structure of American Industry

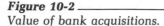

Figure 10-2

Value of bank acquisitions.

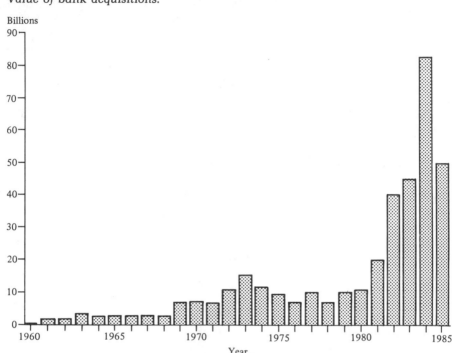

Source: S.A. Rhoades, "Mergers and Acquisitions by Commercial Banks," *Staff Studies,* Board of Governors of the Federal Reserve System, 1985; S.A. Rhoades, personal correspondence for later years.

The release of the revised U.S. Department of Justice merger guidelines in 1982 had a major impact on the number and character of mergers in banking. These guidelines (couched in the Hirschman–Herfindahl Index) seemed to indicate that the higher the concentration level, the greater the likelihood that a merger would be challenged. In unconcentrated markets, no mergers would be challenged. In highly concentrated markets, even relatively small mergers would likely be challenged.

Since the 1963 decision in *U.S.* v. *Philadelphia National Bank,* the Department of Justice had continually opposed horizontal mergers in commercial banking. Commercial banking was defined as *a line of commerce,* meaning that competition from savings and loan associations, credit unions, savings banks, and nondepository intermediaries was ignored in determining the legality of a merger under the Bank Merger Act and the Celler–Kefauver Act. In a market in which the only financial-services firms were commercial banks, a merger of two banks was treated exactly as a merger of two banks in a market with a large number of other specialized financial intermediaries.

The geographic market was considered to be local in nature. Market definitions often followed county or metropolitan-area definitions. Firm size was based on total deposits. The effect of the court rulings, as well as the policy of the regulatory agencies, was that virtually any horizontal merger that increased concentration of bank deposits by even a small amount was illegal. This, however, did not seem to deter mergers of the market-extension variety, which enabled banks to enter new geographic markets without serious exposure to legal challenge.

The relaxation of antitrust limitations opened the door for significant expansion by larger institutions. At the same time, there was increased pressure on these institutions to grow — in anticipation of interstate banking and because of the fear that their markets would be dominated or they would be acquired by large money-center banks.

Mergers and Interstate Banking

If nationwide interstate banking is permitted, this merger process will continue, and it will increase in intensity. The existing antitrust laws will do little to stop major acquisitions by the largest U.S. banks, and this could lead to an overall concentration of resources, which would be unacceptable from a public-policy perspective.

Large interstate mergers in banking would not initially increase national concentration ratios to levels found in other industries. However, banking is a unique industry, and even small increases in the shares of the dominant firms should be subject to careful scrutiny.

A major acquisition movement by the largest commercial banks could impose sufficient social costs to warrant denial. Our national goal has always been to encourage a diffuse banking system, with many independent banks deciding on credit allocation within their own markets and within their regions of the country. If control were increasingly held by a few large banks, potential borrowers could lose access to credit. Although there is no empirical evidence to substantiate this claim, it certainly is a possible consequence of high overall concentration of banking resources in the control of a few firms.

The greatest problem that would result from rapid growth by the very largest banks would be an increase in the risk exposure of the banking system. It is extremely difficult to predict when (and which) banks will encounter major financial stress. They are all highly leveraged and therefore must take great risks in their normal business activities. In some periods, they may encounter financial stress owing to a mismatch of maturities in their balance sheets, for example, lending long and borrowing short. In other cases, stress may be the result of other factors, such as large foreign loans, energy loans, losses on foreign-exchange transactions, or agricultural loans.

These kinds of risks occur almost at random and are not totally subject to management control. No matter how well it is managed, any bank could find itself in a financial crisis, unable to meet its liabilities. The larger the bank that is exposed, the greater the potential impact of its failure on the soundness of the entire system. Because the system is basically run on public trust, we must be careful to keep banks to a size where we can tolerate their failures. A merger movement of the existing large banks would only make the economy more vulnerable.

The same situation would occur if banking were open to insurance companies, real estate companies, or investment banking. Major mergers of the dominant firms could take place without violating current antitrust standards. Moreover, these types of acquisitions would be undesirable from a public-policy viewpoint, because they could increase the actual or perceived risks of the banking system unless great care is taken in protecting depositors.

As commercial banking becomes increasingly deregulated, the failure rate of firms that offer banking services will undoubtedly rise. Their investment opportunities will broaden, and at least some of their activities will be riskier than their present activities. This expansion would probably be in the public interest and should be permitted. By maintaining some degree of diffusion in the banking structure, the possible impact of this increased exposure to risk is minimized.

III.
PERFORMANCE

Because of the pervasive influence of the financial intermediaries on the U.S. economy, there has been a great deal of discussion regarding how well this sector performs. What does society require from the financial services sector? How can we guarantee this performance?

The most important element of performance is inherent in the nature of financial intermediaries and concerns its liabilities. For the system to function effectively, the public must have confidence in the overall integrity of the system. If the public were to lose confidence in the soundness of financial intermediaries, there would be two major effects. First, there would be a reduction in demand deposits to fund commercial transactions. Consequently, there would be a significant contraction in the money supply. Second, savers would begin to pull funds out of the weaker institutions. These institutions would not be able to obtain enough cash to meet the outflows without selling off assets at distress prices. Ultimately, even well-run, conservative institutions could be forced into failure. To prevent both of these effects, public confidence in the stability of the system must be maintained.

The industry has performed very well in this regard, with the help of the regulatory agencies. The actual failure rate for commercial banks, savings and loan associations, and credit unions has been very small, averaging less than one per thousand per year, since the 1930s, but increasing in recent years.

Failing institutions have generally been merged with other institutions, protecting not only small depositors but also the large uninsured depositors. A panic — such as the one in the 1930s when depositors attempted to convert their funds into cash — has not developed.

For the regulatory agencies, the cost of this protection is at times very high. When a large bank is in financial trouble, the liability to the FDIC is substantial. In a recent bank failure, for example, First Republic cost the FDIC over $2.5 billion, to compensate for extremely high loan losses. Although it has been sharply criticized for this form of bailout, the FDIC has argued that there is no choice, because the failure of a very large institution, with its accompanying losses to uninsured depositors, would cause a panic in the national and international markets. As the largest banking firms grow in size, the U.S. economy becomes even more vulnerable to this possibility.

The second most important element of performance — efficiency — is not unique to financial institutions. An efficient system is innovative; it uses the best available technology; its firms are operating at peak efficiency, and they are charging competitive prices. In a system that is performing well, there should be no monopoly rents. There is considerable argument over the efficiency of the U.S. banking system. For example, the banks have aggressively utilized new computer and communications innovations, yet most transactions still use paper checks. This apparent failure to go to electronic transactions may be a failure of the regulatory agencies, rather than the banking system.

The third element of performance is related to resource allocation. The private market should allocate credit to the sectors of the economy and to the geographic areas where it is most needed. Capital should be mobile. However, there are additional credit-allocation goals, including the provision of funds for housing, student loans, and small business. Good performance requires that credit allocation meet these goals. Although the banking structure is highly fragmented, it is generally believed that capital does flow to its most valued use in banking through loan participations and interbank lending.

The final element of performance involves consumer protection. It is generally believed that there have been many abuses in the area of credit in past years. These have involved abusive collection practices, charging of usurious rates, and discrimination against women and minorities in the granting of credit. Good performance is not consistent with any of these practices.

In general, the industry has performed well. Increases in competition, as well as deregulation, have put considerable pressure on the industry to be efficient and innovative in the services it offers, as well as in the delivery of services. However, much of the current regulation is superfluous and creates inefficiency.

Profitability

Industry profitability has been stable and growing, with the glaring exception of 1987. However, the levels of profit are not abnormally high. Unless this is corrected, the industry will continue to find it difficult to raise capital.

Stability of Banks

The goal of public policy has been to promote stability in the banking system by the prevention of failures. The regulatory agencies, and the industry, have been extremely successful in this regard. Very few banks have failed until the last few years (Figure 10-3). Even these failures have not hurt public confidence in the strength of the banking system.

Strength and stability in the banking system have been achieved by a combination of restrictions on bank investment and loan policy, by limitations on competition, by deposit insurance, and by the Federal Reserve standing as a lender of last resort to all banks. While this approach has worked, it may not have been the most effective means of achieving the

Figure 10-3 _____

Total assets of failed banks.

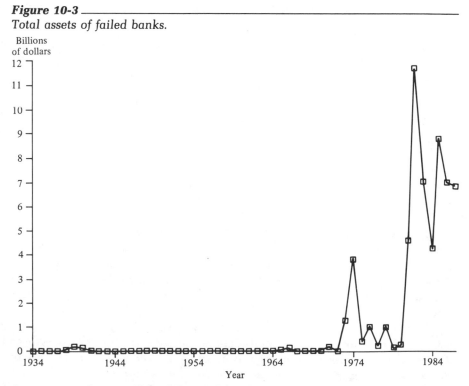

Source: *Annual Report*, Federal Deposit Insurance Corporation, 1987.

desired objective, especially when other public-policy goals for the banking industry are considered.

Throughout most of the period since the 1930s, there has been excessive "soundness" regulation. Competition and management behavior have been controlled to a degree that has limited competition and stifled innovation. Weak, poorly performing management has been protected from failure and permitted to continue to operate.

The 1980s have brought an additional challenge to the stability of the banking system. Deregulation and increased competition in financial services have increased the opportunities for bankers to earn high profits by taking greater risk. This has resulted in the bankruptcy of some large banks, such as Continental Illinois in Chicago. Many smaller banks have also experienced sizable losses in real estate, energy, and agricultural loans, which have led to their failure.

In this environment, there will be a need for the industry and for regulators to develop systems to limit the abuses that lead to failures. This must be accomplished without permitting a return to the policies of earlier periods that led to inefficiencies and poor performance due to excessive regulation.

Innovation

Innovation in banking traditionally has been slow, partly because of regulatory resistance. Banks have been limited in their ability to use new communications and computer technology by regulatory constraints as well as by their own inertia. Similarly, most development in new financial products — such as options, financial features, and securitization — have come from outside the banking industry. Efficient portfolio management was an innovation that spread slowly among the conservative bankers. On the whole, and continuing even now, banking innovation has been somewhat slow. Most innovation has been directed at evading regulations, rather than developing new products or new delivery systems.[14]

Evaluating Regulation

Some policy actions — especially regulation — have been extensive and, in part, probably counterproductive. The regulatory patchwork is complex and costly; it is an industry in itself. It controls much of the activity within the banks. The more thorough regulation is, the more it disrupts the banks' normal operations. The regulators must make thousands of complex judgments about quality, new competition, applications for entry, and mergers.

Much of the banking regulation is excessive, considering its objective of optimum bank stability, which is already assured by deposit insurance and Federal Reserve support for the whole system. Not only are the regulatory resources often used pointlessly, but regulation per se operates to suppress competition and discourage entrepreneurship. This is most evident in the state antibranching regulations, but it pervades the whole system of restraints.

Three possible benefits of regulation offset these costs. (1) Security is increased. (However, deposit insurance probably provides sufficient security.) (2) Regulation keeps banks and industrial firms at arm's length. The abuses and monopoly effects that mingling makes possible (abroad, and before 1933 in the United States) are avoided. (3) The local character of banking may be enhanced, but this, too, is the result of rules (for example, against bank branching), rather than regulation of operations. And "localness" often has led to inefficiency and restrictive behavior.

IV.
PUBLIC POLICY

The ultimate future of banking and the entire financial services industry depends on public policy toward the industry. Just as it was created by public laws and regulations, it will continue to be shaped by the same forces. Deregulation will operate in the consumers' interest with greater efficiency, more innovation, and more services. However, deregulation does lead to greater risk and instability. The challenge is to find the proper balance.

We have discussed most of the specific policy issues; however, many of these issues can be included in one basic question: What role should competition and regulation play in banking? Some observers suggest that competition should become universal, as in any "normal" industry. Others want public regulation and/or public banking to cover essentials, in order to assure stability and meet overall social needs. During the 1970s, prior limits on banking were eroded, and competition (or an overlapping of activities) increased. Should this shift go further?

Recommendations:

1. Regulation should be further reduced—selectively. Deposit insurance should continue, but chartering should be liberalized, and most of the regulatory inspection of banks should cease. Under certain conditions, takeovers of banks should be permitted; but banking operations and accounts should be kept separate from nonbanking activities. The present salvaging of failing banks should continue, but there should be no official commitment to prevent bank failures at any cost.
2. A clear delineation of banking should be developed. Entry into banking should be opened further (perhaps phased in), in order to minimize disruptions. However, in terms of regulation, all firms that provide banking services should be treated equally.

3. Greater pressure should be developed to allow the private markets to control the risk exposure of banking firms. This can be accomplished by forcing the banks to go to uninsured-debt and to equity markets for some portion of their funds (for example, those with high capital requirements) and by providing the public with more information on bank conditions.

V.
CONCLUSION

There is much room for experimenting and learning as technology matures and external conditions change. Together, the aforementioned policies have a balance and depth that cover most of the apparent gaps in banking performance. More competition alone will not suffice, nor will a continuation of the present duplicative nonsystem of "regulation." All of the present standard policy tools—antitrust, regulation, and public enterprise—are appropriate, in varying degrees. In a different form, and in a different balance, they could be optimally effective. We must see them for what they are and then modify them, in order to make a good banking system an excellent one.

NOTES

1. Under the provisions of the Depository Institution Deregulation and Monetary Control Act of 1980, all limitations on rates on time and savings deposits and on most transactions deposits were removed in 1986.

2. For a thorough analysis of this concept, see James L. Pierce, *Monetary and Financial Economies* (New York: John Wiley & Sons, 1984).

3. George Benston and Clifford Smith, "A Transactions Cost Approach to the Theory of Financial Intermediation," *Journal of Finance*, 31 (1976), pp. 215–231.

4. For a thorough discussion of these innovations, see T. D. Simpson and P. M. Parkinson, "Some Implications of Financial Innovations in the United States," *Staff Study*, Federal Reserve Board, September 1984.

5. By the end of 1982, there were 4,289 holding companies, which held 80 percent of total bank deposits. Consequently, the Federal Reserve, by regulating the parent holding companies, has some degree of regulatory control over virtually the entire industry.

6. See *Annual Report*, Federal Reserve Bank of Minneapolis, 1982.

7. This correlation does not imply that limitations on branching are in the public interest. In states that permit branching, customers at the local market level have more options than in a unit banking state. However, the result does not imply that one consequence of interstate banking will be an increase in overall concentration of banking resources as firms combine across the country. To minimize the concentrating effect, considerable attention must be directed to merger policy in an interstate banking environment.

8. For a thorough survey of local market concepts in commercial banking, see John Wolken, "Geographic Market Delineation: A Review of the Literature," *Staff Study,* Federal Reserve Board, November 1984.

9. This has been the judicial standard since *United States* v. *Philadelphia Nat'l. Bank,* 374 U.S. 321 (1963). In recent litigation, however, this simple approximation has been challenged. See *United States* v. *Connecticut Nat'l. Bank,* 418 U.S. 656 (1974).

10. Talley, "Recent Trends in Local Banking Market Structures," Staff Economic Studies, No. 89, p. 5 (Board of Governors of the Federal Reserve System, May 1977).

11. The Hirschman–Herfindahl Index is

$$\sum_{i=1}^{n} S_{i^2}$$

where S_i is the share of the market held by firm i, and where there are N firms in the market. The reciprocal of the Herfindahl Index is the "numbers equivalent," which is the number of equal-size firms that would give a Herfindahl index of a given value. See Adelman, "Comment on the 'H' Concentration Measure as a Numbers-Equivalent," *Review of Economies & Statistics* 51 (February 1969), pp. 99–101.

12. See R. A. Gilbert, "Banking Market Structure and Competition: A Survey," *Journal of Money, Credit, and Banking,* Vol. 16, No. 4, Part 2 (November 1984), pp. 617–644, for a recent and critical survey.

13. For a summary of this research, see David B. Humphrey, "Cost and Scale Economies in Bank Intermediaries," in Aspinwall and Eisenbeis (eds.).

14. See Edward Kane, "Accelerating Inflation, Technological Innovation, and the Decreasing Effectiveness of Banking Regulation," *Journal of Finance,* 36 (May 1981), pp. 355–367.

SUGGESTED READINGS

Books

Aspinwall, R. C., and R. A. Eisenbeis, eds. *Handbook for Banking Strategy.* New York: John Wiley and Sons, 1985.

Hempel, George H., A. B. Coleman, and D. G. Simonson. *Bank Management.* New York: John Wiley and Sons, 1986.

Rose, Peter. *The Changing Structure of American Banking.* New York: Columbia University Press, 1987.

Government Publications

Federal Reserve Bank of New York. *Recent Trends in Bank Profitability.* New York: 1986.

Federal Reserve Bank of Kansas City. *Restructuring the Financial System.* Kansas City: 1987.

CHAPTER 11

THE WEAPONS INDUSTRY

William B. Burnett
*and Frederic M. Scherer**

I.
INTRODUCTION

One of the largest and most fascinating branches of American industry is the cluster of firms supplying advanced weapons and space vehicles. It has a number of distinctive characteristics. It includes producers from a variety of more conventionally defined fields — aircraft, guided missiles, electronics, computers, communication systems, shipbuilding, and ordnance. It is a voracious consumer of the nation's highly skilled scientific and technical resources, performing more than one-third of the research and development undertaken by all U.S. industries. It sustains an extraordinarily rapid pace of technological advance, attended by unusually great uncertainties concerning product characteristics and costs. Because of these uncertainties and the large size of individual defense and space programs, special institutions have been created to shift from producers to government what might otherwise be intolerable financial risks. Assuming the risks of research and production, the government tends also to usurp many decision-making functions traditionally exercised by sellers. The consequence is a set of buyer–seller relationships quite unlike those found in the normal market economy. Indeed, what goes on in the industry lies in the grey area between public and private enterprise. Much of what follows in this chapter attempts to elucidate the nature of this unique "nonmarket" buyer–seller relationship.

II.
MARKET STRUCTURE

The demand for weapons ebbs and flows with changes in defense expenditures, which in turn depend upon international relations and government policy. Figure 11-1 reveals the wide variations in U.S. defense spending

*The authors are indebted to Peter Regen for research assistance and to Swarthmore College for financial support.

Figure 11-1

Long-term movements in defense-related activity.

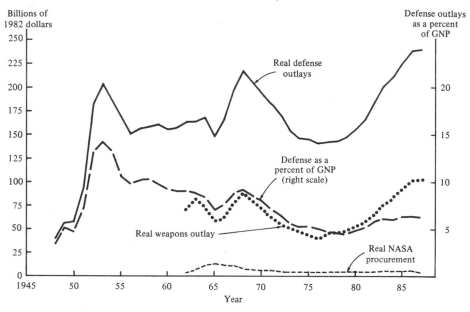

since the return to "normalcy" following World War II. To remove the effects of general inflation, all outlays are measured in terms of 1982 price levels (using the overall gross national product deflator). During peak war years 1943 and 1944, defense expenditures had soared to 39 percent of GNP. They fell sharply, both absolutely and relative to GNP, with postwar demobilization. The Korean war (1950–53) led to remobilization and heavy military spending, followed by lower but, by historical standards, relatively high cold-war activity in the subsequent decades. Escalation of the Vietnam war injected a further spike in the 1960s. Public disillusion and the war's end reversed the trend, but a new peacetime escalation was initiated by the Carter Administration in 1977 and continued by the Reagan Administration.

The weapons industry's contribution to defense activity is shown by the dotted curve "real weapons outlay" in Figure 11-1. It sums three components: outlays in the Department of Defense budget categories for procurement and research and development, plus Department of Energy spending for nuclear materials and weapons. Constant-dollar weapons expenditures exhibit the same fluctuations as overall defense spending, but their share of total defense outlays varies in a further cyclical pattern. Weapons outlays were relatively high, peaking in 1963 at 47 percent of total defense spending, as cold-war efforts sought technological superiority over the Soviet Union. With the shift to a fighting war and later to all-volunteer armed forces, weapons outlays fell relative to expenditures for military personnel, operations and maintenance, and administrative overhead. By 1976, weapons outlays were 29.5 percent of total defense spending. With renewed emphasis on outgunning the Soviet Union, the weapons component then rose steadily to 43 percent of total defense outlays in 1987.

The companies producing advanced weapon systems deploy similar skills to supply the National Aeronautics and Space Administration, whose constant-dollar procurement outlays are charted in the lowest (dashed) curve of Figure 11-1. Peak effort levels were reached with the Apollo moon-landing program in the 1960s. A mild resurgence, led by the Space Shuttle program, is evident in the 1980s.

The Constituent Supply Sectors

The weapons "industry" comprises numerous more detailed specialties, viewed as separate industries or product lines by U.S. Census authorities. It includes both prime contractors, who receive contracts directly from the government, and a host of subcontractors providing specialized components (such as aircraft landing gear, special-design microcircuits, ships' propeller shafts, and so on), exotic materials (such as graphite–epoxy laminates), and standard commercial parts and materials. Table 11-1 reports the 1982 sales, on both prime and subcontracts, of the principal industry groups and subgroups with a distinct military hardware orientation. Comparison with similar

Table 11-1

Value of 1982 Census Product Class Shipments of the Principal Defense-Oriented Industries

Census Code	Description	Value of 1982 Shipments (millions)
36625	Electronic search and detection, navigation, and guidance equipment	$18,092
37211	Military aircraft	9,835
3761	Guided missiles and space vehicles	8,586
37312	New military ships	4,095
37950	Tanks	2,681
37241	Engines for military aircraft (est.)	2,600
3769	Space vehicle equipment	2,574
3764	Missile and space propulsion units	2,199
37314	Military ship repair	1,571
3483	Ammunition, other than small arms	1,359
34891-2	Guns, howitzers, and other ordnance and accessories	1,010
3484	Small arms (incl. machine guns)	896
35730	Specialized electronic computing equipment	859
34436	Nuclear reactor steam supply systems	634
38324	Sighting, tracking, and fire control equipment	505

Source: U.S. Bureau of the Census, *1982 Census of Manufactures,* "Concentration Ratios in Manufacturing," subject report MC82-S-7 (Washington, D.C.: U.S. Government Printing Office, April 1986), Table 6.

data for 1965 reveals that aircraft assemblers lost their first-place position to electronic communication systems makers. This reflects the general trend toward weapon systems that substitute electronic for human functions. For example, some 40 to 45 percent of the cost of the Air Force's new Advanced Tactical Fighter was expected to be for electronic gear.[1]

The Prime Contractors

The Defense Department's annual list of its 100 leading prime contractors includes petroleum refiners, universities (such as M.I.T. and Johns Hopkins), Xerox of copying machine fame, and many electronic component specialists.[2] Yet the leaders from year to year are the major aircraft, missile, and electronic systems companies, along with a few large corporations known best for their civilian goods but with active military systems divisions. Table 11-2 provides comparative listings of the top 15 defense and space prime contractors during World War II, the Korean war, 1960, 1970, and 1987. Seven companies or their merged survivors—General Motors (merged with Hughes), General Dynamics (stemming from a merger of Consolidated–Vultee and Electric Boat), McDonnell Douglas (merging two aircraft makers), United Technologies (previously United Aircraft), Lockheed, Boeing, and Rockwell (merging North American Aviation)—are on all five lists. Three others—General Electric, Martin Marietta (merging Martin with American Marietta), and AT&T (mostly through its Western Electric and Bell Telephone Laboratories subsidiaries) appear on at least three of the lists. The most notable disappearances are Curtiss–Wright, which failed to make the transition from reciprocating to jet aircraft engines; Bethlehem Steel, whose shipbuilding operations atrophied after World War II; and Chrysler, which sold its military tank division to General Dynamics in 1982.

The 15 companies listed as the top 1987 contractors won 41 percent of Defense Department prime contract awards by dollar value in that fiscal year. The top 100 prime contract recipients accounted for 67 percent of 1987 dollar awards. This pattern of prime contract award concentration has been fairly stable, as data on the shares of the leading defense prime contractors for diverse periods reveal:[3]

	Share of Top 25	Share of Top 100
World War II	46.5%	67.2%
Korean war (1951–53)	45.5	64.0
1960	53.5	73.4
1965	48.2	68.9
1970	46.0	69.7
1975	48.6	68.7
1980	45.2	65.9
1987	50.5%	66.9%

Table 11-2

The Leading 15 Defense and Space Contractors in Five Periods, 1940–1987

Rank	World War II (1940–44)	Korean War (1951–53)	1960	Vietnam War (1970)	1987
1	General Motors	General Motors	General Dynamics[a]	Lockheed	McDonnell–Douglas
2	Curtiss–Wright	Boeing	Lockheed	North American–Rockwell[b]	General Dynamics
3	Ford Motor Co.	General Electric	Boeing	General Dynamics	Lockheed
4	Consolidated–Vultee	Douglas	McDonnell	General Electric	General Electric[e]
5	Douglas	United Aircraft	North American	McDonnell Douglas[c]	General Motors–Hughes[f]
6	United Aircraft	Chrysler	Martin	Grumman	Martin Marietta[g]
7	Bethlehem Steel	Lockheed	United Aircraft	AT&T	United Technologies[h]
8	Chrysler	Consolidated–Vultee	AT&T	United Aircraft	Raytheon
9	General Electric	North American	RCA	Boeing	Rockwell[i]
10	Lockheed	Republic Aviation	Douglas	Litton	Boeing
11	North American	Curtiss–Wright	Hughes	LTV[d]	Grumman
12	Boeing	Ford	Raytheon	Hughes	Unisys[j]
13	AT&T	AT&T	Sperry–Rand	Sperry–Rand	Tenneco[k]
14	Martin	Westinghouse	IBM	Textron	Litton
15	Dupont	Grumman	Republic Aviation	Westinghouse	Honeywell

[a]Merger of Consolidated–Vultee, Electric Boat, and others.
[b]Merger of North American with Rockwell.
[c]Merger of McDonnell and Douglas.
[d]Merger of Chance–Vought Aircraft with Temco Aviation and Ling Electronics.
[e]Acquired RCA.
[f]Merger of General Motors and Hughes Aircraft.
[g]Merger of Martin with American Marietta.
[h]Name change from United Aircraft.
[i]Name change from North American–Rockwell.
[j]Merger of Sperry–Rand and Burroughs.
[k]Acquired Newport News Shipbuilding.

Historically, then, a handful of companies has captured the lion's share of prime contracts. The concentration of orders is even higher in narrowly defined product categories such as high-performance fighter aircraft, bombers, long-range ballistic missiles, aircraft engines, nuclear submarines, and electronic navigation systems, in which only a few companies have the skills and physical facilities needed to compete. The Defense Department is nevertheless required by Congress to encourage small-business participation in defense contracting when and where it can. In 1986, companies defined as small businesses (with employment of less than 500 to 1,000, depending upon the industry) obtained 19.7 percent of all domestic defense prime contract awards by dollar volume, including 3.3 percent of the missile contracts, 11.4 percent of the communication equipment contracts, 27.8 percent of services contracts, and 49.7 percent of "other" contracts (for example, contracts for uniforms, fuels, provisions, and much else).[4]

Defense and space prime contractors rely upon thousands of subcontractors, some of whom also occupy important prime contractor roles, but most of whom do not sell to the government directly. Few solid statistics are available on the scope and characteristics of this vast and important infrastructure.

Intramural Government Production

The existence of a weapons industry populated mainly by private corporations is a relatively new phenomenon. Throughout the nineteenth century and the first quarter of the twentieth century, the Army and Navy relied in peacetime primarily on government-owned shipyards and arsenals for specialized military equipment. They turned to private industry only for standard items (such as food and clothing) sold also in civilian markets, and in wartime to supplement their production capacity when the arsenals and shipyards became overloaded. With the advent of aviation, this traditional pattern was challenged. Civilian inventors and entrepreneurs pioneered the development of the airplane, which initially could be used almost interchangeably for military purposes, sport, and mail or passenger transport. When the military officers running government facilities shunned aircraft design and production, the government turned to private industry to meet its needs, which were modest before 1915 and in the interwar period, but which soared to great heights during the two world wars.

Following World War II, and especially after the cold war stabilized armaments demands at high levels, private industry began to play an increasingly important role. There were two main reasons. First, private firms had greater flexibility in offering salaries and working conditions needed to attract large numbers of engineers and skilled technicians. Also, contracting out offered subtle political advantages. Through its industrial suppliers, dispersed across numerous states, the newly organized Air Force found a potent and enthusiastic source of political support for its programs, with more freedom to lobby and mount promotional campaigns than government-owned establishments. These advantages did not escape the notice of the other services, which gradually tempered their advocacy of the arsenal approach and began to depend more and more upon private contractors. In 1982, approximately 14 percent of the Defense Department's weapons production, R&D, and maintenance work was done in arsenals, U.S. naval shipyards, and similar government-owned facilities.[5]

The Cost of Weapons Programs

Technological advance at a forced pace has been the weapons industry's hallmark during the past half century. Much of the effort is program oriented, that is, directed toward designing and developing a new weapons system and then producing the resulting product for the military services' operational inventory. When production begins, efforts to develop more advanced versions of the system often proceed in parallel. Constantly pressing the state of the art to secure weapons of the highest possible technical performance and sophistication has led to program costs that are both high and rising at a remarkable rate.

Once applied research has generated the necessary new technological concepts and a design approach is formulated, weapons programs move into the stage of full-scale development. Designs are refined, prototypes are built and tested, modifications are made to reflect what has been learned, and detailed engineering software is prepared to guide quantity production. How the cost of such activity has risen over time can be illustrated by tracing the evolution of fighter aircraft since the 1950s. The cost of designing and testing the first supersonic fighters, the F-100, F-102, and F-104, ranged between $15 million and $100 million per program at mid-1950s price levels, or $55–365 million at 1982 price levels.[6] The F-16 fighter development program, undertaken in 1975, cost more than $500 million ($730 million in 1982 dollars); the parallel F-18 Navy fighter cost nearly $1 billion. The Air Force's Advanced Tactical Fighter development program, entering full-scale development in 1986, is expected to cost several billion dollars before a decision to commence production can be taken. The Navy's parallel A-12 Advanced Tactical Aircraft development contract was let for $4.4 billion.

A broader perspective is gained by comparing the cost per unit, in every case transformed to 1982 price levels, of operational fighter and bomber aircraft purchased by the U.S. armed forces between World War II and the 1990s. Figure 11-2 shows the approximate date of production on the horizontal axis and the "flyaway" cost per aircraft on the vertical axis (using a logarithmic scale). Imperfectly comparable data had to be tapped, but any inaccuracies are far too small to obscure the reality of rapid exponential growth in unit costs—roughly 11 percent (in constant dollar terms) per year.

Figure 11-2

Unit costs of representative bombers and fighters, 1942–1990.

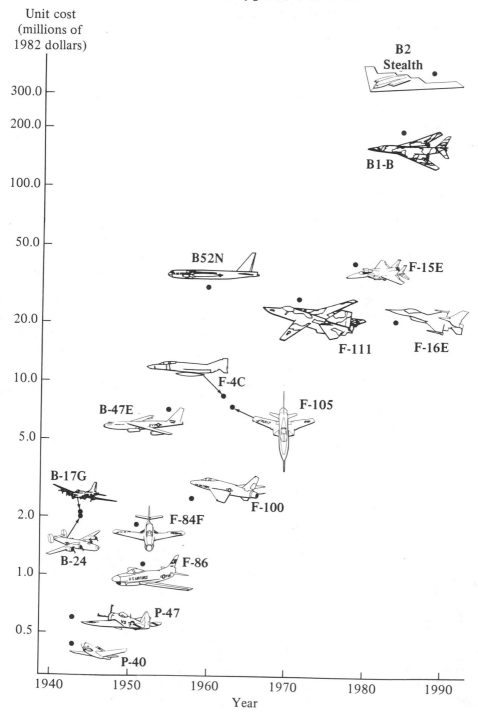

The top-rated P-47 fighter of World War II fame cost $600,000; its 1982 counterpart, the F-15, $40 million. The B-24 bomber, a mainstay of World War II operations, cost $2 million; its B-1B successor $200 million.

The growth of unit costs has been most striking for high-technology weapons. For more mundane items, the comparisons are more even.[7] The World War II M-4 Sherman tank cost $328,000 in 1982 dollars; the M-60 (Patton) tank of the 1970s, $985,000; and the M-1 Abrams tank of the early 1980s (without "active" armor plate), $1.6 million. In 1942, the M-1 (Garand) rifle's cost averaged $381; mass production brought the 1945 unit cost at Springfield Arsenal down to the 1982 equivalent of $159. The M-14 rifle's average cost in 1961–62 was $309 in 1982 dollars. The M-16 rifle's comparable unit cost (as of 1987) was $379.

Why has the cost of high-technology weapon systems risen so astronomically? There are two main reasons: (1) beyond some threshold, achieving higher performance is subject to diminishing marginal returns, while (2) one side's qualitative edge is nullified by the other's countervailing advances, forcing incessant striving for further advantage. Today's aircraft, missiles, and ships can travel faster, fly higher (for airplanes) or dive deeper (for submarines), "see" farther (electronically), deliver more powerful blows with greater precision, and defend themselves against ever more sophisticated threats. Moving out on the potential technological trajectories requires more complex but miniaturized electronics, exotic materials (such as titanium or graphite–epoxy composites in place of aluminum), more refined fabrication techniques, more intricate and skilled workmanship, and more extensive testing of the completed products.

Whether the armed forces should constantly push weapons technology to its limits, with ensuing high costs, is the subject of fierce debate.[8] Restraint is urged because the last increments of performance are so costly, because too much sophistication can degrade reliability, and because the continuous pursuit of technical advantage drives a qualitative arms race in which the parties' efforts eventually cancel each other out. On the other side is the powerful argument, supported often in the history of warfare, that an appreciable technical advantage can mean victory rather than defeat or stalemate. A striking modern example (attributable to superior planning and training as well as to the performance of F-15, F-16, and E-2C aircraft and Shrike missiles) was the Israeli victory over the Syrian air force in June 1982. The Israelis destroyed 61 Syrian Mig-21 and Mig-23 fighters and 19 surface-to-air missile installations while losing only one attack aircraft of their own.[9] Invulnerability and lethal effectiveness of retaliatory forces can also help deter war and sustain the peace. If top performance affects the outcomes of military conflict, actual or potential, so decisively and can be sustained despite the arms race's leapfrogging dynamics, it may be well worth its high cost.

An important influence on the cost of modern weapons is the phenomenon of learning-by-doing. As the production of a complex weapons system progresses, workers become more proficient at their tasks, and engineers come to understand the production process better, devising more effective techniques. As a result, unit costs fall systematically with cumulative output. This is illustrated in Figure 11-3 by the learning curve for B-17 aircraft assembly operations at Boeing's Seattle plant during World War II.[10] As is typical of such data, the unit costs of successive lots (reflected here by production worker hours per pound of airframe) cluster along a downward-sloping straight line when plotted on double logarithmic coordinates. It is customary to describe such learning curves by what happens to unit costs as cumulative output doubles, for example, moving from 100 to 200 units or 1,200 to 2,400 units. The relevant slope in Figure 11-3 is 72 percent; that is, with a doubling of output, unit costs are only 72 percent of previous costs.

Figure 11-3

B-17 learning curve data.

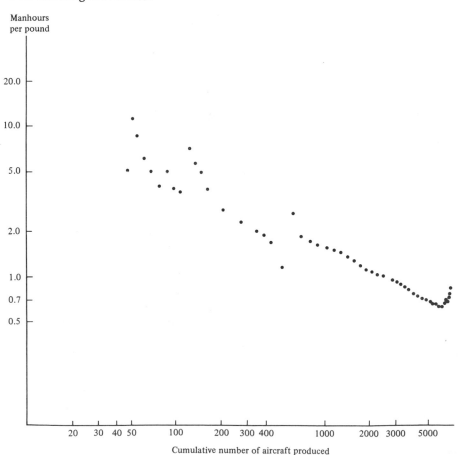

Cumulative number of aircraft produced

This was a slightly faster rate of cost reduction than the 78 percent average computed for all World War II combat aircraft. As is also common, the learning curve in Figure 11-3 is not smooth. It has three distinct segments, corresponding to different versions of the bomber introduced with unit 50, unit 123, and unit 605. Such model changes disrupt work patterns and require new learning to bring costs down. An upturn in unit costs for the last bombers produced reflects the disruptions and slowed work pace as program phaseout occurred.

Because unit costs fall with cumulative volume, exact cost comparisons between weapons generations require that the data be drawn for comparable outputs. This was not done in Figure 11-2, partly because of data limitations, but mainly because the number of units produced in the typical weapons program has tended to fall over time. During World War II, 12,700 B-17 bombers were assembled. The B-52 production run totaled 744, while the B-1B bomber schedule calls for only 100 units. The decrease in production quantities stems partly from modern weapons' greater performance capability, making larger numbers unnecessary, and partly from the limiting interaction between rising but finite budgets and high unit costs. Yet in the high unit costs there is a chicken-and-egg problem, for in addition to the pressure of greater technical sophistication on costs, low production volumes imply relatively high costs by the learning curve phenomenon, and those high costs feed back into the budget equation to limit production volumes.

The high costs of modern weapons programs in turn have profound implications for the structure of competition among weapons makers. During the 1950s, weapons R&D programs cost sufficiently little that the three services could have under active development five heavy bombers, more than a dozen fighter aircraft, and six long-range ballistic missile systems. By the 1980s, development and production costs had risen so much that fewer programs could be supported — two heavy bombers, two advanced fighters, two new ICBMs (MX and Midgetman), and a single sea-launched ballistic missile (with two submarine builders). The government's ability to hedge against technological and strategic uncertainties by supporting multiple programs had been constrained. And for contractors, there were fewer programs than companies with the specialized capability to meet military demands. Each new program opportunity became a life-or-death struggle.

A further implication merits immediate attention. Research and development on a weapons system entails a front-end fixed cost. The more units subsequently produced, the more widely those fixed costs will be spread, giving rise to an important economy of scale. Learning-by-doing leads to another kind of scale economy. Together, these phenomena imply massive economies of scale in advanced weapons development and production. This in turn provides a stimulus to substantial international trade in weapons, for through trade, the advantages of specialization can be realized, and production runs can be extended. Between 1980 and 1985, world-wide arms exports averaged $36.4 billion per year, 49 percent of which originated from NATO nations and 38 percent from the Soviet Union and its satellites.[11] With a defense budget large both absolutely and relative to GNP, the United States has enjoyed comparative advantage among free-world nations in the armaments trade. Its weapons exports between 1980 and 1985 averaged $9.3 billion per year—52 percent of all NATO nation exports. Between 1977 and 1982, exports averaged 28 percent of the value of domestic output for U.S. military aircraft producers, 9 percent for missiles and space systems firms, 51 percent for missile and space-vehicle component suppliers, 33 percent for makers of large-caliber ammunition, and 18 percent for producers of miscellaneous ordnance items.[12] For the same industrial groups, imports hovered at or below one percent of domestic supply.

III.
THE CONDUCT OF WEAPONS PROGRAMS

Weapon systems development and production costs are not only high; they are also subject to substantial prediction uncertainties. For a sample of 11 programs conducted during the 1950s, Peck and Scherer found that on average, actual R&D costs exceeded original predictions by 220 percent, with a standard deviation of 162 percent.[13] For 15 aircraft and missile programs of similar vintage, Robert Summers reported that actual constant-dollar *production* costs per unit, adjusted for learning-curve effects, exceeded the predictions made at early program stages by 171 percent on average, with a standard deviation of 191 percent.[14]

In this environment of high cost and uncertainty, the government adopts a variety of special buying procedures in its efforts to secure good performance. These can be characterized in terms of three main instruments: direct monitoring and control of contractor operations, contractual incentives, and the spur of competition.

The Control Organization

A large bureaucratic organization has evolved to administer the hundreds of thousands of contracts, large and small, issued each year by the Department of Defense. In the late 1980s, it included roughly 22,000 civilians and 3,000 military personnel.[15] For major weapon systems programs, the key contact point between the government and its contractors is the military service program management office, with a staff ranging from dozens for small programs to hundreds for large programs. Program management office personnel monitor company progress, cajole, and participate in a host of detailed design and contractual decisions. Above the program office hovers a superstructure deciding what programs to conduct, which contractors will do the work, the technical goals to be met, guidelines for contractual relation-

ships, and much else. In a continuing struggle to control the weapons acquisition process, the superstructure has grown by leaps and bounds. In the
office of the Secretary of Defense alone, comparably defined executive-level
positions increased from 77 in 1956 to 253 in 1987.[16] That an organization
with 253 top-level executives can escape committee meetings long enough to
do any work at all is one of the Defense Department's more impressive
accomplishments.

The rules by which weapons contracting is conducted have been codified
in minute detail. The basic guidelines are contained in the *Federal Acquisition
Regulations,* a three-volume tome with more than 1,850 pages prescribing
how competition will be used, profit policy, accounting standards, mandates
for dealing with small business, and much else.

Congress has also become increasingly involved in the "micro-manage-
ment" of Defense business. In 1970, Congressional committees made 830
detailed program adjustments while passing financial appropriations and
authorization bills; in 1985, the number of adjustments was 3,163.[17] In 1970,
Congress requested 36 special reports or studies from the Defense Department; in 1985, the comparable number of requests was 458.

Contractual Incentives

To cope with the unique problems of weapons acquisition, the government has evolved unusual contractual instruments. Standardized items such
as filing cabinets and uniforms are obtained through advertised competitive
bidding with contracts very much like those used in the civilian world. But for
weapons programs facing substantial uncertainties, special contracts are employed.[18] The most important variants can be characterized by a simple
formula

$$\text{Realized Profit} = \text{Target Profit} + SP\ (\text{Cost Target} - \text{Actual Cost})$$

Through negotiation, sometimes accompanied by competitive pressure and
sometimes not, the government and contractor agree on a cost target reflecting their consensus belief about the contracted-for work's cost; a target profit
sum related by a complex formula to the cost target; and the parameter SP,
which is called the sharing proportion. When $SP = 1$, a *firm fixed price*
contract exists. If actual costs exceed the cost target, the contractor's profit is
reduced dollar for dollar; if actual costs are less than the target, profit is
increased dollar for dollar. This is the kind of contract used most frequently
in the civilian world. If, however, $SP = 0$, a *cost-plus-fixed-fee* contract exists.
The contractor gets its target profit, whether actual costs turn out to be half
or three times the negotiated target. Under CPFF contracts, all the risk of
cost increases or decreases is assumed by the government as buyer. When SP
is set at values between 0 and 1, one has what is called, somewhat mislead-
ingly, an *incentive* contract. If, say, SP has the fairly typical value of 0.3, the

contractor absorbs 30 percent of any cost increase above the target as a reduction of its profits, and the government picks up the remaining 70 percent; if actual costs are less than the target, the contractor keeps 30 percent of the saving and the government the other 70 percent. Contracts that have ceilings above which the contractor bears 100 percent of further upward cost deviations are called *fixed-price incentive* instruments. Those that lack such caps are called *cost-plus-incentive-fee* (CPIF) contracts.

Complex bargaining occurs over the contract type choice. When cost and technical uncertainties are high, as in the early R&D stages of a program, both government and contractor negotiators may find CPFF or CPIF contracts most suitable. As production experience accumulates, cost uncertainties diminish, and a shift toward fixed-price incentive and then firm-fixed-price contracts occurs. However, if the government has struck a tough cost target bargain, so that actual costs are expected to exceed the target (a *cost-overrun* situation),[19] the contractor prefers a low sharing proportion to minimize its risks. The government may simultaneously favor a high *SP* value to maximize the contractor's incentives for cost control and minimize its profit payments. If the contractor has the upper hand in bargaining, it may prefer a high sharing proportion, while the government faces a dilemma: High *SP* values maximize incentive but increase the likelihood that the contractor will gain unnecessarily high profits.

Concerned about the high incidence of cost overruns and alleged inefficiency on defense contracts, Congress and top Defense Department officials have insisted upon expanded use of firm fixed price and other high sharing proportion contracts. The consequence is seen in Table 11-3. Since 1960 in

Table 11-3

Share of Military Procurement Funds Obligated Under the Principal Contract Types

Contract Type	FY 1952 (%)	FY 1960 (%)	FY 1968 (%)	FY 1976 (%)	FY 1984 (%)	FY 1987 (%)
Firm fixed price[a]	29.8	31.4	52.7	54.6	62.8	65.8
Fixed-price incentive	12.0	13.6	18.7	17.6	17.5	14.1
Cost-plus-incentive-fee	0.0	3.2	9.0	10.5	5.3	3.8
Cost-plus-fixed-fee	17.8	39.0	12.8	12.2	8.4	9.6
All other types[b]	40.4	12.8	6.8	5.1	6.1	6.8

[a]Data for 1952–68 include only firm-fixed-price contracts; for 1976–87, they include both firm-fixed-price and fixed-price-escalation contracts.
[b]Include time and materials, escalation, and redeterminable contracts.

Source: U.S. Department of Defense, *Prime Contract Awards* (Washington: U.S. Department of Defense, annually).

particular, there has been a sharp decline in the share of procurement dollars obligated under CPFF contracts and a more than compensating increase in firm-fixed-price contracts. Although this means that incentives for cost control have been strengthened, the shift has probably been carried too far. The Air Force and Navy, for example, issued fixed-price contracts to cover the technically complex development work on their Advanced Tactical Fighter programs.[20] Constrained by the fear that a significant increase in R&D costs could mean huge, possibly bankrupting, losses, contractors may resist design-refining work that is in the government's interest. Or more likely, they will insist that each improvement not explicitly anticipated in contract specifications be negotiated as a special-contract price-increasing amendment. This generates formidable problems in allocating costs between the original contract and its changes and makes the developmental process more bureaucratic and inflexible — the antithesis of what is needed to achieve top technical results.

The Role of Competition

Competition in the development and production of advanced weapon systems comes nowhere near satisfying the large-numbers requisite of textbook definitions. On the buying side stands the Department of Defense, in effect, a monopsonist. Even when several firms have the technical capability to compete for new programs, once they are locked into a role through experience on initial development and production work, the number of meaningful competitors is reduced to one, or at most, a very few. Bilateral monopoly, with its well-known indeterminacies, exists. In both early and intermediate program stages, the variables on which competition focuses include not only the price paid by the government, but the product's performance capabilities and the schedule on which it will be available.

A particularly important type of competition occurs when the government chooses firms to undertake weapons development assignments, that is, at the *source-selection* stage. The government's approach to source selection has changed dramatically and, to some extent, cyclically over time. During the 1930s and 1940s, contractors were chosen to produce new airplanes only after constructing prototypes (often, but not always, with government funds) and demonstrating their performance. But as the age of high-performance turbojets, guided missiles, sophisticated electronic systems, and nuclear-fueled ships dawned, soaring R&D costs seemed to require a new approach. Key roles in major weapons development programs were then awarded on the basis of a so-called design competition. Would-be contractors assigned their most creative engineers to conjuring up new weapons concepts, proven at best through small-scale model or electronic "breadboard" tests. These paper designs were submitted, along with cost and schedule projections and glowing accounts of the company's capabilities, to a government source selection board. The winner received a contract, sometimes for hundreds of millions of dollars, to develop and test full-scale prototypes and prepare for mass production.

This approach, although sometimes unavoidable, has grave problems. At the start of a complex and ambitious weapons development program, it is virtually impossible to make reliable technical performance and cost predictions. The decision maker who behaves as if design competition projections foretell future events accurately is usually proven wrong. Reinforcing this intrinsic difficulty is a further problem. Under the CPFF or weak CPIF contracts traditionally awarded to cover development work, the contractor has little to lose if costs soar above original predictions, but much to gain if it can lock in a program role by promising attractive features and unrealistically low costs. Optimism is rampant. The military procurement agencies seldom curb this opportunistic contractor behavior. They are advocates for the programs they manage, and they recognize that if too high a pricetag is revealed early in the game, opposition is likely to emerge at high levels in the Defense Department or Congress, preventing the program from getting started. It is better, they reason, to let the cost overruns accumulate in bite-sized increments so that they can say, "Yes, we've had problems, but they're behind us, and to stop now would be a scandalous waste of the huge R&D costs we have already incurred." Thus, the expected costs are understated until so much political and psychological momentum has been gained that program cancelation becomes difficult. The consequences of such behavior include large development and program cost increases, weapons performance that fails to meet original predictions, commitments that would not have been made if the truth had been known early, and waste.

Numerous correctives have been tried. One approach implemented with only modest success and some spectacular failures[21] by Secretary of Defense Robert McNamara in the early 1960s was to centralize program decision-making authority at top levels within the Pentagon. At those levels, greater objectivity and cost consciousness exist, but maximum distance is placed between those who know the truth and those who make the decisions. And at the R&D working level, there are incentives to behave in ways that defeat the top-level controls.

Another McNamara solution, implemented in the C-5A cargo aircraft, F-14 Navy interceptor, and Cheyenne helicopter programs, was "total package procurement." The C-5A program, whose goal was a cargo aircraft of unusually large capacity, illustrates the problems.[22] The technological uncertainties faced in developing subsonic cargo aircraft are typically milder than those encountered with high-performance fighters, bombers, and long-range missiles.[23] As winner of the paper design competition (defeating a variant of Boeing's 747 airliner), Lockheed received a $1.95-billion fixed-price incentive contract for a total package, consisting of development work and the construction of 115 aircraft, including both initial prototypes and operational units. But then, Murphy's Law ("If anything can go wrong, it will") took hold. The total-package procurement concept requires that contract provisions be respected. Lockheed could not meet the maximum weight goal to which it agreed, so in a late development stage, it had to undertake a concerted weight-reducing campaign, redesigning most structural members and remilling many that had already been manufactured. This alone cost more than $100 million, and as other problems surfaced, Lockheed found itself with a billion-dollar cost overrun for the first 58 aircraft. Threatened with the bankruptcy of a major contractor, the government renegotiated the contract, reducing Lockheed's loss to tolerable levels, and loaned it money until it could be restored to health on subsequent contracts.[24] Meanwhile, it turned out that too much weight was shaved from the plane's structure, causing the wings to crack under full loads. Thus, the C5s were required to fly with less than their intended payloads until new wings could be fitted at an additional cost to the government of $1.4 billion.

Finding the total-package approach fatally flawed, the Defense Department began placing renewed emphasis on prototype competition.[25] An early success was the Air Force's lightweight tactical fighter program, which combined a fly-before-you-buy philosophy with willingness to sacrifice top speed and advanced electronic capabilities for simplicity, lower cost, and higher maneuverability. In April 1972, besting several rivals in paper design competitions, General Dynamics and Northrop were given contracts (for approximately $40 million each) to design and build two prototypes each. After a fly-off competition in 1974, General Dynamics was declared the winner, receiving a $417-million contract for the full-scale development of its design into a combat-ready system. The resulting F-16A fighter was less expensive than the earlier, faster, more elaborately armed F-14s and F-15s and, with superior maneuverability, it was a pilot's delight. It is well on its way toward becoming one of the most-produced U.S. military aircraft since the 1950s. However, its evolution did not satisfy all purists, for in the initial full-scale development and further R&D contracts, it lost its simplicity and acquired increasingly elaborate (and expensive) radar and missile capabilities.[26]

"Fly before you buy" is not, however, a game for every season. One reason is the enormous cost of creating prototypes sufficiently refined to demonstrate the capabilities of aircraft, missiles, and submarines advancing technology farther than it was pushed in the F-16 program. In the Air Force's Advanced Tactical Fighter program, two teams were given $691-million contracts in 1987 to build two prototypes each for competitive evaluation. But in the Navy's parallel Advanced Tactical Aircraft program, the cost of such duplication was considered so great relative to eventual planned purchase requirements that a single full-scale development team was chosen in 1988 following a paper design competition.

With or without a prototyping stage, the latest source selection competitions include two new and important wrinkles. For one, attempting to hold contractors to their promises, the Department of Defense has insisted that major new weapon systems development contracts be of the fixed-price type, with severe financial penalties for cost overruns. This is almost certain to limit flexibility and/or necessitate elaborate renegotiation of desirable changes. Also, during the paper design competitions preceding the award of fixed-price prototype or full-scale development contracts, the military authorities have played one contender off against the others, returning to demand "best and final offers" on the cost targets to be included in the winning contract. With huge stakes in the balance, the participating companies established elaborate espionage systems to find out what offers their competitors were making so they could bid slightly lower. When this was discovered in 1988, it was appropriately viewed as a scandal.[27] But the hand-wringing of legislators was in part misdirected, since, given the high level of uncertainty pervading the early stages of weapons R&D programs, it is senseless to award contracts on the basis of low price bids. As former Deputy Secretary of Defense David Packard observed in Senate testimony, the procurement system broke down because of "the attempt by Congress to impose competition in a situation in which real competition in the conventional sense is virtually impossible to achieve."[28]

The high costs and risks of major programs have also led to "teaming," joint ventures between two or more companies to develop a single weapons system. The government encourages teaming to facilitate sharing of ideas and know-how and to preserve companies' ability to participate in future competitions when there are too few programs to let each firm be prime contractor on at least one. For the companies, teaming is a way of remaining in the action and spreading R&D costs not reimbursed by the government—in the case of the Air Force Advanced Tactical Fighter program, expected to be at least $500 million per team.[29] But teaming also poses problems, as one can see from the following team-member constellations in the Air Force and Navy fighter competitions:

Lockheed	Air Force	Northrop
General Dynamics	Advanced	McDonnell Douglas
Boeing	Tactical Fighter	
McDonnell Douglas	Navy Advanced	Northrop
General Dynamics	Tactical Aircraft	Grumman

McDonnell Douglas was teammate to General Dynamics on the Navy program but competitor to General Dynamics on the Air Force program; and before the Northrop–Grumman team was eliminated from the Navy's roster, McDonnell was teamed with Northrop on the Air Force effort but competing against its Navy entry. Sharing know-how and working closely together are difficult when firms are both teammates and rivals in such life-or-death struggles. The eagerness to cooperate is jeopardized even more by the government's stated intent to have teammates compete with one another for production assignments when the development tasks are completed.[30]

Dual Sourcing

Historically, weapons contractors have sustained losses or low profits on R&D contracts but recouped by exploiting their locked-in position when designs emerge from development into the production stage. To combat this bargaining-power reversal, it has become increasingly common for the government to encourage price competition by *dual sourcing,* that is, establishing at least two firms with the necessary capacity and having them compete for production contracts, with the low bidder getting the lion's share of the annual order. Dual sourcing offers obvious benefits: Competition forces firms to accept lower profit rates and squeeze the fat out of their operations, and it may induce intensified quality-control efforts. But there are also costs. Tooling and design documentation sufficient to transfer the original developer's know-how to the second source must be duplicated. To set up General Dynamics as a second source to Raytheon for producing the relatively simple Sparrow air-to-air missile, front-end fixed costs estimated at $38.7 million were incurred.[31] Unless competition spurs the rivals to accelerate their learning, economies stemming from learning by doing may be sacrificed. If, as is typical, unit costs fall by 22 percent with each cumulative doubling of output, dividing production equally between two firms means that a 22 percent incremental cost reduction is forfeited. Also, when the second source is still high on its learning curve, it is not much of a competitive threat to the original developer. In the Sparrow program, for example, Raytheon is said to have doubled its profit rate from 13 to 25 percent in the early dual-source stages, while General Dynamics' costs were still high.[32] And savings that look good on paper may prove illusory on closer scrutiny. In particular, if the government wants its two sources to keep their engineering capabilities intact, they may implement accounting changes that shift engineering overhead costs from the dual-sourced program to other government programs experiencing less competitive pressure.

Although there have been many claims that dual sourcing yields impressive savings,[33] the supporting studies commonly confuse savings spurred by competition and savings that would have occurred in any event through the natural progression down learning curves. A careful review of the available quantitative evidence reached a Scotch verdict: that reductions in program cost had not been proven and that in 10 of the 15 programs with dual sourcing, the most one could say was that prices did not go up following the inception of competition.[34]

Since there are both costs and benefits, a careful tradeoff is required to determine whether competition through dual sourcing is warranted. When the number of units to be produced is small, and/or when designs continue to be modified as production occurs, as is true of nearly all major aircraft and long-range missile programs, the costs of dual sourcing are likely to outweigh the benefits. Only when long production runs are assured, for example, with rifles, simple missiles, ammunition, and widely used electronic systems, is dual sourcing unambiguously advantageous.

IV.
INDUSTRY PERFORMANCE

Appraising the weapons industry's performance is peculiarly difficult, since the standard theories of industrial organization are largely inapplicable. The products supplied press the frontiers of technology. Technological and strategic uncertainties abound. Competition, used in misguided ways, leads to manifold distortions. Contractual instruments take myriad forms and have complex behavioral effects. The bureaucracy in government offices and their contractor counterparts increases, multiplies, and fills the earth.

Yet things get done. The industry is responsible for some of the most spectacular technological achievements of all time. That men have been able to land on the moon and return home safely astonishes even the most callous science watcher. The arsenal of missiles, nuclear weapons, submarines, supersonic fighters, spy satellites, and much else cannot help but impress. There is debate on some comparisons, but the United States has managed to maintain superiority of weapons technology over its perceived rival, the Soviet Union, in many areas, and parity in most others.[35] The acid test of deterring all-out war has been passed, year by agonizing year, for nearly a half century. The success of U.S. weapons is shown inter alia by the robust demand for their export. Great Britain has acquired Polaris and Trident submarines; West Germany, Pershing missiles; dozens of industrialized nations, the top-performance F-15, F-16, and F-18 fighters; and less-developed nations, new or used versions of the F-4 and F-5 fighters. As their export market sales reveal, advanced U.S. weapon systems are produced at costs competitive with those of such foreign competitors as the French Mirage series and the British–German–Italian Tornado fighter.[36] Even the Israelis, who have highly competent engineers and are known for their austere approach, spent the equivalent of $1.5 billion (mostly provided by the United States) developing their Lavi fighter aircraft before canceling the program in 1987 and buying U.S. F-16s.[37]

All this has required an enormous expenditure of resources, including a considerable share of the United States' top technical talent. An appreciable but unknowable fraction of the expended resources was wasted. Congressional speech-making and the newspapers epitomize the waste problem with tales of $435 hammers and $640 toilet seats, but they are only a superficial manifestation of more deep-seated problems. Much more important is the waste incurred in developing and producing major weapons systems. This has two main causes.

Most important, multibillion-dollar program decisions are often faulty because the cost and performance predictions upon which they rely are systematically optimistic. Contractors provide biased predictions because they must do so to win all-important development contracts. The military chiefs pass this biased information on to top Department of Defense officials and the Congress in fear that the truth will precipitate program disapproval. The result has been such fiascos as the F-102 fighter, B-58 bomber, and Bomarc missile in the 1950s; the F-111 fighter, Skybolt missile, and C5-A transport in the 1960s; the AMRAAM missile, Los Angeles class attack submarine program, and DIVAD air defense gun in the 1970s; and, quite probably, the B-1B bomber of 1980s fame.

Even on programs that have achieved a considerable measure of success, the use of resources has often been profligate. Contractors, in league with their military counterparts, include in their weapon systems designs performance features that appeal to aficionado instincts but whose cost far outweighs the likely benefits. And because incentives for stringent cost control are weak, contractor development teams and production staffs are commonly overstaffed by a considerable margin.

The tendency toward overstaffing is in part inevitable, given the rapid technological obsolescence of weapons-making skills and the violent swings in industry demand. When the future is uncertain, when gaining the next major program contract may make the difference between rapid growth or organizational demise, and when winning future competitions depends upon holding one's development and production team intact, every contractor must hoard resources, even when there are more contractor teams than there are jobs to be done. As a result, resources exit the industry very slowly in times of falling demand, such as 1968–76. They shift slowly from companies that lose competitions to those who garner one of the few large plums, as in the late 1970s and early 1980s. And the mix of skills available lags demand, which alters rapidly as technology evolves.

This resource misallocation problem is as much the fault of the Pentagon (and its Congressional overseers) as it is of contractors attempting to secure their uncertain futures. Afraid of being criticized for departing from free-enterprise traditions by systematically "planning" the defense industry's structure, the Defense Department has for decades failed to do the long-run resources planning needed in the markets it controls, nor has it created an "invisible hand" that does the required job automatically.

In a market economy, low profits are the signal that resources must exit; high profits, the lure to the entry of additional resources. In the weapons economy, this invisible hand works at best imperfectly. Profit policy is consciously planned by the Defense Department. Yet, except in its effort to induce *all* contractors to invest more capital in their operations, Pentagon profit policy has not systematically encouraged entry in times of resource shortage and forced exit when and where it was appropriate.

Figure 11-4 presents the longest perspective available on weapons con-

Figure 11-4 _____

Aerospace industry profits, 1956 – 1986.

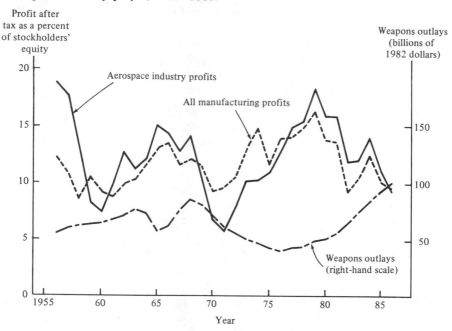

tractors' profits. It focuses on the aircraft and missiles industry, the most important locus of weapons production. Supplementing the aerospace profit time series (solid line) are data on the profits of all manufacturing industries (dashed line) and on demand, that is, constant 1982 dollar outlays for defense research and development and procurement (lowest line).[38] Aerospace companies' profits were high following massive Korean War ordering. They declined as cold-war procurement stabilized and then rose as the Kennedy Administration allocated large sums to ICBM and moon-landing programs and adopted (in 1963) a "weighted-guidelines" profit policy intended to raise the profits of contractors willing to accept incentive-type contracts. The sharp fall in procurement following an early Vietnam War peak brought defense firms' profitability below the average for all manufacturing, but then strange things happened. The surge in profits during the 1970s confounded the further depression of demand. And in the 1980s, as weapons demand boomed, there was a countercyclical fall in aerospace profits, both absolutely and in relation to the averages for all manufacturing (hit hard by the recessions of 1980 and 1982).

Two Department of Defense surveys provide additional insight.[39] For the years 1970 – 83, major contractors reported line-of-business profitability data isolating the financial results of defense-oriented business segments from those for nondefense sales. The findings are summarized in Figure 11-5. The

Figure 11-5
Profitability trends in major defense contracting units compared to all durable
goods manufacturers.

Operating income
as a percent of assets

Year

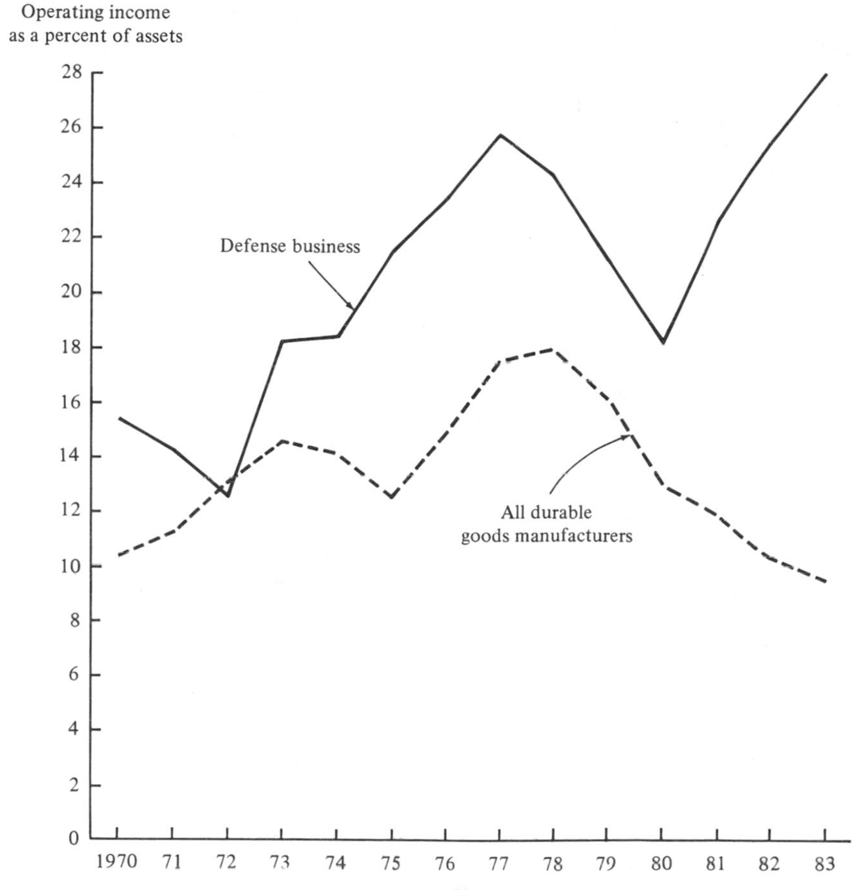

Source: U.S. Department of Defense, *Defense Financial and Investment Review,* June 1985,
p. V-32.

implications are generally similar to those of Figure 11-4. The profitability of
defense business declined to a trough in 1972, rose countercyclically to a
peak in 1977, and then began falling as military procurement increased.
However, unlike Figure 11-4, Figure 11-5 shows rising profitability from
1980 to 1983. In all years but one, military work yielded returns on assets
substantially above the returns for all U.S. durable-goods manufacturers,
chosen as a benchmark in the Defense Department surveys. Averaged over
the 14 years surveyed, defense profitability was 54 percent higher—20.5
percent as compared to 13.3 percent. A further breakdown of the survey data
shows that in the late 1970s and early 1980s, aircraft and missile producers

secured higher profits than business units specializing in electronics—the opposite of what one might have expected from the growth of demand relative to supply.[40]

The Defense Department's guidelines for profit negotiation make no provision for setting higher rates in fields where resources are particularly scarce. To the extent that profitability guides defense-contractor resource allocation in the right directions, it is mainly through discrepancies between the contract profit bargains originally negotiated and actual performance. When there is excess capacity, contractors tend to bid low, incur substantial cost overruns, and suffer reduced outgoing profits. This is less likely when demand presses tightly upon supply. In contracts settled between 1970 and 1974, originally negotiated profit rates averaged 8.8 percent of sales, but the rates actually realized averaged 4.7 percent, or 47 percent less.[41] Costs incurred by contractors, but not allowable for reimbursement under defense regulations, accounted for 2.0 percentage points of the discrepancy between negotiated and realized rates, while increases in cost relative to originally negotiated targets, that is, cost overruns, were responsible for the other 2.1 points.

Criticized by Congress for its wasteful procurement practices, and sensitive to the high profit rates revealed by its 1986 survey, the Defense Department began bringing increased pressure to bear in the expectation that cost overruns and nonreimbursable contractor cost contributions to program efforts would lead to lower realized profit returns. Such pressure was particularly evident in bargaining over Advanced Tactical Fighter development contracts. As an Air Force official explained:

> We looked at the marketplace, we saw what the marketplace was willing to do, and we took advantage of it. Any prudent businessman would do the same bloody thing.[42]

Although the perception of market realities was correct, it carries two risks. For one, the winning firms—those selected to provide fighter development and production capabilities into the distant future—might compete themselves so deeply into financial difficulties that the government would be forced later to bail them out, as it did for Lockheed in the C-5A program, Grumman in the F-14 program, and General Dynamics in the Los Angeles class attack submarine program. Second, if top government officials believed the optimistic cost estimates contractors found themselves compelled to submit, faulty decisions of enormous magnitude could be taken. Surely, there should be a more rational way to conduct the nation's defense business.

V.

PUBLIC POLICY

Few things are more enduring than calls for reform of the system by which the United States acquires weapons. Charles E. Wilson, Secretary of

Defense during much of the Eisenhower Administration, once remarked before Congress that reforming the Department of Defense was like kicking a 100-foot sponge. Blue Ribbon commissions have come and gone with clock-like regularity, but little, if any, improvement is visible.[43]

Nevertheless, some changes cry out for action. The government's weapons-acquisition bureaucracy must be pruned radically. A two-thirds cut in the number of top decision-making participants, that is, to levels like those existing during the Wilson secretaryship, would be appropriate. Reductions are especially needed in the hordes who make and enforce regulations. At the same time, strength must be built to ensure that Pentagon officials can perform well the one really important task that cannot be decentralized: deciding which weapons programs to support and which to reject. This requires staffs with top-rate technical insight and the ability to estimate program costs accurately, free of the biases that pervade contractor bids and military program office projections. At lower levels, as virtually every Blue Ribbon panel since the 1950s has urged, the competence of government officials staffing program and contract management offices must be raised by establishing career paths as well rewarded as those of military line officers, but with terms of service that avoid the 20-and-out syndrome and tempta-tions for the more able individuals to take higher-paying jobs in industry.

In marshaling new weapon systems candidates, it is important to pre-serve a multiplicity of choices carried as far into "breadboard" and prototype demonstration stages as cost conditions permit. Firms should be awarded contracts to conduct such work for the quality of their ideas and their past performance, roughly equally weighted. It is foolish to award development contracts, or to pretend to Congress that they are being awarded, on the basis of predevelopment cost or price quotations. Except in the most urgent cases, occurring only a few times per decade, commitments to production should be made only after development work has progressed sufficiently far that good technical performance is assured and accurate cost projections are feasible. The profit rates awarded on production contracts should be substantially higher in specialties that require additional resources than in fields with excess capacity.

To implement a rational profit policy and to ensure that it has the resources it needs, the Department of Defense should formulate, publicize, and update regularly a ten-year defense industry resource requirements plan. Companies with superior performance records should be assured a place in the allocation of assignments, if not as program leaders, then as performers of advanced research, subcontractors, and backup sources. Companies with poor performance records should be rooted out ruthlessly, despite the politi-cal obstacles.

Finally, the most important thing that can be done to improve the weapons-acquisition process is to bring the qualitative arms race under con-trol. Over the long run, history demonstrates, the most sophisticated weapons soon become obsolete because each major nation feels compelled to match or leapfrog the technical advances of its rivals. During the 1980s, important preliminary strides were made toward arms control verified by both satellite and on-site inspection. Carrying that effort forward is the most important task on any government's public-policy agenda. The scientific, engineering, and management talent released through arms control—without exaggeration, a disproportionate share of the United States' best and brightest individuals—can be used to enrich society in a host of peaceful endeavors.

NOTES

1. "Northrop, Lockheed to Build Prototypes of Jet," *The Wall Street Journal*, November 3, 1986, pp. 2 and 28.

2. U.S. Department of Defense, Directorate for Information Operations and Reports, *100 Companies Receiving the Largest Dollar Volume of Prime Contract Awards: Fiscal Year 1987* (Washington, D.C.: 1988).

3. Drawn from M. J. Peck and F. M. Scherer, *The Weapons Acquisition Process: An Economic Analysis* (Boston: Harvard Business School Division of Research, 1962), p. 117; and annual reports of the Department of Defense. See note 2.

4. *Statistical Abstract of the United States: 1988*, p. 316.

5. U.S. Bureau of the Census, *1982 Census of Manufactures*, "Manufacturing Activity in Government Establishments," subject series report MC82-S-2 (August 1983), Table 1.

6. See Thomas Marschak, "The Role of Project Histories in the Study of R&D," in Marschak, T. K. Glennan, and Robert Summers, eds., *Strategy for R&D: Studies in the Microeconomics of Development* (New York: Springer, 1967), pp. 90–117.

7. The unit aircraft costs are drawn largely from a variety of published sources. We are indebted to the Historical Office of the Air Force for early bomber cost data; to the Army Armament, Munitions, and Chemical Command and the Army Office of Public Affairs for the rifle data; and to the Army Tank–Automotive Command for early tank data.

8. For an insightful analysis of the problem drawing upon several case studies, see Thomas L. McNaugher, *New Weapons, Old Politics: America's Military Procurement Muddle* (Washington: Brookings Institution, 1989), Chapters 5–7.

9. See Lon O. Nordeen Jr., *Air Warfare in the Missile Age* (Washington: Smithsonian Institute Press, 1985), Chapter 8; and "Syrian Action Spurs Massive Air Battle," *Aviation Week and Space Technology* (June 14, 1982), p. 29.

10. The data source is Army Air Forces, Air Materiel Command, *Source Book of World War II Basic Data: Airframe Industry* (Volume I, 1952). For a more general study of the learning-by-doing phenomenon in weapons production, see Harold Asher, *Cost-Quantity Relationships in the Airframe Industry* (Santa Monica: RAND Corporation study R-291, July 1956).

11. *Statistical Abstract of the United States: 1988*, p. 319, reporting U.S. arms control and disarmament agency estimates.

12. U.S. Department of Commerce, Bureau of the Census, *U.S. Commodity Exports and Imports as Related to Output: 1981–82* (Washington, D.C.: Government Printing Office, December 1986), Tables 3A and 3B.

13. Peck and Scherer, *The Weapons Acquisition Process*, p. 429. See also U.S. General Accounting Office, *DoD Needs to Provide More Credible Cost Estimates to the Congress.* GA1.13:NSIAD-84-70 (Washington: 1984).

14. Robert Summers, "Cost Estimates as Predictors of Actual Costs: A Statistical Study of Military Developments," in Marschak et al., eds., *Strategy for R&D*, p. 136.

15. See J. Ronald Fox, *The Defense Management Challenge: Weapons Acquisition* (Boston: Harvard Business School Press, 1988), p. 251.

16. Counted from issues of the *U.S. Government Organization Manual* for 1955–56 and 1986–87 (Washington: U.S. Government Printing Office). The positions counted include secretaries, under-secretaries, assistant secretaries, directors, and their direct deputies along with a few similar but differently named functionaries (such as general counsel).

17. U.S. Senate, Committee on Armed Services, staff report, *Defense Organization: The Need for Change* (Washington: U.S. Government Printing Office, October 1985), pp. 591–593.

18. On these and other contract types and their behavioral effects, see F. M. Scherer, *The Weapons Acquisition Process: Economic Incentives* (Boston: Harvard Business School Division of Research, 1964), Chapters 6–8.

19. A semantic point is in order. The once well-accepted term *cost overrun* has been replaced in Defense jargon by the better-sounding *cost growth*. We adhere to the old custom.

20. See "New Risks in Military Deals," *The New York Times,* February 24,1987, p. D1; and "The Battle for a New Fighter," *The New York Times,* February 20, 1986, p. D1.

21. See, e.g., Robert F. Coulam, *Illusions of Choice: The F-111 and the Problem of Weapons Acquisition Reform* (Princeton: Princeton University Press, 1977).

22. See Ernest A. Fitzgerald, *The High Priests of Waste* (New York: Norton, 1972); and U.S. General Accounting Office, *The C-5A Wing Modification: A Case Study Illustrating Problems in the Weapons Acquisition Process,* PLRD-82-38 (Washington: March 1982).

23. See Summers, "Cost Estimates as Predictors of Actual Costs," p. 157, note 15.

24. See Charls E. Walker and Mark Bloomfield, "The Political Response to Three Potential Major Bankruptcies: Lockheed, New York City, and Chrysler," in Michael Wachter and Susan Wachter, ed., *Toward a New U.S. Industrial Policy?* (Philadelphia: University of Pennsylvania Press, 1981), pp. 423–432.

25. But not before letting two huge contracts for new attack submarines on what amounted to a total-package basis, leading again to billion-dollar cost overruns. See Patrick Tyler, *Running Critical: The Silent War, Rickover, and General Dynamics* (New York: Harper & Row, 1986).

26. Compare James Fallows, *National Defense* (New York: Random House, 1981), pp. 95–106; and Ingemar Dorfer, *Arms Deal: The Selling of the F-16* (New York: Praeger, 1983), Chapters 1 and 4.

27. See "Pentagon Inquiry Hears of Payoffs from Contractors," *The New York Times,* June 16, 1988, p. 1.

28. "Honesty Called 'Impossible' in Pentagon Bidding System," *The New York Times,* July 28, 1988, p. A20.

29. "Military Aircraft: How Much High Tech Is Enough?" *Business Week* (May 11, 1987), p. 80.

30. See William B. Burnett and William E. Kovacic, "United States Department of Defense Weapons Acquisition Policy: Team Agreements and Dual Sourcing," paper presented at the International Institute of Public Finance congress, Paris, August 1987. An earlier teaming arrangement in the F-18 program led to complex lawsuits and countersuits. See *Northrop Corp.* v. *McDonnell Douglas Corp.*, 498 F. Supp. 1112 (1980), 705 F. 2d 1030 (1983).

31. Michael Beltramo, "A Case Study of the Sparrow AIM-7F," *Program Manager* (September–October 1985), pp. 28–35.

32. Donald Pilling, *Competition in Defense Procurement* (Washington: Brookings Institution, 1989), Chapter 1.

33. See "Competition for Contracts Trims Costs for Pentagon," *The New York Times,* March 31, 1988, pp. 1 and D2.

34. Pilling, *Competition in Defense Procurement.*

35. For analyses showing the limitations of Soviet weapons, see Andrew Cockburn, *The Threat: Inside the Soviet Military Machine* (New York: Random House, 1983); and Central Intelligence Agency, Directorate of Intelligence, *The Soviet Weapons Industry: An Overview* (Washington: September 1986).

36. See McNaugher, *New Weapons, Old Politics,* Chapter 8; and "Champagne on a Beer Budget," *The Economist* (September 24, 1988), p. 66.

37. See "Israelis Unveil New Warplane," *The New York Times,* July 22, 1986, p. 9; "U.S. Is Pressing Israelis to Drop Costly Jet Effort," *The New York Times,* August 12, 1987, p. 1; and "Arens Quits Israeli Cabinet Post Over Jet Decision," *The New York Times,* September 3, 1987, p. 6.

38. The "Weapons Outlays" series is an extension of the data in Figure 11-1, with slightly noncomparable statistics spliced in to reach back to 1956.

39. See U.S. Department of Defense, *Profit '76: Summary Report* (Washington: Office of the Assistant Secretary for Installations and Logistics, December 1976); U.S. Department of Defense, *Defense Financial and Investment Review* (Washington: June 1985); and U.S. General Accounting Office, *Government Contracting: Assessment of the Study of Defense Contractor Profitability* (Washington: December 1986).

40. From *Profit '76,* p. II-28; and *Defense Financial and Investment Review,* p. VIII-10.

41. *Profit '76,* p. II-21.

42. "ATF Teams Disdain R&D Dollar Drain," *Defense News* (March 9, 1987), p. 26.

43. See William E. Kovacic, "Blue Ribbon Defense Commissions: The Acquisition of Major Weapons Systems," in Robert Higgs, ed., *Arms, Politics, and the Economy* (San Francisco: Independent Institute, 1989).

SUGGESTED READINGS

Books

Fallows, James. *National Defense.* New York: Random House, 1981.
Fox, J. Ronald. *Arming America: How the U.S. Buys Weapons.* Boston: Harvard Business School Division of Research, 1974.
———. *The Defense Managers: Their Role in Weapons Acquisition.* Boston: Harvard Business School Press, 1988.
Gansler, Jacques S. *The Defense Industry.* Cambridge: MIT Press, 1980.
———, *Affording Defense.* Cambridge, Mass.: MIT Press, 1989

Kaldor, Mary. *The Baroque Arsenal.* New York: Hill and Wang, 1981.

Marschak, Thomas, Thomas K. Glennan, Jr., and Robert Summers. *Strategy for R&D: Studies in the Microeconomics of Development.* New York: Springer-Verlag, 1967.

McNaugher, Thomas L. *New Weapons, Old Politics: America's Military Procurement Muddle.* Washington: Brookings, 1989.

Peck, Merton J., and F. M. Scherer. *The Weapons Acquisition Process: An Economic Analysis.* Boston: Harvard Business School Division of Research, 1962.

Scherer, Frederic M. *The Weapons Acquisition Process: Economic Incentives.* Boston: Harvard Business School Division of Research, 1964.

Government Publications

President's Blue Ribbon Commission on Defense Management. *A Quest for Excellence: Final Report to the President* (The Packard Commission Report). Washington: June 1986.

CHAPTER 12

CONGLOMERATES: A "NONINDUSTRY"

Willard F. Mueller

The large modern corporation typically is not confined to a single industry but embraces many lines of business, and its operations extend over much of the globe. We call such a firm a *conglomerate enterprise.*

Economists developed the theory of *oligopoly* to explain conduct in markets with few sellers. This theory, which explains market power created by the structure of a particular industry, is not adequate to explain many features of an economy that is increasingly dominated by conglomerate firms. The power that conglomerates have within a particular industry depends on their market position, not just in that one industry but in all their other lines of business, at home and abroad. When the same huge firms are among the leading producers in separate industries, the industry lines themselves may become blurred. This does not mean that traditional industrial organization theory and research are meaningless, but rather, that conglomeration should be considered an additional structural variable when explaining behavior in many contemporary industries. This view is shared by Joan Robinson, whose 1933 work, *The Economics of Imperfect Competition,* is one of the pillars of modern oligopoly theory. In the preface to the 1969 edition of this seminal work, Robinson observes that growing conglomeration had largely made obsolete her theory of imperfect competition: "My old-fashioned comparison between monopoly and competition may still have some application to old-fashioned restrictive rings (cartels) but it cannot comprehend the great octopuses of modern industry."

Because all huge firms are conglomerates to varying degrees, Corwin Edwards coined the term *conglomerate bigness.*[1] Because bigness and conglomeration are correlated, increasing centralization of the economy in a relatively few vast corporations is one index of the growing importance of conglomerate bigness in the economy. We therefore begin our discussion of conglomerate bigness by examining the growing centralization of the economy, and especially the unique role that conglomerate mergers have played in this process in recent years.

I.

INDUSTRIAL CENTRALIZATION AND CONGLOMERATE BIGNESS

The great merger movement, around 1900, centralized control over much of manufacturing, which, at the time, represented a relatively small part of the economy. And compared with today's industrial elite, the early twentieth-century business monarchs ruled modest domains. With combined sales of $213 billion in 1988, today's two largest industrial corporations have greater sales (even after adjusting for inflation) than did all manufacturing companies combined in 1900.

The leading corporations have not only grown larger in an absolute sense but in a relative sense as well. Since the mid-1920s, they have expanded substantially their share of the total assets held by corporations engaged primarily in manufacturing. This share increased primarily during periods of rapid growth by mergers: first, during the frenzied movement of 1926–31, then during 1965–1970, and finally during the unprecedented conglomerate merger mania of the 1980s.

These mergers centralized the control of American industry. Between 1965 and 1970, the share of manufacturing assets held by the top 200 industrials jumped from 56.7 percent to 61.0 percent. Indeed, by 1970, the top 100 industrial corporations held a larger share of assets (49 percent) than had been held by the top 200 industrials in 1950, an increase that is attributable primarily to mergers. Although merger activity ebbed during the 1970s, it reached record highs in the 1980s, with the result that the share of industrial assets of the top 200 corporations rose from 61 percent in 1970 to about 63 percent in 1988.

One index of growing conglomerate bigness is the share of assets of industrial corporations in manufacturing, mining, and trade, held by corporations with assets of $1 billion or more (measured in 1988 dollars). In 1929 there were about 65 corporations of this size, whereas in 1988 there were 466. The share of total assets in manufacturing, mining, and wholesale and retail trade held by these billion-dollar corporations grew from 22 percent in 1929 to 67 percent in 1988. Thus, today a few hundred huge corporations control over one-half of all assets in manufacturing, mining, and wholesale and retail trade.

The trend toward growing centralization and conglomerate bigness is even greater because corporate decision making is, in many instances, further centralized by numerous corporate joint ventures among the large corporations. By forming new communities of interest and by strengthening existing ones, joint ventures create the capacity to reduce both actual and potential competition among their large corporate parents.

II.
MERGERS AND INDUSTRIAL CONGLOMERATION

One of the most important characteristics of the post-World War II merger activity is that, as it intensified, the share of horizontal and vertical mergers declined sharply, at the same time that more and more mergers were of the conglomerate type. Horizontal mergers are mergers between companies that produce identical or nearly identical products, for example, two manufacturers of steel products. Vertical mergers are those between companies in a buyer–seller relationship, for example, a shoe manufacturer and a shoe retailer. Conglomerate mergers are those between companies that are neither direct competitors nor in a buyer–seller relationship with one another. Conglomerate mergers may be subdivided into three classes: (1) geographic market-extension mergers, which combine companies that produce identical products but sell in separate geographic (economic) markets, for example, a fluid-milk processor in Chicago who merges with a fluid-milk processor in New York; (2) product-extension mergers, which combine companies that are functionally related in production and/or distribution but sell products that are not in direct competition with each other, such as a fluid-milk company that merges with an ice cream company; and (3) pure conglomerate mergers, which combine companies that fall in none of these categories, such as a railroad and a tire manufacturer.

In the period 1948–1955, most mergers were horizontal or vertical. As the laws that applied to such mergers become more stringent, and as merger activity accelerated, a growing share involved conglomerate mergers. One accurate gage of the changing number and size of large acquisitions is the acquisition of corporations ranked among the *Fortune 500* largest industrials of each year. Since *Fortune* magazine began compiling this list of companies, 319 were acquired (Table 12-1). There were two periods of especially intense merger activity, 1965–69 and 1980–88. Over the entire 25-year period, 1955–1979, only one of the top 50 corporations and only five of the top 100 were acquired. During 1980–88 alone, 7 of the top 50 and 13 of the top 100 companies were acquired. The net effect of these huge mergers has been the further conglomeration and centralization of the economy.

But mergers did much more than increase the absolute size of the acquiring corporations. Today, each of these corporations operates in many geographic and product markets, and most of them have extensive foreign as well as domestic holdings. In a word, they are huge conglomerate enterprises.

III.
CONGLOMERATE MERGERS: MOTIVES

Perhaps no concept so rapidly captured the imagination of so many as the concept that conglomeration yields the benefits of synergism, that is, the

Table 12-1

Number and Total Assets of Acquired Firms Among Fortune's 500 Largest Industrials by Sales Rank and Period of Acquisition (Millions of Dollars)

Fortune Rank (Sales)[a]	Total	Assets $	1980-88	Assets $	1975-79	Assets $	1970-74	Assets $	1965-69	Assets $	1960-64	Assets $	1955-59	Assets $
Top 50	8	65,075	7	64,468	—	—	1	607	—	—	—	—	—	—
51 to 100	11	27,188	6	23,088	—	—	—	—	5	4,100	—	—	—	—
101 to 200	48	71,623	23	54,394	7	8,555	1	465	11	6,804	2	592	4	813
201 to 500	252	100,442	103	70,643	29	11,226	13	2,770	59	11,515	26	2,627	22	1,661
Total	319	264,328	139	212,593	36	19,781	15	3,842	75	22,419	28	3,219	26	2,474

[a]Rank in year before acquisition.

Source: "Fortune 500," Fortune, Time, Inc., New York City, various years.

notion that combining separate substances produces an effect greater than that resulting from using the substances separately. In the popular trade parlance, synergism results in two plus two equaling five. The synergism thesis held that the explanation for the conglomerate merger wave of the 1960s was to be found in the new management techniques of the merger makers. None of the conglomerate miracle workers was more admired than Harold Geneen (ITT), Jimmy Ling (LTV), and Tex Thorton (Litton). They were viewed as a new breed of business manager, omniscient men who could make dynamic firms out of lethargic ones, who could make two blades of grass grow where others struggled to grow one.

For a time, there was superficial evidence that the new conglomerates could, indeed, outperform other corporations. A number of conglomerates showed spectacular increases in their profit performance. This apparent superior profit performance was reflected in seemingly ever-rising stock prices. In what, at the time, seemed indisputable evidence *of synergism,* Tex Thorton's Litton Industries had a magical record of earnings growth during the years of conglomerate expansion. This profit performance was reflected in the astronomical rise in the value of Litton's common stock, as it rose from $6 per share in 1960 to $104.75 in early 1968. Then a precipitous decline set in, as profits fell in 1968, the first annual earnings decline in its history. The initial reaction was one of guarded disbelief. But then the unthinkable happened: 1968 did not prove to be an exception but the beginning of a long downward slide in Litton's fortunes, as its common stock ultimately fell to a low of $2.50 in 1974. Since then, Litton's fortunes have improved as it restructured its conglomerate organization. Yet, in 1988 its common stock sold at an average price of $70, well below the peak price of $104 ¾ in 1968.

Nor was Litton an exception among the leading conglomerates. There was no more enthusiastic proponent of the synergy theory than Jimmy Ling, CEO of LTV. This conglomerate merger propelled the common stock price of his company from $21 per share in 1960 to $108 in 1968. But then the bubble burst, sending the stock on a long plunge. In 1986 LTV filed for protection under the bankruptcy laws, and in 1988 its common stock sold for an average price of around $3.50 per share.

Finally, ITT, the world's largest conglomerate, also performed well during the 1960s: The price of its common stock rose from $32 in 1960 to a high of $124 in 1967. Thereafter its price plummeted to $12 in 1974. Following a massive restructuring during 1980–87, involving divestments of billions of dollars in assets, ITT's common stock price rose modestly, averaging around $45 per share in 1988.

How were some conglomerates able for so long to conceal from their stockholders the truth about their financial health? The answer is that some managements are able to "manage" profit performance by exploiting a host of accounting and tax gimmicks that are available to firms that expand by merging with other companies. The new conglomerate managers did not discover new management techniques; they developed a seemingly endless number of tax, accounting, and financial gimmicks that favored merger over internal growth.

The numerous mergers of ITT offered it a seemingly limitless variety of ways to increase *reported* earnings per share without any real improvement in operating efficiency. Most important was its exploitation of the opportunities of accounting rules that permitted merging companies to pool their interests. (These accounting rules were subsequently changed.) Accounting procedures permitted a company to pay well above the market price of another company and yet show only the book value of the acquired company on its books. A little-publicized Staff Report of the House Antitrust Subcommittee shows how ITT's use of pooling-of-interest accounting permitted ITT to greatly overstate its earnings from 1964 to 1968. During that period, ITT paid $1,278 million in stock for companies with a new worth of $534 million. If this excess payment for "goodwill" had been amortized during a 10-year period, ITT's actual reported net income for 1968 would have been overstated by 70.4 percent.[2] This is only one of several methods used by ITT to increase its profits on common stock. It also increased the company's leverage by increasing the ratio of debt capital and preferred stock to common stock. After acquisition, ITT frequently changed the acquired firm's depreciation policy. Changes in accounting procedures by ITT–Sheraton, Continental Baking, and Rayonier increased ITT's profits by $7.2 million in 1968; this accounting change alone accounted for 11.8 percent of the increase in ITT's earnings from 1967 to 1968. None of these changes was reported in the notes to ITT's financial statements in 1968.

The failure of ITT to disclose the true source of its ever-growing earnings per share came under increasing fire from financial analysts. For example, Mr. David Norr, partner of First Manhattan Company and a member of the Accounting Principles Board, severely criticized ITT's 1970 annual report for not reflecting retroactively the results of the many companies it had acquired. Norr thought that this omission was sufficient grounds for the New York Stock Exchange to halt trading in ITT securities.[3] The Exchange did not, however, see fit to discipline one of its leading members.

Other financial analysts have reported their frustrations in seeking to learn the true source of ITT's rising earnings. In an "Alert for Portfolio Managers," investment analysts Scheinman, Hockstin, and Trotta warned, "ITT continues its financial advertising blitz in the financial media with the eye-catching caption, 'Here's the story again—in case you missed it in the press.'"[4] But after a careful study of ITT's financial statements—and with no help from ITT—these analysts found that, in 1968 and 1969, 34 percent of ITT's increased earnings per share were the result of such nonrecurring sources of income as sale of securities and plants. The report added that it had "good reason to believe that similar or analogous transactions of even greater magnitude took place in 1970." It concluded that "the key to ITT's 'growth' in 1970 share earnings (ex. Hartford Fire) lies in the undisclosed elements which were responsible for the 1970 increase in deferred taxes — equivalent to 40 cents a share of ITT earnings in 1970."

Fortune magazine reported that, in 1971, ITT again reaped large capital gains from its Hartford Fire Insurance Company acquisition and that it was likely to continue to do so for many years to come. Little wonder an ITT executive described it as a gold mine.

Its past financial wizardry seems to have caught up with ITT in recent years, as the company became plagued with operating and financial problems. Even its "cash cow, Hartford Insurance, has been having severe problems."[5] There is now much talk of corporate retrenchment, because ITT has sold off ailing divisions. And as its profits have plunged, the value of its stock has fallen so sharply that ITT frequently has been named as a probable takeover target.

The preceding are some of the most obvious gimmicks and motivations that often have made mergers a preferred method of corporate growth. Several studies document how various tax and accounting rules and practices encouraged mergers for reasons unrelated to economic efficiency. One of the first of these was a 1969 FTC report that concluded, "The balance of evidence so far available lends little support to the view that the current merger movement reflects, in substantial measure, efforts to exploit opportunities to improve efficiency in resource allocation. On the contrary, there are abundant indications that certain institutional arrangements involving tax and accounting methods, aided by speculative developments in the stock market, have played a major role in fueling the current merger movement."[6]

None of this is meant to imply that all mergers are promoted to exploit accounting and tax gimmicks or are for purposes of personal greed or aggrandizement. Although a variety of factors may promote mergers, a consensus is emerging among economic researchers as to what mergers accomplish, or more correctly, what they do not accomplish. In 1970, Thomas F. Hogarty conducted a comprehensive review of fifty years of research on the question of whether mergers are more profitable than alternative investments. He concluded: "A host of researchers, working at different points of time and utilizing different analytical techniques and data, have but one major difference: whether mergers have a neutral or negative impact on profitability."[7]

In 1977, Dennis C. Mueller conducted a similar review of research findings. Perhaps the most important of these findings was that conglomerate mergers generally do not enhance the profitability or stock values of acquiring firms.[8] Among the important conclusions flowing from this finding is that the management of acquiring firms apparently are pursuing "corporate growth or other objectives not directly related to stockholder welfare and economic efficiency." Dennis Mueller believes that this explains "why managers of acquiring firms undertake mergers providing no benefits for their stockholders; why managers of acquisition targets vigorously resist bids which would greatly enrich their stockholders." A corollary of this finding is that acquired companies generally are not less efficient than the acquiring companies.

The most comprehensive analysis of the merger mania of the 1960s and 1970s was recently completed by Ravenscraft and Scherer.[9] These prominent industrial organization economists made an empirical analysis of the pre-merger and postmerger performance of over 600 acquisitions. They found that the typical merger of the period involved the acquisition of a well-managed company with above-average profitability. Following the merger, profitability typically worsened and the acquired company's market share declined. The postmerger profitability was especially dismal for pure conglomerate mergers. Many acquisitions were so disastrous as to trigger a massive sellout mania in subsequent years. Fully one-fifth of a sample of companies acquired during 1974–77 were sold off during 1974–81. Some have heralded the selloffs as creative restructuring; a more accurate characterization of the sales is that they are proof of failed acquisitions.

Ravenscraft and Scherer further found that not only did the mergers result in losses to private parties, but they crippled the economy by reducing manufacturing productivity and R&D outlays. The study also concluded that the mergers did not confirm the theory that mergers occur because acquiring companies that are managed in a superior way take over poorly managed companies, thereby increasing economic efficiency.

The most comprehensive academic study reviewed previously examined mergers of the 1960s and 1970s. But the early findings regarding more recent mergers paint a grim picture for investors as well as the economy as a whole. In 1984, the prestigious business journal *Fortune* analyzed the worst mergers of the past decade, focusing solely on the financial costs to stockholders of the acquiring companies. The findings are unequivocal: Stockholders lost hundreds of millions of dollars because of the mistakes made by the managers of the acquiring company.[10]

The debate over the motives of the current conglomerate merger mania may continue long after it ends. But based on over 30 years of observing the post-World War II merger waves, I suspect the effects of the latest wave will be like its predecessors: While many participants gained handsomely, these personal gains will have come largely at the expense of overall economic efficiency and huge personal losses to many victims of mergers gone sour.

In sum, there is now overwhelming research evidence that considerations other than efficiency motivate most large conglomerate mergers. But a question still remains: Even though large conglomerate mergers generally do not promote efficiency, are there reasons for placing restraints on such mergers? One reason for concern with conglomerate mergers is that they result in greater overall concentration of economic power, with a concomitant increase in corporate political power. Dennis C. Mueller observes that whereas in earlier times economists were inclined to dismiss such concerns as unsubstantiated, "The age of innocence regarding corporate power is now over. Large corporations both have and utilize political power. And it seems reasonable to assume that this power is positively related to company size."[11] We now turn to the events of the 1970s that were responsible for ending "the age of innocence" regarding the interplay of corporate economic power and political power.

IV.
CONGLOMERATE BUSINESS AND THE POLITICAL PROCESS

The recent wave of very larger mergers has not been motivated primarily by a quest for economic efficiency. This fact alone would not necessarily cause a serious public-policy problem if it were not for the fact that our economic system is becoming increasingly centralized in ways that may transform adversely both our political and economic institutions. Corwin Edwards, in his seminal article on the conglomerate enterprise, spelled out how conglomerates are able to parlay their economic power into political power. He made his observations well before the merger mania of recent decades, when vast conglomerate mergers have increasingly centralized the economy and transformed our economic–political order. Many believe this centralization process threatens our pluralistic political processes, which rest on a tradition of diffused, dispersed, heterogeneous patterns of industrial ownership.

In the 1970s the political power of large corporations was unmasked. First came revelations of improper domestic political conduct. International Telephone and Telegraph employed its considerable power in a well-orchestrated drive to receive a favorable antitrust consent decree.[12] The Watergate investigations uncovered numerous illegal political contributions by large corporations. In April 1974, George M. Steinbrenner, chairman of the board of American Shipbuilding Corporation and owner of the New York Yankees, became the first corporate executive ever indicted on felony charges in connection with illegal corporate political contributions.[13] The numerous disclosures of domestic corporate misconduct in political affairs soon were overshadowed by evidence of massive corporate bribery and political intervention in the affairs of other nations. The ITT efforts to overthrow the Allende government in Chile have been documented by the Senate Foreign Relations Committee.[14] United Brands admitted that it made a $1.3-million payment to an official of the Honduras government to reduce that country's banana tax; it subsequently admitted making payments of $750,000 to officials of the Italian government.

Perhaps no observer of the large modern corporation was surprised to learn that America's largest petroleum corporation apparently was also one of the top corporate contributors to foreign elections. From 1965 to 1975, Exxon Corp. contributed more than $59 million to various political parties in Italy alone.[15] Inexplicably, Exxon even contributed $86,000 to the Italian Communist party. It also has admitted making political contributions in Canada, as well as payments in three unnamed countries, to government officials and to officials of government-owned companies.

These are not isolated cases of corporate bribery and illegal political activities. In 1976, the Securities and Exchange Commission (SEC) issued a special report entitled *Questionable and Illegal Corporate Payments and Practices*.[16] The SEC's interest in these matters was triggered by the work of the special prosecutor who was appointed to investigate the illegal activities in the so-called Watergate scandals. As its investigations progressed, the SEC realized that more was involved than a few isolated violations of the federal securities laws and other laws. The violations included illegal or improper political contributions to domestic politicians, various activities in foreign affairs, and dubious accounting practices. The SEC therefore adopted a policy whereby all corporations subject to its jurisdiction were encouraged to make voluntary disclosure of questionable or illegal activities.

As of April 21, 1976, the SEC received 97 disclosures regarding illegal or questionable practices. The two most frequently represented industries were drug manufacturing and petroleum refining. Most of the corporations that engaged in the questionable activities were very large enterprises: 49 had sales exceeding $1 billion in 1974, and 86 had sales exceeding $100 million. About one-third of the 97 reporting companies had made illegal domestic political payments, and all 97 companies reported a total of 183 questionable or illegal practices. The SEC report expressed concern about the extent of past illegal activities but ended on an optimistic note. The reason for the commission's optimism was that many corporations had issued directives ordering the cessation of questionable conduct and adopted written corporate policies prohibiting similar practices in the future. However, four companies told the SEC that they intended to continue the practice of making questionable payments, particularly in foreign trade.

In 1980, *Fortune* magazine (December 15, 1980) examined the extent of "crime in the executive suites" of large corporations in a feature article entitled "How Lawless Are Big Companies?" In *Fortune*'s words, "A look at the record since 1970 shows that a surprising number of them have been involved in blatant illegalities." The *Fortune* study was "limited to five crimes about whose impropriety few will argue — bribery (including kickbacks and illegal rebates); criminal fraud; illegal political contributions; tax evasion; and criminal antitrust violations. The latter consist entirely of price fixing . . . and exclude the vaguer [areas of antitrust]."

Of the 1,043 major corporations examined, 117, or 11 percent, of these had, during 1971–78, committed at least one of the crimes listed in the *Fortune* study. *Fortune* observed that "eleven percent of major American corporations involved in corrupt practices [in an eight-year period] is a pretty startling figure." But the 11 percent figure understates the relative extent of illegal activity by the largest U.S. corporations. The *Fortune* list of offenders included 39 percent of the 100 largest.

How can the pervasive illegal activity of large corporations be explained? *Fortune* believes that "Simple economic incentives explain much illegal behavior: corruption seems to pay, at least in the short term." Perhaps the search for higher profits is the basic force that stimulates such behavior, but if it is, should it be condoned—any more than crimes committed by individuals who hope to improve their personal economic lots?

To Marshall B. Clinard, the leading expert on the sociology of corporate crime, the answer is an obvious no. Clinard believes sactions against corporate offenders are essential because unequal justice is inconsistent with the basic democratic precept of equality before the law.[17]

We must emphasize, however, that many corporations, even very large ones, have not been cited for any violations since 1970. This is persuasive evidence that illegal corporate behavior is not endemic to American capitalism. Corporate behavior can be influenced by the codes of conduct set by top management. Moreover, the fact that most large corporations succeed economically without engaging in such conduct demonstrates that corporate success does not require illegal conduct.

V.
CONGLOMERATE MERGERS AND THE COMPETITIVE PROCESS

Economists have identified a variety of ways in which mergers may injure competition. The most obvious injury occurs when merging companies are direct competitors; these are called horizontal mergers. There also are discernible anticompetitive effects in mergers among companies in buyer–seller relationships, so-called vertical mergers. But the economic effects are less evident in the case of *conglomerate mergers,* that is, mergers between companies that are neither horizontally nor vertically related. Some economists reason that competition is not injured so long as the merging companies are not direct competitors. They reason that there is no link between growing, *overall* industrial concentration and conglomeration, on the one hand, and the quality of competition in *particular* markets, on the other.

This view is based on the simplistic assumption that competition is determined solely by the structure of a particular market. But it overlooks the fact that the multimarket nature of many large industrial corporations enables them to engage in practices that are peculiar to conglomerate firms. It also ignores the fact that the organizational characteristics of the large conglomerate give it a unique capacity to alter the structures of the markets in which it operates. Hence, the conglomerate may not only possess traditional market power — that is, power vis-à-vis customers or suppliers — but power vis-à-vis actual or potential rivals. The nature and extent of such power depend on the relationship between the conglomerate firm's structure, that is, its relative size, diversification, and profit capabilities in its individual markets, and that of its rivals, customers, and suppliers.

Specifically, business conglomeration enlarges two lines of conduct that are unavailable to single-market firms, cross-subsidization and reciprocity. It also widens the scope of mutual interdependence among large firms, which leads to greater competitive forbearance among them. Conglomeration by merger accelerates the development of conglomerate options and mutual interdependence and allows such conduct characteristics to become significantly more pervasive than they would be if conglomeration were achieved by internal growth alone.

This is not meant to imply that conglomerate power always has anticompetitive consequences. Indeed, in some market settings conglomerate power is used to inject new competition into the market. In industries where entry barriers are very high, a conglomerate firm may increase competition by entering the industry by internal growth or by acquiring a small firm in such a market and subsequently expanding it. But competition may be injured when a conglomerate merger eliminates a significant *potential* competitor. Economic theory teaches that when industries are already highly concentrated, a major restraint on the oligopolists' market power is the threat of new entry. Often, the leading potential entrant into an oligopolistic industry is a firm in another industry. In this case, competition may be injured when a firm within an oligopolistic industry acquires one of the leading potential entrants into the industry. The most famous antitrust case involving this kind of conglomerate merger was the Federal Trade Commission's challenge of Procter & Gamble's (P&G) acquisition of the Clorox Corporation, which had a 50 percent share of the household bleach industry. Although P&G did not sell household bleach, the U.S. Supreme Court upheld the FTC's finding that the merger threatened competition because P&G was a leading potential entrant into the household bleach industry.

Cross-Subsidization

An important fact about large conglomerate corporations is that the great majority operate across many industries and hold prominent positions in the most concentrated manufacturing industries. In addition to being especially prominent occupants of concentrated industries, the largest corporations hold leading positions in many industries.

Because the typical large conglomerate enjoys abnormally high profits in at least some of its markets, it may expand its power by coupling these high profits with an ability to "shift marketing emphasis and resources among its various markets," If a conglomerate firm earned a competitive rate of return in each of its product markets, it would have no "excess" profits with which to subsidize particular product lines. But, as we have seen, when a firm operates in many markets, it generally has market power in one or more of its important markets and hence secures noncompetitive long-run profits. The amount of such profits depends not only on the degree of market power that the conglomerate firm has in its various markets but also on its total sales in markets where it has market power.

When a firm enjoys large profits, it has the option of engaging in special competitive tactics that are not available to the firm that earns only a competitive return. Conglomeration is an instrument through which these options can be exercised by using excess profits in some markets to subsidize losses in others, either by price cuts or by incurring a substantial increase in costs — for example, by abnormally large advertising outlays. If the subsidized markets are small, compared with the overall operations of the firm, subsidization may have very little impact on overall profitability. When a firm undertakes this policy after a rational investment decision, it expects to enhance its long-run profits by virtue of the effects of subsidization on the structure of the subsidized markets and because of the firm's relative position in these markets.

Many case studies have demonstrated how large corporations have used their conglomerate-derived power to engage in cross-subsidization.[18] Here we review briefly events in the beer industry, in which a conglomerate merger appears to have played an important role in increasing concentration.[19]

There was a persistent decline in the numbers of brewers following World War II, from 404 companies in 1947 to about 75 in 1970, reflecting in part economies of large-scale production and advertising. But whereas the *number* of local and regional brewers dropped sharply between 1947 and 1970, the total sales of all regional brewers remained about the same. Economists who analyzed the industry during the 1960s and early 1970s commented optimistically on its competitive future. Ira and Ann Horowitz concluded: "It appears unlikely that concentration in the brewery industry, at least with regard to the leading five firms, will increase to any great extent in the near future."[20] Similarly, Kenneth Elzinga concluded, in 1973, that "Even with a generous estimate of the minimum optimum size plant, the industry could support at least 30 efficient and independent firms."[21] Seldom have the predictions of prominent economists been proven wrong so quickly. The reasons for their errors are to be found in events that were not impacting on the industry when they were examining it.

In 1973, a critical change occurred in the evolving structure of the beer industry. In that year, the sales growth of the national brewers began to accelerate at the expense of locals and regionals. In 1975, the regionals experienced the first drop in combined annual volume since 1961. The share of the surviving regionals and local brewers fell from 48 percent in 1972 to 3.0 percent in 1988. By 1988, Anheuser–Busch and Philip Morris–Miller had a combined share of 65 percent. Only two of the other 15 top brewers of 1972 increased their shares after 1975, and both of these, Stroh and Heileman, accomplished this by acquiring other brewers. Since 1972, seven of the top 15 brewers have been acquired—Schlitz, Olympia, Schaefer, Carling, Hamms, Rheingold, and National. In 1988, a mere 10 brewers made 99 percent of all U.S. brewed beer, a far cry from Elzinga's 1973 observation that the industry could "support at least 30 efficient and independent firms."

Because of these dramatic events, it is natural to raise this question: What happened after 1972 to bring about so concentrated an industry structure? The poor showing of the other national and large regional brewers, which had been prospering until 1973, suggests that more than economies of scale were involved. Much of the answer seems to be found in Philip Morris's acquisition in 1969–1970 of the Miller Brewing Company for $229 million.

Prior to its acquisition, Miller was the eighth largest U.S. brewer, with only 4.5 percent of sales in 1969. Miller was a financially successful company, whose operating income during 1967–1969 roughly equaled that of the three other national brewers. But in comparison with its acquirer, Philip Morris, Inc., Miller was a financial midget. Philip Morris is a huge, powerful conglomerate firm, which overshadows all other U.S. brewers except for Anheuser–Busch. Indeed, by 1988 Philip Morris had total sales of $26 billion and net profits of $2,337 million; in 1986 it had a 37 percent share of the highly concentrated U.S. cigarette industry and a 19 percent share of EEC cigarette sales. Philip Morris has substantial expertise and resources with which to promote consumer-type products that are readily transferable to the merchandising of beer. By acquiring in 1984 the General Foods Corp., with sales of $8.6 billion, and in 1988 Kraft, Inc., with sales of $11 billion, Philip Morris became the world's largest consumer products company and the tenth largest American industrial corporation.

Over 25 years ago, economist John M. Blair emphasized the potential anticompetitive consequences that might follow when a conglomerate enters an industry composed of "single-line" firms. According to Blair, "The danger to competition posed by cross-subsidization, whether actual or anticipated, is at a maximum in unconcentrated industries populated largely by single-line firms."[22] The key here is that "What had been a 'symmetrical' oligopoly, with each of the oligopolists having about the same position, might be transformed into an 'asymmetrical' oligopoly, with the new entrant assuming a position of dominance and leadership."

When a conglomerate acquires a small factor in a market, it has a strong incentive to engage in cross-subsidization to expand its position. In 1971 Philip Morris initiated such a policy of subsidizing the expansion of Miller, with the aim of becoming number one in the beer industry. To accomplish this, PM–Miller launched an aggressively orchestrated strategy of demand creation and capacity expansion.

In 1972 Philip Morris acquired the Meister Brau and Lite brands of Meister Brau, Inc. of Chicago, one of the top three brands in the Chicago area. Immediately PM–Miller began accelerating advertising outlays for the Lite brand, from $525,000 in 1973 to $33 million in 1980 and $83 million in 1987. The Lite advertising program has become a classic case study of how to blitz one's way into a market segment with massive advertising outlays. The Lite success story represents the ultimate achievement of advertising-created product differentiation—being able to sell a lower-cost product at a higher price.

Paralleling its enormous outlays for brand creation, Philip Morris poured enormous amounts of money into expanding its existing plant facilities and building new ones. Over a six-year period, 1972–1979, Philip Morris's cumulative capital investment in Miller grew from about $228 million to over $1 billion.

PM–Miller's policy forced other leading brewers to follow its lead. Regional brewers, which historically have spent relatively little on advertising, also substantially increased their advertising outlays. Even Coors, long credited with being able to grow successfully with very little advertising, increased its advertising expenditures manyfold between 1975 and 1988, from $1.1 million to $125 million.

This is the environment in which other brewers struggled for survival. As PM–Miller and Anheuser–Busch increased advertising and further segmented the market with new brands, competing brewers were crowded out of the market unless they could strengthen their brands and increase their offerings. The increased emphasis on advertising especially disadvantaged the regional brewers because they were unable to obtain equal access to the television media.[23]

The extent and significance of PM–Miller's cross-subsidization can be best appreciated if Miller is viewed as an autonomous profit center. This lays bare the financial prerequisites of Miller's expansion in the face of deep and sustained losses. According to my estimates, Philip Morris's Miller division incurred losses every year during 1971–1975, totaling $120 million. In 1976 and 1977, Miller earned very modest profits. Since then its profits have continued to be submarginal. Although it is impossible to determine from public records its net profits from brewing, Philip Morris's annual report for 1988 indicates that during 1985–88 the operating profits (profits before payment of interest expense and corporate overhead) of the Miller division were only 5.1 percent of beer sales; in contrast, the operating profits of its tobacco operations averaged 34.3 percent. At Miller's recent rate of improvement in operating income, Philip Morris may not recoup its accumulated losses and subcompetitive profits until well into the 1990s. Thus, after years of subsidized expansion, causing massive structural reorganization in the beer industry, Philip Morris will have converted Miller into a profitable operation; it will have moved Miller from its position in eighth place in a relatively unconcentrated industry to second place in a highly concentrated one.

The PM–Miller conglomerate merger triggered an inexorable trend toward shared monopoly, in which price competition was replaced by escalating promotional competition and higher prices, an environment in which survival and success often depended on market power, not efficiency. The end result to date has been the creation of a highly concentrated industry: Whereas in 1972 four brewers made 47 percent of sales, by 1988 four brewers made 86 percent of all beer sales.

Reciprocal Selling

We now turn to another competitive strategy that is available to conglomerate firms, *reciprocal selling*. Simply defined, this practice involves taking your business to those who bring their business to you. It becomes a potentially harmful competitive strategy under two conditions: (1) when the market structure creates special *incentives* in the promotion of a firm's sales; and (2) when the product and organizational characteristics of a business create extensive *opportunities* for engaging in the practice. In short, both the incentive and the opportunity are prerequisites to the successful use of reciprocal selling.

A firm has an incentive to engage in reciprocity when doing so promises to increase its profits. In purely competitive markets there would be no incentive. In the absence of product differentiation, price alone would govern sales and purchases. But in markets of relatively few firms, sellers recognize their interdependence. Each, knowing that it may influence the price level by its decisions, avoids price competition. Firms in these markets, therefore, have an incentive to engage in various nonprice strategies to promote sales, for example, by advertising, innovation, promotion, and tying arrangements. Reciprocal selling is another such nonprice strategy.

In markets where firms sell a specialized product to firms similarly organized, generally there are few opportunities to practice reciprocity. The opportunity arises only when each firm produces something that is required in the operations of the other. An enterprise must purchase goods or services from companies that are potential customers for its products in order to make possible the arrangement "You buy from me and I'll buy from you."

The volume of sales that may be influenced by reciprocal trading depends on the number, volume, and type of products that are bought and sold. A single-line producer will have relatively few opportunities for reciprocal dealings, whereas a firm that buys and sells a large variety and volume of products has the best opportunity to engage in reciprocal dealing. It is in the large conglomerate enterprise that reciprocal dealing develops into a major strategy for expanding sales.

Some economists, relying on a simple theoretical model, contend that reciprocity is an insignificant anticompetitive problem. This position is most categorical among economists of the Chicago School, who reason thus: (1) In perfectly competitive markets reciprocity can have no adverse effects; (2) firms with monopoly power can exploit their own power without resorting to reciprocity; and (3) reciprocity is prompted primarily by a desire to increase efficiency by eliminating selling costs. After dismissing reciprocity on these theoretical grounds, members of the Chicago school usually close their argument by echoing George Stigler's observation that, in any event, "Reciprocity is probably much more talked about than practiced and is important chiefly where prices are fixed by the state or a cartel."[24]

This problem is too complex to be disposed of with such simplistic logic. Analysis of reciprocity must begin with the recognition that most contemporary markets, although falling short of monopoly, are sufficiently concentrated so that price competition already is somewhat muted. In such markets oligopolists have an incentive to resort to a variety of nonprice strategies to promote their sales. Reciprocity is such a strategy, but, unlike most other sales strategies, the capacity to practice it depends on the overall size and conglomeration of the firm, not on its position in an individual market.

In the real world, reciprocity is found in the broad spectrum of markets falling between the polar extremes of perfect competition and monopoly. Stigler et al. fail to explain adequately the competitive process in such markets and therefore minimize the potential market power that reciprocity may confer on its users. They find some "frictions" in imperfectly competitive markets, but conclude that "A plausible explanation for reciprocity under effectively competitive conditions is the desire to minimize costs of searching and selling."[25] Thus, they believe it is "plausible" that most reciprocity is merely a means of cutting the costs of locating and persuading customers, something to be applauded rather than condemned. The only exceptions they find to reciprocity that is motivated by the quest to minimize selling costs are in markets in which firms have monopoly power or in markets that are subject to regulation. But here, again, they see reciprocity mainly as having a beneficial influence, because reciprocity either reduces the producers' surplus that would go to the monopsonistic buyer or it enables the market to approach a more optimal allocation of resources in regulated markets.

This analysis is wrong because of the unrealistic assumptions concerning the structural environment in which reciprocity is practiced. The analysis greatly underrates the capacity and propensity of large conglomerate firms to practice reciprocity. These economists apparently have not looked at, or have ignored, the considerable evidence showing that in imperfectly competitive industrial markets—covering a wide range of competitive structures— reciprocity is a pervasive, and often decisive, factor in determining the allocation of sales. It can restructure markets by increasing concentration and by raising entry barriers to new competitors, and it can make prices more rigid.

It is a mistake to assume that reciprocity forecloses entry of only small firms. In a well-documented case, entry into an industry by even a billion-dollar corporation can be prevented by reciprocity-created entry barriers when the market has become tied up by larger rivals. For example, in the 1960s the Cities Service Corporation found that its entry into the rubber–oil market was blocked because the major tire companies had developed extensive reciprocity arrangements with other large petroleum companies.[26]

Nor is there legitimate basis in fact for the argument expressed by Stigler: that reciprocity generally "restores flexibility of prices" in oligopolistic markets. Logic and industrial experience show that the reverse is more likely to be the case. When firms become associated as reciprocity partners, outsiders soon learn that it is futile for them to compete for such accounts; doing so promises to spoil the open portion of the market (that not covered by reciprocity agreements) and fails to divert business from reciprocity partners, who, at most, simply renegotiate transaction prices. Indeed, once reciprocity becomes pervasive in an industry, reciprocity partners tend to minimize price as a factor in their transactions.

This is not idle speculation. The available evidence demonstrates that reciprocity creates tight trading bonds among practitioners. And, whereas reciprocity partners often claim that they only deal with one another on an all-other-things-being-equal basis (and, indeed, this is often the case), reciprocity partners often short-circuit the market so completely that they do not adequately test it to discover their lowest-price alternatives. In fact, it is not uncommon for reciprocity partners to pay prices above the going market price, although not for the reason Stigler assumes (that is, to grant secret price concessions to customers); rather, they do so in order to not rock the boat in an otherwise stable market. This is illustrated by an Atlantic–Richfield trade relations manual, which outlined buyers' procedures for selecting vendors. The manual directed Atlantic–Richfield buyers to place business with bidders offering the lowest cost, "unless other factors, *including trade relations,* make it advisable to pay a higher price."[27] This is not an isolated incident. Not only do firms frequently pay higher prices to their reciprocity partners; at times they even accept lower-quality products in their drive to maintain an equitable balance of payments.[28] Such facts cannot be reconciled with the Chicago school's statements that, in oligopolistic markets, reciprocity (1) is practiced mainly as a device to discover new customers; (2) erodes price rigidity; and (3) generally improves the allocation of resources.

The manner in which conglomerate mergers enhance the reciprocity opportunities of already huge corporations and the use of the practice are well documented. Space prevents a review of this literature.[29]

Continued conglomerate expansion—both by merger and internal growth—promises to increase reciprocity opportunities, thereby threatening to result in closed-circuit markets from which medium and small businesses are excluded. Oligopoly in individual markets would be magnified by circular integration, in which purchases of the leading firms would be tied to sales, thus precluding the opportunities of firms without substantial reciprocity opportunities to gain access to the inner circle of firms. Indeed, as a *Fortune* study concluded, "The United States economy might end up completely dominated by conglomerates happily trading with each other in a new kind of cartel system."[30]

Conglomerate Interdependence and Competitive Forbearance

We have seen how the post-World War II merger movement contributed to the creation of a dual economy, in which a few hundred enormous corporations are expanding their control over the bulk of industrial activity, leaving the literally thousands of smaller businesses to share the remainder. We also have seen how the conglomerate mergers, which propel this centralization, have greatly increased the reciprocity opportunities of large corporations as they expand their product lines, thereby increasing the potential buyer–seller linkages with other corporations.

But growing reciprocity opportunities are only the most obvious manifestation of the changed competitive environment. Reciprocity is but a symptom of the larger problems of conglomerate interdependence and competitive forbearance, which is the inevitable concomitant of an economy in which most commerce is controlled by a relatively few huge corporations.

It is now well recognized in economic theory and industrial experience that, in a market of few sellers, firms tend to behave interdependently. That is, each seller takes into account the direct and indirect consequences of its price, output, and other market decisions. This is called *oligopolistic interdependence.*

The theory of oligopoly explains the behavior of firms operating in a single market in which their discretion in pricing is constrained by certain structural characteristics of the market. Especially relevant characteristics are market concentration, product differentiation, and barriers facing would-be entrants.

The competitive-conduct characteristics of particular markets may be influenced not only by these three traditional structural characteristics but also by the conglomerate character of some of the firms operating in the market. We have just seen that a conglomerate enterprise possesses a unique capacity to practice reciprocal selling. In addition, however, the multimarket characteristics of firms may result in what we will call *conglomerate mutual interdependence and competitive forbearance* among actual and potential competitions—an interfirm relationship that differs from *oligopolistic interdependence* as it is traditionally viewed.

Conglomerate interdependence and forbearance can arise because (1) the same or related decision makers have simultaneous access to both firms, or (2) the firms share contact points in input–output markets, which creates an awareness of common interests. Interlocking directorates, intercorporate stockholdings, and joint ventures represent the first set of factors that facilitates coordinated relationships among firms. A *firm's conglomerate* structure constitutes the second set of factors that creates a commonality of interest with other conglomerate firms. By increasing both size and diversification, the conglomerate merger increases the number of contacts shared with competitors, suppliers, and customers, thereby increasing the mutual awareness of common interests among firms. Simply put, growing conglomeration and overall industrial concentration greatly broaden and extend traditional communities of interest among key industrial decision makers.

The continuing merger movement of recent decades has greatly increased the contact points among large corporations and, therefore, the likelihood that conglomerates will exercise forbearance in their competitive confrontations.[31] Perhaps the simplest form of conglomerate interdependence is related to price decisions. Firms that meet as competitors in many markets are likely to regard each other with greater deference than if their pricing decisions were constrained solely by structural conditions in particular markets.

But conglomerate interdependence may take more subtle forms, as conglomerates accommodate and harmonize their behavior. Although they are generally ignored or overlooked by many economists, antitrust proceedings provide rich evidence of such behavior, which goes back more than half a century. This evidence demonstrates the inherent logic of conglomerate power: To possess such power inevitably invites its use.

For example, after DuPont became a large, diversified corporation in the early 1920s, it developed a community of interest with other leading national and international corporations. The evidence demonstrates that when these corporations met as actual or potential competitors, they often exercised mutual forbearance. As early as 1923, a DuPont vice president explained his company's policy toward Imperial Chemical Industries of Great Britain (ICI), the world's second largest chemical firm, which DuPont met in many international markets:

> It is not good business sense to attempt an expansion in certain directions if such an activity is bound to result in a boomerang of retaliation. It has been the DuPont Company's policy to follow such lines of common-sense procedure. . . . [32]

DuPont's philosophy of self-restraint in dealing with ICI was summed up succinctly:

> This was done on the broad theory that cooperation is wiser than antagonism and that in the matter of detail the chances in the long run were that the boot was just as likely to be on one leg as on the other.

Irenée DuPont pointed out in 1927 that it was his company's policy to encourage the establishment of esprit de corps among the country's "great corporations." As he put it, the DuPont company felt "that the great corporations of the country, especially those that are leaders in business ethics and in service to the economic structure, should stand together without fear of veiled threats from companies which are more predatory."

"Standing together" may sometimes prove to be a euphemism for avoiding actual or potential competition with one another. For example, Union Carbide and Carbon in 1931 purchased rights to a process for manufacturing a transparent wrapping material that Carbide thought might be competitive with DuPont's cellophane. Lammot DuPont reported a conversation on this topic with Carbide officials:

> They assured me repeatedly they did not wish to rush into anything; most of all a competitive situation with DuPont. Their whole tone was most agreeable. . . . In the course of the conversations, various efforts at cooperation between Carbide and DuPont were referred to and in every case assurances of their desire to work together.

There also is evidence that, in recent times, DuPont has continued the "common-sense procedures" it embraced earlier in its history as a conglomerate enterprise.

A recent example of conglomerate interdependence in action was General Foods' (GF) response to an invasion of its eastern markets by Procter & Gamble (P&G) following its acquisition of the Folger coffee company. The Folger brand was especially strong west of the Mississippi, whereas General Foods' Maxwell House brand was the leading brand east of the Mississippi. When P&G–Folger invaded GF's eastern market, GF took counter-strategies to repel the invasion. As one of its strategies, GF invaded Folger's large-share western markets to "drain considerable funds from Folger which could be used in the new markets."[33] The chairman of Ogilvy & Mather, GF's advertising agency, colorfully characterized the retaliation as "the same as bombing Hanoi." As one GF official put it:

> [The] idea was to go into the West . . . into one of their markets where they had very high share levels in and were very dependent on profits. . . . Because our volume base was so small and their volume base was so high in those areas, in order for them to meet our deal rate structure, they would have to spend an awful lot of money. . . . [34]

This illustrates that when one huge conglomerate considers entering another conglomerate's market, the invaded party has competitive strategy options not open to the single-market enterprise, no matter how large it may be.[35]

This and other evidence cited previously demonstrates how shared contact points can induce forbearance and interdependence among potential conglomerate competitors. The exchange of reciprocal favors among conglomerate corporations involves shared contact points, but the contemplated consequences of such sharing need not be limited to reciprocal buying. The interfirm structural framework characterized by the shared contact points leads to the consideration, proposal, and possible realization of acts of conglomerate interdependence and forbearance that can affect market shares, entry, and pricing practices. It may well represent a serious long-run threat to competition resulting from the growing merger-achieved centralization of economic resources among a relatively few conglomerates, which meet as actual or potential competitors or customers in many markets. The ultimate result is a closed economic system in which price and other business decisions by vast conglomerates become largely immune to the disciplining influence of the market. Such a system runs counter to the basic assumptions of a free, competitive enterprise system that relies on the market to discipline the use of private economic power.

Conglomeration by merger accelerates the development of such a system, and when it involves large firms, it widens the market-power differential between the largest firms and other firms in the economy. There thus exists a causal relationship between the growing merger-achieved centralization of control over American industry and the competitive structure and behavior found in particular markets occupied by giant conglomerate enterprises. It is extremely difficult to quantify how growing aggregate concentration and conglomeration change the structure and behavior of particular markets. However, the available case studies of cross-subsidization, reciprocity, and conglomerate interdependence provide insightful evidence of the effects. This case-study evidence is reinforced by an increasing number of statistical analyses.[36]

These findings have rich implications for public policy concerning conglomerate mergers. They may provide an important bridge between the concern with overall centralization of economic power, as it was expressed by the Congress when it enacted the Celler–Kefauver Act, and the language of the Act that focuses on competition in specific markets. We turn now to the question of whether existing legislation and its enforcement are adequate to cope with the problems created by the increasing conglomeration of American industry.

Deconglomeration Promotes Horizontal Mergers

One generally ignored byproduct of the conglomerate merger mania of the 1980s is the indirect way it has promoted horizontal mergers in many markets. This occurs in the following situations: (1) when a conglomerate merger goes sour, as occurs in one out of five, and the acquiring company disposes of all or large parts of the acquired company; (2) when management resists a takeover, with the assistance of investment bankers, by outbidding the unfriendly suitor with a leverage buyout (LBO); and (3) when investment bankers take over a conglomerate with an LBO for the sole purpose of selling off the parts piecemeal.

In each of the latter LBO situations, the party ultimately controlling the company pays for it with huge debt borrowings based on the assets of the acquired company. The management and investment bankers involved in the LBO make only small equity investments in the company they end up owning. The new owners then pay off the debt by divesting parts of the company piecemeal.

Under the Reagan Administration the antitrust agencies have greatly relaxed the standards toward horizontal mergers, permitting increases in market concentration that would not have been tolerated in earlier administrations of either party. This often has given the green light to divesting the pieces of the conglomerate to direct competitors.

The way in which deconglomeration may restructure an industry is well documented by recent happenings in the food retailing industry. (Large retail food chains are conglomerate enterprises because they operate across a large number of separate geographic markets.) Space permits examination of only the most recent examples.

In 1986, Dart Group Corp. attempted to acquire Safeway Stores, Inc., the nation's largest supermarket chain, with sales of $19.7 billion at the time. To prevent the "unfriendly" takeover, Safeway agreed to a $4.25-billion leveraged buyout by Kohlberg Kravis Roberts & Co. (KKR), the leading leveraged buyout (LBO) house in the country. KKR paid well above the going stock market price to acquire Safeway's common stock, after which the company become a private corporation. KKR paid for the stock with huge debt borrowings guaranteed by the assets of the acquired company. KKR then began selling off Safeway's operations in various markets. During 1987 and 1988, KKR sold off hundreds of Safeway stores with billions of dollars in sales, in many cases to direct competitors. The most important selloff came in 1988, when Safeway sold its entire southern California division, with sales of $1.8 billion, to Von's Companies, Inc., with sales of $3.4 billion. Safeway and Von's were direct competitors in all important southern California markets. Although the Federal Trade Commission initially questioned the legality of the merger, it entered into a consent agreement with the parties that required only token divestiture.[37]

Another potential dismemberment of a huge supermarket chain involves the Kroger Co., the second largest grocery chain, with sales of $17.1 billion in 1987. For over a year Kroger had been mentioned as a potential takeover target. Thus the company was "in play," the trade jargon for a company whose stock is being accumulated by speculators in anticipation of a buyout. In September 1988, Kohlberg Kravis Roberts & Co. (KKR), while still in the process of dismembering Safeway, announced plans to acquire Kroger in a leveraged buyout valued at $4.64 billion.[38] Kroger management immediately took steps to resist the buyout. It proposed paying $40 in cash for each common share, plus a subordinated debenture with deferred 20-year interest with a trading value of about $8, and what was left of the company's shares would trade as so-called stub equities, allegedly valued at $5 to $7 a share.[39] As the first step in paying off the huge borrowings necessary for this deal, Kroger immediately announced it planned to sell off assets worth $333 million, including three of its supermarket divisions. Kroger's creative financial restructuring plan was developed by that prominent merger maker, Goldman, Sachs & Co. KKR subsequently abandoned the takeover attempt. Nonetheless, Kroger must now go through with its restructuring plan, which presumably will require it to sell many of its stores to pay off the huge debt it incurred to ward off KKR. Significantly, had KKR gained control of Kroger, it would simultaneously have controlled all or parts of three supermarket chains: Safeway, Kroger, and Stop & Shop, with combined sales of about $40 billion.

At least 11 other food chains were acquired in leveraged buyouts, with combined sales of $21 billion, since early 1987. Since direct competitors have the most to gain by acquiring the parts of a deconglomerating firm, they often are the highest bidders, absent antitrust constraints. Given the lack of enforcement policy of the Reagan antitrusters, LBOs in food retailing and many other industries, as well as the numerous divestitures of failed conglomerate acquisitions, create a great potential for anticompetitive horizontal mergers. This is a largely ignored fallout of the deconglomerating mergers of the 1980s. The matter has received virtually no attention by industrial organization economists.

VI.
PUBLIC POLICY

Public policy must begin with the premise that large conglomerate enterprises will not wither away. Even very inefficient large corporations do not disappear from the economic landscape. Because of anticipated catastrophic consequences to stockholders, employees, and entire communities when a large corporation's survival is threatened, either the government bails it out—for example, Lockheed Aircraft and Chrysler—or permits it to merge with another large corporation, even a direct competitor—for example, the merger of McDonnell Co. and Douglas Aircraft.

Without adequate funding, the antitrust agencies are hopelessly undermanned and outgunned in most litigation against the large corporations. An order of magnitude is given to this mismatch by noting that AT&T reportedly budgeted at least $50 million to "defend" itself in the recent suit brought against it by the Antitrust Division. This is greater than the *total* annual budget of the Antitrust Division.

In the face of the merger mania of the 1980s, between 1981 and 1987 the Reagan Administration cut the staff of the Antitrust Division from 939 to 645 (31 percent) and recommended an additional cut of 100 for 1988.[40]

Quite clearly, unless antitrust enforcement is to remain a charade, the antitrust agencies must receive adequate funding and once more be enthused with a will to enforce vigorously the existing laws.

Strengthening the Merger Law and Its Enforcement

In 1956, the historian Richard Hofstadter concluded that antitrust enforcement had become solidly institutionalized, resulting in little change of enforcement policy from one administration to another.[41] All this changed in the 1980s. In his campaign for the presidency Ronald Reagan said that efforts to slow the conglomerate merger tide were "arbitrary, unnecessary and economically unsound."[42] He proved true to his word. After his election he appointed Chicago school lawyer–economists to head the Antitrust Division and the Federal Trade Commission.[43] Both agencies adopted new merger guidelines that gave a green light to conglomerate mergers. Indeed, his first appointee as Federal Trade Commission Chairman, James C. Miller, III, proudly proclaimed that under his regime the FTC did not open an investigation into a single conglomerate merger.[44] His successors have lived by the same code. This is the environment that has encouraged the greatest conglomerate merger movement in American history, unmatched in other advanced capitalistic economies. Obviously, unless the current administration changes enforcement policy, the conglomerate merger mania of the past eight years will continue.

The antitrust agencies must be especially alert to a little-noticed by-product of the current conglomerate merger tide. Often, increases in market-concentrating mergers follow in the wake of leveraged buyouts by investment bankers and others. To pay off the huge debts incurred in such takeovers, investment bankers systematically sell off the individual parts of the conglomerate to the highest bidders. Not surprisingly, direct competitors often are the highest bidders for the divested parts. As shown previously, such deconglomeration, when left unchecked by antitrust authorities, increase concentration in the industries affected.

More vigorous antitrust enforcement alone will not deal effectively with conglomerate mergers and the problems resulting from existing levels of conglomeration. If the traditional case-by-case antitrust approach is used, it could take a decade or more to explore the outer boundaries of the existing antitrust laws. Even before the Reagan Administration, the U.S. Supreme Court under Chief Justice Warren Burger had become increasingly tolerant of mergers, leading to the charge that the Burger court had an "anti-antitrust bias." Quite clearly, existing law, as interpreted by the current Supreme Court, is not capable of preventing all undesirable conglomerate mergers. A more direct approach is called for: legislation that applies special legal standards to very large mergers. This legislation should recognize explicitly that such mergers pose serious economic and political dangers, which transcend the economist's narrow preoccupation with a merger's competitive impact on an isolated market.

In 1979, a conglomerate merger bill was introduced in the United States Senate aimed at mergers among large corporations and acquisitions of firms holding large market shares. Specifically, this bill called for the prohibition of mergers among companies where each had sales of $350 million or more or where a company with sales of $350 million acquired a company with a market share of 20 percent or more in any significant market. The bill provided that a merging company could provide the following affirmative defenses: (1) The merger "will have the preponderant effect of substantially enhancing competition"; (2) the merger "will result in substantial efficiencies"; or (3) within one year before the merger the parties shall have divested one or more viable businesses with revenues at least equal to revenues of the smaller merger partner. (These affirmative defenses would not apply where each of the merging companies had revenues exceeding $1 billion.) Sponsors of the bill had expressed concern that existing law was unable to cope with the rising tide of conglomerate mergers, which were viewed as antithetical to our system on political, social, and economic grounds.

Such strict restraints on large conglomerate mergers would prevent much merger-induced conglomeration and would contribute to the erosion of existing market concentration. By preventing large corporations from entering new industries by acquiring other large corporations, especially those holding large market shares, these firms would be encouraged to enter other industries—by building new capacity or by acquiring small concerns. Then, instead of merely being substitutes for an already large competitor in an industry, they would increase the number of significant competitors, thereby eroding the market position of entrenched firms.

Eliminating Corporate Secrecy via Federal Chartering

Even at best, the aforementioned measures will not provide sufficient safeguards to ensure that conglomerate power will be disciplined by the marketplace. Because of the enormous economic and political power of modern conglomerate corporations, it should be made very clear that conglomerates are not purely *private* institutions. Congress should explicitly declare that the large conglomerate corporation's business is very much the *public*'s business. Simply put, the huge conglomerate enterprises that control most industrial resources are quasi-public institutions because they have been granted the privilege—but not the explicit responsibility—of running the American economy. Former ITT chairman Harold Geneen acknowledged this when he said, "Increasingly, the larger corporations have become the primary custodians of making our entire system work."[45] This quite naturally raises questions of legitimacy—whether these powerful corporations are running the economy in the public interest.

Justice William O. Douglas identified the problem more than four decades ago when he observed: "Enterprises . . . which command tremendous resources . . . tip the scales on the side of prosperity or on the side of depression, depending on the decisions of the men at the top. This is tremendous power, tremendous responsibility. Such men become virtual governments in the power at their disposal. In fact, if not in law, they become affected with a public interest."[46]

An appropriate first step toward recognizing that the large corporation is not a purely private enterprise is to require that all very large corporations receive a corporate charter from the federal government rather than from individual states. In the more than one hundred years since New Jersey amended its constitution (1875) to liberalize greatly the incorporation process, state chartering statutes have become increasingly framed to suit the interests of corporate enterprises. The whole thrust of this development has been to confer on the corporation the rights and privileges of private citizens. Yet, during the period, as more and more of the economy has become the domain of enormous corporate enterprises, corporations increasingly have taken on the characteristics of public enterprises, in that they influence, directly and indirectly, the livelihood of all Americans.

A federal chartering statute should spell out a set of corporate *responsibilities* as well as *rights*. A major purpose of such a charter should be to remove the veil of secrecy covering much corporate decision making that is vital to the public interest. It should be restricted to only the very largest corporations, perhaps those controlling assets of $1 billion or more. (The 333 manufacturing corporations of this size controlled about 69 percent of all manufacturing assets in the fourth quarter of 1988). Among the possible provisions of such a charter are the following:

1. Establish guidelines to be applied by management and directors when contemplating merger with other huge corporations, involving either friendly or unfriendly takeovers. The provisions might spell out a corporation's responsibilities to its employees, the communities in which it operates, and other matters affecting significantly the public interest when two huge corporations merge.
2. Prohibit leveraged buyouts by management that are not in the interest of stockholders.
3. Much more extensive public reporting of the sources of investment, revenues, and profits than is now required by the SEC.
4. Extensive public disclosure of the volumes of all products manufactured and sold, including such information that corporations currently supply to the Bureau of the Census under strict rules of confidentiality.
5. Disclosure of the social costs of certain corporate actions.
6. Disclosure of publicly owned facilities operated or leased by private corporations.
7. Disclosure of various details of a corporation's foreign operations and

prohibitions against political intervention in the affairs of other nations.
8. Publicly appointed representatives on the board of directors, who would obtain relevant information on corporate affairs, thereby insuring that the public interest receives some direct representation in the affairs of the giant conglomerate.

This, in skeletal form, is a program for providing greater public responsibility of corporate affairs. This is intended to outline the general approach; it is not a claim that the specific provisions mentioned are those that are best suited to ensure that the huge conglomerate corporations perform in the public interest. This is not an attack on our market economy, but an effort to perfect it. Although federal chartering is not a panacea, it recognizes the large modern corporation for what it is — an essentially public institution.

Nor is this proposal a substitute for a vigorous program to make competition more effective wherever possible or for the other reforms mentioned in this chapter. On the contrary, it complements such efforts. It recognizes that giant conglomerate corporations enjoy great discretion in making numerous decisions that affect our social, cultural, political, and economic welfare. Therefore, more complete disclosure by large corporations would serve the dual objective of aiding natural market forces and of providing the broader benefits to society that flow from more complete information on corporate affairs. The belief in the elimination of unnecessary corporate secrecy is based on what Justice Louis Brandeis emphasized as being "the essential difference between corporations and natural persons."

The author holds no illusions that any of these proposals will be adopted in the near future. Proposals to restrain conglomerate mergers have received scant support in recent years. For the past eight years, the Antitrust Division and the Federal Trade Commission have been headed by individuals who are hostile to the basic tenets of the antitrust laws as articulated by the authors of these laws and by judicial precedents interpreting the laws.[47] But those concerned with shaping public-policy alternatives that would improve our economic system must not be swayed by the popular moods of the times. To do so would silence all voices of reform.

NOTES

1. Corwin D. Edwards, "Conglomerate Bigness As a Source of Power," in *Business Concentration Price Policy* (Princeton, N.J.: Princeton U.P., Conference of National Bureau of Economic Research, 1955), pp. 346–347.

2. U.S. Congress, House, Antitrust Subcommittee of the Committee on the Judiciary, *Investigation of Conglomerate Merger, Staff Report,* 92nd Cong., 1st sess., June 1, 1971, p. 414.

3. "Accountant Urges Better Reporting Practices," *The New York Times,* July 24, 1971.

4. Scheinman, Hochstin, and Trotta, "Alert for Portfolio Managers," Supplement P, July 1971, p. 1.

5. "The Trouble That Led to ITT's Dividend Shocker," *Business Week* (July 23, 1984), p. 77.

6. FTC, *Staff Report, Economic Report on Corporate Mergers* (Washington, D.C.: U.S. Government Printing Office, 1969), p. 159.

7. T. F. Hogarty, "Profits from Mergers: The Evidence of 50 Years," *St. Johns Law Review*, special ed., 44 (Spring 1970), p. 389.

8. D. C. Mueller, "The Effects of Conglomerate Mergers: A Survey of the Empirical Evidence," *Journal of Banking and Finance*, 1 (1977), p. 339.

9. David J. Ravenscraft and F. M. Scherer, *Mergers, Sell-Offs, & Economic Efficiency* (Washington, D.C.: Brookings Institution, 1987).

10. "The Decade's Worst Mergers," *Fortune* (April 30, 1984), p. 263.

11. D. C. Mueller, op. cit., p. 342.

12. W. F. Mueller, "The ITT Settlement: A Deal with Justice?" *Industrial Organization Review*, 1 (1973), p. 67–86.

13. "Before and After the Felony," *The New York Times*, September 6, 1975, sec. 3, p. 1. Steinbrenner and the corporation subsequently pleaded guilty to reduced charges and were fined $15,000 and $20,000, respectively.

14. U.S. Congress, Senate, Subcommittee on Multinational Corporations, *The International Telephone and Telegraph Company and Chile, 1970–71*, 93rd Congress, 1st sess., June 21, 1973.

15. "Exxon Concedes That Donations in Italy Were for Promoting 'Business Objectives,'" *The Wall Street Journal*, July 17, 1975, p. 2; "Exxon Says Donations in Italy Exceed $46 Million; Communists Got $86,000," *The Wall Street Journal*, July 14, 1975, p. 10; "Exxon Discloses More Foreign Payments in Filing, Says SEC May Demand Details," *The Wall Street Journal*, September 26, 1975, p. 6.

16. SEC, *Questionable and Illegal Corporate Payments and Practices* (Washington, D.C.: U.S. Government Printing Office, 1976).

17. M. B. Clinard and P. C. Yeager, *Corporate Crime* (New York: Macmillan, 1980), p. 298.

18. FTC, *Merger Report*, op. cit., pp. 406–457; John M. Connor, R. T. Rogers, B. W. Marion, and W. F. Mueller, *The Food Manufacturing Industries: Structure, Strategies, Performance, and Policies* (Lexington, Mass.: Lexington Books, 1985), pp. 244–270.

19. The following discussion of the beer industry is based in part on W. F. Mueller, testimony before the Subcommittee on Antitrust and Monopoly, Committee on the Judiciary, U.S. Senate, the 95th Cong., 2nd sess., May 12, 1978, pp. 78–124.

20. I. Horowitz and A. R. Horowitz, "Firms in a Declining Market: The Brewing Case," *Journal of Industrial Economics*, No. 152 (March 1965). In a subsequent article, these authors concluded that "the 4 majors will ultimately claim about 40.3 percent and the widely marketed regionals 23.6 percent of the market." See "Entropy, Markov Processes and Competition in the Brewing Industry," *Journal of Industrial Economics*, No. 205 (March 1967–68).

21. K. G. Elzinga, "The Restructuring of the U.S. Brewing Industry," *Industrial Organization Review*, 1 (1973), p. 114.

22. J. Blair, "The Conglomerate Merger in Economics and Law," *Georgetown Law Journal*, 86:672 (Summer 1958), p. 693.

23. See W. F. Mueller, paper submitted to the Department of Justice, January 15, 1979: "Competitive Significance for the Beer Industry of the Exclusive Advertising

Rights Granted National Brewers in Major Network Sport Events." (Available from the author.)

24. See George Stigler, "Reciprocity," Working Paper IV, Nixon Task Force on Productivity and Competition, February 18, 1969, reproduced in *Antitrust Law & Economics Review* (Spring 1969), p. 52.

25. J. H. Lorie and P. Halpern, "Conglomerates: The Rhetoric and Evidence," *Journal of Law and Economics,* 13 (April 1970), pp. 149–166.

26. FTC, *Merger Report,* op. cit., pp. 383–384. For an extensive discussion of the scope and practice of reciprocity, see FTC, *Merger Report,* op. cit., pp. 332–297.

27. FTC, *Merger Report,* op. cit., p. 387.

28. Ibid., pp. 392–393.

29. For examples of the use of reciprocity, see Willard F. Mueller, "Conglomerates: A Nonindustry," in W. Adams (ed.), *The Structure of American Industry,* 7th ed. (New York: Macmillan, 1986), pp. 374–377.

30. *Fortune,* 71 (June 1965), p. 194.

31. The frequency of horizontal and vertical contact points among large conglomerate corporations is examined in some detail in an earlier edition of this book. *See* Mueller, "Conglomerates . . . ," op. cit., pp. 378–79.

32. Cited in Willard F. Mueller, *DuPont: A Case Study of Firm Growth* (Ph.D. dissertation, Vanderbilt University, 1955), p. 393. All of the following references to DuPont are from this source at pp. 202 and 393.

33. J. M. Connor, et al., op. cit., pp. 261–63.

34. Ibid., p. 263.

35. A growing number of economists are discovering anew what we have called "conglomerate interdependence and mutual forbearance." Porter, in alluding to the P&G–GF and other similar confrontations, says that they involve a "cross-parry" competitive strategy. Such strategies are possible, Porter explains, "when firms compete in different geographic areas or have multiple product lines that do not competitively overlap." M. E. Porter, *Competitive Strategy* (New York: The Free Press, 1980), p. 84. Some economists have labeled multimarket contact points as "parallel integration." See William J. Adams, "Should Merger Policy Be Changed?" in L. E. Browne and E. S. Rosengren (eds.), *The Merger Boom* (Boston: Federal Reserve Bank, 1987), p. 186.

36. FTC, *Merger Report,* op. cit., pp. 230–234. For an analysis of this study, see Leonard Weiss, "Quantitative Studies of Industrial Organization," in M. D. Intriligator (ed.), *Frontiers of Quantitative Economics* (Amsterdam: North Holland, 1971), pp. 378–379; L. L. Deutsch, "Entry and the Extent of Multimarket Operations," *Journal of Industrial Economics,* 32 (June 1984), pp. 477–487; John T. Scott, "Multimarket Contact and Economic Performance," *The Review of Economics and Statistics* 64 (1982), pp. 368–375; Stephen Rhoades and Arnold Heggestad, "Multimarket Interdependence and Performance for Banking: Two Tests," *Antitrust Bulletin* 30 (1985), pp. 975–95.

37. Federal Trade Commission, *Von's Companies, Inc. and Safeway Stores, MC.,* Agreement Containing Consent Order, File No. 881-0038, May 25, 1988.

38. "KKR Makes an Unsolicited Offer for Kroger Totaling $8.464 Billion," *The Wall Street Journal,* September 23, 1988.

39. "Kroger Team Campaigns for Restructuring Plan," *Supermarket News* (October 3, 1988), pp. 1, 62.

40. "Rodino Announces Hearings to Consider Impact of Antitrust Cutbacks on U.S. Competitiveness," Committee on the Judiciary, U.S. House of Representatives, February 25, 1987.

41. Richard Hofstadter, "What Happened to the Antitrust Movement?" in E. F. Cheit (ed.), *The Business Establishment* (New York: Wiley, 1964), p. 116.

42. "Government May Abandon Fight to Stem Conglomerate Takeovers," *The Wall Street Journal,* November 14, 1980, p. 23.

43. Willard F. Mueller, "A New Attack on Antitrust: The Chicago Case," *Antitrust Law & Economic Review,* 18 (1986), pp. 29–66.

44. E. W. Barnett, "Interview with James C. Miller III, Chairman, Federal Trade Commission," *Antitrust Law Journal,* 53 (1984), p. 11.

45. Quoted in A. Sampson, *The Sovereign State of ITT* (New York: Stein & Day, 1973), p. 125.

46. William O. Douglas, *Democracy and Finance* (New Haven, Conn.: Yale U. Press, 1940), p. 15.

47. Willard F. Mueller, "The New Attack on Antitrust," in A. A. Heggestad (ed.), *Public Policy Toward Corporations* (Gainesville, Fla.: University of Florida Press, 1987), pp. 53–79.

SUGGESTED READINGS

Books

Clinard, M. B., and P. C. Yeager. *Corporation Crime.* New York: The Free Press, 1980.

Connor, J. M., R. T. Rogers, B. W. Marison, and W. F. Mueller. *The Food Manufacturing Industries: Structure, Strategies, Performance and Policies.* Lexington, Mass: D.C. Heath Co., 1984.

Ravenscraft, David J., and F. M. Scherer. *Mergers, Sell-Offs, & Economic Efficiency.* Washington, D.C.: Brookings Institution, 1987.

Journal Articles

Bradford, Ralph M. "Conglomerate Power Without Market Power." *American Economic Review,* 70 (June 1980).

Deutsch, Larry L. "Entry and the Extent of Multiplant Operations." *Journal of Industrial Economics,* 32 (June 1984).

Mueller, Willard F., "A New Attack on Antitrust: The Chicago Case." *Antitrust Law & Economics Review,* 18 (1986).

Mueller, Willard F. "The ITT Settlement: A Deal with Justice?" *Industrial Organization Review,* 1 (1973).

Scott, John T., "Multimarket Contact and Economic Performance." *Review of Economics and Statistics,* 64 (1982).

Government Publications

Federal Trade Commission, Staff Report, *Economic Report on Corporate Mergers.* Washington, D.C.: U.S. Government Printing Office, 1969.

U.S. Congress, Senate, Subcommittee on Multinational Corporations. *The International Telephone and Telegraph Company and Chile, 1970–1972,* 93rd Cong., 1st sess., June 21, 1973.

CHAPTER 13
PUBLIC POLICY IN A FREE ENTERPRISE ECONOMY
Walter Adams

When Congress passed the Sherman Act of 1890, it created what was then—
and has largely remained—a uniquely American institution. Heralded as a
magna carta of economic freedom, the Sherman Act sought to preserve
competitive free enterprise by imposing legal prohibitions on monopoly and
restraint of trade. The objective of the act, according to Judge Learned
Hand, was not to condone *good* trusts or condemn *bad* trusts, but to forbid *all*
trusts. Its basic philosophy and principal purpose was "to perpetuate and
preserve, for its own sake and in spite of possible cost, an organization of
industry in small units which can effectively compete with each other." In
elaborating on the goals of the Sherman Act, Judge Hand stated: "Many
people believe that possession of unchallenged economic power deadens
initiative, discourages thrift, and depresses energy; that immunity from competition is a narcotic, and rivalry is a stimulant, to industrial progress; that the
spur of constant stress is necessary to counteract an inevitable disposition to
let well enough alone. Such people believe that competitors, versed in the
craft as no consumer can be, will be quick to detect opportunities for saving
and new shifts in production, and be eager to profit by them. . . . True, it
might have been thought adequate to condemn only those monopolies which
could not show that they had exercised the highest possible ingenuity, had
adopted every possible economy, had anticipated every conceivable improvement, stimulated every possible demand. . . . Be that as it may, that was not
the way that Congress chose; it did not condone 'good' trusts and condemn
'bad' ones; it forbade all. Moreover, in so doing it was not necessarily ac-
tuated by economic motives alone. It is possible, because of its indirect social
or moral effect, to prefer a system of small producers, each dependent for his
success upon his own skill and character, to one in which the great mass of
those engaged must accept the direction of a few. These considerations,
which we have suggested only as possible purposes of the Act, we think the
decisions prove to have been in fact its purposes."[1]

349

I.

THE ANTIMONOPOLY LAWS

Specifically, the Sherman Act outlaws two major types of interference with free enterprise: collusion and monopolization. Section 1 of the Act, dealing with collusion, states: "Every contract, combination . . . or conspiracy, in restraint of trade or commerce among the several States, or with foreign nations, is hereby declared illegal." As interpreted by the courts, this made it unlawful for businesses to engage in such collusive action as agreements to fix prices; agreements to restrict output or productive capacity; agreements to divide markets or allocate customers; agreements to exclude competitors by systematic resort to oppressive tactics and discriminatory policies — in short, any joint action by competitors to influence the market. Thus, Section 1 was, in a sense, a response to Adam Smith's warning that "people of the same trade seldom meet together even for merriment and diversion, but the conversation ends in a conspiracy against the public, or in some contrivance to raise prices."[2]

Section 2 of the Sherman Act, which deals with monopolization, provided that "Every person who shall monopolize or attempt to monopolize, or combine or conspire with any other person or persons to monopolize any part of the trade or commerce among the several States, or with foreign nations, shall be deemed guilty . . . and . . . punished." This meant that businesses were deprived of an important freedom, the freedom to monopolize. Section 2 made it unlawful for anyone to obtain a stranglehold on the market either by forcing rivals out of business or by absorbing them. It forbade a single firm (or group of firms acting jointly) to gain a substantially exclusive domination of an industry or a market area. Positively stated, Section 2 attempted to encourage an industry structure in which there are enough independent competitors to assure bona fide and effective market rivalry.

As is obvious from even a cursory examination of the Sherman Act, its provisions were general, perhaps even vague, and essentially negative. Directed primarily against *existing* monopolies and *existing* trade restraints, the Sherman Act could not cope with specific practices that were, and could be, used to effectuate the unlawful results. Armed with the power to dissolve existing monopolies, the enforcement authorities could not, under the Sherman Act, attack the *growth* of monopoly. They could not nip it in the bud. For this reason Congress passed, in 1914, supplementary legislation "to arrest the creation of trusts, conspiracies and monopolies *in their incipiency and before consummation.*"[3] In the Federal Trade Commission Act of 1914, Congress set up an independent regulatory commission to police the industrial field against "all unfair methods of competition." In the Clayton Act of the same year, Congress singled out four specific practices that past experience had shown to be favorite weapons of the would-be monopolist: (1) price discrimination—that is, local price cutting and cutthroat competition; (2) tying contracts and exclusive dealer arrangements; (3) the acquisition of stock in competing companies; and (4) the formation of interlocking directorships between competing corporations. These practices were to be unlawful whenever their effect was to substantially lessen competition or to create tendencies toward monopoly. Thus, price discrimination, for example, was not made illegal per se; it was to be illegal only if used as a systematic device for destroying competition—in a manner typical of the old Standard Oil and American Tobacco trusts.[4] The emphasis throughout was to be on prevention rather than cure. The hope was that—given the provisions of the 1914 laws to supplement the provisions of the Sherman Act—the antitrust authorities could effectively eliminate the economic evils against which the antitrust laws were directed. The thrust of the Celler–Kefauver Anti-Merger Act of 1950 was aimed at the same objectives.

II.

THE CHARGES AGAINST MONOPOLY

What those evils were never has been clearly stated and perhaps never has been clearly conceived by the sponsors of antitrust legislation. In general, however, the objections to monopoly and trade restraints—found in literally tons of antitrust literature—are of ancient vintage and can be summarized as follows:

1. *Monopoly affords the consumer little protection against exorbitant prices.* As Adam Smith put it, "The price of monopoly is, upon every occasion, the highest which can be got. The natural price, or the price of free competition, on the contrary, is the lowest which can be taken, not upon every occasion indeed, but for any considerable time taken together. The one is upon every occasion the highest which can be squeezed out of the buyers, of which, it is supposed, they will consent to give; the other is the lowest which the sellers can commonly afford to take, and at the same time continue their business."[5] The consumer is, under monopoly conditions, open prey to extortion and exploitation—protected only by such tenuous self-restraint as the monopolist may choose to exercise because of benevolence, irrationality, concern over government reprisals, or fear of potential competition.

The monopolist generally can charge all the traffic will bear, simply because the consumer has no alternative sources of supply. The consumer is forced to pay the monopolist's price, turn to a less desirable substitute, or go without. His freedom is impaired, because his range of choice is artificially limited (see Figure 13-1).

An example, while admittedly extreme, serves to illustrate this point. It involves tungsten carbide, a hard-metal composition of considerable importance in such industrial uses as cutting tools, dies, and so on. In 1927,

Figure 13-1 _____

Free competition versus price fixing.

Economics of a Free Market

Producers   Consumer

Economics of Security

Producers   Consumer

Source: Thurman W. Arnold, *Cartels or Free Enterprise?* Public Affairs Pamphlet No. 103, 1945. Reproduced by courtesy of Public Affairs Commission, Inc.

tungsten carbide sold in the United States at $50 per pound; but after a world monopoly was established by General Electric (GE) and Friedrich Krupp A.G., of Germany, under which GE was granted the right to set prices in the American market, the price promptly rose to a maximum of $453 per pound. During most of the 1930s the price fluctuated between $225 and $453 per pound, and not until 1942—when an indictment was issued under the antitrust laws—did the price come down. Thereafter, it fluctuated between $27 and $45 per pound.[6]

2. *Monopoly causes a restriction of economic opportunity and a misallocation of productive resources.* Under free competition, it is the consumer who, through his dollar votes in the marketplace, decides how society's land, labor, and capital are to be used. Consumer tastes generally determine whether more cotton and less wool, more cigarettes and less pipe tobacco, or more aluminum and less steel shall be produced. Under free competition, the consumer

is in this strategic position because businesses must, if they want to make profits, do as the consumer demands. Because a business, under competition, is free to enter any field and to produce any type and quantity of goods it desires, the tendency will be for it to do those things that the consuming public (in its wisdom or ignorance) deems most valuable. In short, under a truly competitive system, the business can improve itself only by serving others. It can earn profits only by obeying the wishes of the community as expressed in the market.

Under monopoly, by contrast, the individual business finds its freedom of enterprise limited. It cannot do as it pleases, because the monopolist has the power of excluding newcomers or stipulating the terms under which newcomers are permitted to survive in an industry. The monopolist can interfere with a consumer-oriented allocation of resources. It, instead of the market, can determine the type and quantity of goods that shall be produced. It, and not the forces of supply and demand, can decree who shall produce what, for whom, and at what price. In the absence of competition, it is the monopolist who decides what *other* businesses shall be allowed to do and what benefits the consuming public shall be allowed to receive.

A good illustration of this is the Hartford-Empire Company, which once was an undisputed monopolist in the glass-bottle industry. Through its patent control over glass-bottling machinery, Hartford-Empire held life-and-death power both over the producers already in the industry and those attempting to enter it. As one observer described the situation,[7] Hartford had become benevolent despot to the glass container. Only by its leave could a firm come into the industry; the ticket of admission was to be had only upon its terms; and from its studied decision there was no appeal. The candidate had to subscribe to Hartford's articles of faith; it could not be a price cutter or a troublemaker. It could not venture beyond its assigned bailiwick or undermine the market of its partners in the conspiracy. Each concern had to accept the restrictions and limitations imposed by Hartford. Thus, the Buck Glass Company was authorized to manufacture wine bottles for sacramental purposes only. The Sayre Glass Works was restricted to producing "such bottles, jugs, and demijohns as are used for vinegar, ciders, sirups, bleaching fluids, hair tonics, barber supplies, and fluid extracts." Knox Glass Bottle Company was allowed to make only amber-colored ginger ale bottles. Mary Card Glass Company could not make products weighing more than 82 ounces. Baurens Glass Works Inc. was licensed to provide bottles for castor oil and turpentine, but none to exceed 4 ounces in capacity. Here, indeed, was a shackling of free enterprise and a usurpation of the market—a private government more powerful than that of many states. Here, indeed, was a tight little island, where the law of the monopolist was supreme and unchallenged. Only through antitrust prosecution were the channels of trade reopened and the Hartford dictatorship dissipated.[8]

3. *Monopoly often restrains technological advances and, thus, impedes eco-*

nomic progress. As Clair Wilcox points out, "The monopolist may engage in research and invent new materials, methods, and machines, but he will be reluctant to make use of these inventions if they would compel him to scrap existing equipment or if he believes that their ultimate profitability is in doubt. He may introduce innovations and cut costs, but instead of moving goods by price reduction he is prone to spend large sums on alternative methods of promoting sales; his refusal to cut prices deprives the community of any gain. The monopolist may voluntarily improve the quality of his product and reduce its price, but no threat of competition compels him to do so."[9]

Our experience with the hydrogenation and synthetic rubber processes is a case in point. This, one of the less illustrious chapters in our industrial history, dates back to 1926, when I. G. Farben of Germany developed the hydrogenation process for making oil out of coal — a development that obviously threatened the entrenched position of the major international oil companies. Soon after this process was patented, Standard Oil Company of New Jersey (now Exxon) concluded an agreement with I. G. Farben, under which Farben promised to stay out of the world's oil business (except inside Germany) and Standard agreed to stay out of the world's chemical business. "By this agreement, control of the hydrogenation process for making oil outside Germany was transferred to the Standard Oil Company in order that Standard's petroleum investment might be fully protected. In the United States, Standard licensed only the large oil companies which had no interest in exploiting hydrogenation. Outside the United States, Standard . . . proceeded to limit use of the process so far as the threat of competing processes and governmental interest [of foreign countries] permitted."[10] As a result, this revolutionary process was almost completely suppressed, except in Germany, where it became an effective tool for promoting the military ambitions of the Nazi government.

The development of synthetic rubber production in the United States was similarly retarded by the Farben–Standard marriage of 1928. Because Buna rubber, under the agreement of 1928, was considered a chemical process, it came under the exclusive control of I. G. Farben — both in and outside Germany. Farben, however, was not interested in promoting the manufacture of synthetic rubber anywhere except in Germany, and proceeded, therefore — both for commercial (that is, monopolistic) and nationalistic reasons — to forestall its development in the United States. Farben had, at least, the tacit support of its American partner. As a result, the outbreak of World War II found the United States without production experience or know-how in the vital synthetic rubber field. In fact, when the Goodrich and Goodyear tire companies attempted to embark on synthetic rubber production, the former was sued for patent infringement and the latter formally threatened with such a suit by Standard Oil Company (acting under the authority of the Farben patents). This happened in November 1941, one month before Pearl Harbor. Not until after our formal entry into World War II was the Farben–Standard alliance broken under the impact of antitrust prosecution, and the production of vital synthetic rubber started in the United States. Here, as in the case of hydrogenation, monopolistic control over technology had serious implications not only for the nation's economic progress but also for its military security.[11]

4. *Monopoly tends to impede the effectiveness of general stabilization measures and to distort their structural impact on the economy.* Monopolistic and oligopolistic firms, as John Kenneth Galbraith suggests, may insulate themselves against credit restrictions designed to curb investment and check inflation. They may do so by raising prices to offset higher interest costs, by raising prices to finance investment out of increased profits, or by resorting to the capital market rather than to banks for their supply of loanable funds. Competitive firms, by contrast, cannot raise prices to compensate for higher interest charges. They cannot raise prices to finance investment out of higher profits. They cannot readily turn to the capital market for funds. Their lack of market control makes them the weakest borrowers and poorest credit risks, and they must, therefore, bear the brunt of any "tight-money" policy. In short, monopolistic and oligopolistic firms not only can undermine the effectiveness of monetary control in their sector of the economy, but also shift the burden of credit restrictions to the competitive sector and, thus, stifle its growth. The implications for concentration need not be belabored.[12]

5. *Monopoly threatens not only the existence of a free economy, but also the survival chances of free political institutions.* Enterprise that is not competitive cannot for long remain free, and a community that refuses to accept the discipline of competition inevitably exposes itself to the discipline of absolute authority. As Henry Simons once observed, the enemy of democracy is monopoly in all its forms, and political liberty can survive only within an effective competitive system. If concentrated power is tolerated, giant pressure groups will ultimately gain control of the government or the government will institute direct regulation of organized pressure groups. In either event, free enterprise will then have to make way for collectivism, and democracy will be superseded by some form of authoritarianism.[13]

This objection to monopoly, this fear of concentrated economic power, is deeply rooted in American traditions—the tradition of federalism, the separation of church and state, and the tripartite organization of our governmental machinery. It is the expression of a sociopolitical philosophy of the decentralization of power; a broad base for the class structure of society; and the economic freedom and opportunity for new firms, new ideas, and new organizations to spearhead the forces of progress. It stands in stark contrast to the older European varieties of free enterprise, which merely involve curbs on governmental powers without similar checks on excessive private power.[14] The seriousness of the danger is not easy to evaluate. "Who can say whether any particular warning is due to overcautiousness, timidity, or even superstition or, on the other hand, to prudence and foresight? . . . It is, of course, possible that 'monopoly' is merely a bugbear frightening the believers in free enterprise and free society; but it is equally possible that we have underestimated the danger and have allowed the situation to deteriorate to such a degree that only a very radical effort can still save our social and political system."[15]

III.

THE CHALLENGE OF ECONOMIC DARWINISM AND THE NEW LAISSEZ-FAIRE

In recent years, it has become fashionable to deprecate the traditional philosophy underlying the antitrust laws and to urge its replacement by a latter-day economic Darwinism. The leaders of this movement—primarily members of the Chicago School—treat property rights and freedom of contract as near-absolutes and believe that untrammeled laissez-faire will assure a natural selection of what is best and most worthy—a survival of the fittest.

Professor Robert H. Bork, probably the most incisive and sophisticated exponent of the *nouvelle vague,* sees a striking analogy between a free market system and the Darwinian theory of natural selection and physical evolution.[16] Says Bork: "The familiarity of that parallel, and the overbroad inferences sometimes drawn from it, should not blind us to its important truths. The environment to which the business firm must adapt is defined, ultimately, by social wants and the social costs of meeting them. The firm that adapts to the environment better than its rivals tends to expand. The less successful firm tends to contract—perhaps, eventually, to become extinct. The Stanley Steamer and the celluloid collar have gone the way of the pterodactyl and the great ground sloth, basically for the same reasons. Since coping successfully with the economic environment also forwards consumer welfare (except in those cases that are the legitimate concern of antitrust), economic and natural selection has normative implications that physical natural selection does not have. At least there seems to be more reasons for enthusiasm about the efficient firm than about the most successful physical organisms, the rat and the cockroach, though this view is, no doubt, parochial."[17]

There is little justification, Professor Bork argues, to interfere with the "natural" operation of a free market system. Laissez-faire, he says, can be trusted to produce optimum results in the operation of the system: "It is a common observation of biologists that whenever the physical environment provides a niche capable of sustaining life, an organism will evolve or adapt to occupy the place. The same is true of economic organisms, hence the fantastic proliferation of forms of business organization, products, and services in our society. . . . To expand, or even to survive, every firm requires a constant flow of capital for employees' wages, raw material, capital investment, repairs, advertising, and the like. When the firm is relatively inefficient over a significant time period, it represents a poorer investment and greater credit risk than innumerable alternatives. If the firm is dependent upon outside capital, the firm must shrink, and, if no revival in its fortunes occurs, die."[18] Monopoly or market power, according to Bork, are of little social concern because neither is endowed with significant durability: "A market position that creates output restriction and higher prices will always be eroded if it is not based upon superior efficiency."[19] Of course, if it is based on superior efficiency, Bork would say that it serves the best interest of consumers and should, therefore, be immune from public attack.

In this view, then, a firm achieves market power or giant size because of superior efficiency, and it would be wrongheaded for public policy to punish such a firm for its success. The winner of the race deserves the prize—the right to take all he can get. He won the race because he was the best, and punishing him would deprive others of incentives to excel. Punishing industrial success, the Darwinists argue, would not only lessen competition, but would inevitably result in a diminution of consumer welfare. Besides, the successful firm will retain its dominance only as long as its performance remains superior. As soon as it becomes slothful, lethargic, inefficient, or unprogressive, it will surely be replaced by greedy newcomers aspiring to preeminence and leadership.

This doctrine of economic Darwinism, which seems to have become official U.S. government policy during the 1980s, suffers from several defects:

1. It is based on the *post hoc ergo propter hoc* fallacy. It assumes that a monopolist, oligopolist, or conglomerate giant has achieved its market position exclusively or predominantly because of superior performance. This is no more than an assertion—devoid, more often than not, of any empirical substantiation.

2. Although economic Darwinism makes superior economic performance the centerpiece of its policy position, its supporters concede that economic performance is difficult, if not impossible, to measure scientifically. Professor Bork, for example, concedes that "the real objection to performance tests and efficiency defenses in antitrust law is that they are spurious. They cannot measure the factors relevant to consumer welfare, so that after the economic extravaganza was completed we should know no more than before it began. In saying this I am taking issue with some highly qualified authorities. Carl Kaysen and Donald Turner proposed that 'an unreasonable degree of market power as such must be made illegal,' and they suggested that all the relevant dimensions of performance be studied. Their idea, essentially, is that a court or agency determine, through a litigation process, whether there exists in a particular industry a persistent divergence between

price and marginal cost; the approximate size of the divergence; whether breaking up, say, eight firms into sixteen would reduce or eliminate the divergence; and whether any significant efficiencies would be destroyed by the dissolution."[20] Bork seems to despair about the possibility of measuring performance even though he posits superior performance as the ultimate goal of economic activity.

3. The new Darwinism is concerned primarily with static, managerial efficiency rather than with dynamic social efficiency. It thus falls victim to the sin of suboptimization. The relevant policy question is not whether General Motors produces automobiles powered by the internal combustion engine at the lowest possible cost, but whether it should be producing such automobiles at all. The relevant policy question is whether the tight oligopoly that presently controls the U.S. automobile industry is more likely to "reinvent the automobile" — a safer, more fuel-efficient, more pollution-free prototype — than a competitively structured automobile industry.

4. The new Darwinism assumes that any firm that no longer delivers superior efficiency will automatically be displaced by newcomers. This underestimates the ability of established firms to build private storm shelters — or to induce the government to build public storm shelters for them — to shield them from the Schumpeterian gales of creative destruction. It ignores the difference between legal freedom of entry and the economic realities barring the entry of potential newcomers to concentrated industries. It underestimates the ability of powerful firms in concentrated industries to parlay economic power into political power to insulate their dominance from competitive erosion. Here, as elsewhere, the economic Darwinists are so wedded to formal logic that they carry their logic one step beyond the realm of realistic applicability.

5. Economic Darwinism fails to make the crucial distinction between individual freedom and a free economic *system*. As Bentham pointed out, it is not enough to shout laissez-faire and oppose all government intervention: "To say that a law is contrary to natural liberty is simply to say that it is a law: for every law is established at the expense of liberty — the liberty of Peter at the expense of the liberty of Paul."[21] If individual rights were absolute and unlimited, they would mean license to commit the grossest abuses against society, including license to curb the freedom of others. Moreover, as Lord Robbins suggests, public policy must "distinguish between [government] interventions that destroy the need for intervention and interventions that tend to perpetuate it."[22]

Viewed in this light, Professor Bork's admonition not to penalize the winner of the race is quite irrelevant for policy purposes. The relevant policy problem is how to reward the winner without including in his trophy the right to impose disabling handicaps on putative competitors, or the power to determine the rules by which future races shall be run, or the discretion to terminate the institution of racing altogether. The policy challenge is how to maximize a *bundle* of freedoms and opportunity, not only at a point in time but over the long run as well.

6. Finally, the new economic Darwinism fails to appreciate the linkage between industrial structure and market behavior and the consequences, ultimately, for economic performance. As John Bates Clark warned more than half a century ago, "In our worship of the survival of the fit under free natural selection we are sometimes in danger of forgetting that the conditions of the struggle fix the kind of fitness that shall come out of it; that survival in the prize ring means fitness for pugilism, not for bricklaying nor philanthropy; that survival in predatory competition is likely to mean something else than fitness for good and efficient production; and that only from strife with the right kind of rules can the right kind of fitness emerge. Competition is a game played under rules fixed by the state to the end that, so far as possible, the prize of victory shall be earned, not by trickery or mere self-seeking adroitness, but by value rendered. It is not the mere play of unrestrained self-interest; it is a method of harnessing the wild beast of self-interest to serve a common good—a thing of ideals and not of sordidness. It is not a natural state, but like any other form of liberty, it is a social achievement, and eternal vigilance is the price of it."[23]

The fundamental objective of antitrust is not only—as the economic Darwinists contend—to promote efficiency and consumer welfare. These are ancillary benefits that are expected to flow from economic freedom. The primary purpose of antitrust is to perpetuate and preserve, in spite of possible cost, a *system of governance* for a competitive, free enterprise economy. It is a system of governance in which power is decentralized, in which newcomers with new products and new techniques have a genuine opportunity to introduce themselves and their ideas, in which the "unseen hand" of competition instead of the heavy hand of the state performs the basic regulatory function on behalf of society.

Antitrust, like the political system prescribed by our Constitution, calls for a dispersion of power, buttressed by built-in checks and balances, to protect individuals from potential abuse of power and to preserve not only individual freedom but, more importantly, a free system. According to antitrust precepts—to paraphrase Justice William O. Douglas—power that controls the economy should not be in the hands of an industrial oligarchy. Since all power tends to develop into a government in itself, industrial power should be decentralized. It should be scattered into many hands so that the fortunes of the people will not be dependent on the whim or caprice, the political prejudices, the emotional stability of a few self-appointed men. The fact that they are not vicious men but respectable and social-minded is irrelevant. That is the philosophy and the command of the antitrust laws.

They are founded on a theory of hostility to the concentration in private hands of power so great that even a government of the people can be trusted to have it only in exceptional circumstances.[24]

Antitrust, then, is — above all — a *system of governance.* It is a system for distributing and harnessing economic power. It is a traditional and peculiarly American response to the perennial questions of social organization: Who shall make what decisions on whose behalf at what cost and for whose benefit? To whom shall the decision makers be accountable, and what safeguards shall be built into the system to guard against abuse?

The competitive market, of course, is the prime instrument for implementing the antitrust philosophy. It is to make social decisions. It is to function as the regulatory mechanism in the economy. It is to serve as the safeguard of the public interest. But the competitive market is not an academic model-builder's abstraction adumbrated in basic economic tests. Nor is it — contrary to the preachments of the Chicago School — a gift of nature. It is a social artifact that must be nurtured by constant vigilance and shielded from private subversion (collusion, predation, exclusion, and concentration) as well as governmental subversion (the public storm shelters built to protect special interests from the Schumpterian gales of creative destruction). In short, the competitive market can perform its social role only under certain structural and behavioral preconditions. And the maintenance of these preconditions is the function of antitrust.

IV.
THE NEW LAISSEZ-FAIRE IN ACTION[25]

With the advent of the Reagan Administration in 1981, economic Darwinism and the "new laissez-faire" were enshrined as official government policy. The "new learning" doctrines of the Chicago School became holy writ, and served as the official rationalizations for one of the most spectacular merger movements in American industrial history.

The statistics summarized in Table 13-1, tell the story: The combined reported value of corporate mergers and acquisitions totaled two-thirds of a trillion dollars over the years 1980–86, while the rate of individual mergers involving assets of more than $1 billion escalated tenfold. In all, fully 75 of the 100 largest corporate mergers in American history were consummated between 1981 and 1984.

As these statistics imply, the nation's very largest firms have been the principal protagonists in this merger mania. They have not only bought small- and medium-sized firms, but increasingly have merged with one another. During the Reagan era, DuPont (the 15th largest industrial firm in the nation at the time of the merger) acquired Conoco (the 14th largest at the time of the acquisition); United States Steel (the 19th largest) acquired Marathon Oil

Table 13-1

Value of Corporate Acquisitions (1980–88)

Year	No. of Acquisitions	Total Reported Value (in billions)	No. of Takeovers ($1 billion or more)
1980	1565	$ 33.06	3
1981	2326	$ 66.96	8
1982	2295	$ 60.39	9
1983	2345	$ 52.25	7
1984	3064	$125.23	19
1985	3165	$139.13	26
1986	4022	$190.00	34
1987	3701	$167.50	—
1988	3487	$226.60	—

Source: Information published in *Mergers & Acquisitions*. Information on value compiled only for those transactions for which a purchase price is available.

(the 39th largest); Occidental Petroleum (the 20th largest) acquired Iowa Beef Processors (the 81st largest); Allied Corporation (the 55th largest) acquired both Bendix (the 86th largest) and Signal companies (the 61st largest); Standard Brands (the 128th largest) and Nabisco (the 152nd largest) merged, and the resulting firm Nabisco Brands (the 54th largest) was merged into R.J. Reynolds (the 23rd largest); Philip Morris (the 32nd largest) and General Foods (the 39th largest) merged; and General Electric (the 9th largest) acquired RCA the (2nd largest diversified service company, including the NBC network).

Consolidation between large firms in the same industries has been equally dramatic. The petroleum industry has, since 1980, witnessed mergers between Occidental Petroleum and Cities Service (the 12th and 19th largest oil firms); Texaco and Getty Oil (the 3rd and 13th largest oil firms); and Chevron and Gulf (the 5th and 6th largest oil firms). Also notable have been the 1984 merger between Mobil, the 2nd largest integrated oil company, and Superior Oil, the nation's largest independent explorer and producer of oil and natural gas; and Occidental's acquisition of Midcon, one of the nation's largest gas pipeline operators. In airlines, the Administration has presided over a massive consolidation movement concentrating the field in the hands of a few megacarriers. (See Chapter 8.) Concentration and consolidation through mergers among large firms in the same industries also have been permitted in paper, consumer appliances, and video entertainment.

In addition, the Administration has permitted U.S. firms to merge with their largest foreign rivals. For example, L'Air Liquide, a French firm and the world's largest producer of industrial gases, has acquired Big Three Industries, a leading American industrial gas producer. Through its acquisition of Glidden (at the time, the 3rd largest paint producer in the U.S.), the British firm ICI has become the world's largest paint maker. Hoechst, a German

chemical group, has acquired U.S. Celanese. Union Carbide sold its agricultural chemicals operations to Rhone-Poulenc, a leading French producer of
inter alia agricultural chemicals. Electrolux, the largest producer of appliances in Europe, has acquired White Consolidated Industries (formerly the
3rd largest appliance maker in the U.S.). B. P. Nutrition Ltd., Europe's
largest feed company, acquired Purina Mills, the largest commercial feed
company in the U.S. Unilever and Chesebrough-Ponds (leading British and
American consumer products firms) have merged, as have Nestle and Carna-
tion (both leading food products concerns). Perrier, the world's largest pur-
veyor of mineral water, has acquired five U.S. mineral water concerns, including Arrowhead, the largest U.S. processor and distributor of bottled
water. Britain's largest glassmaker, Pilkington Brothers, has acquired Libbey-
Owens-Ford's U.S. glass production operations. And Grand Metropolitan
PLC, one of the world's largest distillers, has acquired Heublein, the 2nd
largest producer of wines and spirits in the American market.

At the same time — but not included in these merger statistics — the
Administration has countenanced quasi-consolidations, or "joint ventures,"
between the American automobile oligopoly and most of its major foreign
rivals: GM/Toyota; GM/Daewoo; GM/Suzuki; GM/Isuzu; GM/Lotus; Ford/
Mazda; Ford/Mazda/Kia; Ford/Volkswagen; Chrysler/Mitsubishi; Chrysler/
Mitsubishi/Hyundai; Chrysler/Samsung; and Chrysler/Maserati.

Finally, the Administration pursued an active policy of nonenforcement.
Overall, according to one recent count, the Justice Department challenged
only a handful of the approximately 10,000 merger applications filed with it
during the 1980s. In the few instances where mergers were challenged,
Professor Eleanor Fox points out, "almost all were settled upon the filing of a
complaint along with a consent decree, requiring only minor divestiture or
other obligations."[26] Budgets and staff were drastically reduced. Between
1981 and 1987, the number of attorneys in the Antitrust Division was slashed
by 44 percent; the agency's full-time staff (including economists, paralegals
and clerical/secretarial support) was cut by 39 percent; and further personnel reductions were planned, so that by 1988 the staff would be little more
than half of what it was when President Reagan took office in 1981.

From the outset, the Administration assiduously sought to vitiate Section
7, or abolish it altogether. William F. Baxter, President Reagan's first chief of
the Justice Department Antitrust Division, candidly articulated the Administration's position. "Merger activity in general," he opined, "is a very, very
important feature of our capital markets by which assets are continuously
moved into the hands of those managers who can employ them efficiently."
Interfering with mergers "would be an error of very substantial magnitude."
He dismissed concerns about excessive concentrations of economic size and
power. "There is nothing written in the sky that says that the world would not
be a perfectly satisfactory place if there were only 100 companies. . . . I
certainly do not see a war against aggregate concentration as part of this

department's mission." He declared that in evaluating the legality of mergers, an "industry trend toward concentration is not a factor that will be considered. . . ." He told Congress that "vertical and conglomerate mergers have ceased to be a major enforcement focus of the [Antitrust] Division." And Mr. Baxter defiantly announced his break with legal precedent in these respects, admitting, "It's perfectly true that I am disregarding some of the things that the Supreme Court and other courts have from time to time said about the antitrust laws."[27]

The Administration pressed the assault with relentless determination all along the battle front. Attorney General William French Smith declared, "Bigness doesn't necessarily mean badness." His successor, Edwin Meese III, pronounced that loosening restrictions on corporate mergers would "make the United States more competitive." Charles F. Rule, later chief of the Antitrust Division, warned, "It's important we don't stop mergers based on some ephemeral fear of cost to society, when we might be foregoing substantial efficiencies." Rule's successor, Douglas H. Ginsburg, announced, "we are not concerned with aggregate concentration or with absolute size," adding that he "never saw a conglomerate merger that [he] disliked that much."

The late Malcolm Baldrige, Secretary of Commerce, was perhaps the Administration's most indefatigable champion of corporate consolidation. "The world economy has changed," he tirelessly reiterated, "trade patterns have changed, but the antitrust laws have not. It is not just that some parts of those laws are irrelevant today; it is the fact that they place additional and unnecessary burdens on the ability of U.S. firms to compete." He argued, "Repeal of Clayton 7 will increase the efficiency of U.S. firms and strengthen their competitiveness in world markets." He exhorted Congress not to be deterred by what he called "outdated notions about firm size."

The Administration's verbal attack was soon translated into action (or more accurately, inaction). With considerable fanfare the Justice Department unveiled its Merger Guidelines in 1982. They were a triumph of technocratese. Traditional concentration ratios were declared to be *déclassé* in merger analysis. Instead, modernization was said to dictate that merger guidelines be cast in terms of "Hirschman-Herfindahl Indexes," replete with mathematically precise pre- and post-merger "safe" zones, "danger" zones, and intermediate zones.

Camouflaged by the hubris of scientism and numerology, the new guidelines marked a significant departure from established merger policy. First, as the Justice Department admitted in 1984, the guidelines significantly relaxed merger policy. According to DOJ: "The 1982 Guidelines did *not* simply clarify the Department's merger policy. . . . One of the most important advances of the 1982 Guidelines was the increased freedom they gave to American industries to enhance efficiency through mergers. Implicit throughout the Guidelines," Justice asserted, "is the recognition that the efficiency-enhancing potential of mergers can increase the competitiveness of firms and result in lower prices to consumers." Second, for all practical purposes, the Guidelines largely exempted vertical and conglomerate mergers from prosecution. Third, by greatly overstating the breadth of product and geographic markets, therefore understating the degree of market power, the new methodology for defining "relevant" markets almost inevitably permitted even the largest mergers to pass prosecutorial muster. That emasculation, not "modernization," was the primary objective is evidenced, not only in the guidelines themselves, but by the Administration's subsequent willingness to permit mergers that violated them.

In 1986, the Administration launched its "Merger Modernization Act," a broadside effort to have Congress transmogrify Section 7 by legislative action. Once again, the rationale was the Administration's belief that "mergers, in general, have important procompetitive and efficiency-enhancing effects," and that merger policy should "not interfere with the ability of American firms freely to reorganize through mergers and acquisitions."

In addition, the Administration proposed companion legislation empowering the President to grant antitrust immunity for mergers and acquisitions in import-impacted industries. In these cases, too, the Administration believed that unrestricted corporate consolidation would "strengthen American firms' abilities to compete with imports."

This public policy posture leaves a number of crucial questions unanswered.

1. Is Economic Power Benign?

1. Is Economic Power Benign? Implicit in the new laissez-faire, and undergirding it, are the interrelated assumptions that economic power is a rarity; that it is largely innocuous in the rare instances where it operates; and that free market forces will almost always nullify it, so long as government refrains from intervening. In other words, the free market is an all-powerful, ubiquitous regulator of economic affairs and guardian of the public interest.

This view is not only incongruent with contemporary facts, but a mythical rendition of industrial history. The "free market" was hardly an effective regulator of Rockefeller's Standard Oil Trust — an industrial combine that effectively controlled some 90 percent of the American oil industry. The "free market" did not prevent Eastman Kodak from forcing exclusive dealership arrangements on more than 90 percent of the nation's photographic products dealers, or monopolizing color photo-finishing, or obstructing camera innovation for decades. The "free market" did not prevent the Big Five motion picture studios (Paramount, Loew's, RKO, Warner Bros., 20th Century-Fox) from gaining a group monopoly over more than 70 percent of big city, first-run theaters across the country, and exercising vertical monopoly control over the production, distribution and exhibition of motion pictures. The "free market" never succeeded in curbing the American automobile oligopoly that for decades tacitly colluded to suppress safety innovations, tacitly colluded to withhold small fuel-efficient models, and explicitly colluded in a cartel designed to retard innovation and commercialization of automotive smog controls. Contrary to the "new laissez-faire" doctrine, the free market is *not* immutable and omnipotent. It *is* susceptible to erosion and subversion from within by powerful private interests bent on evading its regulatory discipline. Vertical and conglomerate power are not optical illusions. Nor is economic power fleeting or inconsequential.

But the problem of economic power is not limited to economic affairs narrowly construed. In a representative democracy, disproportionate economic size has *political* consequences in the public policy arena as well. Once they attain massive size, corporate bigness complexes unavoidably wield political power. Once they attain giant size, corporate bigness complexes can mobilize the vast political resources at their command—executives and employees, subcontractors and suppliers, governors and mayors, senators and representatives, Republicans and Democrats—to capture government agencies and pervert public policy. By virtue of their disproportionate size, they can manipulate the state to insulate themselves from the compulsions and discipline of the competitive market. They can elicit precisely the kinds of antisocial government interventions that the "new laissez-faire" devotees so vociferously decry.

Corporate bigness complexes, typically acting in concert with powerful labor unions, can compel the state to immunize them from foreign competition, and to protect them from the self-inflicted consequences of their own deplorable performance, but at exorbitant cost to the public (as in the case of the steel quotas and "voluntary" Japanese auto import restraints). Corporate bigness complexes can lobby the state for succor, subsidy and financial sustenance (as the commercial nuclear power industry has done for decades). They can extract tax favors, tax privileges and tax loopholes from government. They can usurp the power of the market (or government) to act as a planning agent, but with no safeguards to insure that their own planning will be in the public interest. And if they are big enough and incompetent enough, they can demand the ultimate perversion of free enterprise, government bailouts, because they are considered to be too big to be allowed to fail. They can assure their survival, not because they are better, but because they are *bigger* (or as a cynic would put it, not because they are fitter, but because they are fatter).

For the economic power problems which bedevil a representative democracy, the "new laissez-faire" has no answers, save for making government less responsive and less accountable to the citizenry. The modern *deus ex machina*, "global competition," is hardly a solution, when large powerful firms can neutralize foreign competition by lobbying the state for special interest protectionist policies in the form of tariffs, quotas, "voluntary" import restraints, "orderly" marketing agreements and the like. Instead, as the conservative British *Economist* points out, "in a political system where special interests hold sway, big really can be bad."

2. Does Merger-Induced Giantism Promote Good Economic Performance?

2. Does Merger-Induced Giantism Promote Good Economic Performance? Contrary to "new laissez-faire" ideology, the weight of empirical evidence suggests that merger mania and corporate bigness do *not* enhance economic performance. Instead, the evidence suggests that more often than not they undermine efficiency in production, sabotage innovation and technological advance, and compound, rather than cure, America's competitiveness problem.

In American steel, bigness is the product of decades of virtually untrammeled mergers and consolidations, beginning at the turn of the century, and continuing to the present day. But merger-induced bigness has been anything but a panacea for Big Steel. Today it is an easy target, not only for foreign competitors, but for vastly smaller, nonintegrated, superefficient, hyperadvanced U.S. "minimill" producers. These small, efficient, innovative minimills have prevailed in the market, not only against domestic giants, but against such "awesome" rivals as "Japan Inc."; they have driven foreign producers from the American markets in which they compete. The collapse of the LTV-Republic combine into bankruptcy in 1986 (only two years after its formation) underscores the point that merger-induced giantism does not guarantee good economic performance.

In automobiles, General Motors (itself the product of numerous mergers and acquisitions) has long stood as the world's largest auto concern. Measured in dollar volume, its annual sales exceed those of the two largest Japanese auto companies combined. But bigness has been a liability, not an asset, for the firm: GM suffers the highest per-car production costs in the industry. Its high degree of vertical integration in parts production impairs the firm's flexibility and adaptability. Indeed, by its own admission, GM has been forced to turn to "joint ventures" with smaller foreign rivals in a struggle to learn how to make cars economically. According to *Business Week,* the "basic question nagging this biggest, most diverse, and most integrated of car companies is whether it is just too big to compete in today's fast-changing car market."[28]

Giant U.S. conglomerates have fared no better. Far from unleashing a synergistic *elan vital,* they have enmeshed American industry in a snarl of ill-fitted bureaucratic disorder. In fact, giant conglomerates like ITT and Gulf+Western (now Paramont Communications), which gorged themselves on acquisitions in the 1960s and 1970s, are today divesting hundreds of previously acquired operations. As summarized by Donald P. Jacobs, dean of Northwestern University's Kellogg School of Management: "The thinking used to be that once a conglomerate was put together, the whole was more valuable than the parts. Now the parts seem more valuable than the whole."[29]

Nor are megamergers felicitous instruments for inducing innovation and technological advance. In a recent cover story, for example, the *Wall Street Journal* reports that the "vast majority of acquisitions of high-technology companies by large corporations [including Exxon, Raytheon, Burroughs, 3M, and Westinghouse] have ended in disaster." An important reason? The "giants' many layers of bureaucracy often paralyze the free-wheeling entrepreneurial style typical in the high tech world."[30] Conversely, innovativeness is observed to substantially increase among divested operations and management buyouts, once they are freed from the chokehold of bureaucratic parental control.

Generalized statistical studies further support these findings. Based upon their extensive analyses, David Ravenscraft and F. M. Scherer find that the average merger is followed by deteriorating profit performance, that these productivity and efficiency losses cast doubt on the efficiency-enhancing faith in mergers, that there is no credible evidence that mergers enhance research and development (R&D) and technological performance, that the adverse performance consequences of mergers have been responsible for a not inconsiderable part of declining productivity in the U.S. economy, and that in the case of leading acquisition-active conglomerate firms, "investors got less return on average with more risk." The implication of these findings, they conclude, is "a skeptical public policy stance toward mergers."[31]

Summarizing his statistical studies Dennis C. Mueller reports: *"No* support was found for the hypothesis that mergers improve efficiency. . . ."[32] In their general survey of mergers and takeovers, Edward S. Herman and Louis Lowenstein find: "Almost as often as not the performance of [corporate acquisition] targets exceeded that of the successful bidders. Furthermore, while there were performance improvements in the early acquisitions in our study period, the post-merger performance deteriorated sharply in the later ones." Murray Weidenbaum, former chief of President Reagan's Council of Economic Advisers, reports from his statistical studies that "the widely held belief that shareholders generally benefit from takeovers does *not* hold up to serious analysis."[33] And with respect to import-impacted industries, a Federal Trade Commission study finds that the "evidence suggests that mergers may not be a more significant source of efficiencies in declining industries than in industries generally," and that "the results do not indicate that mergers are a particularly efficient form of rationalization."[34]

The untoward performance consequences of merger mania are also reflected in the startlingly high failure rate for corporate mergers and acquisitions. As summarized by *Business Week,* "a half to two-thirds of all mergers don't work; one in three is later undone. In 1985, for every seven acquisitions, there were three divestitures."[35] Similarly, a McKinsey & Co. study of the merger record of 56 large U.S. firms over the period 1972–83 concludes that most (39 of 56) of the firms "that embark on diversification programs fail," and that the danger of failure is greatest for "large unrelated acquisitions."[36] According to Peter Drucker, two mergers out of five are "outright disasters," two "neither live nor die," and one "works."[37]

Especially revealing is the recent study by Professor Michael E. Porter who examined the merger and diversification record of 33 large, prestigious U.S. firms over the 1950–86 period. Porter found "that most of them had divested many more acquisitions than they had kept," and that "the corporate strategies of most companies have dissipated instead of created shareholder value"—in short, that the track record of their acquisition strategies has been "dismal."[38]

Clearly, then, merger-induced giantism scarcely marks the path to enhanced economic performance. This evidence is not new. In one analysis of the turn-of-the-century merger movement in the United States, for example, nearly one-half of the consolidations consummated between 1888 and 1905 were found to have subsequently failed; if "success" attributable to patents and monopoly power is excluded, the failure rate exceeded 50 percent.

Nor is evidence regarding the failures of merger-induced giantism limited to the United States. Beginning in the 1950s, and for two decades thereafter, Western European governments encouraged merger and consolidation in order (they believed) to create corporate colossi capable of competing against giant American firms. But the results (such as British Steel and British Leyland) have proven disastrous. As summarized by Geroski and Jacquemin, "The new super-firms do not give rise to a new competitive efficiency in Europe. Indeed, by creating a group of firms with sufficient market power to be considerably sheltered from the forces of market selection, the policy may have left Europe with a population of sleepy industrial giants who were ill-equipped to meet the challenge of the 1970s and 1980s."[39]

These facts are no longer a secret—at least among practical people in the real world. Prominent business periodicals have been ablaze in recent years with articles carrying such revealing titles as "Smaller is Beautiful Now in Manufacturing," "Do Mergers Really Work?" (the magazine's answer: "Not Very Often—Which Raises Serious Questions About Merger Mania"), "Big Goes Bust," "Soap and Pastrami Don't Mix," and "Splitting Up: The Other Side of Merger Mania"—hardly ringing testimonials for the laissez-faire efficiency-through-merger dogma.

3. Are Mergers Costless to Society Over the Long Run?   Undeterred by the evidence, antitrust critics theorize that merger mania is costless to society. After all, the market will punish errant acquisition behavior: mergers that are not efficiency-enhancing will fail; they will be undone; the managements responsible will be chastened and disciplined; hence, no social damage will be done; thus, the market will automatically correct itself with no need for antitrust intervention. As then-Assistant Attorney General Baxter put it, the correct policy approach is to "assume that the people who are spending their money to bring about those mergers and whose motivation can only be to make more money are those most likely to be right in judging which mergers will enhance productivity. . . . Some, of course, will be failures. But, when they make mistakes, they pay heavy penalties; and the market works there, too."[40]

Unfortunately, this argument neglects the fundamental economic principle of opportunity cost. It ignores the fact that with mergers, as elsewhere in economic life, every choice necessarily means forgoing other alternatives (or opportunities). Baxter's argument fails to consider the fact that a society which devotes its efforts and resources to merger mania and paper entrepreneurship must, at the same time, forgo the opportunity of using those resources and energies for real investment in the real productive wealth and competitive capacity of the nation.

Thus, two decades of managerial energies devoted to playing the merger game (organizing raids, designing golden parachutes, devising poison pills and shark repellants, etc.) are, at the same time, two decades during which management attention has been diverted from the critically important job of building new plants, bringing out new products, investing in new production techniques and creating new jobs. The billions spent on shuffling paper ownership shares are, at the same time, billions not spent on productivity enhancing investments to reindustrialize America and to restore U.S. international competitiveness.

So, too, the billions absorbed in the legal fees and banking commissions concomitant with merger mania, expenses incurred at the initial corporate nuptials and again at the subsequent divorce proceedings, represent funds *not* plowed directly into the nation's industrial base. (According to some estimates, the three leading mergers and acquisitions (M&A) houses on Wall Street, Goldman Sachs, First Boston, Morgan Stanley, generated some $250 million in merger commissions in 1988. These fees, says *Forbes*, "may do more to explain current merger mania than all the blather about synergy and diversification."[41]

Placed in an opportunity cost context, America's merger mania represents a possibly unprecedented diversion, dissipation and misallocation of scarce resources and entrepreneurial energies. Table 13-2 provides a graphic illustration. Particularly noteworthy is the fact that, in 1986, spending on mergers exceeded the *combined* expenditures for privately financed R&D *and* net new private investment in plant and equipment.

Thus, merger mania is not costless. Instead, it represents what Adam Smith called "unproductive labour," and what Thorstein Veblen once described as destructive games of chicane and intrigue—intricate arrangements for doing things which ought not to be done, while ignoring the important things that must be done. It is a monumental exercise in social suboptimization which bodes ill for a nation struggling to reindustrialize and regain global competitiveness.

Table 13-2

U.S. Corporate Expenditures on Mergers, R&D, and Net New Investment, 1980–87

	Mergers and Acquisitions	(Billions of Dollars) Industry-Financed R&D	Net New Nonresidential Investment
1980	$ 33.0	$30.9	$ 88.9
1981	67.3	35.9	98.6
1982	60.4	40.1	65.5
1983	52.6	43.5	45.8
1984	126.0	49.1	91.1
1985	145.4	52.6	101.5
1986	204.4	55.7	81.0
1987	167.5	58.8[a]	na

[a]Estimated

Sources: *Mergers & Acquisitions*, May/June 1988; *Statistical Abstract of the United States,* 1988; *Economic Report of the President,* 1988.

V.

THE MISSION OF PUBLIC POLICY

Industrial giantism, whether or not accompanied by monopoly power in specific markets, is not benign and therefore cannot be ignored. At the very least, it breeds an arrogance of power and tends to divert entrepreneurship from risk-taking, investment, research and development, productivity enhancement and market expansion into efforts to manipulate the state for protectionist ends. It transforms the firm from an economic organism, which seeks to maximize profits by excelling in the marketplace, into a quasipolitical institution which seeks the quiet life in an *Ordnungswirtschaft* guaranteed by the state.

Therefore, the basic public policy question, posed earlier, remains, especially in a democratic society: Who shall make what decisions, on whose behalf, at what cost, and for whose benefit? It is a question not for economics, but for political economy. Throughout, the challenge is to design an exogenous control mechanism, largely immune from manipulation by special-interest groups, with built-in safeguards against abuse by concentrated power clusters, so that the system will operate not only to *permit* but rather to *compel* decisions in the public interest (see Figure 13-2).

Thomas Jefferson and the founding fathers believed that "it is not by the consolidation or concentration of powers, but by their distribution, that good government is effected."[42] It is a proposition applicable to the organizational structure of economic as well as political institutions. The alternative, as Stocking and Watkins observed three decades ago, is "to accept some collec-

Figure 13-2

Public policy alternatives: the road ahead.

| Security Through Government Control | Free Enterprise | Security Through Monopoly |

Source: Thurman W. Arnold, op. cit.

tivistic alternative that may give more short-run basic security, but in the long run will almost certainly provide less freedom, less opportunity for experiment, less variety, less economic progress, and less total abundance."[43]

NOTES

1. *United States* v. *Aluminum Company of America*, 148 F.2d 416 (C.C.A. 2d, 1945).

2. *The Wealth of Nations*, Book 1, Chap. 10.

3. U.S. Congress, Senate, Committee on the Judiciary, S. Rep. 695, 63rd Cong., 2nd sess., 1914, p. 1 (italics supplied).

4. A Congressional committee explained the background of the price-discrimination provision of the Clayton Act as follows:

"In the past it has been a most common practice of great and powerful combinations engaged in commerce—notably the Standard Oil company and the American

Tobacco Company, and others of less notoriety, but of great influence—to lower prices of their commodities, oftentimes below the cost of production in certain communities and sections where they had competition, with the intent to destroy and make unprofitable the business of their competitors, and with the ultimate purpose in view of thereby acquiring a monopoly in the particular locality or section in which the discriminating price is made.

"Every concern that engages in this evil practice must of necessity recoup its losses in the particular communities or sections where their commodities are sold below cost or without a fair profit by raising the price of this same class of commodities above their fair market value in other sections or communities.

"Such a system or practice is so manifestly unfair and unjust, not only to competitors who are directly injured thereby but to the general public, that your committee is strongly of the opinion that the present antitrust laws ought to be supplemented by making this particular form of discrimination a specific offense under the law when practiced by those engaged in commerce." (U.S. Congress, House, Committee on the Judiciary, H. Rep. 627, 63rd Cong., 2nd sess., 1914, pp. 8–9).

5.   Smith, op. cit., Book 1, Chap. 7.

6.   See C. D. Edwards, *Economic and Political Aspects of International Cartels*, Senate Committee on Military Affairs, Monograph No. 1 (Washington, D.C.: U.S. Government Printing Office, 1946), pp. 12–13.

7.   See W. H. Hamilton, *Patents and Free Enterprise*, TNEC Monograph No. 31 (Washington, D.C: U.S. Government Printing Office, 1941), pp. 109–115.

8.   See *United States* v. *Hartford-Empire Co., et al.*, 323 U.S. 386 (1945).

9.   Clair Wilcox, *Competition and Monopoly in the American Economy*, TNEC Monograph No. 21 (Washington, D.C.: U.S. Government Printing Office, 1941), pp. 16–17.

10.   Edwards, p. 36. For a popular discussion of the I. G. Farben–Standard marriage, see also G. W. Stocking and M. W. Watkins, *Cartels in Action* (New York: Twentieth Century Fund, 1946), Chap. 11, especially pp. 491–505.

11.   See W. Berge, *Cartels: Challenge to a Free World* (Washington, D.C.: Public Affairs Press, 1944), pp. 201–214; G. W. Stocking and M. W. Watkins, *Cartels or Competition* (New York: Twentieth Century Fund, 1948), pp. 114–117; J. Borkin and C. A. Welsh, *Germany's Master Plan* (New York: Duell, Sloan, 1943). For a contrary view, see F. A. Howard, *Buna Rubber* (New York: Van Nostrand, 1947).

12.   "Market Structure and Stabilization Policy," *The Review of Economics and Statistics*, 39 (May 1957), pp. 131, 133. For further discussion of sellers' inflation, administered price inflation, and inflation in the midst of recession—in short, the relation between market structure and general price stability—see also U.S. Congress, Senate, Judiciary Committee, *Hearings on Administered Prices Before the Subcommittee on Antitrust and Monopoly*, Part 1, 1957, and Parts 9 and 10, 1959; and U.S. Congress, Joint Economic Committee, *The Relationship of Prices to Economic Stability and Growth*, 85th Cong., 2nd sess., 1958.

13.   H. C. Simons, *Economic Policy for a Free Society* (Chicago: U. of Chicago P., 1948), pp. 43–44. See also F. A. Hayek, *The Road to Serfdom* (Chicago: U. of Chicago P., 1945); R. A. Brady, *Business as a System of Power* (New York: Columbia U. P., 1943); G. W. Stocking, "Saving Free Enterprise from Its Friends," *Southern Economic Journal*, 19 (April 1953), p. 431.

14.   This point was well made by Senator Cummins in 1914, when he pressed for adoption of the Federal Trade Commission Act and the Clayton Act:

"We have adopted in this country the policy of competition. We are trying to preserve competition as a living, real force in our industrial life; that is to say, we are endeavoring to maintain among our business people that honorable rivalry which will prevent one from exacting undue profits from those who may deal with him. . . . We are practically alone, however, in this policy. . . . England long ago became indifferent to it; and while that great country has not specifically adjusted her laws so as to permit monopoly they are so administered as to practically eliminate competition when the trade affected so desires. France has pursued a like course.

"I pause here to say, and I say it emphatically and earnestly, that I believe in our course; I believe in the preservation of competition, I believe in the maintenance of the rule that opens the channels of trade fairly and fully to all comers. I believe it because it seems to me obvious that any other course must inevitably lead us into complete State socialism. The only monopoly which civilized mankind will ever permanently endure is the monopoly of all the people represented in the Government itself." *Congressional Record,* June 30, 1914, p. 11,379.

Since World War II, the contrast between the American and European approaches to the monopoly problem has been considerably reduced. Several nations in Western Europe have enacted restrictive practices legislation that, although not as farreaching as the American prototype, nevertheless reflects a growing awareness of the problem. See European Productivity Agency, *Guide to Legislation on Restrictive Business Practices,* 2 vols. (Paris: Organization for Economic Cooperation and Development, 1960).

15. F. Machlup, *The Political Economy of Monopoly* (Baltimore: Johns Hopkins U.P., 1952), pp. 77–78. See also Walter Adams and Horace M. Gray, *Monopoly in America* (New York: Macmillan, 1955).

16. A somewhat less sophisticated version is offered by George Gilder, who assures us that monopoly positions "are not at all unlimited, because they are always held — unless government intercedes to enforce them — under the threat of potential competitors and substitutes at home or abroad. To the question of how many companies an industry needs in order to be competitive, economist Arthur Laffer answers: one. It will compete against the threat of future rivals. Its monopoly can be maintained only as long as the price is kept low enough to exclude others. In this sense, monopolies are good. The more dynamic and inventive an economy, the more monopolies it will engender," *Wealth and Poverty* (New York: Basic Books, 1981), pp. 37–38.

17. Robert H. Bork, *The Antitrust Paradox* (New York: Basic Books, 1978), p. 118.

18. Ibid., p. 119.

19. Ibid., p. 133.

20. Ibid., pp. 124–125.

21. *The Works of Jeremy Bentham,* J. Bowring, ed., Vol. 3., p. 185.

22. Lord Robbins, *Politics and Economics* (London: Macmillan & Co. 1963), pp. 50–51.

23. John B. Clark, *The Control of Trusts* (New York: Macmillan, 1912), pp. 200–201.

24. *U.S.* v. *Columbia Steel Corp.,* 334 U.S. 495 (1948).

25. This section is loosely adapted from Walter Adams and James W. Brock, "Reagonomics and the Transmogrification of The Merger Policy," *Antitrust Bulletin,* **33** (Summer 1988), pp. 310–48.

26. Quoted in "Scales Tip Against Antitrust Statutes," *Insight, Washington Times,* June 15, 1987, p. 12.

27. For these and other statements by Administration officials, see citations in Adams and Brock, op. cit., 25 *supra,* pp. 315–21.

28. "General Motors: What Went Wrong," *Business Week,* March 16, 1987, p. 110.

29. "A Growing Disillusionment with Conglomerates," *The New York Times,* January 27, 1985, Section 3, p. 4.

30. "Raytheon Is Among Companies Regretting High-Tech Mergers," *The Wall Street Journal,* September 10, 1984, p. 1.

31. David J. Ravenscraft and F. M. Scherer, *Mergers, Sell-Offs, and Economic Efficiency* (Washington, D.C.: Brookings, 1987), pp. 212, 121, 202–03, 210, and 221.

32. Dennis C. Mueller, "Mergers and Market Share," *Review of Economics and Statistics,* **67** (May 1985), p. 266 (emphasis added).

33. Edward S. Herman and Louis Lowenstein, "The Efficiency Effects of Hostile Takeovers: An Empirical Study," Center for Law and Economics, Columbia University School of Law, *Working Paper No. 20* (January 1986), p. 54.

34. *Antitrust Policy for Declining Industries,* Bureau of Economics, Federal Trade Commission, October 1985, pp. viii–ix.

35. "Inside a School for Dealmakers," *Business Week,* July 7, 1986, p. 82.

36. "Diversification Blues," *Mergers & Acquisitions,* May/June 1987, p. 13.

37. "Why Some Mergers Work and Many Don't," *Forbes,* January 18, 1982, p. 36.

38. Michael E. Porter, "From Competitive Advantage to Corporate Strategy," *Harvard Business Review* (May–June 1987), pp. 43, 45, 47.

39. Geroski and Alexis Jacquemin, "Industrial Change, Barriers to Mobility, and European Industrial Policy," *Economic Policy* (November 1985), p. 175.

40. U.S. Senate committee on Labor and Human Resources, *Hearings on Productivity in the American Economy,* 97th Congress, 2d session (1982), p. 495.

41. "Fuel for the Flames?" *Forbes,* November 16, 1985, p. 122.

42. Paul L. Ford (ed.), *The Writings of Thomas Jefferson* (New York: Putnam, 1904), Vol. 1, p. 122.

43. G. W. Stocking and M. W. Watkins, *Monopoly and Free Enterprise* (New York: Twentieth Century Fund, 1952), p. 526. We might profit from British experience, which the conservative London *Economist* has summarized as follows: "The fact is that British industrialists, under the deliberate leadership of the Tory Party in its Baldwin-Chamberlain era, have become distinguishable from British Socialists only by the fact that they still believe in private profits. . . . If free, competitive, private-enterprise capitalism is to continue to exist, not throughout the national economy, but in any part of it, then it needs rescuing from the capitalists fully as much as from the Socialists." *The Economist,* **139** (June 29, 1946), p. 22. Copyright *The Economist.* Reprinted by permission of the publishers.

SUGGESTED READINGS

Books

Adams, W., and J. W. Brock. *The Bigness Complex.* New York: Pantheon Books, 1986.
———, *Dangerous Pursuits: Dealmaking in the Age of Wall Street.* New York: Pantheon Books, 1989.
Adams, W., and H. M. Gray, *Monopoly in America: The Government as Promoter.* New York: Macmillan Publishing Company, 1955.
Adams, W. J. *Restructuring the French Economy: Government and the Rise of Market Competition since World War II.* Washington, D.C.: The Brookings Institution, 1989.

Bain, J. S. *Barriers to New Competition.* Cambridge, Mass.: Harvard University Press, 1956.

Blair, J. M. *Economic Concentration.* New York: Harcourt Brace Jovanovich, 1972.

Bork, R. H. *The Antitrust Paradox.* New York: Basic Books, 1978.

Breit, W., and K. G. Elzinga, *The Antitrust Casebook: Milestones in Economic Regulation,* 2nd ed. Chicago: Dryden Press, 1989.

Caves, R. E. *American Industry: Structure, Conduct, Performance,* 3rd ed. Englewood Cliffs, N.J.: Prentice-Hall, 1987.

———, and M. Uekusa. *Industrial Organization in Japan.* Washington, D.C.: Brookings Institution, 1976.

Dirlam, J. B., and A. E. Kahn. *The Law and Economics of Fair Competition: An Appraisal of Antitrust Policy.* Ithaca, N.Y.: Cornell University Press, 1954.

Edwards, C. D. *Maintaining Competition.* New York: McGraw-Hill Book Co., 1949.

Galbraith, J. K. *The New Industrial State.* Boston: Houghton Mifflin Company, 1967.

Goldschmid, H. J., H. M. Mann, and J. F. Weston (eds.). *Industrial Concentration: The New Learning.* Boston: Little, Brown and Company, 1974.

Greer, D. F. *Industrial Organization and Public Policy,* 2nd ed. New York: Macmillan Publishing Company, 1984.

Herman, E. S. *Corporate Control, Corporate Power.* New York: Cambridge University Press, 1981.

Kahn, A. E. *The Economics of Regulation.* 2 vols. New York: John Wiley & Sons, 1971.

Kaysen, C., and D. F. Turner. *Antitrust Policy.* Cambridge, Mass.: Harvard University Press, 1959.

Lindblom, C. E. *Politics and Markets.* New York: Basic Books, 1977.

Mansfield, E. (ed). *Monopoly Power and Economic Performance,* 4th ed. New York: W. W. Norton & Co., 1978.

Phillips, A. (ed.). *Promoting Competition in Regulated Markets.* Washington, D.C.: Brookings Institution, 1975.

Reid, S. R. *The New Industrial Order.* New York: McGraw-Hill Book, Co., 1976.

Scherer, F. M. *Industrial Market Structure and Economic Performance,* 2nd ed. Chicago: Rand McNally & Co., 1980.

Schultze, C. L. *The Public Use of Private Interest.* Washington, D.C.: Brookings Institution, 1977.

Schumpeter, J. A. *Capitalism, Socialism and Democracy.* New York: Harper & Row, 1942.

Shepherd, W. G. *Market Power and Economic Welfare.* New York: Random House, 1970.

———. *The Treatment of Market Power.* New York: Columbia University Press, 1975.

——— et. al. *Public Enterprise: Economic Analysis of Theory and Practice.* Lexington, Mass.: Heath-Lexington Books, 1976.

Simons, H. C. *Economic Policy for a Free Society.* Chicago: University of Chicago Press, 1948.

Stigler, G. J. *The Organization of Industry.* Homewood, Ill.: Richard D. Irwin, Inc., 1968.

Stocking, G. W., and M. W. Watkins. *Cartels in Action.* New York: Twentieth Century Fund, 1946.

———. *Cartels or Competition?* New York: Twentieth Century Fund, 1947.

———. *Monopoly and Free Enterprise.* New York: Twentieth Century Fund, 1951.

Weidenbaum, M. L. *Business, Government, and the Public,* 2nd ed. Englewood Cliffs, N.J.: Prentice-Hall, 1981.

Wilcox, C., and W. G. Shepherd. *Public Policies Toward Business.* Homewood, Ill.: Richard D. Irwin, Inc., 1975.

Williamson, O. E. *Markets and Hierarchies.* New York: The Free Press, 1975.

Government Publications

FTC, *Economic Report on Corporate Mergers.* Washington, D.C.: U.S. Government Printing Office, 1969.

Hamilton, W. H. *Antitrust in Action.* Temporary National Economic Committee Monograph No. 16. Washington, D.C.: U.S. Government Printing Office, 1940.

U.S. Congress, Congressional Budget Office, *The Effects of Import Quotas on the Steel Industry,* July 1984.

U.S. Congress, Senate, Subcommittee on Antitrust and Monopoly, Judiciary Committee, *Hearings,* Parts 1–10, 85th and 86th Congresses, 1957–1960.

U.S. Congress, Senate, Subcommittee on Antitrust and Monopoly, Judiciary Committee, *Economic Concentration,* Parts 1–8A, 88th–91st Congresses, 1964–1970.

U.S. Congress, Senate, Subcommittee on Antitrust and Monopoly, Judiciary Committee, *The Industrial Reorganization Act, Hearings on S.* 1167, 93rd–94th Congresses, Parts 1–9, 1973–1975.

U.S. Congress, Senate, Subcommittee on Antitrust and Monopoly. *Mergers and Industrial Concentration, Hearings,* 95th Cong., 2nd sess. 1978.

U.S. Congress, Senate, Subcommittee on Multinational Corporations, Foreign Relations Committee, *Multinational Corporations and U.S. Foreign Policy, Hearings,* 93rd–94th Congresses, Parts 1–11, 1973–1975.

Journal and Magazine Articles

Adams, W. "The Military-Industrial Complex and the New Industrial State." *American Economic Review,* **58** (May 1968).

———, and J. W. Brock. "The 'New Learning' and the Euthanasia of Antitrust." *California Law Review,* **74** (October 1986).

Adams, W. J. "Firm Size and Research Activity: France and the United States." *Quarterly Journal of Economics,* **84** (August 1970).

———. "Market Structure and Corporate Power." *Columbia Law Review,* **74** (November 1974).

Comanor, W. S., and T. A. Wilson. "Advertising and the Advantages of Size." *American Economic Review,* **59** (May 1969).

Mason, E. S. "Current Status of the Monopoly Problem." *Harvard Law Review,* **62** (June 1949).

Shepherd, W. G., "'Contestability vs. Competition," *American Economic Review,* **74** (Sept. 1984).

Stigler, G. J. "The Case Against Big Business." *Fortune,* **45** (May 1952).

NAME INDEX

A

Abernathy, W. J., 125
Ackoff, R. L., 159
Acs, Z. J., 99
Adams, W., 70, 71, 98, 99, 100, 105, 125, 126, 127, 347, 373, 374, 376
Adams, W. J., 347, 376
Adelman, M. A., 69, 70, 71
Amdahl, G., 172
Anderson, J., 262
Anderson, R., 213
Arnold, T. W., 352, 370
Asher, H., 314
Aspinwall, R. C., 288
Atanasoff, J., 161
Austin, B. A., 214, 216
Aylen, T., 100

B

Badan, J., 71
Baer, H., 276
Bailey, E. E., 240, 241, 242, 243
Bain, J. S., 69, 374
Baldrige, M., 363
Baldwin, R. E., 100
Balio, T., 213, 214, 216
Barnett, D. F., 75, 94, 97, 99
Barnett, E. W., 348
Baron, S. W., 159
Baumol, W. J., 181, 241, 242, 243
Baxter, W. F., 362, 368, 369

Beebe, J. H., 215
Beltramo, M., 316
Benston, G., 287
Berge, W., 372
Blair, J. M., 242, 331, 346, 374
Blaney, J. C., 52
Bloomfield, M., 315
Blumberg, P., 125
Bohi, D. R., 70
Bollier, D., 127
Bolter, W., 250
Bork, R. H., 356, 357, 358, 373, 374
Borkin, J., 372
Boyle, S. E., 127
Bradford, C., 76
Bradford, R. M., 348
Brady, R. A., 372
Brandeis, Justice L., 344
Brenner, M. A., 240, 242, 243
Breton, T. R., 52
Brock, G. W., 181, 182, 262
Brock, J. W., 70, 99, 126, 127, 373, 374
Browne, L. E., 347
Bull, D., 159
Burck, C. G., 159
Burger, Chief Justice W., 342
Burgess, J., 182
Burke, J., 278
Burnett, W. B., 316
Bush, G., 88
Bush, V., 161
Bussey, J., 127
Butler, R. V., 243

377

Subject Index